THE ROYAL NAVY,

This book explores innovation within the Royal Navy from the financial constraints of the 1930s to war, 1939–45, the Cold War, and on to the refocusing of the Royal Navy after 1990. Successful adaptation to new conditions has been critical to all navies at all times and to naval historians the significance and process of change is not a new area of study. The technical requirements of war at sea have focused attention on changing naval technology for many years. However, in recent years innovation has been increasingly studied within a number of other disciplines, providing new theoretical positions and insights. War at sea is a highly complex process which demands the integration of technology with many other social processes for successful innovation. This book aims to examine case studies of innovation, some successful, others less so, which place the experience of the Royal Navy within a variety of economic and strategic contexts. They explore the impact of technology, politics, organization and economics on the process of innovation. Together these studies will provide new insights against which to set recent ideas on innovation and provide a stimulus to more research by historians and scholars in other disciplines.

Richard Harding is Professor of Organisational History at the University of Westminster.

CASS SERIES: NAVAL POLICY AND HISTORY

Series Editor: Geoffrey Till

ISSN 1366-9478

This series consists primarily of original manuscripts by research scholars in the general area of naval policy and history, without national or chronological limitations. It will from time to time also include collections of important articles as well as reprints of classic works.

1 *Austro-Hungarian Naval Policy, 1904–1914*
Milan N. Vego

2 *Far-Flung Lines: Studies in Imperial Defence in Honour of Donald Mackenzie Schurman*
Edited by Keith Neilson and Greg Kennedy

3 *Maritime Strategy and Continental Wars*
Rear Admiral Raja Menon

4 *The Royal Navy and German Naval Disarmament 1942–1947*
Chris Madsen

5 *Naval Strategy and Operations in Narrow Seas*
Milan N. Vego

6 *The Pen and Ink Sailor: Charles Middleton and the King's Navy, 1778–1813*
John E. Talbott

7 *The Italian Navy and Fascist Expansionism, 1935–1940*
Robert Mallett

8 *The Merchant Marine and International Affairs, 1850–1950*
Edited by Greg Kennedy

9 *Naval Strategy in Northeast Asia: Geo-strategic Goals, Policies and Prospects*
Duk-Ki Kim

10 *Naval Policy and Strategy in the Mediterranean Sea: Past, Present and Future*
Edited by John B. Hattendorf

11 *Stalin's Ocean-going Fleet: Soviet Naval Strategy and Shipbuilding Programmes, 1935–1953*
Jürgen Rohwer and Mikhail S. Monakov

12 *Imperial Defence, 1868–1887*
Donald Mackenzie Schurman; edited by John Beeler

13 *Technology and Naval Combat in the Twentieth Century and Beyond*
Edited by Phillips Payson O'Brien

14 *The Royal Navy and Nuclear Weapons*
Richard Moore

15 *The Royal Navy and the Capital Ship in the Interwar Period: An Operational Perspective*
Joseph Moretz

16 *Chinese Grand Strategy and Maritime Power*
Thomas M. Kane

17 *Britain's Anti-submarine Capability, 1919–1939*
George Franklin

18 *Britain, France and the Naval Arms Trade in the Baltic, 1919–1939: Grand Strategy and Failure*
Donald Stoker

19 *Naval Mutinies of the Twentieth Century: An International Perspective*
Edited by Christopher Bell and Bruce Elleman

20 *The Road to Oran: Anglo-French Naval Relations, September 1939–July 1940*
David Brown

21 *The Secret War against Sweden: US and British Submarine Deception and Political Control in the 1980s*
Ola Tunander

22 *Royal Navy Strategy in the Far East, 1919–1939: Planning for a War against Japan*
Andrew Field

23 *Seapower: A Guide for the Twenty-first Century*
Geoffrey Till

24 *Britain's Economic Blockade of Germany, 1914–1919*
Eric W. Osborne

25 *A Life of Admiral of the Fleet Andrew Cunningham: A Twentieth-Century Naval Leader*
Michael Simpson

26 *Navies in Northern Waters, 1721–2000*
Edited by Rolf Hobson and Tom Kristiansen

27 *German Naval Strategies, 1856–1888: Forerunners to Tirpitz*
David Olivier

28 *British Naval Strategy East of Suez, 1900–2000: Influences and Actions*
Edited by Greg Kennedy

29 *The Rise and Fall of the Soviet Navy in the Baltic, 1921–1940*
Gunnar Aselius

30 *The Royal Navy, 1930–2000: Innovation and Defence*
Edited by Richard Harding

THE ROYAL NAVY, 1930–2000

Innovation and Defence

Editor
Richard Harding

LONDON AND NEW YORK

First published 2005 by Frank Cass

This edition published 2012 by Routledge
2 Park Square, Milton Park, Abingdon, Oxon OX14 4RN

Simultaneously published in the USA and Canada by Routledge
711 Third Avenue, New York, NY 10017

Routledge is an imprint of the Taylor & Francis Group, an informa business

Typeset in Great Britain by Keyword Publishing Services Ltd

British Library Cataloguing in Publication Data
A catalogue record for this book is available from the British Library

Library of Congress Cataloging in Publication Data
A catalog record for this book has been requested

ISBN 0-714-65710-7 (hbk)
ISBN 0-714-68581-X (pbk)

CONTENTS

LIST OF ILLUSTRATIONS

Figures

Tables

CONTRIBUTORS

Professor Norman Friedman is an internationally known strategist and naval historian. His 28 books include *Seapower and Space*, an analysis of the way that space systems have changed naval warfare; *Seapower as Strategy*, an account of modern naval strategy; *Terrorism, Afghanistan, and America's New Way of War*, an account of the war in Afghanistan, including its maritime aspects; and a history of the Cold War, *The Fifty-Year War*, which won the 2001 Westminster Medal (given by RUSI) as the best book of military history published in 2000. He has lectured widely on defence issues in forums such as the National Defense University, the Naval War College and the Royal United Services Institution.

Lt-Commander W.J.R. Gardner served for nearly 30 years in the Royal Navy, specialising in anti-submarine warfare. He became a historian in the Naval Historical Branch of the Ministry of Defence in 1994 and has specialised in the Second World War, the Battle of the Atlantic and intelligence. His publications include *Anti-Submarine Warfare* (London: Brassey's, 1996) and *Decoding History: The Battle of the Atlantic and Ultra* (Basingstoke: Macmillan, 1999).

Anthony Gorst is a Lecturer in History at the University of Westminster. He has published on post-war British foreign and defence policy and is currently researching the Royal Navy and the aircraft carrier in the 1960s.

Dr Eric Grove, a graduate of Aberdeen and London Universities, became a civilian lecturer at the Royal Naval College, Dartmouth, in 1971, leaving as Deputy Head of Strategic Studies. He then worked as a self-employed strategic analyst and defence consultant. Since 1993 he has been at the University of Hull where he now directs the Centre for Security Studies. His books include *Vanguard to Trident* (the standard work on post-1945 British naval policy), *The Future of Sea Power, Sea Battles in Close-Up: World War Two, Fleet to Fleet Encounters* and *The Price of Disobedience* (a reassessment of the Battle of the River Plate). He was the co-author of the 1995 edition of the official publication BR1806, 'The Fundamentals of British Maritime Doctrine', and is completing a major new study, *The Royal Navy 1815–2000*. Dr Grove appears frequently on television as a contributor to programmes on modern naval history.

Professor Richard Harding is Professor of Organisational History at the University of Westminster. He is honorary editor of the *Mariner's Mirror* (Society for Nautical Research). He is author of *Amphibious Warfare in the Eighteenth Century* (Woodbridge: Royal Historical Society, 1991), *The Evolution of the Sailing Navy* (London: Macmillan, 1995) and *Seapower and Naval Warfare 1650–1830* (London: University of London Press, 1999). He is also co-editor of *Precursors of Nelson: British Admirals of the Eighteenth Century* (London: Chatham, 2000).

Commander David Hobbs, MBE, RN, joined the Royal Navy in 1964 and specialised as a pilot. He has flown Gannet, Hunter and Canberra aircraft as well as Wessex commando helicopters in a number of front- and second-line squadrons. His service afloat included the aircraft carriers *Victorious*, *Hermes*, *Albion*, *Bulwark*, *Centaur*, *Ark Royal* (IV) and *Ark Royal* (V). After retirement from the active list as a commander in 1997 he became Curator and Principal Historian of the Fleet Air Arm Museum at RNAS Yeovilton. His publications include *Aircraft of the Royal and Commonwealth Navies* (1996), *Aircraft of the Royal Navy since 1945* (1982), Naval Staff Study, *The Invincible Class and their Air Groups* (1997) and *Ark Royal – the Name Lives On* (1985). He has contributed to *The Battle of the Atlantic 1939–45* (1994), *Men of War: Great Leaders of World War II* (1992) and has read papers at major historical conferences in the UK, France, the USA and Australia as well as establishing a reputation as a broadcaster on naval aviation matters on UK radio and television.

Dr Lewis Johnman is Principal Lecturer in History at the University of Westminster. He is, with Hugh Murphy, the author of the Anderson Medal-winning book, *British Shipbuilding and the State since 1918*. He has contributed widely to journals and books on maritime history, is Secretary of the British Commission for Maritime History and a councillor for the Society of Nautical Research.

Malcolm Llewellyn-Jones retired seven years ago from the Royal Navy after 26 years' service, mainly in the Fleet Air Arm. In 2004 he was awarded a Ph.D. at King's College, London, for a thesis 'The Royal Navy on the Threshold of Modern Anti-Submarine Warfare, 1944–49'. For the last two years he has been employed in the Naval Historical Branch, MoD. He has published papers on the British preparations to defeat the

Type XXI U-boat, the anti-submarine submarine, training against the fast submarine, and large convoy studies by Professor Blackett.

Dr Hugh Murphy has held two Caird Research Fellowships at the National Maritime Museum, Greenwich, and is currently a Research Associate at the Centre for Business History, University of Glasgow, and a Visiting Lecturer at Greenwich Maritime Institute. He has published widely in business, banking and maritime history. He is co-author, with Lewis Johnman, of the Anderson Medal-winning book for 2002, *Shipbuilding and the State since 1918.*

Philip Pugh is engaged in consultancy on matters of cost and operational analysis, principally in association with HVR Consulting Services Ltd and for clients in the defence industry and government both in the UK and abroad. Aside from numerous engineering technical and econometric publications, his most significant historical contributions have been the book *The Cost of Sea Power* (Conway, 1986) and a contribution entitled 'Military Need and Civil Necessity' to *The Battle of the Atlantic 1939–1945* (Greenhill and Naval Institute Press, 1994). For his current technical work see, for example, 'Concept Costing for Defence Projects: The Problem and its Solution', *Defence and Peace Economics*, Vol. 14(6), 2003.

Dr Ian Speller is a Lecturer in the Department of Modern History at the National University of Ireland, Maynooth. He also lectures in defence studies at the Irish Defence Forces' Command and Staff School. Prior to this he was a Lecturer in Defence Studies at King's College, London, and the UK Joint Services Command and Staff College. His research interests include post-1945 British foreign and defence policy, maritime strategy and expeditionary warfare, and he is the author of *The Role of Amphibious Warfare in British Defence Policy, 1945–56* (London: Palgrave, 2001).

FOREWORD

Richard Harding, the editor of this collection of essays, reminds us that the concept of military innovation has attracted growing scholarly interest in recent years. To a large extent this has reflected a general societal preoccupation with the nature and management of change, especially technological change. The rate of change at the beginning of the twenty-first century seems quite unprecedented and aspects of it seem unsettling, even threatening, to many people. Of course, it is possible to argue that this has always been the case; that coping with a changing world over which it has imperfect control is an inevitable part of the human condition. Perhaps, but there do seem to be some quite 'objective' criteria that suggest we really are going through an unprecendented (and maybe unending) period of upheaval at the moment. Moore's law, for one example, tells us that computer power now doubles, exponentially, every 18 months. For many people, global warming is also objective evidence of equally unprecedented change.

Military change has been part and parcel of this – to a great extent simply reflecting this change, to some degree being responsible for it. It has become a major focus of scholarly attention partly because, in the nuclear age, of its possible impact on the planet and partly because, more mundanely, it can so influence operational military outcomes. Navies that manage change better, fight better. So we need to know how change – or military innovation – comes about and how is it best managed. This collection of essays on various military projects that affected the Royal Navy in the twentieth century provides a fascinating series of case studies that help us explore these issues. They throw up all sorts of questions. Perhaps one of the most interesting is the extent to which we can hope to generalize about military innovation anyway. If one project provides a list of 'does and don'ts' for military innovators, can these be usefully applied to other projects, for example?

There is another even more fundamental issue too – and this is the very nature of military innovation. Does it apply mainly to the technological area or does it apply across the board, to training and education, manpower policy, strategy and so on? And when is change to be regarded as evolutionary and when revolutionary? How useful is the old Soviet concept of the 'Revolution in Military Affairs' which so preoccupied Western military analysts and historians towards the end of the Cold War? The current emphasis on 'Transformation' in military circles, especially American ones, seems in large measure to be the modern equivalent of this concept. Whether as a decision-maker trying to manage change or as a historian wanting to understand and chronicle military innovation at the beginning of the twenty-first century, a sound appreciation of how arguably similar problems have been approached in the past can only help. Accordingly, this immensely valuable collection of essays and the huge diversity of experience they explore will help us understand the concept of military innovation then and now and also the way in which successful change has helped determine operational success in the past.

Geoffrey Till

PREFACE

In 1977 Professor Bryan Ranft edited a series of essays exploring technological change in the Royal Navy between 1868 and 1939. The purpose of the authors in that collection was to explain how changes in the Royal Navy occurred and how they were reflected in the relative naval power of Great Britain up to the outbreak of the Second World War. Over the last twenty-five years the question of change has remained a constant feature of naval warfare and a matter of discussion for historians and analysts. Furthermore, the concept of innovation has become a major subject of investigation by scholars in other disciplines. Some of this new work lies on the margins of traditional naval studies, such as maritime economic history, strategic studies, studies of armies and air forces, organisational studies, the economics and politics of innovation and organisational change. It has been recognised for a while that naval historians can both contribute to the debates on subjects hotly discussed by other disciplines, such as innovation, as well as usefully draw upon this work to inform their own insights. This is all the more significant as naval history has become increasingly important and popular within academia and with the public in general.

This collection of essays is a response to that challenge. It focuses on just one issue – innovation. The Society for Nautical Research and the British Commission for Maritime History supported a one-day conference, 'Adapting to Change: The Royal Navy and the Maritime Industries 1850–1990' on 31 October 1998. From this it became clear that there was a need to explore the idea of innovation in the Royal Navy from a range of perspectives. In order to make the project manageable it was decided to limit our contributions to the period 1930 to 2000. It is hoped that the results provide a stimulus to further research and questioning, not just for the period under discussion but for other times and in other navies.

I am grateful to all the contributors to this volume and to the conference for their enthusiasm and support. I am grateful for the support of the SNR, the BCMH and the National Maritime Museum for the conference and, particularly, to Dr Lewis Johnman, the original moving force behind the organisation of the conference. I also owe a debt to Professor Andrew Lambert, whose unpublished paper, 'The Prospects for Naval History', delivered at Royal Naval Museum, Portsmouth, in 2000, provided another stimulus, and to Professor John Hattendorf and Rear-Admiral Richard Hill for their time in commenting on the original proposal.

Richard Harding

INTRODUCTION

Richard Harding

There can be few concepts as central to naval history as that of innovation. Victory or defeat depends upon an ability to overcome an intelligent enemy. Strategy, operations and tactics revolve around an understanding of the interaction between competing material, technology and organisation. Creating surprise by doing something different, such as using new weapons or handling them in different ways, are well established means of taking the initiative and defeating the enemy. The importance of such 'innovation' in method or technology in explaining success or failure is acknowledged in most fields of study. For over well one hundred years, military and naval history, economics, politics, human relations, anthropology and even biology have placed innovation or adaptation at the centre of explanation or analysis. So much has been written on the subject and yet at the same time innovation remains extremely problematic. The reason for this is not the poverty of the studies that have been carried out, but rather their richness. Innovation has been studied by such a wide range of disciplines, each with their own perspectives and claims to provide critical insights, that it is difficult to see clearly how this phenomenon has influenced events in any particular context.

Traditionally, in naval history, innovation has been considered from a technological viewpoint. There is a simple and attractive logic that for the maritime dimension of human life to develop, it must be preceded by technological advances to sustain human life afloat. Existence, let alone innovation, upon the sea requires the utilisation of complex technologies. The substitution of iron and later steel technologies for wood, steam for sail, refrigeration for salting, geosatellite positioning for stellar navigation have all made the modern maritime world more developed and sustainable. The passing of one maritime technology in favour of another forms the basic theme of many books. The same is true for naval history. Whether it is the development of an existing technology, such as the battleship and the naval gun – the armour versus arms race – or introduction of a new technology, such as submarines, naval aviation or guided missiles, the technology of naval warfare takes centre stage in the story of historical development.

While this is an essential perspective, it does have its limitations. The idea of technological substitution can carry within it a notion of inevitable progress – that innovation is driven by inexorable scientific and technological invention and that 'superior' technology must prevail. While this does have application in specific arms races, it raises as many problems as it solves.[1] The co-existence of different technologies over many years has to be explained. The success of some military organisations with technologically inferior equipment, the premature abortion of promising technologies, the failure to adopt or adapt technologies, the life cycle and possible trajectories of development for any particular technology all need exploration. The relationship between fundamental science and it application (or non-application) to naval warfare is often unclear. In some cases, the contribution of social, economic and political factors to the successful development of a particular technology is also relatively under-explored.

Naval historians have done a great deal of work to integrate technology with other factors to help explain the role of technological innovation in naval affairs. For example, Arthur Marder explored the interplay of politics, diplomacy and technology in the navy after 1880.[2] John Beeler has developed this in more detail for a part of the period. The relationship between the social structure of the Royal Navy and the new realities brought on by the *Dreadnought* have been explored by Andrew Gordon. The importance of the convoy system – an essentially non-technological response to the submarine – has been explained. Geoffrey Till has shown why aircraft carrier technology was adopted at different rates between 1919 and 1939 by Britain, the United States and Japan. Not just the technologies, but the concept of innovation itself has been under intense scrutiny.[3]

The development of naval studies from technology to the study of technology within specific contexts has accompanied, and probably been stimulated by, harsh economic considerations. The obvious relationship between the financial costs of seapower and its potential benefits has made it the subject of economic analysis. Money is the sinews of power and keeping ships at sea costs a lot of money. However, it is not just the immediate costs of building navies, but the long-term investment planning, the impact of naval building on the physical infrastructure of sectors of the economy that have important and long-lasting effects.[4] Innovation costs money, so the willingness and ability of the public to pay this price is central to changes in navies. The ability to explain the mission and function of the service has always been important in the competitive bidding for funds between the services. After 1918 the favoured position the Royal Navy enjoyed from the last quarter of the nineteenth century remained largely intact, although forced to bid for relatively smaller pots of money. Innovation was not prevented, but innovation to save money without compromising the mission was the order of the day. The development of Operational Research as a discipline after the Second World War and the tools of 'management science' which the successful prosecution of that war seemed to provide encouraged the examination of innovation and operations from a rational decision-making perspective. By the early 1960s, cost–benefit analysis had been applied to different aspects of naval power and Operational Research had evolved into the far more ambitious Systems Analysis.[5]

By the late 1980s, the reality of Systems Analysis had not always lived up to some of the more exaggerated expectations, and economics was providing another way of looking at innovation. The Systems of Innovation Theory developed from 1987. Technical change was taken as the key to productivity growth. However, change takes place within dynamic social systems. Organisations of all types act and react together within rules determined by the institutions of that system. Whereas classical economics provided a vision of development as a self-balancing model of rational decision-making based upon a traditional physics, Systems of Innovation borrowed from biology. Any system was akin to an organism that develops incrementally as the rules and organisations alter in response to various stimuli. Here, there is no idea of equilibrium. Change is not linear, but depended on the current interrelationship of the parts and even possibly random environmental changes. In order to understand change in this context, it is important to understand the relationship between the parts and, most important, the capacity of the organisations to learn or adapt as conditions altered. This is not new. Indeed, a similar emphasis on discontinuous or organic development can be seen in the work of Adam Smith in the eighteenth century and Joseph Schumpeter (1883–1950) in the twentieth.[6] When looking at innovation from this perspective, it is not the individual hero innovator, the rational calculation of the bureaucrats or service chiefs, nor the impersonal technological imperatives that determine innovation, but the manner in which the system as a whole responds to the possibility of change.

This need to understand the whole system may have had a role in the revival of naval and military history. At the beginning of the twentieth century, the study of history played an important part in the development of thinking related to naval warfare. In the absence of large-scale operations involving the new steel and steam navies, guidance for the employment of fleets was sought in historical example. The disappointing results of naval power during the 1914–1918 war, and the rise of other disciplines such as psychology and business administration, led to the eclipse of history in the inter-war period. After 1945, the lack of large-scale employment of new technologies in combat, the changing missions of naval forces and the growing significance of interdisciplinary studies has led to the re-emergence of history as a discipline contributing to the re-evaluation of naval power. In the last decade, military and naval historians have tackled the broader question of innovation with much more explicit attention than before. Stephen Rosen has examined the idea in the context of contemporary military affairs. The trilogy edited by Williamson Murray and Alan Millett provide an excellent example of this concern for innovation. More recently, H.R. Winton and D.P. Mets have edited a valuable collection of essays on innovation and the army in the inter-war period. In these volumes technology plays a prominent part, but always within the specific geographical, social and chronological context.[7]

It is not just naval historians who have responded to this revival of interest in history.[8] Historians of all kinds have been quick to exploit the techniques and approaches of other disciplines where they appear to offer new insights. One of these disciplines has been psychology. Psychology seemed to offer insights into how organisations performed, based securely upon empirical studies of behaviour. Leadership, motivation, creativity have been examined and theories presented related to performance.[9] Linked to the contributions of anthropology and sociology, this has been extended to groups both large and small. The sheer variety of conclusions drawn by researchers produced a complicated range of possible explanations for innovation. On the other hand, by the 1960s confidence had grown in these techniques to raise another discipline – organisation development (OD). OD postulated that it was possible to bring about directed, predictable change across an entire organisation.[10] Whatever the individual results of such studies and activities, a great many valuable additions to our understanding of how navies work have been made as a result of these enterprises. Nevertheless, the confidence in the social-psychological approach to analysing organisations, like all other approaches, was shown to have its limits. Studies of leaders, of groups, of OD interventions, innovations and change programmes have yielded ambiguous results. A major reason for this was that the studies showed that innovation was far more complex than simple experiments anticipated. In the case of OD, illusions of manageability, linearity, predictability and control were seen to distort the programmes and expectation. Multiple group memberships, complexities between leaders and followers, the difficulty of locating a useful definition of creativity, the focus of the studies and the limited research techniques adopted have all made conclusions relating to innovation far more partial and insecure than the initial studies had hoped. One conclusion drawn by a leading scholar in this field was that what was lacking was good organisational histories.[11] Without understanding the history of an organisation, understanding a specific decision is impossible.

Despite the caution with which scholars in these disciplines approach their subject, and the complexity of their research, the demands of contemporary society for a simple explanation of innovation and an easy method of effective implementation have spawned a huge literature on innovation. The quality is highly variable, but it often highlights and reinforces common perceptions of innovation. The role of the hero innovator fighting against the forces of bureaucratic reaction is prominent. A strongly determinist view of the inevitable triumph of advanced technology or industrial muscle is another theme.

Such approaches are not unknown among historians. The desire to focus on a particular aspect of conflict, an individual officer or inventor and assess their contributions to events is common in works on the Second World War. For example, individuals have been ascribed decisive roles in invention and organisation. The Allied industrial capacity, their possession of particular technologies or weapons, such as the Spitfire or radar, its exploitation of technologies such as Ultra, the competitive, destructive nature of Nazi political organisation have all been held up as decisive factors in the Allied victory in the Second World War. While they all played a part, historians have, for the most part, approached teleological history with scepticism.[12] There is nonetheless a tension between those who see history as a means of establishing universal principles of innovation that can be applied to all situations and others who insist that each case demonstrates such uniqueness and complexity that meaningful generalisations are impossible.[13] Navies have a long tradition of using history to inform themselves about the nature of change and innovation. The rapidly changing technology of the last quarter of the nineteenth century changed the shape, power and potential of warships and fleets. There was not the experience of war to determine how these innovations had changed the ways wars might be fought. Senior officers and latter scholars turned to history to find what might be considered the principles of war at sea. At the United States Naval War College, Captain Alfred Thayer Mahan, and in Britain, Vice-Admiral Philip Columb, Professor Sir John Knox Laughton and Sir Julian Corbett all applied historical research to the question of maritime power. Their influence before 1914 was large, but dwindled in the wake of the Great War when other disciplines competed with history as the dominant intellectual force for the development of doctrine. Perhaps at that critical point before 1914 too much was expected by policy-makers from history as a universal predictive tool and as historians they did too little to emphasise the partial nature of their conclusions. Recent studies on these historians have demonstrated that they were not crude 'universalists', but the complexity of their arguments was lost in the rush to influence policy.[14] There has been some revival in the use of history and it is now an important element in developing doctrine and understanding how innovation might be managed effectively.[15] This study is in part motivated by the belief that historical analysis can make an important contribution to our understanding of how the Royal Navy adapts itself to planned, or even unplanned, changes.

In trying to understand the role of innovation in defence, it is easy to become bogged down in interesting, but ultimately futile, 'self-indulgent verbosity' about definition.[16] The definition of innovation is a major issue in economics, where the debate over 'Evolutionary Economics' and particularly the contribution of Joseph Schumpeter is central to the discipline's understanding of its own development.[17] In other contexts the debate over definition has more limited value. Indeed, the tendency to demand precise definition may owe more to the market for books on innovation, of which there is a massive output jostling for the consumer's attention, than any insight such precision might provide. Having said this, there is value in highlighting some features of definitions that could be useful to our study.

Innovation as a deliberate social process

Innovation might be seen as that process that takes an idea or invention and converts it into a new product, structure or operational activity. It is most familiar in the field of technology as turning 'ideas into ironmongery'.[18] One feature of innovation that it is useful to consider is to see it as a planned process of change. With this view, innovation is a deliberate process by which someone defines a particular change and plans to achieve it. The result is not always what has been anticipated. Its impact might be greater or lesser than expected and, indeed, a whole range of unintended outcomes may result. Nor is it a single act or event, but a complex series of interactions between various actors and environments within which the change is taking place.[19] It might be 'an untidy cocktail of power quest, competition, rationality, manipulation and momentum building', but it is not an exogenous single act of fate.[20]

From this perspective it is clear that innovation is embedded in its social context. It is a process consciously willed by certain actors within a social environment and it takes place over time, influencing and being influenced by an interaction with that social environment. Whatever the assumed objective advantages of a technology or organisational form, its application is ultimately a social phenomenon. Adjustment to social, political or economic conditions is often the most challenging aspect of innovation. It is impossible to understand the superiority of British naval power towards the end of the eighteenth century without understanding Britain's relative advantage in the creation and maintenance of effective dockyards and shipbuilding. In the twentieth century, a good example of the importance of the social context is the manner in which the tank was adopted in a number of industrialised countries after the First World War.[21] Similarly the development of the Luftwaffe, with an emphasis on tactical support of the army, had less to do with differing doctrinal views on strategic air power than the relationship that developed with the army after it became an independent organisation.[22] Some innovations may demand significant social change. The shift from sail to steam technology and the rise of the engineer officer raised significant social problems in the Royal Navy during the last quarter of the nineteenth century compared to the United States Navy.

Innovations can even have their origins in social change rather than technology. The shift to mass conscript armies was a social and political change, but combined with the increasing effectiveness of small arms and artillery (a technological change), in the last quarter of the nineteenth century, imposed serious demands on the state in wartime. For Britain this created particular problems as the implications of a continental commitment were fought out in the fierce political debate over conscription.[23] The extent to which military organisations are changed by domestic social, economic or political pressures is highly variable. Their ability to adapt and absorb these changes while retaining their own distinctive features is the subject of many studies and demonstrates how different results can be both for the organisations concerned and for doctrine. The Russian army prior to 1914 and in the wake of the Bolshevik Revolution was faced, respectively, by changing ideas of professionalism and becoming the servant of a new ideology of war. In both cases, the army adapted, absorbed and, to an extent, diverted these pressures.[24] Another clear example of innovation being driven by factors other than technology is Britain's experience in the light of her relative economic decline post-1918. The cost of defence technologies plays an important part in decisions and doctrine. Imperial defence, and particularly the defence of Singapore, was a matter of great debate, with the Royal Navy and the Royal Air Force framing their strategies around the cost of the technology as much as its tested effectiveness.[25] The lack of a clear purpose was a critical feature in the weak investment in the army during the same period. After 1945, financial weakness was an important factor in the development of British carrier technology and deployment. It was impossible to build new larger carriers for the new generation of heavier jet carrier-borne aircraft, so the angled deck, steam catapult and the ski ramp were alternative solutions to the problem.

Innovation as a disruption of the status quo

According to Schumpeter, an important characteristic of innovation is its 'creative destruction', its disruption of the status quo.[26] The advent of the self-propelled torpedo and the emergence of the *Jeune Ecole* at the end of the nineteenth century disrupted the status quo for a number of years.[27] While the armour versus firepower race during the same period can be considered as an evolutionary process, the *Dreadnought* initiated a step change in the technology and another cause of disruption, disquiet and debate. The debate over air power and battleships, or air power and home defence, created tensions throughout the inter-war years. The inventions of the atom bomb, the submarine-launched nuclear missile and the cruise missile have all shifted power relations between services, if not always between nations.

Innovation as revolutionary or evolutionary change

The question as to whether innovation must be change that is discontinuous is vexed. It goes to the heart of one of the key debates about innovation – is innovation best defined as an evolutionary or a revolutionary process? The examples listed above are presented clearly as cases of revolutionary change and to some the whole significance of innovation lies in the disruption it causes to the status quo.[28] While this idea has a long history, its current popularity owes a great deal to Thomas Kuhn, whose 1962 book, *The Structure of Scientific Revolutions,* suggested that science progresses by investigations that gradually undermine current orthodoxy and at a critical, revolutionary, point replace it with a new orthodoxy or 'paradigm'.[29] This has been reinforced more recently by works applying chaos and complexity theory to organisational and technical innovation. It is attractive in that it coincides with the anxiety of many people who experience the turbulence of the modern business environment and are searching for solutions that seem to have a sound scientific rationale.[30] However, to others, successful innovation depends on stable evolution. Change can be effective only if it builds on existing practice, ideology and expectations. Innovation occurs within the boundaries of accepted theory and practice. Its significance lies in its contribution to cumulative change.[31] The design of the battleship was a long evolutionary process. The tank evolved from an infantry support vehicle to a major element in mobile warfare within twenty years. Strategic bombing took a similar amount of time to reach its apogee by 1945. The effective use of land-based artillery was a matter of evolution. Submarine and anti-submarine warfare was essentially an evolutionary process. The large-scale amphibious operations against defended shore positions demanded evolution across a range of technologies at sea, in the air and on land.

There is wide acceptance that innovation can be both evolutionary and revolutionary, but its nature will depend on the relationship innovation has to fundamental science. Revolutionary innovation is likely to be far more successful if it emerges from fundamental science. Where innovation is taking place in response to change in the environment, evolutionary innovation is more likely to succeed.[32] While this sounds a simple and attractive distinction, it is rather more complicated than it appears. For example, the atomic bomb and nuclear propulsion owed their development to nuclear physics. Radar, high-frequency communication and direction finding built upon electronics. The science was essential, but neither would have been successful without the political will to adapt research, development effort and the military services in order to make effective use of the new science in an operational context. Thus, the ability of the scientists to influence and persuade the political and organisational leadership could be critical to successful 'revolutionary' innovation. Likewise an ability to understand, encourage and convert the science among that leadership provides the other side of the coin. It can go wrong. The science may suggest military applications that turn out to be impracticable for a whole range of reasons from the abstract theoretical to the social, financial and political. The linkage of science to military innovation has been both a major strength and a weakness of United States military planning since the 1960s.[33] On balance it seems likely that where the fundamental science remains unchanged, innovation will arise out of adapting to operational changes and experience of use. Yet this obscures some major changes that have built on existing technologies but still provided a step change in operational application.

Innovation as a response to crisis

The question as to the evolutionary or revolutionary nature of innovation leads to questions about the causes of innovation. Revolutionary change suggests an urgency or crisis within the existing systems, be they intellectual, technical or operational. Thus crisis might precipitate revolutionary change. Examples of change occurring when there was an evident inability to meet the challenge posed by new design, weapons or organisation are not difficult to find. The Liberty Ship, *Dreadnought*, the self-propelled torpedo, mass conscription or military professionalization, all seem to fit into this explanation of innovation. On the other hand, innovations do occur when there is no clear evidence of pressing operational necessity. The all-metal stressed-skin monoplane developed from commercial as well as military requirements during the early 1930s. During this period, it was an immature technology, unproven but with clearly perceived potential. In the same period, changes in armoured forces in Britain were occurring without any urgency. After the First World War the tank and the structure of the British armoured division gradually emerged from exercises, experiment and discussion, but their importance to future operations of the British Army was less clear. Both seem to have developed on the back of a technology that had attained a certain momentum, internal logic and trajectory by 1918 for which adequate interest and resources were available, despite the lack of external stimulus.[34]

Similarly, too much pressure might inhibit innovation. Innovation takes up precious resources, which cannot be diverted from the front line in times of severe crisis. One of the great advantages of the Royal Navy in its formative years between 1540 and 1700 was that it was never placed in a position of continuous crisis over a long period. The pressure placed on it by naval competition was severe during wartime, but never overwhelming, and the space provided by periods of peace and by a growing maritime economy enabled the Royal Navy to innovate at a pace at which both the quantity and quality of its naval resources could be developed to meet threats. A slim lead in formal naval power, which had been established by 1713, was the foundation for continued investment during the ensuing peace. By the mid-eighteenth century British naval supremacy had deep structural and economic roots which enabled it to extend its relative power during the long period of wars in the second half of the century. There were periods of considerable crisis, but overall, the deep strength of the Royal Navy enabled it to resist the spectacular, but more shallow, periodic rise in naval capability achieved by France and Spain.[35]

The Royal Navy and innovation

These essays do not seek to produce an overarching theory of innovation in the Royal Navy since 1930, but to explore a variety of contexts that influence the process of innovation. They shed light on the sheer variety of innovation, and constraints on it, that a global navy experienced over a significant period. They raise questions for further investigation, particularly into the relationship of formal scientific and technical research and developments in operational capability, the relative influence of factors such as institutional politics, the national economy and the impact of war on making fundamental changes to capability.

After 1918, the Royal Navy remained the most powerful maritime force in the world, although challenged by the new realities of the post-war environment. The lapse of the 'Ten Year Rule' in March 1932 brought to an end the most restrictive conditions of the post-war period and the Royal Navy was better placed than the other services to take advantage of the new environment. While some of the central issues of this period have been dealt with in recent work,[36] other issues of adapting to the new conditions remain to be explored. The Second World War posed the most dramatic problems for the Royal Navy, but the post-war Navy was faced with major challenges. Most obviously, it had been eclipsed in size by the United States Navy. As significant as this change was, however, there was more to be concerned about – the navy's mission within a NATO and global context, rapid changes in maritime and missile technology, were fertile ground for contested defence budgets.[37] Structural changes in British industry and changes to government departments were additional dynamic elements within the Royal Navy's operating environment.

It is this changing context of innovation that prompted these essays. The period was one in which the restraints and requirements of the Royal Navy changed enormously. From peace to total war and then Cold War; from the world's most powerful navy to severe fiscal limitations and the constraints of national economic capability; and from independent naval power to reliance on other services and other nations, the Royal Navy has had to adapt to huge changes in the exercise of naval power. The contributors to this volume, all with different research interests related to the Royal Navy in this period, were asked to examine the matter of innovation. Authors were given a broad outline of the project with an early draft introduction and asked to explore the question of innovation as they saw it. The resulting essays present case studies of individual weapon or ship types, through particular technologies such as welding and electronics, to mission capabilities such as amphibious operations and anti-submarine warfare. They demonstrate just how difficult it is to pin down the essential or consistent characteristics of innovation over the period of about seventy years. Nevertheless, they tell us something about innovation in a complex organisation such as the Royal Navy.

The relationship with technology is fundamental to the development of the navy. Yet strategic, operational, tactical, political and financial considerations drive technological developments rather than vice versa. Few resources are wasted on speculative investment in technologies that do not shape up in early experimentation or on technologies that do not have a clear operational value. The navy is usually focused, intellectually and materially, upon its core functions. This provides tremendous strength. Winning the long war in the Atlantic between 1939 and 1945 was critical to Britain's survival. There was no question as to the priority given to anti-submarine warfare. Lt-Commander Gardner shows how innovation in submarine detection and anti-submarine weapons depended on careful adaptation in the light of operational experience. Lt-Commander Llewellyn Jones shows that even when the immediate danger of the U-boat passed, the Admiralty retained a focus on defeating a future submarine threat. Extrapolating the potential capability of the fast submarine by experimentation provided the vital experiential base for anti-submarine measures to be developed which met the presumed threat by 1954. The Admiralty was aware that operational effectiveness could not be rapidly improvised. The usefulness of any technology depends upon its effective integration into existing systems by training and the development of doctrine. An important feature of effective adaptation is Operational Research (OR). This powerful analytical tool played an important role in many aspects of the Second World War, but Philip Pugh's examination of

OR in shipboard anti-aircraft defence in 1931 shows that the tools themselves must be embedded in the organisational procedures for them to provide effective information for innovation.

Problems also emerged when the technologies changed rapidly, requiring profoundly different equipment. In peacetime, investments in unproven or questionable technologies weakened both the political and operational position of the navy. Where the mission has been unclear, or when the technology developed in areas not immediately central to the mission, investment in experiment or adaptation was limited and gaps soon become apparent in operational capability. In amphibious operations the developments in radio, mobile armoured forces and fighter aircraft were known to the navy during the 1930s, but developing a doctrine and capability to incorporate these developments was never a priority. Commander Hobbs shows how both the peacetime organisation of naval aviation and its development during wartime left Britain with gaps in operational capability between 1939 and 1945 and incapable of maintaining modern fleet carriers in the post-war environment. The problem then became one of playing 'catch-up'. In wartime, with the mission and priorities clearer and the resources available, this was done. In peacetime it is far less easy. Tony Gorst's exploration of the attempt to jump a generation with the CVA-01 project between 1957 and 1966 demonstrates how such large-scale projects can become mired in changing operational requirements and financial limitations. Professor Friedman shows how the rapid development of electronic systems after 1945 could hardly be accommodated with the existing naval platforms. Changes had to be introduced slowly. Priorities had to be identified, compromises made and large, if temporary, gaps in capability had to be accepted as a norm in the planning process. The story of CVA-01 shows that planning proceeded with an eye open to the possible use of the technological investment in the event of the cancellation of the original project.

Any operation at sea requires the mastery of highly complex operations. Adding or changing capabilities imposes strains that are not easily accommodated. The requirements for effective amphibious operations during the Second World War could hardly have been anticipated and were only perfected over four years of development. They required a level of inter-service collaboration unimagined before the war and difficult to maintain post-1945 given the other missions of the services during the Cold War. Dr Speller shows how the level of enthusiasm which the Royal Navy demonstrated to collaboration varied according to the degree of control the navy would have over operations and how other, more direct, challenges to British seapower fluctuated.

A further issue was the relationship with the British economy. In almost all aspects of war at sea the navy usually wanted more than it could get for the resources it possessed. It is dependent upon industry to deliver what it requires, and changes to the management of the shipbuilding industry and production engineering played an important part in ensuring the right quantity of materials for the war at sea between 1939 and 1945. The wartime development of the aircraft carrier imposed demands that exceeded British shipbuilding capacity and the post-war development strained the capability of the Admiralty Ship Department. To keep up with the rapid development of maritime electronics, it demanded different approaches to research and development and to the sharing of costs. On the whole, the recovering British economy was not well positioned to resource modern naval power. The small domestic market for electronics in Britain after 1945 made a self-sustaining electronic industry to service the defence requirements almost impossible.[38] The need for an export market to ensure adequate returns has been important for these products and seems to have been an important exception to the usual focus on the primary mission in British naval innovation. By the early 1960s, the lack of experience of private contractors in tendering for carrier construction was an additional obstacle to the progress of CVA-01.

However, as Drs Johnman and Murphy show, with the story of ship welding, industrial organisation itself could hinder innovation. In this case, the failure of the industry to develop a technology lay in its poor industrial relations, poor management practices and a general unwillingness to invest in hostile market conditions. So deeply entrenched was the pattern of labour practices that even at the height of a national crisis, in 1942, the Admiralty felt unable to push through organisational changes that would have expanded welding in ship construction. One other issue that retarded innovation which emerges quite clearly, is the failure of inter-organisational collaboration or understanding. Dr Grove and Professor Friedman show how diplomatic relations with prospective partners shaped the adoption and adaptation of missile and electronic systems. The dominant role of the RAF in naval aviation had a negative effect on carrier aviation between the wars and after. While the strategic deterrent was an important part of post-war developments, it involved uneasy relationships with the RAF and Aldermaston. Likewise, there was a failure of the three services to develop amphibious capability in the same period. The patchy collaboration after 1945 over amphibious warfare and the battles that took place whilst CVA-01 was being developed indicate that service ambitions had a significant and damaging impact on innovation.

While it is possible to see these failures as the result of prejudice and conservatism, they were also quite understandable responses to the limited capacity of Britain to sustain all its possible defence options and the long-standing political processes used to allocate scarce resources. All three services had to determine their roles in a changing environment. Technology, strategy and finance all had to balance to make the overall mission practicable. Losing sight of this by focusing on unrealistic ambitions and technologies could undermine the very basis of service capability. The services could co-operate very well at all levels when the occasion demanded. The air attacks on the German submarine production system had an important impact on the anti-submarine effort. Collaboration concerning amphibious operations in the 1930s did not require large investment or commitment, but it existed and provided a foundation for development when war came. When amphibious operations moved up the strategic list of priorities, both during the Second World War and during the 1960s as well as after 1997, the services have committed energy and resources to make them work.

An important aspect of innovation in any service was its alignment with the current mission and resources. It is a low-key form of innovation, emerging out of testing and developing existing resources. It was a key feature in the development of anti-submarine warfare, where the improvement of command, control and communication of the convoy system, the gradual improvements to detection and anti-submarine weapons, as well as the extension of Operational Research, all contributed to the eventual defeat of the U-boat threat and the maintenance of an effective post-war anti-submarine capability. British carrier aviation shows a similar trajectory of development. While the basic hull size remained limited, new angled decks and landing mirrors improved operational capability after the Second World War. The use of shore stations and the fleet train gave the Royal Navy an operational reach in the Pacific undreamed of in the 1930s when carrier operations were based on North Sea scenarios. The ability of the Royal Navy to develop in missile and electronic capability has been based on developing existing technologies and forging partnerships with private electronics companies such as Marconi and Ferranti or making bilateral agreements with other nations to share costs. The development of the helicopter from transport to anti-submarine and ground attack roles is another example of this important low-profile innovation.

Despite the challenges, the Royal Navy was and remains one of the largest, most comprehensive and technologically advanced fleets in the world. It remained so despite the heavy concentration of attention on the European Central Front during the Cold War, and the decline of the British mercantile marine. This was not inevitable within the context of the United States naval and nuclear umbrella. The choices lay in Britain and the decisions lay in the hands of the British public, politicians and service chiefs. The decision to use submarines as the platform for Britain's ballistic nuclear weapons in 1962, the lessons of the Falklands War in 1982, the collapse of the Soviet Union and the Warsaw Pact in 1989–90, have all focused British defence planning around a powerful and flexible maritime capability.

The problem of innovation has particular implications for understanding the history of the Royal Navy. Innovation is far too important and complex to make general conclusions as to cause and effect. There is no simple cause and effect relationship between perceived operational need, technological possibility and innovation. One has to look closely inside an organisation and see it in relation to its specific environment to understand why innovation is taking place or not. It is a phenomenon with many layers. Turning ideas into effective operations can involve changes in science; changes in technology; changes in the relationship between the scientists or experts and the military organisations they assist; changes in the relationship with other interested parties in society, from industry to voters; or changes in the relationships between the services and within individual services. What is clear is that innovation is as much a social phenomenon as a technical one. History, politics, economics and psychology have all contributed to an understanding of innovation as something more than a technical process.

No doubt the changes experienced by the Royal Navy between 1930 and 2000 were not universally welcomed within the naval command, especially as joint operations with the other services have taken a larger share of resources. In some quarters there remains the view that the navy could never innovate to bring about deep or significant change in such a traditional organisation. Nevertheless, it is unlikely that the political choices that have shaped the modern navy over a long period would have been made had it not been for the fact that the Royal Navy could demonstrate its ability to develop itself to perform new tasks satisfactorily. Thus, innovation – the capacity to recognise a changing environment and integrate its essential elements into organisational activities and purpose – lies at the centre of the Royal Navy's success.

Notes

1 For some of the issues related to the development of military thinking along linear trajectory and propositions regarding its antecedents in the nineteenth century, see M. de Landa, *War in the Age of Intelligent Machines* (New York: Zone, 1991). See also A. Beyerchen, 'Clausewitz, Nonlinearity and the Unpredictability of War', *International Security*, 17(1992–3), 59–90.

2 A.J. Marder, *The Anatomy of Power: A History of British Naval Policy in the Pre-Dreadnought Era, 1880–1905* (London: Frank Cass, 1964).

3 J. Beeler, *Birth of the Battleship: British Capital Ship Design, 1870–1881* (London: Chatham Publishing, 2001); A. Gordon, *The Rules of the Game: Jutland and British Naval Command* (London: Murray, 1996); P.P. O'Brien (ed.), *Technology and Naval Combat in the Twentieth Century and Beyond* (London, Frank Cass, 2001); G. Till, 'Adopting the Aircraft Carrier: The British, American and Japanese Case Studies', in W. Murray and A.R. Millet (eds), *Military Innovation in the Interwar Period* (Cambridge: Cambridge University Press, 1996), 191–226; S.P. Rosen, *Winning the Next War: Innovation and the Modern Military* (Ithaca, NY: Cornell University Press, 1991).

4 G.A.H. Gordon, *British Seapower and Procurement Between the Wars: A Reappraisal of Rearmament* (London: Macmillan, 1988); P. Pugh, *The Cost of Seapower: The Influence of Money on Naval Affairs from 1815 to the Present Day* (London: Conway, 1986). See also M. Smith, *British Air Strategy Between the Wars* (Oxford: Oxford University Press, 1984) and B. Bond, *British Military Policy Between the Two World Wars* (Oxford: Clarendon Press, 1980). For a general work on the matter of finance and military power in the early modern period, see J. Brewer, *The Sinews of Power* (London: Unwin, 1989).

5 M. de Landa, *War in the Age of Intelligent Machines,* 101–2. Operational Research is primarily a study of how to get the best operational results from a known weapons system. Systems Analysis is aimed at designing the systems to resolve a known military problem. See also *The Origins and Development of Operational Research in the Royal Air Force* (London: HMSO, 1963).

6 A. Smith, 'The History of Astronomy', in *Essays on Philosophical Subjects,* ed. W.P.D. Wightman and J.C. Bryce (Oxford: Oxford University Press, 1980), 33–105; D.D. Raphael, *Adam Smith* (Oxford: Oxford University Press, 1985), 109–13; E. Roll, *A History of Economic Thought* (London: Faber, 1992, 5th ed.), 541–2.

7 Besides the works noted in previous notes, see M. Howard, 'Miltary Science in an Age of Peace', *Journal of the Royal United Services Institution* (hereafter *JRUSI*), 119(1974), 3–11.

8 See A. Kransdorf, *Corporate Amnesia: Keeping Know-How in the Company* (Oxford: Butterworth, 1998).

9 For an interesting collection of essays on this theme, see M.A. West and J.L. Farr (eds), *Innovation and Creativity at Work: Psychological and Organisational Strategies* (London: Wiley, 1990).

10 W.L. French and C.H. Bell, *Organization Development: Behavioural Science Interventions for Organization Improvement* (New York: Prentice-Hall, 1995), 26–62.

11 E. Rogers, *Diffusion of Innovations* (New York: Free Press, 1983, 3rd edn), 358.

12 R. Overy, *Why the Allies Won* (London: Cape, 1995); W.J.R. Gardner, *Decoding History: The Battle of the Atlantic* (London: Macmillan, 1999).

13 The desire to draw useful conclusions can lead to generalisations that in the course of time look questionable. The classic historical study of innovation in Britain by Burns and Stalker in 1962 drew some very important conclusions regarding a variety of aspects of the phenomenon, but the careless reader might infer too much from notions of ideal organisational forms. See T. Burns and G.M. Stalker, *The Management of Innovation* (Oxford: Oxford University Press, 1962). For the development of business history as a sub-branch related to this study, see L. Hannah, *The Rise of the Corporate Economy* (London: Methuen, 1976). See also J.F. Wilson, *British Business History, 1720–1994* (Manchester: Manchester University Press, 1995), 1–20. For the problem of complexity, see D. Edgerton, *Science, Technology and British Industrial Decline, 1870–1970* (Cambridge: Cambridge University Press, 1996), 16–19.

14 See the introduction by B. Gough in P. Columb, *Naval Warfare: Its Ruling Principles and Practice Historically Treated* (Annapolis, MD: Naval Institute Press, 1990), 2 vols, vol. 1, xiii–xxx; D.M. Schurman, *Julian S. Corbett, 1854–1922: Historian of British Maritime Policy from Drake to Jellicoe* (Woodbridge: Royal Historical Society, 1981); A. Lambert, *The Foundations of Naval History: John Knox Laughton, the Royal Navy and the Historical Profession* (London: Chatham Publishing, 1998); J.T. Sumida, *Inventing Grand Strategy and*

Teaching Command: The Classic Works of Alfred Thayer Mahan Reconsidered (Baltimore, MD: Johns Hopkins University Press, 1997).

15 The literature is vast, but an overview of the state of naval history can be obtained from J.B. Hattendorf (ed.), *Ubi Sumus: The State of Naval and Maritime History* (Newport, RI: Naval War College Press, 1994). A specific example of the relationship between strategy and naval history can be found in J.B. Hattendorf (ed.), *Mahan is Not Enough: Proceedings of a Conference on the Works of Sir Julian Corbett and Admiral Sir Herbert Richmond* (Newport, RI: Naval War College Press, 1993).

16 J. Elster, *Explaining Technical Change: A Case Study in the Philosophy of Science* (Cambridge: Cambridge University Press, 1983), 112.

17 J. Schumpeter, *Capitalism, Socialism and Democracy* (London: Allen & Unwin, 1976), 82–8. Schumpeter's notion of 'creative destruction' and the role of the entrepreneur is acknowledged by many to be the basis upon which ideas on innovation have been developed. As such, what Schumpeter actually meant has become an important element in the debate. For an early example of the genre, see, E.E. Morison, *Men, Machines and Modern Times* (Cambridge, MA: MIT Press, 1966); J. Elster, *Explaining Technical Change*, 112.

18 A. Rupert Hall, 'What Did the Industrial Revolution Owe to Science?', in N. McKendrick (ed.), *Historical Perspectives: Studies in English Thought and Society* (London: Europa, 1974), 131.

19 J. Tidd, J. Bessant and K. Pavitt, *Managing Innovation: Integrating Technological, Market and Organisational Change* (London: Wiley, 2001), 5, 50.

20 D. Buchanan and D. Boddy, *The Expertise of the Change Agent: Public Performance and Backstage Activity* (New York: Prentice-Hall, 1992), 62.

21 Compare E.C. Keisling, 'Resting Uncomfortably on its Laurels: The Army of Interwar France', in H.R. Winton and D.R. Mets (eds), *The Challenge of Change: Military Institutions and New Realities, 1918–1941* (Lincoln: University of Nebraska Press, 2000), 1–34; J.S. Corum, 'A Comprehensive Approach to Change: Reform in the German Army in the Interwar Period', in Winton and Mets, *The Challenge of Change*, 35–73; H.R. Winton, 'Tanks, Votes and Budgets: The Politics of Mechanization and Armored Warfare in Britain, 1919–1939', in Winton and Mets, *The Challenge of Change*, 74–107.

22 J.S. Corum, 'A Comprehensive Approach to Change: Reform in the German Army in the Interwar Period', in Winton and Mets (eds), *The Challenge of Change*, 51–54.

23 R.J.Q. Adams and P. Poirier, *The Conscription Controversy in Great Britain, 1900–18* (London: Macmillan, 1987); K. Grieves, *The Politics of Manpower, 1914–18* (Manchester: Manchester University Press, 1988). See also J. Ellis, *The Social History of the Machine Gun* (London: Random House, 1976; 1993 edition). For a wider discussion, which, despite a great deal of new research, still retains its force, see A. Marwick, *The Deluge: British Society and the First World War* (London: Bodley Head, 1965).

24 D.A. Rich, *The Tsar's Colonels: Professionalism, Strategy and Subversion in Late Imperial Russia* (Cambridge, MA: Harvard University Press, 1998); J.W. Kipp, 'Military Reform and the Red Army 1914–1941: Bolsheviks, Voyenspetsy and the Young Red Commanders', in Winton and Mets (eds), *The Challenge of Change*, 108–161.

25 For the RAF case regarding the effectiveness of air defence for Singapore in preference to heavy naval guns, see Public Record Office (hereafter PRO), Air 8/102 (Singapore Defences, 1928–1930).

26 N. Rosenburg, *Inside the Black Box: Technology and Economics* (Cambridge: Cambridge University Press, 1992), 5; Morison, *Men, Machines and Modern Times*, 9.

27 H. Coutau-Bégarie, 'Réflexions sur l'Ecole Française de la Pensée Navale Moderne', in H. Coutau-Bégarie (ed.), *L'Evolution de la Pensée Navale* (Paris: Commission Française d'Histoire Maritime, 1990), 31–56.

28 Good examples of this type of literature are R. Foster, *Innovation: The Attacker's Advantage* (London: Guild Publishing, 1986); G. Hamel and C.K. Prahalad, *Competing for the Future: Breakthrough Strategies for Seizing Control of Your Industry and Creating the Markets of Tomorrow* (Cambridge, MA: Harvard Business School Press, 1994); G. Hamel, *Leading the Revolution* (Cambridge, MA: Harvard Business School Press, 2000).

29 T.S. Kuhn, *The Structure of Scientific Revolutions* (Chicago: University of Chicago Press, 1962). For an example of how this has been applied in naval history, see J.S. Sumida and D.A. Rosenberg, 'Machines, Men, Manufacturing, Management and Money: The Study of Navies as Complex Organisations and the Transformation of Twentieth Century Naval History', in J.B. Hattendorf (ed.), *Doing Naval History: Essays Towards Improvement* (Newport, RI: Naval War College Press, 1995), 25–40.

30 A good example of how this has been absorbed into the field of popular management literature is T. Peters, *Thriving on Chaos* (New York: Knopf, 1987). For a good introduction to the subject as a whole, see R. Lewin, *Complexity: Life at the Edge of Chaos* (New York: Macmillan, 1992).

31 Rosenburg, *Inside the Black Box*, 6–7; see also Burns and Stalker, *The Management of Innovation*, 20–7.

32 Hall, 'What Did the Industrial Revolution Owe to Science?', 131–2.

33 F. Kaplan, *The Wizards of Armageddon* (New York: Simon & Schuster, 1983). For other examples, see R. Clark, *The Rise of the Boffins* (London: Phoenix House, 1962); R.V. Jones, *Most Secret War: British Scientific Intelligence, 1939–1945* (London: Hamish Hamilton, 1978).

34 J.P. Harris, *Men, Ideas and Tanks: British Military Thought and Armoured Forces, 1903–1939* (Manchester: Manchester University Press, 1995).

35 For discussions of the internal development of the Royal Navy, see R. Harding, *The Evolution of the Sailing Navy, 1519–1815*, (London: Macmillan, 1994). For a discussion of comparative seapower, see J. Glete, *Navies and Nations: Warships, Navies and State Building in Europe and America, 1500–1860*, 2 vols (Stockholm: Almquist & Wiksell, 1993) and R. Harding, *Seapower and Naval Warfare, 1650–1830* (London: University of London Press, 1999).

36 See, for example, G.A.H. Gordon, *British Seapower and Procurement Between the Wars: A Reappraisal of Rearmament* (London: Macmillan, 1988).

37 This has been recounted in some detail in E. Grove, *From Vanguard to Trident: British Naval Policy since World War II* (London: Bodley Head, 1987).

38 G. Owen, *From Empire to Europe: The Decline and Revival of British Industry since the Second World War* (London: HarperCollins, 1999), chap. 10.

1

MANAGING THE AERIAL THREAT

Provisions for anti-aircraft warfare during the 1930s

Philip Pugh

Aims of the chapter

The Royal Navy entered the Second World War confident in its readiness, in its doctrine, in its equipment and of its central rôle in the defence of Britain. This is not to say that it would not have wished for even more and better ships. But, especially given that the foe was then Germany, rather than Japan – against whom so much of planning had been directed – the qualitative adequacy and quantitative superiority of the British battle line seemed to be more than enough. Moreover, it was that gun-armed battle line that was expected still to be the final arbiter of naval war. Threats from submarines and from aircraft had been faced and, it was thought, disposed of. New equipment for capital ships and their escorts and additional secondary armament for the former had together nullified these new threats, it was believed. The Royal Navy had faced change and, as it imagined, had adapted successfully to that change. The primacy of the battleship remained intact, it was assumed.

Disillusionment was rapid. The Norwegian campaign of early 1940 convinced the Admiralty that the battle fleet could not operate within range of the German air force. At 8.07 p.m. on 7 September 1940, just 102 days after the conclusion of the failed Norwegian campaign, the massing of barges along the now hostile French and Belgian coasts and calculations of moon and tide prompted the issuing of the signal 'Cromwell' – that invasion of Britain was imminent. The Royal Air Force braced itself for an even more intense phase of the Battle of Britain which it had been fighting for almost two months and in which it had already lost over 430 aircraft. The battered, scarcely yet reorganised and imperfectly re-equipped Army came to instant readiness at improvised defences across south-east England. The ill-armed Home Guard stood to. But the Home Fleet did not stir from Scapa Flow. Safety from German air attack took precedence over any move to reduce the 600 miles by which it was distant from where it might justify its oft-repeated claim to be Britain's first line of defence against invasion.

As Italy entered the war, so the British Mediterranean Fleet withdrew to Alexandria. The island of Malta, the base from which that fleet had been supposed to dominate the sea for which it was named, became a fortress under siege – a siege enforced not by some opposing battle fleet but by a none too numerous and none too well-equipped air force.

Worse was yet to come. When war with Japan approached, the two capital ships that might be spared were sent promptly to Singapore and when war broke out they were even more promptly sunk by air attack. Next, just four months later, news of the approach of a Japanese carrier force to Ceylon sent the British Far Eastern Fleet from there and into hiding at Addu Atoll – again some 600 miles away from the action. Then, but a further three months later, came what must count as one of the blackest days of any navy when dozens of merchantmen and hundreds of crew were abandoned to death by the withdrawal of the escort from the Russian convoy PQ-17. The proximate cause of this blunder may have been that the First Sea Lord was labouring under the illusion that that the escort was about to be overwhelmed by the German battleship *Tirpitz* – in fact, nowhere near the convoy but in port. However, no such decision would have been imposed upon an ailing mind had it not become by then the unquestioned policy that no British units of size and number sufficient to counter *Tirpitz* could ever be risked within range of German air power.

In brief, in September 1939 the Royal Navy entered war confident that the aerial threat to its battle fleet had been foreseen and met. By June 1942 the British battle fleet was available to prevent invasion, to protect its own bases, to defend British possessions or to safeguard seaborne transport if, and only if, it could first be guaranteed immunity from enemy air attack.

The aim of this chapter is to examine how this came to pass – how was it that the Royal Navy formed so erroneous an expectation of its performance in anti-aircraft warfare? In such a context, it is necessary to appreciate that capital ships have long time scales. Even in the 1930s each took years to build – even just to modify. They then had long service lives. Industrial capacity, then as now, is thus geared to replacing the fleet over a period of, say, two decades. Even to cycle a complete fleet through major modifications must therefore take the best part of a decade. So, if we are to understand why British capital ships were as they were in 1939, then it is towards the beginning of that decade that we must look.

Looking thus, one finds that the matter of anti-aircraft warfare and the aerial threat were subjects of much inquiry then. At the forefront of that was the work of the Anti-Aircraft Gunnery Committee of 1931. This followed, and made reference to, a similarly entitled committee but of 1921. However, the work of 1931 seems to have been upon a much bigger scale, drawing upon all relevant sources, examining proposals from outside the Royal Navy, commissioning intramural work specifically for its purposes and essaying a comprehensive review of the problem with the aim of recommending what, if any, new equipment and/or armament should be fitted to Royal Navy ships of various types in order to meet the aerial threat.

It is upon the work of the Anti-Aircraft Gunnery Committee of 1931 that the present chapter concentrates. It does so for two reasons. First, the Anti-Aircraft Gunnery Committee of 1931 merits particular attention for its exemplification of Royal Navy thinking during the relevant period. Second, it is worth studying for its methodology also. Both in its general approach and in its use of mathematical modelling it attracts attention as one of the earliest examples of what would today be termed an operational research study – the usual recourse today when requiring to evaluate an emerging military problem and to find means for its resolution. To determine where such an approach succeeded and why, overall, it failed has, therefore, special pertinence to an appreciation of innovation and of how it is handled at present.

It was in that context exactly that the present author came across a copy of the report of the Anti-Aircraft Gunnery Committee of 1931 resting among numerous much more recent reports and books on the shelves of the Main Library of the (UK) Ministry of Defence (MoD) at Great Scotland Yard, off Whitehall, London. This was during the late 1980s when he was engaged in cost analysis and related operational research within MoD. Naturally, he was fascinated by so early an example of the practice of his trade and returned to it upon numerous occasions to take careful and extensive notes. Alas, enquiries recently (late 2003) proved this document to have been the victim of various reorganisations, transfer of catalogues to electronic format and moves of stock in the interim. Kind efforts on the part of MoD librarians could no longer trace it. It is probable that it has been archived with the Public Records Office; but, until it surfaces again, this chapter may serve the additional function of providing access to the data methods and conclusions of what must have been one of the very first pieces of operational research in a form recognisable to practitioners of that art today.

This is all the more important since reviewing critically this seminal piece of operational research offers the opportunity – all too rare – for comparing predictions with the actual outcomes of later events. For that purpose we shall concentrate upon two episodes of the Second World War which, as will become clear later, correspond closely to circumstances that the Anti-Aircraft Committee of 1931 had most in mind during their deliberations. These episodes are the loss of HMS *Prince of Wales* and

Repulse off Malaya on 10 December 1941 and the passage of the English Channel on 12 February 1941 by the German battlecruisers *Scharnhorst* and *Gneisenau* and the heavy cruiser *Prinz Eugen.*

Throughout this chapter, dimensions, masses, etc., are given in SI units rather than in the Imperial system employed by the committee in its report. Similarly, the now more familiar standard deviation is used as the statistical measure of variability in place of probable deviation (i.e. inter-quartile range in modern terminology) as used by the committee in accord with customary usage of its time (conversions here being based upon the committee's assumption of a Gaussian form for probability distributions). Such practice is anachronistic, but may be excused by greater ease of understanding for a modern audience and greater facility in such calculations as are necessary in what follows.

Background

The Anti-Aircraft Gunnery Committee of 1931 did not begin its work in a vacuum. On the contrary, the aerial threat to the battleship had been for some time the subject of widespread lively debate both within military circles and beyond.

Proponents of an enlarged, even predominant, rôle for aircraft pointed particularly to the sinking in 1921 of the ex-German battleship *Ostfriesland* by bombers of the United States Army Air Force (USAAF). This battleship of 24,701 tonnes full load displacement and then but ten years old withstood hits and near-misses from some 24 shells and 80 bombs but then succumbed to 6×1,000 kg bombs from aircraft directed by Brig.-General William ('Billy') Mitchell. Sceptics pointed to this demonstration having been carried out in perfect weather and with the target ship stationary and unable to fight back. Matters would be very different in war, they asserted.

Nevertheless, it had been demonstrated that aircraft could now carry bombs of a size sufficient to sink major warships. Some defence against aircraft was therefore necessary. In new designs and during major refits, passive defence was added to many battleships in the form of heavier horizontal armour. Active defence, added more readily, took the form of installing a number of guns for anti-aircraft purposes. These, usually of 76 mm and later 114 mm calibre, were changed little, if at all, from designs for surface action save for being married to mountings permitting their elevation to high angles (almost 90° in the case of the British Mk I anti-aircraft gun).

Requirements for passive defence might be stated quite simply and precisely in terms of resisting penetration by a bomb of armour-piercing type and of standard size (*c.* 1,000 kg being assumed usually) falling vertically at its terminal velocity. Designing to meet such a requirement lay well within contemporary knowledge of terminal ballistics.

But passive defence can only mitigate, not preclude altogether, damage from a hit. Moreover, far from all of a battleship could be armoured. Active defence was essential. Ideally, this would prevent attackers from getting into any position to make a hit and/or would inflict deterrent losses upon the attackers. At the least, active defence must reduce the probability of each attacker making a hit to a level such that, when compounded with good passive defence, battleships had a high probability of emerging from intense and prolonged aerial attack with their (surface) fighting capacity sensibly undiminished.

The nature of such active defence was not in doubt. The only type of weapon with sufficient range was the gun – a weapon in whose effective use at long range the Royal Navy felt itself to be well versed. So, however widely an initial brief might be drawn, the central question for those seeking in the early 1930s to counter the aerial threat to the battle line came rapidly down to the simple one of how many guns of medium calibre and on high-angle mounts should be added to each battleship.

In non-technical ways also, any study during the early 1930s of British naval affairs could not but be a product of its times. In common with the rest of the world, Britain was suffering from the effects of the Great Depression. It was a time for economy. The year 1931 was a year of political and financial crisis, of the National Government and of cuts in unemployment benefit, of increases in taxation and of cuts in pay and of the mutiny at Invergordon that those provoked. It was no time to be proposing expensive solutions, whatever the problem.

Of course, all economic troubles pass eventually – even those of the Great Depression. But, even were contemporary analysts to look beyond immediate economic woes, there was little to be seen for their comfort even supposing economic recovery. Britain had accepted parity with the United States in battleship numbers under the terms of the Washington Naval Armament Limitation Treaty of 1922. She had done so not out of any spirit of international altruism but reluctantly and as the lesser of two evils. The alternative, that of being outbuilt by the United States in the course of the armaments race then burgeoning, would have been even less palatable than accepting parity.

Even within the narrower context of Europe or in rivalry with Japan, Britain no longer had superior economic power. No longer could she hope to outbuild decisively any rival. Much hung, therefore, upon preserving, as central to naval power, Britain's legacy of past industrial predominance – an ageing, but still effective, battle line.

Also to be considered as background to studies of anti-aircraft gunnery during the 1930s is the state of aeronautics – the origin of the threat. This was evolving rapidly – a characteristic that, as will be argued later, seems to have been central to the failure of the Royal Navy to anticipate the severity of the aerial threat during the Second World War.

Aircraft had come of age during the First World War in the sense of being transformed from rare and expensive examples of equipment for a dangerous sport into mass-produced means of transport and weapons of war. However, even in 1918 they were still immature in terms of deficiencies of their essentially empirical design. Nevertheless, such was the evident potential of aeronautics that its advancement attracted continuing sponsorship – both government and private – after the end of the First World War. Such was the intellectual challenge of the problems that advancing aeronautics threw up that it attracted many of the finest mathematical and engineering brains of the era. Results followed rapidly.

By the mid-1920s enlarged understanding of structures and of the mechanisms of lift and drag production had resulted in the definition of the stressed-skin cantilever monoplane as the optimum layout and one capable of vastly increased performance as compared to the aircraft of the day. Its realisation commenced with racing and record-breaking aircraft but spread quickly into commercial use. Problem after problem was solved in rapid succession until by the middle of the 1930s airliners such as the Boeing 247D, the Douglas DC-2 and the Douglas DC-3 (later to become ubiquitous as the Dakota) were cruising in long-distance revenue service at speeds of around 300 km/hr, matching the world absolute speed record of 1920.

Military users were slower to respond. The new knowledge was applied first in respect of details but not initially to overall layout. As fighter aircraft were 'cleaned up' by ameliorating the worst drag-producing features, so their maximum speed moved up from the *c.* 175 km/hr of 1918 to the 320 km/hr of the British Hawker Fury of 1929. However, the average was considerably worse than this best with the biplane layout, strut bracing, fixed undercarriages and open cockpits remaining the norm. Bomber aircraft were slower yet, typified by the assumption of the Anti-Aircraft Gunnery Committee of 1931 that high-altitude bombers would approach their targets at 110 knots (203 km/hr) and torpedo bombers at 125 knots (230 km/hr).

The military attractions of the cantilever monoplane were not to be overlooked for long, however. By the outbreak of the Second World War, remarkable performance gains had been achieved. Pertinent to the present study is the Japanese Mitsubishi G4M Type 1 as used in the attacks on HMS *Prince of Wales* and *Repulse*. These cruised at 314 km/hr and had maximum speeds of 435 km/hr at 4,600 m altitude and 422 km/hr at 2,000 m altitude.

Only in the remotest corners of Empire and in the Royal Navy did the fabric-covered, fixed undercarriage, open cockpit biplane last much into the Second World War. In the case of the Royal Navy it lasted until seven years after that war ended as the Swordfish torpedo-bomber laboured on into the supersonic era with its maximum speed when laden with a torpedo of just 220 km/hr – about half that of the Mitsubishi G4M Type 1. Even when the Royal Navy did acquire a cantilever monoplane in the Blackburn Skua, it soon got rid of it.

Quite why the Royal Navy of the 1930s was so indifferent to the performance of its aircraft is a subject for study in its own right. What matters here is the fact that it was so indifferent and the possibility that, failing thus to be exposed day by day to advances in aircraft performance, it might fail to see a need to re-examine conclusions based upon levels of aircraft performance long past.

But the Royal Navy had first to reach any conclusions concerning countering any level of aerial threat. In its way stood the obstacle that confronts all military operational research in peacetime – the lack of direct empirical evidence.

Methodology

Empirical evidence may have been lacking in the sense of there being no contemporary wartime attacks by aircraft upon major ships to analyse; but there were more detailed technical data in quantity available from trials on firing ranges and elsewhere – in which respect, analysts of 1931 may well have been better placed than their counterparts today when the cost of weapons severely limits the extent of live-fire testing and training. The problem was thus one of employing a mass of data on the performances of diverse components in a synthesis of the probable performance of a complete anti-aircraft system.

The approach adopted is worthy of note as being probably the first instance within operational research of what would be termed today a hierarchy of models. In this, the mathematical modelling of the whole system is kept to a manageable level of complexity through simplicity in the modelling of each subsystem. However, fidelity to the real world is assured through the ability of each sub-model to replicate essential aspects of a much more detailed model of the respective subsystem. So, each element of the model of the complete system is validated by reference to more detailed modelling which, in turn, is justified by its replication of empirical data from trials.

In this way, for example, trials provided a large volume of data concerning the masses, velocities and spatial distributions of fragments generated by exploding shells of various sizes and types. Other trials provided statistics concerning the results of the impact of shell fragments of varying mass and speed upon different components of an aircraft. All this information was represented in the final model of a complete engagement by the rule that a shell was to be taken as destroying an aircraft if, but only if, it exploded while it was within a 'lethal volume' of cylindrical shape, aligned with the trajectory of the shell and with the pilot of the aircraft at its centre. There is, of course, no such precisely defined lethal volume of simple shape and at whose boundary the effectiveness of an exploding shell ceases abruptly. But such a representation is justified by being shown to provide, under the circumstances of a typical engagement, a good approximation to results from much more elaborate models following closely and in detail the empirical evidence. Being thus justified, the simple concept of a 'lethal volume' characteristic of each calibre of shell enables an entire engagement to be described in the very simple mathematical terms that follow and for the influence on this of factors such as shell calibre to be appreciated readily.

The investigations of 1931 followed modern practice also in that the engagement was not considered as an end in itself. Rather, probable circumstances under which the engagement would take place and, thence, the objectives of each of the engaged forces were set out. In modern terms, a clear scenario and set of objectives were postulated. Thence followed readily a clear view of what would constitute success on the part of the defending ships, i.e. what was to be aimed for in any enhancement of their anti-aircraft defences.

In all, the methodology of the Anti-Aircraft Gunnery Committee of 1931 is not to be faulted as an approach calculated to resolve a complex problem in the evaluation of an emerging threat and of possible counters to that.

Scenario

Beginning with the principal scenario adopted by the committee, it has to be said that if it emerged from any specific consideration of geopolitical possibilities, then these were not recorded in its report. Rather, it was simply stated as a given – a fact significant in itself since it would indicate that this was not a matter requiring to be argued but, rather, a matter of consensus within the Admiralty of the time. The scenario thus laid down was that of the passage of a fleet through disputed waters during the transit of which the fleet would expect to come under attack from land-based enemy aircraft.

From whence the fleet was sailing and what was its destination was not set down; but it would not be difficult to imagine such circumstances during the course of a campaign in the Pacific Ocean such as occupied much British naval thinking at the time. Departing northwards from Singapore or in the vicinity of the Japanese home islands, such a situation might arise readily enough.

Three issues flow from this being the scenario within which the adequacy of anti-aircraft gunnery was to be evaluated.

First, this was not the decisive battle. The fleet was en route elsewhere – in search, presumably, of the decisive battle with the enemy fleet, which remained the central aim of British naval strategy as it had been since before the days of Nelson.

Second, attack by ship-based enemy aircraft was not the concern. Evidently, the decisive battle to which the fleet was steaming was to be one between battle lines of big-gun ships, aircraft having only scouting and artillery-spotting rôles.

Third, the objective of the fleet was to complete its passage unscathed – and thus fully fit for the decisive battle yet to come. Success did not involve defeat of the opposing air force in any sense other than its failure to inflict significant damage upon the fleet. Inflicting casualties upon attacking aircraft was not the goal save in as far as that would diminish the weight of the attack and make avoiding damage to ships easier to achieve. In no sense were the ships to seek and win a 'stand-up fight' with aircraft. Rather, the object was to avoid damage during an exposure to air attack that would be kept as brief as possible – an exposure if not to be evaded then certainly not to be sought and to be minimised in so far as that might be done without prejudice to the primary objectives of fleet operations.

Put simply, the aim of anti-aircraft defences was seen not as that of taking on and defeating an opposing air force but, rather, that of making opposing aircraft an irrelevance – unable significantly to prevent the battle fleet from pursuing its traditional goals by its traditional means.

The operations that anti-aircraft defence was meant to allow were, therefore, precisely those upon which Admiral Phillips embarked when, in search of a Japanese invasion fleet, he took *Prince of Wales* and *Repulse* within range of Japanese air bases or that Vice-Admiral Ciliax faced as *Scharnhorst*, *Gneisenau* and *Prinz Eugen* exited the harbour at Brest.

The central problem

To kill an aircraft with a shell is a matter simple of statement but difficult of achievement. It is a matter of getting a shell to explode in the right place and at the right time. As described earlier, the 'right place and right time' came down to having the shell explode within a cylindrical volume whose axis was aligned with the flight path of the shell and whose centroid coincided (and therefore moved) with the pilot of the aircraft (see Fig. 1.1).

Dimensions of this 'lethal volume' for various calibres of shell were as shown in Table 1.1. It will be seen that the linear dimensions of the lethal volume increase somewhat more rapidly than in proportion to the calibre, an attraction of using the largest calibre for which rapid fire might be

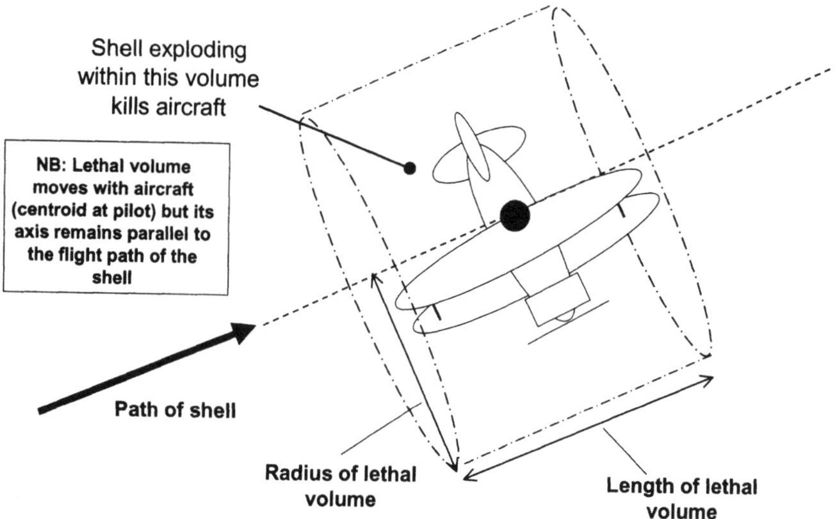

Figure 1.1 The 'lethal volume'.

sustained with manual loading (as was then universal for these weapons). However, even with the largest calibre of 120 mm (British nominal 4.7 inch), the base of the lethal volume subtended an angle of only 9.5 milliradians at a slant range of 5,000 m while, even though such shells lost much of their initial velocity over such a range, such a shell passed through the length of the lethal volume in under 37 milliseconds. Anti-aircraft gunnery demanded precise as well as rapid fire.

The first requisite of placing a shell within this lethal volume was to aim the gun appropriately; that is to say, not at the target aircraft, but at where the aircraft (and thus the lethal volume) would have moved to during the time taken by the shell to travel from gun to target.

The extent to which the gun had thus to be 'aimed off' was considerable. Flight time of shells from gun to target was of the order of $12\frac{1}{2}$ seconds for a British 120 mm gun and a slant range of 5,000 m.

Table 1.1 Lethal volume

	Lethal volume	
Shell calibre (mm)	*Radius (m)*	*Length (m)*
76	11.9	6.4
102	15.5	9.1
120	23.8	10.1

During that time even the slow military aircraft of 1931 would have travelled some 700 m.

This aiming problem attracted much attention. The Anti-Aircraft Gunnery Committee of 1931 examined contemporary Royal Navy equipment and a wide range of proposals for its improvement that came from firms and from individuals both within and outside the service. In essence, however, there were but two forms of system.

In the form favoured by the Royal Navy and taken by it into the Second World War, the location of the target was first determined by traditional means of optical range finding. That location was then adjusted using the flight time of the shell and the estimated course and speed of the target. The gun was then laid upon this adjusted target location. This process being conducted continuously throughout engagement of the target, estimates of target course and speed were refined and corrected via observation of the positions of shell bursts in relation to the target. Data available to the Anti-Aircraft Gunnery Committee of 1931 indicated that this sighting, prediction and gun-laying process was unbiased (i.e. aiming errors averaged to zero over a large number of shots) but that the aiming of individual shots was subject to significant quasi-random variability in both bearing and elevation.

The alternative form of aiming was the 'tachymetric' system as used by the British Army and to be adopted by the United States and German navies. In this the range of the target was measured in the usual optical range-finding way, but target bearing and elevation were measured directly as were rates of change of these. Thus, adjusted target bearing and elevation for gun laying were obtained simply from their current values and current rates of change together with flight time of the shell derived from target range. Again, aiming errors were unbiased, but this 'tachymetric' system exhibited much less variability in the aiming of each shot, as is shown in Table 1.2.

The difference between the accuracies of the two types of system and the failure of the Royal Navy to adopt the better of the two has been remarked upon by a number of commentators. Beyond doubt, it is

Table 1.2 Aiming errors

	Aiming error, standard deviation (milliradians)	
System	*Bearing*	*Elevation*
Royal Navy (HACSI)	18.9	18.9
Tachymetric	7.3	7.3

significant; but its importance can be exaggerated by forgetting that aiming errors are not the only cause of shells diverging from their intended trajectories. Even when aimed perfectly, there remains substantial shot dispersion, i.e. round-to-round deviations from the average trajectory both in bearing and in elevation. The measurement of shot dispersion is shown in Fig. 1.2.

Values of shot dispersion collated by the Anti-Aircraft Gunnery Committee of 1931 were as given in Table 1.3. Since shot dispersion and aiming error can be taken to be statistically independent, overall standard deviations of divergences from the nominal (average) trajectory were, for example, with the 120 mm calibre weapon $\surd(18.9^2 + 11.6^2) =$ 22.2 milliradians with the Royal Navy system of aiming and $\surd(7.3^2 + 11.6^2) =$ 13.8 milliradians with tachymetric fire control. Such a reduction in spread about the nominal trajectory by 38 per cent is significant, but is considerably less than the 61 per cent reduction that would be deduced from aiming error alone.

Having sent the shell along the right trajectory, it is then necessary that it explode at the right time into its flight. Here a change was in progress with Type 206 time mechanical fuses replacing older, powder-train types of fuse. For both types there were again no systematic differences between the actual times of operation and those set. There was, however, considerable fuse-to-fuse variation in this difference with the new time

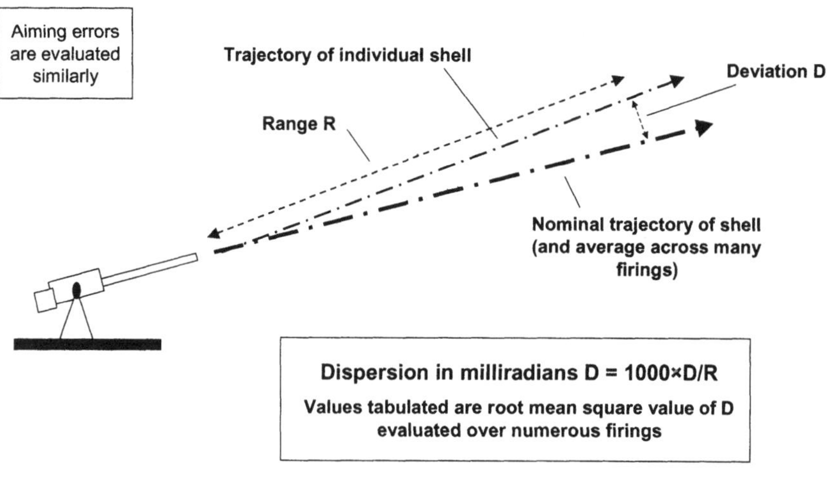

Figure 1.2 Measurement of shot dispersion.

Table 1.3 Shot dispersion

Gun calibre (mm)	Dispersion standard deviation (milliradians) Bearing	Elevation	Note
12.7	1.2	1.2	Machine gun, automatic fire
40	0.9	0.9	2-pdr 'Pom-pom', rapid single shot
40	4.4	4.4	2-pdr 'Pom-pom', automatic fire
102	11.6	11.6	British 4 in. QF Mk V
120	11.6	11.6	British 4.7 in. QF Mk VIII

mechanical fuse being notably more repeatable as is shown in Table 1.4. For shell velocities typical of shells towards the top of their trajectory, a variation in time of 200 ms corresponded to a distance of *c.* 55 m.

Comparing this distance with lengths of typical lethal volumes (Table 1.1) and comparing shot dispersion and aiming error with the angle subtended by the radius of that volume makes evident immediately that there was but a small chance of any individual shot effecting a kill. Anti-aircraft gunnery was therefore a matter of probability. It was a question of mounting a volume of fire sufficient for the small probability of each individual shot producing a kill to accumulate over a large number of shells into a high probability that one would do its intended business.

We are now in a position to follow the Anti-Aircraft Gunnery Committee of 1931 in the calculation of the overall effectiveness of a single gun firing upon a single aircraft at a given slant range. By way of example, we shall consider the British 4.7 in. QF Mk VIII gun firing shells fitted with the Type 206 time mechanical fuse at a slant range of 5,000 m under Royal Navy HACSI fire control. Gaussian probability distributions will be assumed throughout.

The calculation is straightforward. As Fig. 1.3 indicates, it involves computation separately of the probabilities of the shell being at the right height (elevation), on the right course (bearing) and bursting at the right time. These statistically independent probabilities are then multiplied to

Table 1.4 Fusing errors

Fuse type	Variability of time of shell burst, standard deviation milliseconds	Notes
Powder train	400	
Time mechanical	200	Type 206

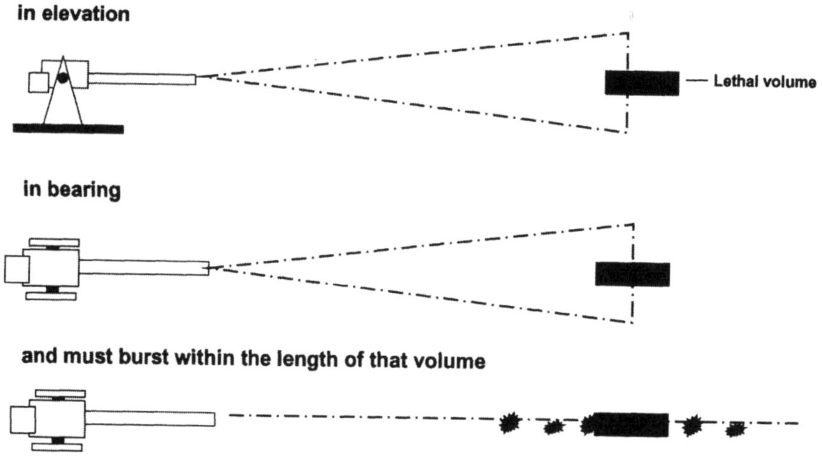

Figure 1.3 To kill an aeroplane.

give the overall probability of all three conditions being met and, hence, of a kill being made. It is sufficient here to reproduce the results as in Table 1.5 below and to show them graphically in Fig. 1.4. A slant range of 5,000 m is around that at which the Royal Navy expected to open fire upon an attacking aircraft. As this calculation makes clear, anti-aircraft fire at that range must be for purposes such as alerting other ships to the presence of an aircraft rather than in the hope of a kill. An aircraft is reasonably safe at that range, unless all the guns of the fleet concentrate upon it.

Table 1.5 Effectiveness of AA fire

Slant range (m)	*Single shot kill probability*	*Average no. of shots per kill*
500	6.9%	15
1,000	3.7%	27
2,000	1.2%	82
3,000	0.6%	175
4,000	0.3%	310
5,000	0.2%	472

British 4.7 in. QF Mk VIII gun, shells fitted with Type 206 time mechanical fuse, Royal Navy HACSI fire control.

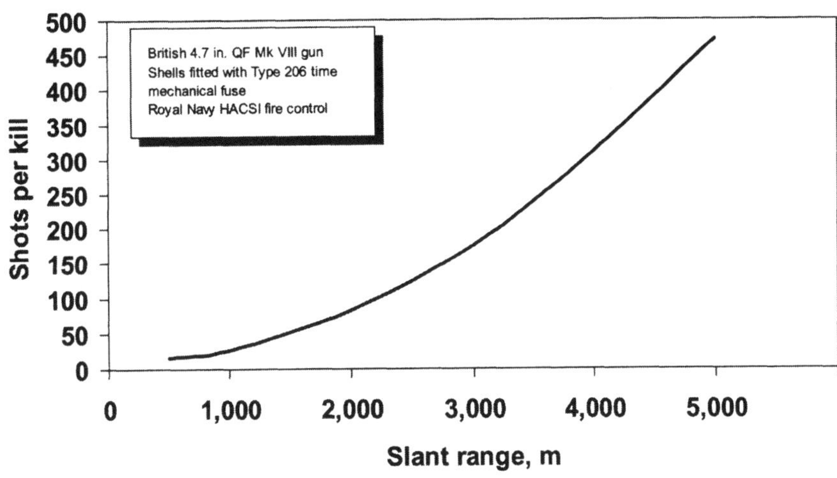

Figure 1.4 Average number of shells fired per aircraft killed.

However, as Fig. 1.4 shows, matters change as the aircraft closes with the ship. At, say, 1,000 m slant range a kill requires only 27 shells to be fired upon average. A capital ship might typically be able to bring 4 AA guns to bear and each might, for a brief period, fire at a rate of 12 rounds per minute. These guns together thus firing a shell every $1\frac{1}{4}$ seconds, the average life expectancy of the aircraft would be just under 34 seconds.

The probability of a kill within a given period (one second, say) varies directly as the number of guns firing (N) and over much of the variation of slant range shown above it varies inversely as the square of the slant range (R). We may suppose that the aircraft commences its attack at a long distance from the ship but ceases to be the attention of anti-aircraft fire when slant range has fallen to a value R' – because, for example, it then releases its weapons and anti-aircraft fire control switches to other incoming aircraft concerning whose menace something may yet be done. We can then deduce as an approximate, but useful, relationship that the probability of shooting down an aircraft while it is on an attacking run towards the ship is proportional to the number of anti-aircraft guns brought to bear on it and inversely proportional both to the speed of the aircraft and to the slant range at which it releases its weapons, i.e. the probability of the aircraft being destroyed is proportional to $N/(V \times R')$.

The merits, from the attacker's point of view, of approaching the target at high speed and with weapons that can be released at long range are obvious. Implications for defence of the fleet depend upon fleet tactics to which the discussion now turns.

Fleet tactics

Throughout the considerations of 1931, the primary threat was assumed to be from bombers releasing (free-fall) bombs while in level flight at high altitude. This was how air forces the world over expected then to operate. They had a healthy respect for anti-aircraft gunnery, and over-flying defences at altitudes of typically 3,000 m was no more than prudent. The accuracy of bombing from such altitude was not good; but it was certainly sufficient to pose a serious threat to vessels of the size of battleships if as much from the cumulative effects of near-misses as from direct hits.

At first sight, the figures just derived for the effectiveness of anti-aircraft gunfire would seem to offer little hope of defence against such attack. An aircraft bombing from level flight at an altitude of 3,000 m would release its bombs when at a slant range of around 3,300 m when, as interpolation within Table 1.5 indicates, some 211 shots would be required to make a kill.

However, fleet tactics did not rely upon the guns of the attacking ship alone. Capital ships in company and the destroyer screen were expected to lend their aid. Most importantly also, some air cover was expected to be available, either from friendly air bases nearby or from aircraft carriers with the fleet. In those pre-radar days, continuous defence by aircraft could be provided only via standing air patrols. These were expensive in effort and, hence, only one or two fighters could be expected to be aloft when an attack came. Nevertheless, their presence was crucial.

One or two fighter aircraft were not expected to inflict many losses upon an attacking bomber force. However, they were expected to oblige the bombers to fly in close formation in order to provide mutual support from their defensive armaments in accord with the standard air force doctrines of the day.

Shooting at a tight formation rather than at a single aircraft transformed the anti-aircraft gunnery problem. With shells being spread in course (bearing) and height (elevation) by typically more than 70 m at a slant range of 3,300 m, a shell was as likely to hit a neighbouring aircraft as the one being aimed at. Putting, say, 6 aircraft into close formation multiplied the chances of hitting one of them by almost 6. Further, it was supposed that shooting down one aircraft of a formation would so disrupt the attack as to cause them all to miss their target.

So, the Anti-Aircraft Gunnery Committee recommended a minimum anti-aircraft armament for capital ships of 8 guns of calibre 4 in (102 mm) or greater, approximately doubling the contemporary outfit of such ships. They reasoned that at least 4 of these guns would to be able to bear, that the number of guns firing would be at least doubled by the efforts of other ships, and that bombers would attack in formations of at least 6 aircraft. Then, with a rate of fire of 12 rounds per minute from each gun, the shooting down of aircraft close to the point of bomb release should be accomplished at a rate of around one every 20 seconds or so and with that attack by the entire formation defeated.

In brief, the expected form of air attack could be fended off with relative ease – given conditions as supposed then and illustrated here in Fig. 1.5.

Other aerial threats

Analysis was not confined to the expected primary mode of air attack. In particular, the airborne torpedo was given extensive consideration. However, it soon becomes clear that torpedo-bomber pilots had to be made of stern stuff. A typical lightweight torpedo of the day had a maximum range of 1,500 yards (1,372 m) and a maximum speed of around 40 knots. Hence, an attacking torpedo-bomber would have to close to within a slant range of at most 1,070 m in order to attack a ship moving at, say, 25 knots. As has been shown above, life expectancy at that range would be brief. Few torpedo-bombers would be expected to survive to release their weapons, while a ship under command and with an alert bridge crew could be expected to evade those few torpedoes that were released.

The Anti-Aircraft Gunnery Committee gave consideration also to reports of a new form of aircraft supposedly under development in the United States. This, it was said, was capable of approaching its target at high altitude (and thus with relative immunity from anti-aircraft gun fire)

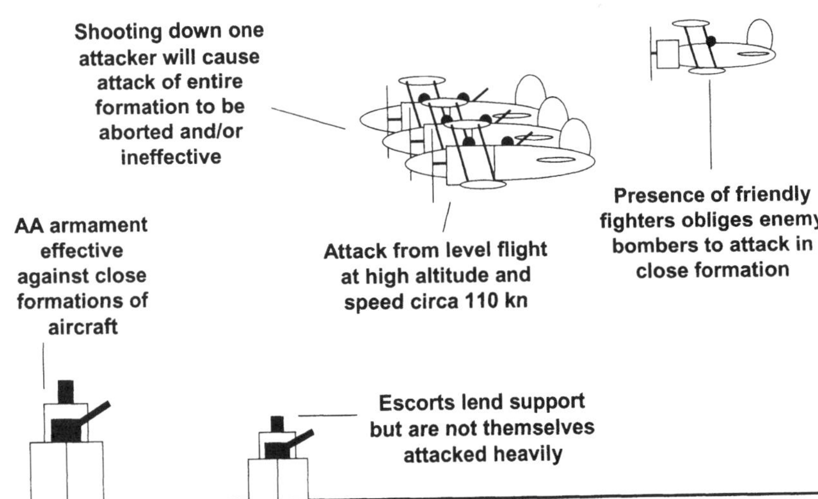

Figure 1.5 Defence of the fleet: suppositions of 1931.

and then of diving vertically at speeds of around 550 km/hr (so presenting a difficult fleeting target) to deliver its bombs with great accuracy.

Expert advice, solicited by the committee from the Royal Air Force, pointed out major difficulties of control in vertical dives and observed that, at the suggested speed, pullout from the dive to level flight would have to commence at high altitude if the pilot and aircraft were to survive the experience. This mode of attack was dismissed as impracticable and/or conveying no advantage, therefore.

The committee and its expert advice seem to have had in mind such a form of dive-bombing attack by aircraft designed for other purposes (e.g. as fighters or as conventional bombers). They were right to regard that as infeasible. They erred, however, in overlooking the possibility of designing aircraft specifically for the dive-bombing rôle. In so doing, they failed to spot that a very steep (but not absolutely vertical) dive would have the claimed advantages of presenting a difficult target and of facilitating accurate bomb aiming while aerodynamic devices (speed brakes) could be devised to limit speed in the dive (typically to around 330 km/hr) and thus permit the dive to be maintained until close to the surface. Since dive-bombers of this kind were in squadron service with the United States Navy by 1934, theirs was a short-sighted view indeed.

As indicated in Fig. 1.6, this oversight was especially unfortunate in respect of destroyers and other small warships. The main armament of

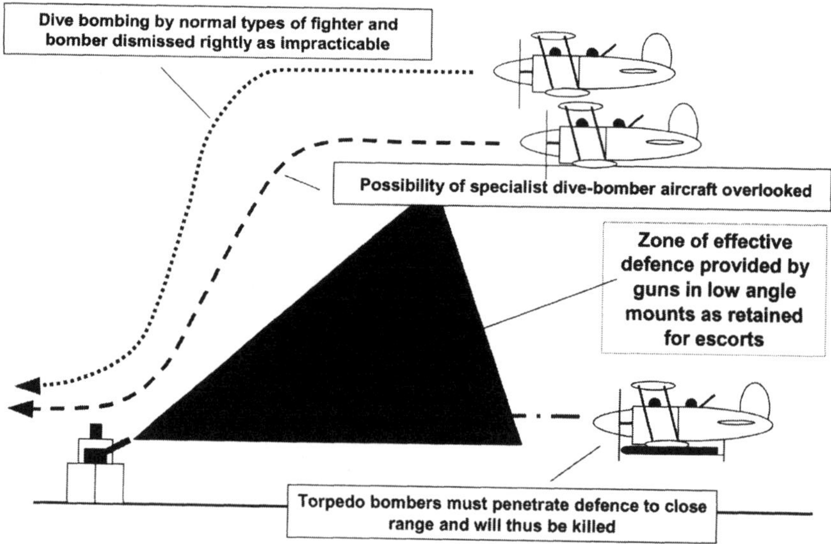

Figure 1.6 Other forms of attack: retention of low-angle gun mounts for escort vessels.

such vessels was of much the same calibre as the anti-aircraft armament of capital ships. Smaller vessels could be given effective anti-aircraft armament – almost as effective as that of capital ships – by mounting their main armament in high-angle mounts and so fitting them for anti-aircraft use as well as surface action. Unfortunately, this involved some modest sacrifice of reliability and speed of (hand) loading when in the anti-surface ship rôle.

The committee considered, not unreasonably, that the speed and small size of destroyers meant that bombing from level flight at high altitude posed little threat to them. Issue of anti-aircraft ammunition and fitting of anti-aircraft fire control (but with retention of low-angle mounts) enabled destroyers to engage torpedo-bomber aircraft very effectively (see above and recall that a destroyer might bring typically 6 × 102 mm or 120 mm guns to bear on the beam). The same arrangements enabled destroyers when screening the fleet to engage aircraft passing at some distance en route to attack a capital ship.

Having dismissed the possibility of dive-bombing, there was no advantage to be seen to compensate for even a modest loss of effectiveness in traditional (anti-surface) destroyer rôles. The Royal Navy paid heavily for this mistake. In the Second World War, as shown in Fig. 1.7, the predominant cause of loss of destroyers was to air attack, much of that by dive-bombers. Losses to aircraft were more than double those to surface warships. Clearly, the wrong balance was struck.

The rapid contemporary pace of change in aeronautics was touched upon earlier in this chapter. No hint of that is present in the report of the Anti-Aircraft Gunnery Committee of 1931. Herein lays its great failure – not so much as in what it did as in what it failed to do. It saw the anti-aircraft problem as one of providing a counter to the contemporary threat

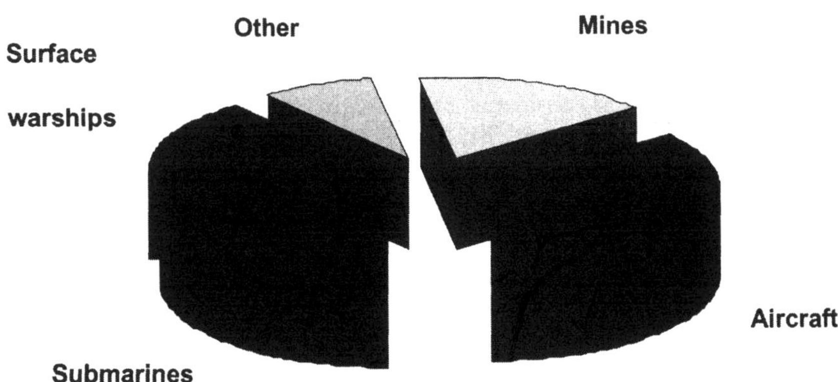

Figure 1.7 Losses of Royal Navy destroyers 1939–45: analysis by cause.

and not that of determining what the situation would be by the time that any recommended changes (i.e. its doubling of the anti-aircraft armament of capital ships) could be brought into effect. Its analysis was conceived as being a once-for-all solution to a problem and not as but one move in a continuing battle between offence and defence.

What happened

We come now to the two incidents during the Second World War that were identified earlier as exemplifying well the scenario envisaged by the analysts of 1931.

First, consider the 'Channel Dash' – the passage of the English Channel by the German ships *Scharnhorst*, *Gneisenau* and *Prinz Eugen*. This is remembered best for the attack on these ships by six Swordfish torpedo-bombers lead by Lt-Cmdr Esmonde. Such aircraft were of exactly the performance assumed for torpedo-bombers in the 1931 analysis.

The defence was also just as envisaged in 1931 save that the air cover had the advantage of radar direction from aboard the fleet. That, however, can be balanced against the provision of fighter escort (albeit smaller than intended) for the attacking aircraft. In the event, German fighter cover appears to have been engaged effectively by the British escorts, with only one of six Swordfish falling to German fighters before crossing the German destroyer screen.

The engagement that followed was thus between torpedo-bombers and the anti-aircraft guns of the fleet – both close in performance to those envisaged in 1931, albeit the German ships had the modest advantage of tachymetric fire control. The outcome was just as predicted in 1931. The torpedo-bombers closed with the ships sufficiently to launch their weapons (without result), but at such short slant ranges their lives became nasty and short. All were lost along with 13 of their 18 crew.

Off Malaya the *Prince of Wales* and *Repulse* were attacked by both bombing from high altitude and with torpedoes. The armament of the ships was as had been considered sufficient in 1931. The attacking aircraft were very different, however. Moreover, no British fighter aircraft were present.

The attacking aircraft were thus not obliged to adopt a tight formation, so knocking away much of the foundation upon which effective defence against bombing from high level had been predicated. Then, also the speed of the Japanese aircraft – roughly twice that which had been envisaged in 1931 – reduced yet further their exposure to the ships' defences. It is just as the analysis of 1931 would predict, therefore, that the high-level bombers appear to have come away unscathed. Equally as expected in 1931, even crews of the quality of the Japanese at this stage of the war found accuracy hard to come by from high altitude, just one hit being made by 27 aircraft.

The torpedo-bombers also took advantage of freedom from need for tight formation and attacked simultaneously from different directions, thus making evasion of their weapons much more difficult. Improved torpedoes meant that the aircraft carrying them needed to close only to within 2,000 yards (1,829 m) before releasing their weapons. As Table 1.5 shows, that reduces risk to the attacking aircraft by a factor of around 2.4, with which must be compounded a reduction by a factor of about 1.8 on account of aircraft speed relative to that assumed in 1931. Overall, then, the risk to the attacking aircraft was reduced by a factor of *c.* 4.3 relative to the assumptions of 1931. It is unsurprising, therefore, that the loss of just fewer than 7 per cent of the attacking force of torpedo-bombers was the modest price for sinking two capital ships

In brief, if given appropriate input data, the model generated by the Anti-Aircraft Gunnery Committee of 1931 predicts well the outcomes of engagements fought a decade later but corresponding closely to the principal scenario that the Royal Navy then postulated.

Conclusions

We conclude, therefore, that:

1. In the early 1930s the Royal Navy was faced with the problem of evaluating and countering the then novel threat posed to its battle fleet by the possibility of attack from the air. Its technical analysis of the problem was exemplary, exhibiting innovative methodology and achieving a standard of operational research which, in purely technical and mathematical terms, would be difficult to better even now after decades of experience of this discipline.
2. The Royal Navy failed, however, in its application of this analysis. It appears to have viewed the problem as one capable of a once-for-all solution rather than as just one further episode in the ever-continuing struggle between offence and defence. In particular, it seems to have failed to take into account the rapid contemporary pace of advance in aeronautics that would vitiate much of the conclusions of its work even before the decade was out.
3. The conclusion drawn in 1931 that, given modest enhancement of anti-aircraft gun armament, the fleet had little to fear from air attack was thus specific to its time as well as to a particular scenario – a brief transit of a limited extent of disputed waters within range of enemy air bases. In so far as the vulnerability of the fleet to air attack came as a shock to the Royal Navy during the Second World War, it must have

been because these limitations and caveats had been forgotten and the conclusions of 1931 over-generalised.

4. Nothing in the analysis of 1931 saw air power as other than a possible distraction and restriction of the ability of the fleet to sail where it would in search of the decisive battle between lines of gun-armed capital ships, which remained the central object of Royal Navy planning and attention.
5. When harsh experience of war demonstrated the vulnerability of battleships to air attack, a perceived imperative to preserve such ships against loss became at times the primary determinant of naval decisions, taking precedence over defence of the nation, its possessions and its trade.

So, the response of the Royal Navy during the early 1930s to the emerging aerial threat can thus be characterised as having been innovative in matters of analysis but profoundly conservative and somewhat myopic in the interpretation of the fruits of such analysis in terms of policy and strategy. In part this may be because within the economic and geopolitical circumstances of the time, any doubting of the rôle and significance of the gun-armed capital ship would have had profoundly difficult consequences for the place of the Royal Navy in the world. But, however that may have been, the treatment during the 1930s of the emerging aerial threat to the British battle fleet constitutes an instructive example of the dangers of first conducting an exemplary piece of analysis but then over-generalising its conclusions and failing to revisit the analysis when circumstances change – as they were then doing with rapid advances in aeronautics. The more comfortable a conclusion, the more the need is for it to be reappraised regularly.

Notes

This chapter is based primarily on the unpublished Admiralty report 'Anti-Aircraft Gunnery Committee: 1931'. The following works also informed the text:

'Anti-Aircraft Gunnery Committee: 1931', unpublished Admiralty report, 1931, Ministry of Defence, Main Library, London

Ships of the Royal Navy: Statement of Losses During the Second World War (London: HMSO, 1947)

Bennett, G., *Naval Battles of World War II* (London: Batsford, 1975)

Busch, Fritz-Otto, *Prinz Eugen* (London: Futura, 1975)

Chesneau, Robert, *Conway's All the World's Fighting Ships: 1922–1946* (London: Conway, 1980)

Gibbons, Tony, *Battleships and Battlecruisers* (London: Salamander, 1983)

Green, William, *Famous Bombers of the Second World War*, 2nd series (London: MacDonald, 1960)

Morse, Philip M. and Kimball, George E., *Methods of Operations Research* (New York: The Technology Press of the Massachusetts Institute of Technology and Wiley, 1950)

Pugh, Philip G., *The Cost of Seapower* (London, Conway, 1986)

Richards, Denis, *Royal Air Force 1939–45*, Vol. I: *The Fight at Odds* (London: HMSO, 1953)

Richards, Denis, *Royal Air Force 1939–45*, Vol. II: *The Fight Avails* (London: HMSO, 1954)

Schofield, B.B., *The Russian Convoys* (London: Batsford, 1964)

Stevens, James Hay, *The Shape of the Aeroplane* (London: Hutchinson, 1953)

Taylor, A.J.P., *English History 1914–1945* (Oxford: Oxford University Press, 1965)

2

AMPHIBIOUS WARFARE, 1930–1939

Richard Harding

Britain in 1929 was in the depth of a depression, and ten years after the Peace of Versailles the international order looked more threatened by deep and intractable economic malaise rather than crises on the diplomatic front. That this changed rapidly during the 1930s is common knowledge and looking back after the passage of seventy years and across the divide created by the Second World War, it is easy to see an apparently sluggish response of the armed services to massive technological and operational demands. In almost all aspects of defence policy, Britain seemed to have moved slowly and, with hindsight, only just enough to survive the catastrophic onslaught of 1939–42. Amphibious warfare is no exception to this. It was neglected both in material and organisational terms almost until the last moment. That Britain eventually took her place alongside the United States to form part of the Allied amphibious armadas of 1943 to 1945 is seen as the product of adaptation and innovation in response to the most urgent demands of war.

There is a great deal of truth in this and it fits neatly into a well-developed view of the British approach to warfare – that Britain is a civil society only shaken out of its neglect of defence by periodic crises.[1] This view of implicit institutional conservatism in Britain in the 1930s has been strengthened by the great influence of Basil Liddell Hart, whose contrast of a more ancient 'British Way in Warfare' with the 'continentalist' views of the British military establishment was extremely influential from the early 1930s until after his death in 1970.[2] This perspective is clearly an important element in the historiography of amphibious warfare. The early histories of amphibious operations emerged out of the participants' own stories, supported by the meticulous recording processes that had been developed by the staff historians. They were stories consistent with the tradition of conservatism and resistance to innovation.

The first significant history published after 1945 was by Rear-Admiral L.E.H. Maund in 1949.[3] As Captain Maund, he had been appointed the first Director of the Inter-Service Training and Development Centre (ISTDC) in March 1938 and from June 1940, Naval Member of the Directorate of Combined Operations. There could hardly be a better source than the man who had been appointed at the eleventh hour to give some substance to Britain's amphibious capability. He had recorded his memories of the events leading to the war in September 1943[4] and developed them in his published history. He had extensive experience of the pre-war investigations into the problems of amphibious warfare and his memoirs provided the basis for its history. Such operations were earnestly discussed by the three services at combined exercises and radical proposals made, but they were of little interest to the Departments of State. No service was anxious to pay for any specialised materials such as landing craft, so the matter was left in the hands of a Landing Craft Committee that 'met about once a year, had a yarn and went away again'.[5] What was produced, Motor Landing Craft 10 (MLC 10), was of no use, being unarmoured and noisy. Even after the Italian invasion of Abyssinia in October 1935 there was general neglect. Maund witnessed the Japanese landing at Tientsin in 1937 in which a landing craft carrier greatly assisted the operations. Despite this, the authorities continued to insist that amphibious landings in a future war would be made impossible due to air attack. Suddenly, it was agreed to set up the ISTDC and Maund began the process of catching up.

The same picture emerges from Bernard Fergusson's *Watery Maze*.[6] Fergusson drew heavily upon the history drawn up by the Combined Operations Headquarters, and reflects Maund's view of the inter-war years. For Fergusson this was part of a 'tradition of neglect' (the title of his chapter on the subject). The defeat at Gallipoli dominated all discussions of amphibious operations, distorting analysis both because of the scale of the calamity and the unrepentant attitudes of its chief protagonists who remained powerful in public service – Winston Churchill and Sir Roger Keyes.[7] Daylight attack was abandoned. *Ad hoc* manoeuvres and joint staff exercises took place and a 'surprisingly useful' *Manual* was produced and revised, but it was not until the Director of the Royal Naval College Greenwich, Captain Bertram Watson, pulled together the experiences of the staff exercises over the preceding years in a paper of 22 February 1936 that the Admiralty began to take the matter seriously. Even then, nothing happened until the Deputy Chief of the Imperial General Staff, Sir Ronald Adam, presented a paper, supported by the Deputy Chief of the Naval Staff, Sir Andrew Cunningham, which led eventually to the ISTDC.[8] The reason for this sudden interest and why the Chiefs of Staff 'waved their wand' is not made clear. Nevertheless, the impression is clearly that serious work on amphibious operations only really commenced in the latter part of 1938. This has largely been supported by subsequent writers. The exercises and experiments had no impact. There was no organisational memory or commitment and no political support – facts that appeared more stark when compared to developments that were occurring in the United States and Japan.[9] David Massam has provided a much more sophisticated picture of development in this period: that of an essentially pragmatic approach that kept ideas developing through both formal and informal channels.[10]

Viewed in this light, innovation – the disruption of a comfortable status quo by the deliberate introduction of new technologies and operational procedures to meet new and clearly specified objectives – was the offspring of a catastrophic crisis. It presents the British state as being remarkably incapable of responding to all but the most imminent threats. The 1930s were full of threat and change. Financial fragility, a rapidly changing strategic balance in Europe, the Mediterranean and the Far East, and technological changes, particularly in aeronautics, were all clearly perceived threats to Britain. There was a sense of crisis, yet little seems to have been done. This chapter sets out to explore what was done in relation to these emerging threats, how Britain's capacity to wage an amphibious war changed and what may have hindered more dramatic innovation.

Amphibious warfare: the strategic position 1919–1930

The problem of innovation in amphibious warfare can be viewed at different levels, ranging from the strategic/political through the operational to technical/tactical levels. They are all interrelated, but the pressures and strains are different at different levels and at different times.

In the 1920s, amphibious warfare was a part of 'combined operations', which were defined as 'operations where naval, military or air forces in any combination are co-operating with each other, working independently under their respective commanders, but with a common strategic object'.[11] This captured the variety of possible operations ranging from opposed landings to supporting land or air forces on allied soil. Amphibious operations were a part of this, but not defined separately. Nonetheless, amphibious operations – using sea power to land forces in overseas territories for military advantage – was central to the idea of combined operations. Unlike in the United States, where the amphibious role was clearly the domain of the US Navy and its Marine Corps, Britain's interests were too varied and the Royal Navy's interest in large-scale amphibious operations too marginal to develop forces that could act alone.[12] The Royal Marines were adequate for limited operations, but large-scale amphibious operations were 'combined operations' in which the navy was an equal partner with the army and air force.

At senior levels within government and the service there is little doubt that amphibious warfare received very little attention. The ability of the services to work together towards effective combined operations was both expected by their history and limited by the new conditions emerging after 1919.

The key factor in the services' planning between 1919 and 1932 was the constant financial stringency. Public hostility to arms races, the arms control movements in Europe, economic slowdown and eventually depression provided the domestic political imperatives for the tremendous Treasury influence over budgets and policy, which was given expression in the 1919 planning assumption that war would not break out for at least ten years – the 'Ten Year Rule'. In the early post-war years, as a new peacetime *modus vivendi* had to be created, it fostered an environment of intense inter-service rivalry over their very purpose. The Washington Treaty of 1922 provided a ten-year holiday for battleship, carrier and cruiser expansion. While the Royal Navy avoided a potentially crippling arms race, it also put in doubt the long-term preservation of shipbuilding capacity and left it with a fleet inappropriately structured to meet the perceived defence needs of the empire.[13] It coincided with the RAF aggressively asserting its role in imperial and home defence. Having survived the immediate post-war possibility of disbandment, and the loss of representation in the Cabinet between 1921 and 1923, the RAF, under Hugh Trenchard, Chief of the Air Staff (1919–29), utilised both the economic stringency and the untested technological possibilities of air power to bolster the RAF's portion of the budget. The navy had lost the Royal Naval Air Service on the creation of the RAF on 1 April 1918. Control of air power at sea remained a constant irritant between the services until the Fleet Air Arm came back under Admiralty control in 1937.[14] As early as 1920 the RAF argued against battleship building not on the grounds of the ability of air power to destroy battleships, but on the potential for this to be the case within the lifespan of any battleship to be built.[15] This potential capability, which could be initiated, but not guaranteed, by current investment in air power – significantly less than the cost of maintaining a fleet – remained the trump card of the RAF during the whole inter-war period. The Admiralty rejected this unproven hypothesis and countered by denying both the competence and economy of an independent air force. The government decided in favour of the likely maintenance of the status quo in the medium term – that battleships would be the key to maritime supremacy and that an independent air force was the best use of national resources – but the dispute at the heart of national defence was to remain.

The promise of air power was even more of a challenge to the army. After 1918 the future commitment of an expeditionary army to Europe was in doubt, but the army had found its imperial policing role expanded in the new mandated territories.[16] However, an economic alternative to imperial policing with an effective diplomatic weight seems to have been proved by the RAF action in Somaliland in 1919 and Iraq in 1922, where the RAF got its first independent command. The £8 million bill for air power in Iraq, associated with very few casualties, contrasted with the £20 million estimate from the War Office. Further operations in Waziristan in 1923 and Aden in 1928 confirmed the value of air power in imperial policing.[17] The concerted opposition of the War Office, Colonial Office, Admiralty and India Office prevented the extension of this policy, but by then the RAF had effectively staked its claims in imperial defence, home defence and offensive strategy. Trenchard's theory of 'strategic interception', fully developed by 1928, anticipated the services working together to defeat an enemy. The Royal Navy held the ring, ensuring resources were channelled to the army in the field, while strategic air power denied these vital resources to the enemy. Deprived of support the enemy would crumple under an assault delivered by the army.[18] Therefore, by 1929, there seemed to be a way in which strategy could encompass a role for the three services on an equal footing. It was, however, rather misleading. There remained a great deal of ambiguity, in so far as it blurred the key question of the past ten years: what support were the army and navy to expect for their operations? It was quite clear to the Air Council and Air Ministry that this need for effective support would generate future demands for the absorption of the air force into the other two services. Trenchard's doctrine accepted there would be support, but what weight it might be given compared to independent attacks on strategic centres of enemy industry was left unresolved.

By 1930, therefore, the inter-service battles of the preceding decade had left marks on all the services, but amphibious operations had not been a particular casualty. The legacy of the Versailles Treaty demanded limited amphibious and combined operations. Air power provided a powerful striking force, but airfields needed to be defended and supported, In 1923 the aerodrome at San Stefano needed combined operations to defend it against possible Turkish attack. Imperial outposts and positions as far apart as Kuwait and Saldanha Bay provided the opportunities to practise embarkation and disembarkation.[19] Amphibious operations were also expected. Ships and garrisons on imperial stations practised embarkation and disembarkation as part of colonial policing and defence. In 1928, HMS *Emerald* landed forces and maintained a defensive position at an improvised airfield in Kuwait against the threat of Saudi incursion. During the 1930s HMS *Durban* carried out landing exercises in the West Indies. HMS *Dorsetshire* led a practice exercise at Saldanha Bay, South Africa, in 1934.[20] Larger exercises were carried out in the Far East during 1924 and 1925, simulating attacks on Singapore both to test the vulnerability of the defence and the resources needed to reconquer if it were lost.[21]

The navy's interest in amphibious operations was not limited to Singapore. The Washington Treaty largely prohibited the development of fortifications or naval facilities east of 110° longitude. The government's position on the defence of Hong Kong was that it could not be defended in a crisis. It had not been used for capital ships since 1905 and its defences and facilities were thoroughly out of date. Yet the Admiralty war plan against Japan depended on the defence of this island as it was vital for blockading operations against the Japanese home islands.[22] However, to defend Hong Kong demanded the dispatch of a relief fleet from the Mediterranean or around the Cape via Singapore and fuelling bases further east. Unable to develop such bases, at least until the expiry of the Washington Treaty in 1931, the problem required alternative solutions. One such solution was the Mobile Naval Base Organisation (MNBO), which was in the process of development since 1920. Six MNBOs were estimated for war against Japan. A war against the United States would demand four.[23] These bases required a significant amphibious capability based largely around the Royal Marines, but with possible army and RAF contributions. During the 1920s the Admiralty continued to work independently on this type of operation, making their conclusions available to the other services for information.[24]

Thus, by 1930, there were real prospects of amphibious operations, but they were likely to be limited in scope, either for imperial policing or for the rapid deployment of substantial naval forces. Exercises, together with other initiatives, captured experiences, developed techniques and suggested improvements to procedures and practices.[25] Yet, at the strategic level, there was no particular pressure to force forward any innovation. At this point there is no particular animus against amphibious operations, but few indicators within the international situation, from known technological developments at home or abroad, or from war plans, to demand substantial investment in this type of warfare. This was taking place against a background of financial pressures and differing service positions on strategy that threatened the core capabilities of each service, but which was to change dramatically in the next nine years.

Amphibious warfare: the strategic position 1930–1939

The diplomatic situation that had provided the foundation for limiting defence budgets crumbled by 1934. The London Naval Disarmament Conference of 1931 continued the battleship expansion moratorium for another five years and extended the controls to cruisers, but it was the last gasp of the disarmament movement. The Japanese invasion of Manchuria in September 1931, and the German walkout from the Geneva Disarmament Conference in October 1933, left little doubt that planning assumptions had to change. Concern within the services led to a concerted and successful effort to abandon the Ten Year Rule in March 1932, but the expansion of budgets created as many tensions as their restrictions.[26]

In November 1933 the Defence Requirements Committee was set up to try to co-ordinate the process of correcting the worst deficiencies of the services in line with perceived threats. The Admiralty view of future war requirements had not fundamentally altered. Naval defence of the home islands, the Eastern Mediterranean and the Far East were three great challenges, with Japan as the most immediate threat. However, to meet it, the ageing battle fleet, lack of cruisers and diminished war stocks all needed urgent attention and huge investment. The Royal Air Force, however, was developing its views on future war on a fundamentally different basis. The view that the potential destructive power of air forces was growing to the point when air power alone would be able to force an industrialised enemy to sue for peace was growing in the early 1930s. The growth of the Luftwaffe during 1934, and the recognition by the Defence Requirements Committee that Germany was the main potential enemy – with its growing air force within practicable flying time of London – pushed the airmen's claims for priority to the top. The doctrine of the effective bomber force had major implications for defence decisions for the rest of the decade, not least for amphibious warfare.[27]

The need for a field force to hold the line until air power crippled the German war effort and then drive to Berlin was now called into question. Indeed, whether a field force could even get to Europe or be supplied once there was questionable if German air power could destroy facilities in Britain. The need to defend France and the Low Countries was also in doubt if German air forces could fly around them. This argument was reinforced over the next few years by the development of new stressed-skin metal monoplanes with more powerful engines and greater potential bomb load. It was not until the collapse of the 'Little Entente' and the fall of Czechoslovakia in March 1939 that the Cabinet accepted that in the event of war a new British Expeditionary Force must be sent to support France. It was not a refutation of the bomber doctrine, but recognition that without it France may not withstand German pressure.

The bomber doctrine did not just cover the idea of strategic destruction of an enemy's capacity to make war. It also laid claim to decisive tactical results. The defence of Singapore was a major issue of contention between the Royal Navy and the RAF. The Admiralty had long held concerns about an amphibious attack on Singapore and the best method of defending the island and anchorage. As early as 1928 the Air Staff rejected the Admiralty's fears; 'there is simply no chance of the Japanese being able to bring their fleet all the way to Singapore to carry out either the land operations, or the prolonged bombardment necessary, in the time that would be available'.[28] Their arguments at this time rested on an analysis of naval operations, judging that the risks and obstacles to the Japanese of such long-range operations outweighed the possibility of success. Over the next five years the delays in fortifying Singapore greatly increased

Admiralty worries about the security of the base.[29] The Air Staff never fully accepted these concerns, and by 1937 saw the defence of the island as being possible directly by air power.

As early as 1925 the torpedo-bomber was seen as a real threat to concentrations of shipping.[30] Flying boats and submarines could reconnoitre the approaches and, once located, the Japanese aircraft carriers could be destroyed by shore-based aircraft at Singapore. After this any invasion convoy would be at the mercy of air attack.[31] While an exercise along these lines was a success, the results were not entirely convincing. It was blessed by good flying weather and the old HMS *Hermes,* making 18 knots, representing the Japanese force, was not the exact equivalent of the newer 30-knot Japanese carriers. Nevertheless, it did not dispel the belief that air power could effectively prohibit amphibious operations and it is against this that the apparent neglect and the much quoted remark of an unidentified senior officer at the Admiralty in 1939, that combined operations were unlikely in this war, must be viewed.[32] By then, the planning assumptions of both the Royal Navy and the RAF made large-scale amphibious operations highly unlikely. In the Far East, the Committee of Imperial Defence (CID) had never expected that Hong Kong would be successfully defended. The Japanese advance southwards along the Chinese coast during 1938–9 made the survival of the island base even less likely. The Admiralty clung to the possibility of its relief and consequently the utility of the MNBO operations – but only as a pre-requisite for a traditional naval blockade – and it was only in August 1940 that the plan was definitively abandoned. In the Eastern Mediterranean, the Italian threat to Abyssinia in 1935 sent ripples of concern through the defence establishment and stimulated the first MNBO deployment to Alexandria in September of that year.[33] Nevertheless, sustained amphibious operations were not seen as central to a military solution of the crisis.

When war finally broke out in September 1939, Britain had taken the decision to commit herself to a continental campaign and the movement of the BEF to France over the autumn was a highly successful unopposed amphibious operation. From the spring of 1939 army plans were clearly linked to a long-term continental campaign. The deployment of large forces from the sea to an enemy coast was not central to this immediate concern. Neither naval nor air plans foresaw the need for substantial amphibious operations. The world had changed dramatically since 1930, but it had not raised the likelihood of amphibious operations. On the contrary, they were somewhat less likely. If the bomber doctrine were correct – which, even if the wilder predictions of the air enthusiasts were dismissed, was strongly assumed at governmental level – the decisive battle would be taking place in the air. If the nation survived strategic bombardment, substantial amphibious operations anywhere near an industrialised enemy were likely to be destroyed by tactical air power. The proximity of Japanese forces to Hong Kong made the Admiralty ambition of its relief through an effective MNBO less likely, whilst at this time the distance of Japanese forces from Singapore made a successful assault unlikely and the need for an amphibious reconquest unnecessary. That these assumptions were grossly misplaced is now clear, but it would have taken a huge leap of imagination to move from past history and current preoccupations. The services were straining to build up their core capabilities in the face of an immediate threat. It was not complacency, but the great pressures that lay in the defence threats as they were then perceived, that made it highly unlikely that resources would be diverted to what was recognised as highly complex but less likely amphibious warfare. It is largely with hindsight that the disbandment of the ISTDC during the Munich Crisis in October 1938 and its virtual disbandment in September 1939 look like mistakes.

If it should not be expected that documents related to the strategic direction of a future war would reveal much regarding innovation in amphibious warfare, it is pertinent to ask what impact the planning assumptions had on the operational and tactical preparations for war and vice versa. Some evidence here certainly suggests neglect. In July 1938 a practice landing exercise on Slapton Beach, Devon, was not a great success and it is quoted as an example of the unpreparedness of British forces.[34] When the crisis came in 1940, powered, armoured landing craft were not available in any numbers. Was there a failure to innovate or respond to reasonable challenges?

Amphibious operations: operational development 1930–1939

The evidence for neglect of the operational concerns of amphibious warfare is partly found in comparison with developments in other countries, particularly the United States and Japan. Maund himself witnessed the Japanese landings at the mouth of the Yangtze near Shanghai in 1937 and was impressed by their use of a specialised landing craft carrier, *Shinshu Maru,* and landing craft.[35] The US Marine Corps went into the war against Japan in 1941 with a clear doctrine and technical equipment suited to an island war. The Corps could point to an offensive vision in the Pacific dating from the early 1920s. They had a dedicated marine assault force, the Fleet Marine Force, from 1933. They had a *Tentative Landing Operations Manual* in place by 1935 which became 'the Bible of amphibious warfare' or the foundation of later documents that were 'the Holy Writ of modern amphibious warfare' adopted by the navy and army.[36] The Fleet Exercises (Flex 1–7) from 1935 to 1941, which employed progressively larger landing forces, reaching two divisions by 1941, extensively tested equipment and procedures.

Set against the very limited British activity, the gap between Britain, Japan and the United States looks enormous. However, it is possible to overstate the contrasts. The operational developments in Japan and the United States were largely products of the second half of the 1930s, the very point when British strategic interest began to wane. Japanese landing resources were limited both in number and capability. The converted whaler, *Shinshu Maru,* was probably adapted as much for rapid unloading at quays as assault landings in open waters.[37] The Japanese amphibious advances in South-East Asia and the Pacific from December 1941 to April 1942 were seldom against prepared resistance, and it is important not to read back into the 1930s Japanese doctrine that was consolidated in this period.[38] It was not until after the outbreak of the war in Europe that the US Marine Corps came close to solving fundamental aspects of amphibious operations, such as supporting naval bombardment, ship to shore movement, landing craft and tracked vehicle design.[39] During the majority of the post-1919 period the operational gap between Britain, the United States and Japan was far closer than the perspective of 1939–41 suggests. In the early 1930s British amphibious development looks very like US developments. The amphibious nature of imperial policing and rapid response to external threats to the empire had demanded close co-operation between the services since the eighteenth century. At the beginning of the twentieth century, this close interrelationship was clearly understood. In 1905 it had been agreed to establish a joint committee to examine the conquest of the German colonies in the event of war. In 1913 a *Manual on Combined Naval and Military Operations* was created to capture current procedures for these joint operations.[40] This does not mean that operational policy, procedures and practices were fully developed, agreed and understood. In a discussion on this matter at the Royal United Services Institution in 1907, despite agreement about the need for the services to work together, the speaker, G.G. Aston, had to conclude with the hope that 'with the hour will arise the man'.[41]

The First World War challenged many of the assumptions about combined operations. The only strategic amphibious offensive of the war, on the Dardanelles peninsula, had not been planned in detail or rigorously prepared. Before the war, operations were perceived as enabling an army to land with massive naval superiority against an isolated European enemy or a hostile force lacking first-class training or weaponry. At the Dardanelles, the naval superiority had counted for far less than has been assumed. The Turkish defenders were seriously underestimated, as was the impact of just a few machine guns and some barbed wire. The tragedy cast a huge shadow over post-war political and operational thinking,[42] but it did not stop innovation. Technological changes during the war, such as the tank, the aeroplane, wireless communications and artillery plotting, were integrated into operational plans on the Western

Front by 1918.[43] In many ways the end of the war led to the services slipping back into pre-war habits, but the ability to integrate change, demonstrated particularly in 1917–18, was not lost and was applied to amphibious operations.

By 1930, the Gallipoli campaign had been examined in detail at the staff colleges. The *Manual* had been re-examined by the services and a revised version was prepared during 1921–2. The tank promised an offensive power that could overcome opposition on the beach and from 1920 the matter of transporting tanks to the beaches was seriously taken in hand. The effectiveness of naval gunfire in support of the landing, particularly against indirect targets, had been a problem at Gallipoli.[44] The army needed to land its own artillery as soon as possible. This demand for speed and the infantry demand for protection against small arms on the approach to the beach were fed into the debates on the production of a powered, armoured landing craft. By 1926 the Beach Motor Boat or Motor Landing Craft 1 (MLC 1) was a design that the army and navy could work with for the rapid landing of troops, stores and guns. The issue of landing tanks was more complex. The weight of the Vickers medium tank (13 tons) made hoisting out a loaded landing craft from the standard mechantman's davits impossible. Experimentation with the light tanks (4 tons) and tankettes (2 tons) indicated that a practicable solution might be possible with existing material. In the event, it had to be accepted that specially modified transport ships would be required for carrying tanks overseas and a new landing craft, the MLC 10, similar to the MLC 1, was completed in September 1929.

The role of air power in amphibious landings was not ignored. The need for complete local air superiority over the invasion fleet, convoy and beachhead area was the primary role for aircraft. This required the destruction of enemy air forces in the area. Reconnaissance out to sea and inland was important. Disruption of the enemy's lines of communication by land and sea and the bombing of enemy targets in front of the battlefield were to be followed up.[45] Exercises during the 1920s put some flesh on these operational objectives. Concentration of adequate air power was the key problem. An enemy air force would be able to concentrate aircraft on the landing zone very quickly – far quicker than it was possible to process intelligence of the move and pass it on to the commanders of the amphibious forces.[46] There would seldom be enough aircraft on the navy's carriers to carry out all the operations expected and it was vital that aircraft allocated to defend the fleet should not be diverted to operations ashore. The RAF could not expect to undertake large-scale operations until a base had been established ashore. There would therefore be a period when the troops were ashore fighting to establish a lodgement large enough to support an operational airfield during which assistance from the air forces would be extremely limited. The floatplane was examined as a solution to this gap in air protection. Floatplanes could operate from any calm piece of water, supplied, rearmed and refitted by floatplane tenders.

Exercises in the Baltic between 1927 and 1929, where Britain lacked any land bases, tested these ideas. The early exercises led to experiments with the Fairey 3F, a standard fleet carrier and spotter plane, the Westland Wapiti, and Hawker Horsley torpedo-bomber. These indicated that floats could be fitted in place of the standard land undercarriage. These aircraft were chosen because they were single-engined machines with an armed weight of less than 12,000 lb. The thrust required for take-off on water was found to be adequate, although supercharging could give a margin of greater safety. In so far as training was concerned, limited experience of training pilots of land-based aircraft to fly floatplanes during the China crisis of 1927 indicated that it could be done in time for any expedition. A proposal was made to ensure that all land-based aircraft should have interchangeable land and float landing gear.[47]

This last suggestion was not acted upon. A basic requirement for any solution to the problems of amphibious warfare at this time was that it did not incur additional costs. A fundamental planning assumption that remained in place after the abandonment of the Ten Year Rule in March 1932 was that there would be time during the period of increasing tension before a war broke out to build up the required material and train the forces. The landing craft fitted this requirement very well. Their design and construction were simple. They were designed to be carried by a standard merchant ship with limited conversion work. Likewise it was assumed that the Board of Trade would be able to hire vessels for conversion to seaplane or floatplane carriers within six months. It was not necessary to keep the old seaplane tenders *Ark Royal* and *Pegasus* on the lists.[48] The training of service personnel on the landing craft or the floatplanes was assumed to be matter of weeks rather than months. However, the adaptation of all serving aircraft to land as well as float undercarriage and the modification of aircraft with folding wings was both expensive and unnecessary in the immediate term. The proposal was 'in accordance with Air Staff policy, though it has not yet been possible to put that policy fully into effect'.[49] The floatplane provided an answer to the air cover problem, which imposed few immediate costs, but it was far from perfect. The Air Ministry disliked the operational limitations and cost implications. As the Director of Training pointed out, floatplanes could not operate in bad weather or with ice on the water. *Ad hoc* training was no substitute for training in units. He concluded, 'I feel that only in exceptional circumstances could an operation such as this be successfully brought off, and that in the majority of cases we shall have to operate aircraft from carriers and accept the risk to the carriers until a suitable aerodrome can be provided'.[50] The Air Ministry agreed, but it was, predictably, totally unacceptable to the Admiralty.

By 1930 there had been considerable progress on providing technical solutions to some of the operational problems identified by fairly extensive research into the practicalities of amphibious warfare. Other operational problems had also been addressed. It is sometimes claimed that daylight operations were considered to be impossible after the Gallipoli débâcle, hence no real progress was made towards solving the problems of opposed landings by large forces. Instead, it has been suggested that the daylight attack was reinvented independently by the USMC during the 1930s.[51] This is not entirely true. Undoubtedly, the daylight assault landing became much more of an operational focus for the USMC after 1933, but during the 1920s, when both the USMC and the British services saw amphibious operations as potentially much more varied, ranging from major opposed landings to small shore parties, advanced naval base construction and reinforcement of allies, innovations were made to meet the needs of this variety of action. In 1919 it was assumed that initial landings would take place at night to secure the beach for the main landings after dawn. This was incorporated in the revised *Manual of Combined Operations*.[52] Night landings were preferred by the Royal Navy, but the army had doubts about the advantages. During an exercise at Kasid Bay, India, in December 1925, the Royal Marine 'defenders' on 'B' beach sighted the first tows at 0550 – fifteen minutes before the first boats beached. At 0603 searchlights were directed from the covering warships in the hope of blinding the defenders, but it just had the effect of showing up the tows approaching the beach. On 'A' beach the tows were also seen fifteen minutes before the first boat landed. The second tow took twenty minutes to cover the last one hundred yards to the beach; 'All this time the whole tow was under close fire in adequate light'.[53] The senior army commander concluded that armoured landing craft, supported by tanks, were needed for this type of operation in future.

The development of the self-propelled semi-armoured landing craft – capable of landing all arms – by 1929, made landing a slightly more precise prospect, but the problems of accurate navigation, landing on time and avoiding beach obstacles had still to be negotiated. By 1934, the procedure of putting an officer ashore the previous night to check conditions on the beach was adopted. An experiment was made, landing at dawn twilight to conceal the approach, but giving enough light for final navigation and first movement ashore. It was the worst of all possible worlds. The tows were seen between 300 and 800 yards offshore – hopelessly exposed if met by machine guns – and they were denied covering naval fire in order to preserve secrecy. The recommendation was that landings should take place in daylight. Naval gunfire and light tanks and smoke screens would more than compensate for the loss of night cover. The 1938 *Manual of Combined Operations* had dropped the assumption of a night landing and included an assumption of a tank-supported landing. Although night landings were not ruled out – indeed the landings in the 1938 exercise in Devon was undertaken at night – the key objective was to attain maximum concentration on the point of attack, which the navigational problems of night attacks directly threatened.[54] Thus before 1939 British doctrine, like USMC doctrine, was moving with the technological possibilities of powered, armoured landing craft and tanks to effect opposed daylight landings.

The daylight landing was not the only aspect of amphibious warfare to evolve over these years of apparent neglect. One of the major prospects for improving combined operations was wireless. It was being tested by most services and the need to control and co-ordinate the three services operating in a few square miles of beachhead was an obvious problem. During 1933 it was decided that the focus for the 1934 combined exercises would be inter-service wireless communications. One of the great achievements of the British Army by 1918 was the effective co-ordination of artillery and infantry. A major element in this success was the development of wireless communications. Although the Royal Navy did not see its primary role as providing tactical firepower for the army, it was, nonetheless, an important function. The *Manual* of 1925 had something to say about wireless. The need for wireless communication between the Forward Observation Officers (FOOs) or spotter aircraft and the director of the bombarding squadron was clear. A Combined Signals Directing Staff was appointed to keep an eye on the issues arising from this complex area of development. A uniform signal code and procedure between the services had been agreed for supporting fire. Ships had wireless that was capable of communication with spotter aircraft and special gear could be fitted to enable the ship to receive 'zone calls' from RAF aircraft.[55] The Beach Organisation was important, but at this stage the signals arrangements were not spelt out. Each service needed to transmit to and receive from its own units, at sea and ashore. There had to be communication between the services to ensure effective support. The volume of traffic that these communications would generate and the staff required to handle it were potentially enormous. Given that it was assumed that the land and sea commanders would be accommodated on the same ship, it raised serious questions about the practicability of a combined Head Quarters Ship.

Before the full exercise a preliminary exercise was carried out at Sandhurst by the Combined Signals Board in December 1933 regarding the best type of HQ ship.[56] The conclusion was that it was not possible for an existing warship to operate such a number of high-power wireless transmission lines without creating unacceptable interference. To reduce interference in its own wireless transmission, the Royal Navy operated a system of 'guard ships'. These guard ships were detailed to answer all calls on specified frequencies by high-power transmitter, while the Flag Ship kept a watching ear on all the frequencies but did not transmit except by low power to the guard ships when necessary. This kept the commander in chief informed, but imposed some delay in replies. However, it required large numbers of warships to be kept on this duty to ensure a complete complex network, and the loss of a vessel could disrupt the communication system. It was therefore not an ideal solution. Tests were carried out on HMS *Iron Duke* to see if grouping receivers and transmitters at different ends of the ship would reduce interference. Equally worrying was that most wireless telegraphy equipment on British battleships was by 1933 obsolescent by RAF and Army standards. They used frequency ranges unsuited to mobile shore-based sets. The RAF had not at that point completed the conversion of its aircraft from medium- to high-frequency transmission. So far as the Staff College syndicates were concerned, it would be possible to use a capital ship, such as HMS *Nelson,* as an HQ ship but only if she were re-equipped with modern equipment.

An alternative was the conversion of a merchant liner. This would be a large undertaking, but result in the provision of purpose-built facilities for each service. While it would release the warships from signals duty, it would put all communications in the hands of an ill-protected, unarmed, unmanoeuvrable vessel. It would take at least three months to fit out and even then would be unlikely to meet the wireless needs of each service.

The initial examination was, thus, inconclusive. The Air member of the Combined Signals Directing Staff agreed with the general conclusions and was concerned that the limitation on frequencies would simply be inadequate for all the communication functions required by the air force during a landing. The Army member, Colonel Chenevix Trench, suggested that a capital ship would not provide the necessary signals capacity and that prior to a landing the General Officer Commanding should move to a dedicated Army HQ ship, with low-power links to the naval and RAF HQs. A single HQ ship could be used for planning, when the full wireless capacity would not be needed, but was impracticable for the operation itself.

It was also unfortunate that the consideration of this matter was taking place at a time when wireless technology was in a state of change. By 1935, the Air member claimed, all aircraft would be operating on high frequency and five day bomber squadrons would be equipped with it in time for the live exercise in late 1934. A greater matter was the development of ultra-short wave, being developed by Marconi. This required far less power for clear and fast transmission. It was only set up experimentally at this time, between Marconi's Electra House in the Strand and their Chelmsford offices, but it was possibly an effective answer to the problem of interference on an HQ ship.[57]

The exercise to test these ideas was carried out off the Yorkshire coast between 10 and 13 September 1934.[58] The HQ ship was HMS *Nelson*. The suggested scenario gives an insight into the expected use of amphibious operations at this time. It was supposed that the Royal Navy would continue to dominate the seas and an enemy fleet could not be induced to give battle on the high seas. Instead the enemy would confine himself to posing a potential threat as a 'fleet in being'. However, new weapons meant that this fleet was no longer safe in its anchorage. The enemy could now be destroyed by air attack. Sufficient air power could only be supplied by land-based bombers operating within striking distance. To this end an expeditionary force, up to three divisions strong, had to be landed on enemy territory in a defensible spot to set up an air base for these operations against the enemy fleet. To ensure effective supply from the sea, a MNBO had to be established or a port had to be captured. These last actions were to be carried out by the Royal Marines.

The purpose was to test staff planning and wireless communications, so many other matters were put on one side. It was to be an unopposed landing. It was assumed that the enemy would have only a brigade of infantry and a regiment of cavalry in the general vicinity. To represent a landing by three divisions, about 2,000 troops of the 5th Division would be landed on two beaches by brigade. The follow-up operation of landing their vehicles and stores was to be deduced from sample activities based partly on the performance of the one MLC 10 carried by HMS *Hood*. It was assumed that a compulsory delay of one hour would represent the time required for the arrival of necessary vehicles and stores for an advance inland. Operational navigation aids, such as taut wire gear, were to be simulated. Specialised landing craft were simulated by using local drifters. The Fleet Air Arm was to cover the fleet and invasion convoy against air or sea attack. The Royal Navy would supply spotter planes, linked to the shore-based FOOs and their own bombarding ships. It was assumed that in the previous four days an air battle had been won and the RAF had air superiority over the landing zone. The RAF role was 'strategic reconnaissance' on hostile airfields. For air defence the RAF and Fleet Air Arm would operate on a single frequency. The HQ ship, Flag Officer Carriers and the Advanced Air HQ would maintain a listening watch. Anti-submarine aircraft from the fleet would operate on a completely separate frequency.

Officers were put ashore the previous night to test the beach and surf conditions. The landings went ahead in excellent weather. All the dawn landings took place on time and in the right place. Army and Navy beach signals offices were set up, along with a visual signals post. The army advanced to positions expected. The Royal Marines successfully captured Hornsea (the 'enemy' port) by 1700 on the first day to open up port facilities. After three days the exercise concluded to general satisfaction. It was a landing in nearly ideal conditions, but a large amount was learned about the practicality of such operations.

The twilight was no protection. The tows were seen at least 300 yards offshore by coast watchers. A few machine guns covering the approaches would have proved lethal. The recommendation was that light tanks, armoured landing craft, smoke screens and effective naval bombardment more than compensated for the lack of darkness and that these should be seriously tested.

The signals traffic was handled satisfactorily in general and it was concluded that, with a few modifications, HMS *Nelson* could act as an effective HQ ship. The main problem was that *Nelson* could not accommodate enough receivers to provide adequate monitoring for all three services. The air radio traffic did have problems as the Flag Officer Carriers on HMS *Courageous* reported serious interference, particularly among the spotting aircraft. The carrier flag did not have transmission access to the Advanced Air HQ and this impeded co-ordination of RAF and FAA air defence fighters. RAF medium-range reconnaissance went through the officer commanding the covering force (the initial landing force) through the HQ ship to the Senior Naval Officer Landing (SNOL). This was found to be unnecessarily lengthy as the navy's beach signals office could route it directly.

Aerial spotting was a problem from the first day when it was difficult to identify the positions of the advancing troops. On 12 September the weather deteriorated, which made spotting impossible. This put more emphasis on the FOOs' communication with bombarding ships. The naval FOOs were installed near the army signals units and worked closely with them. Working with gridded maps and an army liaison officer, the FOOs each had their own frequency for contact with their ship. The navy wireless sets (Type 30A) were found to be too fragile for the mobile beach offices and it was recommended to replace them with the army 'C' set. The need to ensure constant communications indicated that an additional low-power set was needed to back up the high-power set on the Admiral's wave. While it was agreed that a decentralised battery control was important, the system of each ship operating on a different frequency with its own FOO was questioned. A common frequency monitored by the HQ ship could streamline the process and prevent dramatic loss in bombardment effectiveness. However, the most obvious issue was the need to create a combined call signs and cipher office with direct transmission to the Senior Officer Bombardment.

There were other matters that raised problems. Before the covering force could move inland, the main body and stores had to be landed. The army wanted to be able to move off within four hours of landing. It was assumed that 80 MLC 10s would be available for every division, but from the operations of *Hood*'s MLC 10 it was deduced that it would take at least eight hours to land all the necessary stores. By reducing the stores required, the time could be reduced to four and a half hours, but still many questions remained about the MLC operations. Given that a beach landing in divisional strength was the most likely scenario, the only method that the navy considered to be adequate was the use of large numbers of MLC 10s. For this there had to be enough modified transports. The weather and sea conditions had to be calm enough to hoist them out and the beach had to be right for an effective landing.

Finally, anti-aircraft defences had not been seriously tested. Every stage was subject to disruption by enemy aircraft. Anti-aircraft defences were needed not just for the ships but for the beach signals offices. Overall, the reports did not hide the fact that the exercise had not replicated the experience of a large-scale landing on a hostile shore. It had shown how a foothold might be gained by an assault force, but not how the main force could land and secure territory. Many of the issues related to the use of current technology were highlighted and solutions proposed. Some were easy, such as reorganising transmission frequencies to ensure less interference and more direct communications. Others were extremely important, yet not immediately soluble, particularly the requirements for armoured landing craft and tanks operating in daylight and the need for large number of MLC 10s for support operations.

Any exercise such as this could not lead to instant changes. The interests of the services and the Board of Trade had to be considered and the recommendations were couched in terms of further tests and experiments. Nevertheless, each department was expected to respond and over the next four years minor adjustments were made. Tests were carried out with smoke shells. The Admiralty accepted that the Motor Landing Craft 'is the most important material question at present outstanding in connection with combined operations and that they consider that the proposal to build nine of these vessels and to proceed with the production of armoured protection for them to be a necessary preliminary to further progress in Combined Operations, and to be now a matter of some urgency'.[59] The Admiralty also agreed with the recommendation that the old disputes about who paid for the boats had to end. Landing was an Admiralty responsibility, and the agreement reached with the War Office in the 1920s that the army would provide them and the Admiralty maintain them could not be sustained. The Admiralty needed to accept full responsibility for landing craft.[60] MLC 10s could take loads of up to 12 tons, but most army loads were less than 5 tons. This suggested that more, smaller, landing craft could be produced and carried more easily to the landing zone, but the Admiralty was not convinced that these advantages would compensate for the loss of buoyancy in the smaller vessels.[61] On the other hand, smaller landing craft were precisely what the Director of Sea Transport at the Board of Trade saw as important to solve the shipping problem, and further lifting tests of the MLC 10 took place in July 1935.[62] The Director of Naval Construction was also not convinced that the recommendations took the discussions much further than earlier considerations of the problem four or five years earlier.[63] This did not stop consideration of various types of craft for beach landing over the next few years.[64]

The importance of landing tanks with the first flight in a daylight operation remained. The Vickers light tank came into service in 1931. Although two of these vehicles could be carried by each MLC 10, the new design revived interest in amphibious tanks. Experiments with tanks for river crossings and landings from the sea had taken place soon after 1919 and a committee on sea transport and landing of tanks in 1922 had concluded that the 'true solution' to the problem lay with amphibious tanks. However, the current tank in service, the Vickers Medium C, could not be made to float satisfactorily.[65] By 1931 the development of an amphibious tank based on the Vickers light tank design was under consideration, but after experiments in 1932, the design again failed to meet requirements of seaworthiness on water and robustness ashore.[66] Further experiments in 1940 failed to solve the problem.[67] The armoured landing craft was the only alternative and in June 1937 the War Office renewed its request for an armoured tank landing craft. In August the Admiralty, War Office and Board of Trade agreed to build six experimental landing craft to conduct tests in landing light tanks. The trials took place in October 1938, by which time the ISTDC had been established.[68]

Perhaps the most important conclusion of the 1934 exercise was the observation that much more practice would be required to make a large-scale opposed landing practicable. Here lies one of the most significant factors distinguishing invention, innovation and operational capability. Staff exercises could identify problems, inter-service committees could guide the invention of new equipment such as landing craft, exercises and committees could test and evaluate the equipment and revise manuals to bring about innovation in procedures, but only constant practice could move this invention and innovation to operational effectiveness. However, substantial exercises were impossible given British planning assumptions. Planning was based on the assumption that the material for combined operations could be produced in the period of heightening tension before war broke out. To some extent this was justified by the rapidly changing technology of the time. Landing craft could be built fairly quickly, so to build and lay up large numbers of these vessels for no clear purpose was questionable. By 1934 the rapid expansion of the Luftwaffe was absorbing the attention of the RAF. Both Chiefs of the Air Staff, Sir Edward Ellington (1933–37) and Sir Cyril Newall (1937–40), were hampered in their plans for expansion by the rapidly changing technology of air power.[69] The highest denominator of technical superiority was the objective in this rapidly changing environment. Co-operation with an amphibious landing force was conceived in terms of air superiority, reconnaissance and long-range interdiction – tasks suited to the modern fighters and bombers being designed and developed – not close support. Indeed, in the late 1930s army co-operation was looking increasingly problematic as the contemporary army co-operation aircraft, the Hawker Hector, Westland Lysander and Bristol Blenheim, could hardly defend themselves against modern fighters. It would not be until 1941 and the introduction of the Curtiss Tomahawk, that army co-operation would have an aircraft that could be used effectively in contested skies.

The long-term testing of equipment and procedures during the last five years of the decade is the most obvious difference between the British and American experience. During the early 1930s there was little difference between British capability and that of the USMC. In equipment, experience and doctrine there were great similarities. Landings were made in tows under the cover of naval gunfire. In the landing of tanks and heavy equipment, and in naval gunfire direction, the USMC was less advanced that the British. Except on the subject of naval gunfire and air support, the 1935 *Tentative Manual* said little different from the 1925 or 1931 *Manual of Combined Operations*. The differences began to emerge from the US fleet exercises from 1935. Like the British they tested equipment for landing and radio communications. Also like the British they found that tows were inadequate, that night landings were not as effective as expected, and that naval wireless sets were not robust enough for operations ashore. However, over the years the number and scale of the operations allowed for much more. While the exercises were conducted under almost ideal conditions, live firing from bombarding vessels gave data for changes to ammunition type and target identification. Aircraft attacks on beach targets and strongpoints gave evidence both for the need for modern ground attack aircraft and their capabilities. Systematic combat loading of vessels could be tested and refined. Still, much remained to be done to remedy defects when Pearl Harbor was attacked in December 1941.[70]

At the heart of the difference between the USMC tactical development and that of the British was the clear purpose of the former. The move across the Pacific in time of crisis with Japan provided strategic objectives and identifiable tactical problems that could be planned and tested. Likewise intervention in the Caribbean provided clear objects and obstacles. For Britain the experience of joint exercises and committees provided some vital lessons but also far more ambiguity about purpose. The evolution of the *Manual* in the last years of peace gives a good impression of how ideas were developing.

Between 1925 and 1938 the *Manual* expanded from 22 to 31 chapters. Both *Manuals* accepted that training would be *ad hoc* and lay in the hands of local commanders who were willing to work together. The general tenor of the 1925 *Manual* put an emphasis upon expounding established procedures and was naturally much more limited in its discussion of tanks and landing craft, while the 1938 *Manual* still contained many vital details of procedures and practice. In some areas the exercises seemed to have provided greater certainty. The importance of tanks was more clearly emphasised and the inadvisability of night landings more apparent.[71] However, it also focused much more on explaining the context for strategic planning, the responsibilities of the services and their broader roles in an operation. The types of combined operation are more fully discussed and the need to remain open-minded about who would exercise command. The 1925 emphasis on the Advanced Sea Base organisation gave way to an emphasis on the variety of operations. This followed through into presenting more flexible approaches to centralisation and decentralisation of command and function. There is more detail on the types of landing craft, more information on the semi-armoured self-propelled landing craft, and more emphasis on anti-aircraft defence.

The last significant test of Britain's amphibious capability before the outbreak of war occurred in the summer of 1938, when a small-scale landing to test technical and tactical aspects of landing, including naval gunfire support, was undertaken. While it had its successes, the subsequent analysis revealed worrying elements. Naval spotter aircraft provided direction for indirect fire, but a mechanised enemy moving quickly to reinforce the defences was a new problem that aircraft could not easily identify. Naval aircraft were vulnerable to modern land-based fighters. Supply was difficult despite the good performance of equipment for landing vehicles. Overall, despite the Japanese experience in 1937, it was felt that such a landing was only possible by complete surprise or against an enemy without modern weapons.[72]

Conclusions: innovation and amphibious warfare?

Amphibious operations were not at the centre of British military thinking throughout this period. However, they were never entirely ignored. There was always enough ambiguity in British defence policy to demand that military operations overseas be considered. On the whole the period has been characterised as lacking innovation. Financial constraints and complacency encouraged drift until almost too late. Nevertheless, the British attempts to come to terms with the changing world of amphibious operations may tell us something about how innovation operated at this time. If successful innovation requires careful and determined navigation through complex social situations, then there is no doubt that the political and organisational complexity of the situation in the 1930s was enough to defeat most of the efforts of the amphibious operations visionary. The three services were required to integrate efforts on three levels – strategic, operational and tactical. There was never deep agreement between the services on the strategic need for amphibious operations. There were never the resources to provide the fine detail of tactical integration. Equipment was not available for long-term and large-scale training. On the other hand, operational planning throughout the period, in staff colleges, limited exercises and special committees, provided important pointers to organisational and material requirements.

If innovation is defined by its disruption of the status quo, then again the period was not innovative. Amphibious warfare was a British tradition, which was integrated into the doctrine of the Royal Navy by 1910.[73] It was innovation elsewhere that disrupted the status quo of pre-1914 British 'navalism'. Despite popular reaction to the slaughter on the Western Front during the First World War and the miserable budgetary situation of the army throughout the 1919–39 period, the continental commitment remained an important factor in defence planning, which undermined any possibility of clear focus on the significance of amphibious power. Even more significant was the untried threat of air power. It was an innovation that increasingly questioned the practicality of amphibious operations wherever a world-class air power existed. The technological advances in aircraft design throughout the 1930s were a constant unsettling factor.

If innovation is a function of crisis, then again, amphibious warfare does not demonstrate any serious innovation. Through successive crises in the 1930s, there was not consistent development of amphibious doctrine or material. The demands of the Second World War in Europe and the Pacific brought forth diverse materials, technologies and operational procedures that were unthought of before the war. However, it took a long time, exposure to failure and dedicated teams to develop everything that was needed. For example, while photographic reconnaissance was recognised as important during the 1914–18 war, it was not until the 'Bideford Bar' tests in 1943 that effective photo-reconnaissance interpretation of beach gradients, depths and obstacles was available.[74] Likewise the wide variety of ships and craft, doctrine for gunfire support, landing, beach control, close air support, and command and control were produced and worked out in the light of hard experience.[75] During the 1930s, financial constraint and a very different view of the strategic threat inhibited the development of a strategic necessity and thus the materials for tactical deployment.

However, at the operational planning level evolutionary change was going on. Here, it can be said that important innovation was taking place. The difference between the *Manual* of 1938 and that of 1925 shows a clear development in thinking and intention. The British forces did not enter the Second World War with the mind-set of 1914–18. Nor was it only the vision of the ISTDC and the Combined Operations Head Quarters experts, working on the experiences of 1939–42, that bridged the huge gap that had opened up in amphibious needs and British capability. If one looks for innovation only in the dramatic and the material, then the war years were undoubtedly years of tremendous innovation and the 1930s were static and conservative. However, if innovation includes the deliberate development of relationships to build on existing experience and make allowance for changes, then the 1930s were more innovative than is usually allowed. Throughout the 1920s and 1930s there had been a level of collaboration, testing and refining that enabled the Royal Navy to adapt and act effectively with the other services. Perhaps the key contribution of this period was to attune the services to the possibilities and practicalities of working together and establishing the boundaries of responsibility and possibility. The limitations on capacity of the defence establishment to judge relative strategic threats caused real division between the services,[76] but the practice of exercise and planning pulled them together. It was small-scale and partial, but without it, it is likely that levels of inter-service friction would have been much higher and the painful lessons of the early war years might have taken much longer to learn.

Notes

1 G. Searle, *The Quest for National Efficiency: A Study of British Politics and Political Thought 1899–1914* (Oxford: Blackwell, 1971).

2 B. Liddell Hart, *The British Way in Warfare* (London: Faber, 1932); B. Bond, *Liddell Hart: A Study in Military Thought* (London: Cassell, 1977), 65–118; J.P. Harris, *Men, Ideas and Tanks: British Military Thought and Armoured Warfare, 1903–1939* (Manchester: Manchester University Press, 1995), 291–4.

3 L.E.H. Maund, *Assault from the Sea* (London: Methuen, 1949).

4 The National Achive (TNA): Public Record Office (PRO), DEFE 2/699, History of Combined Operations, 1915–1942, 'Early History'. The ISTDC was approved by the Deputy Chiefs of Staff (Interservice Training) in March 1937, but it did not begin to operate until September of that year. See TNA: PRO, DEFE 2/782A, Early History of Combined Operations.

5 Maund, *Assault from the Sea,* 4.

6 B. Fergusson, *The Watery Maze: The Story of Combined Operations* (London: Collins, 1961). This is the main conclusion of K.J. Clifford, *Amphibious Warfare Development in Britain and America from 1920 to 1940* (New York: Edgewood, 1983).

7 Churchill's and Keyes' sensitivity regarding the Dardanelles can be seen in correspondence with Brigadier-General Cecil Aspinall Oglander, who wrote the official history of the campaign. Isle of Wight Record Office, Oglander Papers, OG 112, Churchill to Oglander, 28 Apr. 1932; OG 112, Keyes to Oglander, 1 Jan. 1931.

8 Fergusson, *Watery Maze,* 37; TNA: PRO, DEFE 2/699, History of Combined Operations, 'Major-General MacLeod's amplifications'.

9 A. Whitehouse, *Amphibious Operations* (London: Muller, 1964), 179–88; J.D. Ladd, *By Sea By Land: The Authorised History of the Royal Marine Commandos* (London: HarperCollins, 1998), 28–30; J. Thompson, *The Royal Marines: From Sea Soldiers to a Special Force* (London: Pan, 2001), 227–37; A. Millett, 'Assault from the Sea: The Development of Amphibious Warfare Between the Wars. The American, British and Japanese Experience', in W. Murray and A. Millett (eds), *Military Innovation in the Interwar Period* (Cambridge: Cambridge University Press, 1996; paperback ed. 1998), 50–95.

10 D.R. Massam, 'British Maritime Strategy and Amphibious Capability, 1900–1940' (unpublished D.Phil. thesis, Oxford University, 1995).

11 TNA: PRO, Air 10/1206, *Manual of Combined Naval, Military and Air Operations,* 1925, 11

12 Thompson, *The Royal Marines,* 227–9.

13 G.A.H. Gordon, *British Seapower and Procurement Between the Wars: A Reappraisal of Rearmament* (London: Macmillan, 1988), *passim*; S. Roskill, *Naval Policy Between the Wars,* vol. 1: *The Period of Anglo-American Antagonism, 1919–1929* (London: Collins, 1968).

14 See Roskill, *Naval Policy,* vol. 1, 234–68, 356–99, 467–97; vol. 2, 194–212, 392–415. For the RAF interpretation of the situation, see TNA: PRO, Air 9/2, Staff History: Fleet Air Arm 1914–1930.

15 TNA: PRO, Air 41/45, Staff History: RAF-Maritime Operations, 63.

16 B. Bond, *British Military Policy Between the Two World Wars* (Oxford: Oxford University Press, 1980), 22, 72–81, 85–6.

17 M. Smith, *British Air Strategy Between the Wars* (Oxford: Oxford University Press, 1984), 28–9.

18 Ibid., 57–64.

19 TNA: PRO, Air 5/283, Command and Defence of RAF Aerodromes in Combined Naval and Military Operations.

20 I am grateful to Lt-Cmdr John Bingeman for showing me photographs of the operation by HMS *Emerald* and to John Parkinson for the references to HMS *Durban* and HMS *Dorsetshire.*

21 TNA: PRO, Adm 203/84, Combined Exercise, Salsette Island, Dec. 1924; Adm 203/74, Combined Exercise, Kasid Beach, 7–8 Dec. 1925.

22 I. Cowman, *Dominion or Decline: Anglo-American Naval Relations in the Pacific, 1937–1941* (Oxford: Berg, 1996), 13–15.

23 TNA: PRO, Adm 116/2335, Mobile Naval Base Organisation, 1920–1928. For the Admiralty position regarding war in the Far East, see I. Cowman, *Dominion or Decline,* 13–46. See also TNA: PRO, Adm 203/47, RN Staff College, Greenwich (Session 1922–3), 'The Possibility of Losing Hong Kong in a War with Japan in 1926', Lt-Cmdr R.R. Stewart, 9 May 1923.

24 D.F. Bittner believes that the commitment to the MNBO was a 'blind alley' for the Royal Marines. This is certainly true in the light of the development of amphibious warfare 1939–45 and the Royal Marines' own self-perception as a striking force by 1937, but for much of the period between 1920 and 1936 it was, from the Royal Navy's perspective, the most likely amphibious function. See D.F. Bittner, 'Britannia's Sheathed Sword: The Royal Marines and Amphibious Warfare in the Interwar Years – A Passive Response', *Journal of Military History,* 55(1991), 345–64.

25 R. Harding, 'Learning from the War: The Development of British Amphibious Capability, 1919–1929', *Mariner's Mirror,* 86(2000), 173–85.

26 Bond, *British Military Policy Between the Two World Wars*, 94–5.

27 U. Bialer, *The Shadow of the Bomber: The Fear of Air Attack and British Politics, 1932–1939* (London: Royal Historical Society, 1980), *passim.*

28 TNA: PRO, Air 8/102, The Defence of Singapore, 1928–1930, Paper prepared by the Air Staff, 16 Jan. 1928.

29 TNA: PRO, Adm 116/3472, Defensive Measures in the Far East, 1933, Admiralty to C in C. China, Draft Telegram (Most secret) No. 428 and following correspondence.

30 TNA: PRO, Air 10/1206, *Manual of Combined Naval, Military and Air Operations*, 1925, 97.

31 TNA: PRO, Air 20/183, Report on Combined Operations Exercise Singapore, Feb. 1937.

32 Fergusson, *The Watery Maze,* 41.

33 S. Roskill, *Naval Policy Between the Wars, vol. 2: The Period of Rearmament, 1930–1939* (Collins: London, 1976), 258–61. For the general background, see L.R. Pratt, *East of Malta, West of Suez: Britain's Mediterranean Crisis, 1936–1939* (Cambridge: Cambridge University Press, 1975).

34 Fergusson, *The Watery Maze,* 39–40.

35 Maund, *Assault from the Sea,* 5–6; TNA: PRO, DEFE 2/782B, Combined Naval and Military Landing Operations Special Landing Craft Carrier and Special Military Landing Craft, Report, 12 Oct. 1937. These landings impressed the US Marine Corps, which had a force defending the international settlement at Shanghai. See V.J. Croizat, *Across the Reef: The Amphibious Tracked Vehicle at War* (London: Arms and Armour Press, 1989), 36.

36 J. Robert Moskin, *The Story of the US Marine Corps* (London: Paddington Press, 1979), 223; J.A. Isely and P.A. Crowl, *The US Marines and Amphibious Warfare: Its Theory and Practice in the Pacific* (Princeton: Princeton University Press, 1951), 36. See also K.J. Clifford, *Progress and Purpose: A Developmental History of the United States Marine Corps, 1900–1970* (Washington, DC: USMC, 1973), 33–48. I am grateful to Professor Dinardo of the USMC Combat Development Command, Quantico, for locating a copy of the 1935 *Manual* that I could consult.

37 TNA: PRO, DEFE 2/782B, Japanese Combined Naval and Military Landing Operations, 12 Dec. 1938.

38 For Japanese doctrine by April 1942, see H.G. von Lehmann (trans. M.C. Halbig), 'Japanese Landing Operations in World War Two', in M.L. Bartlett (ed.), *Assault from the Sea* (Annapolis, MD: US Naval Institute Press, 1983), 195–201.

39 G. E. Rothenberg, 'From Gallipoli to Guadalcanal', in M.L. Bartlett (ed.), *Assault from the Sea,* 177–82.

40 TNA: PRO, Cab 21/3, Offensives against German Colonies, Hankey to Asquith, 5 Aug. 1914.

41 G.G. Aston, 'Combined Strategy for Fleets and Armies or Amphibious Strategy', *JRUSI*, 1907, 984–1004.

42 For an interesting view of how almost twenty years of historical writings, literature and current military debates blended in the mid-1930s to influence a view of the Gallipoli campaign, see J. North, *Gallipoli: The Fading Vision* (London: Faber, 1936).

43 S. Bidwell and D. Graham, *Fire Power: British Military Weapons and Theories of War, 1904–1945* (London: Allen & Unwin, 1982), 133–7.

44 TNA: PRO, Adm 116/1451, Gallipoli Peninsula: Reports of Ships' Gunnery Firing. The conclusions drawn from this enquiry led to a realistic appreciation

of the likely support the navy would be able to give in the *Manual*. See TNA: PRO, Air 10/1206, *Manual of Combined Naval, Military and Air Operations*, 1925, 74–87. The debate led to the suggestion of the Royal Artillery to provide howitzer fire support on Royal Navy vessels. See TNA: PRO, Adm 116/2086, Proposed matters for discussion during Major-General Ironside's spring cruise with the Atlantic Fleet, 5 Jan. 1922.

45 TNA: PRO, Air 10/1206, *Manual*, 1925, 90–101.

46 TNA: PRO, Air 10/1206, *Manual*, 1925, 101.

47 TNA: PRO, Air 9/1, Combined Operations, 1914–1930, Item 10, 'Employment of Seaplanes and Seaplane Carriers in Combined Operations: Extracts from the Reports of the Commandant RAF Staff College and remarks thereon by Branches of the Air Ministry'.

48 TNA: PRO, Air 9/1, page 5, Deputy Chief of Air Staff to Director of Staff Duties, minute 9, no date.

49 TNA: PRO, Air 9/1, page 5, 1929 Operations in the Baltic, Extract of Commandant's Covering Letter, no date. Also page 8, Air Ministry's reply to Commandant's report, no date.

50 TNA: PRO, Air 9/1, page 6, Director of Training to Deputy Chief of Air Staff, no date.

51 J.P. Campbell, 'Marines, Aviators and the Battleship Mentality, 1923–1933', *JRUSI*, Feb. 1964, 45–50, esp. 45; Isely and Crowl, *The US Marines and Amphibious Warfare,* 20–1.

52 See TNA: PRO, Air 10/1206, *Manual of Combined Naval, Military and Air Operations*, 1925, 107.

53 TNA: PRO, Adm 203/74, Report on Combined Naval and Military Exercise at Kasid Beach, 7–8 Dec. 1925, p. 48, Observations from shore.

54 TNA: PRO, DEFE 2/709, *Manual of Combined Operations*, 1938, 110–12. For the 1938 exercise, see TNA: PRO, Adm 1/9552, Combined Report, Combined Operations Exercise, 5–6 July 1938.

55 TNA: PRO, Air 10/1206, *Manual of Combined Naval, Military and Air Operations*, 1925, 83.

56 TNA: PRO, Adm 116/3674, Notes on the HQ ships in a Combined Operation by the Signals Directing Staff, 14 Dec. 1933.

57 TNA: PRO, Adm 116/3674, Notes on HQ ships. For a general introduction to telecommunications, see D.R. Headrick, *The Invisible Weapon: Telecommunications and International Politics, 1851–1945* (Oxford: Oxford University Press, 1991), particularly 203–4 for short wave.

58 The information in the following paragraphs can be found in TNA: PRO, Adm 116/3395, Report on Landing Operations 1934.

59 TNA: PRO, Adm 116/3395, Memo of the Director of Training and Staff Division (DTSD), 7 Jan. 1935.

60 Ibid.

61 Ibid.

62 TNA: PRO, Adm 116/3395, Memo, Director of Sea Transports, 8 July 1935.

63 TNA: PRO, Adm 116/3395, Memo of the DNC, 15 June 1935.

64 TNA: PRO, Adm 226/42, Reports to Director of Naval Construction (DNC), Reports on new X lighter, 5 Aug., 12 Oct. and 5 Dec. 1938 ; Adm 116/4059, Material and Personnel for Landing Attacks, 1939. It is noted here that preliminary investigations were underway regarding a landing craft carrier before being suspended at the establishment of the ISTDC.

65 TNA: PRO, WO 33/1015, Interim Report of the Committee on Sea Transportation and the Landing of Tanks, 1922.

66 Anon., 'An Amphibious Tank', *JRUSI*, 76(1931), 812–13; D. Fletcher, *Mechanised Force: British Tanks Between the Wars* (London: HMSO, 1991), 52–4, 86–7.

67 Tests in 1940, using the tank's tracks as the propulsion mechanism, found the method to be highly inefficient. This became the basic propulsion system for the very successful US Landing Vehicle Tracked (LVT), but the buoyancy characteristics of a LVT and a tank were very different. See TNA: PRO, Adm 226/46, Reports to DNC, p. 38, Report 100/40, Amphibious Tank, 29 Oct. 1940.

68 National Maritime Museum, NMM 461A, MLC Nos. 14–19, *passim*. The contracts were given to Philips and Son of Dartmouth (4 boats) and Rowhedge, near Colchester (2 boats).

69 Smith, *British Air Strategy*, 152–3, 160, 230–1.

70 Isely and Crowl, *The US Marines and Amphibious Warfare*, 37–56.

71 Compare TNA: PRO, Air 10/1206, *Manual of Combined Naval, Military and Air Operations*, 1925, and PRO, DEFE 2/709, *Manual of Combined Operations*, 1938. The 1931 edition of the *Manual* has differences related to landing operations, but is very similar to the 1925 edition. See TNA: PRO, DEFE 2/708, *Manual of Combined Operations*, 1931.

72 TNA: PRO, Adm 1/9552, Landing Exercise, pp. 10–13.

73 J.S. Corbett, *Some Principles of Maritime Strategy* (London: Longman, 1911).

74 TNA: PRO, Adm 1/15678B, Development of Amphibious Assault Technique 1944, New Section on Beach Reconnaissance, pp. 1–4.

75 TNA: PRO, Adm 1/15678B, *passim*; B.F. Cooling (ed.), *Case Studies in the Development of Close Air Support* (Washington DC: Office of Air Force History, 1990); I. Howcroft, 'The Role of the Royal Navy in Amphibious Assaults in the Second World War' (unpublished Ph.D. thesis, University of Exeter, 2003).

76 P. Kennedy, 'British "Net Assessment" and the Coming of the Second World War', in W. Murray and A.R. Millett (eds), *Calculation: Net Assessment and the Coming of World War II* (New York: Free Press, 1992), 19–59.

3

NAVAL AVIATION, 1930–2000

David Hobbs

The development of the aircraft carrier

The fusion of aircraft, warship, marine engineering and what would become known as 'command, control and communications' technologies into a weapons system revolutionised naval warfare. They did so during a period little longer than a single human lifespan.

The air component of the Royal Navy in the early 1930s was the legacy of the great strides made by the Royal Naval Air Service before and during the First World War. Progress after the war had naturally slowed but had been adversely affected by the creation of the independent Royal Air Force. From 1918, the control of aircraft that embarked in warships was split, with the Admiralty responsible for operational command at sea and the RAF responsible for administration and training ashore. Many of the epoch-making first carriers remained in use but a new generation of aircraft, showing slight improvements over their wartime predecessors, had evolved. Specialist aircraft designs were relatively easy and cheap to procure and so different types were used as fleet fighters, spotters, torpedo attack and reconnaissance aircraft. The political hope that airmen from the RAF would be equally able to operate ashore and with the fleet at sea had already proved to be unrealistic. From 1924 all observers and telegraphist air gunners together with 70 per cent of pilots were to be provided by the Royal Navy, and the term 'Fleet Air Arm' was coined by the Admiralty to describe the sea-going air force that operated from its ships at sea. Despite many administrative changes, that name applied throughout the period in question.

Split control slowly emaciated naval aviation. Its effects were not, at first, technically apparent, although the need for aircrew to be trained in naval warfare was obvious. There were many senior officers in the RAF who had served in the RNAS and were able to influence new designs at first, but as their knowledge of naval warfare faded the RAF became dominated by the protagonists of independent bomber warfare. There were few senior officers in the Royal Navy with practical experience of aviation and it was thus difficult to argue the case against them and for tactical aviation within the Senior Service. It is, thus, all the more creditable that the Admiralty never lost sight of its aim to recover full control of its air arm and did so in 1939 despite opposition from the Air Ministry and indifference from the majority of politicians. In the United States and Japan, both navies retained control of naval aviation and made rapid progress, which soon overtook the Royal Navy's early lead.

Early aircraft operated in small numbers from the prototype carriers, which included *Hermes*, the first ship in the world to be designed and built as an aircraft carrier. Flag hoists told the pilots when to land after the ship had turned into wind. They made individual approaches, judging their approach to the deck by eye, and landed without arrester systems or even brakes since the relative speed of approach was often not much more than the speed of the wind felt over the deck. A handling party held the aircraft steady while its wings were folded and it would be struck down into the hangar leaving the deck clear for the next aircraft to land in turn. It could not do so until the lift platform was locked back at flight deck level. This procedure had the advantage that it left a clear deck for a pilot to take off again after a baulked approach, but the huge disadvantage that up to two minutes elapsed between landings and even longer if the squadron was not worked up to operational efficiency. Landing on a torpedo strike and its escort could, thus, take over half an hour with the ship forced to steam steadily into wind for all that time. This method of operation led to a British concept that aircraft were generally kept in the hangar and only brought to the deck when needed to fly. Neither the Americans nor Japanese adopted the same concept, preferring to keep aircraft on deck in large 'deck parks', able to launch in large numbers.

To launch, aircraft were 'ranged' aft and took off freely down the deck at short intervals, usually becoming airborne just forward of the 'island' structure. Thus the deck run required by the lead aircraft in the range limited the size of a 'deck load' or 'Alpha' strike, as the maximum attack force a carrier could launch became known. *Glorious, Courageous* and *Furious*, all converted from large cruisers, had flight decks much smaller than their foreign contemporaries. All had two hangars, one above the other, another manifestation of the British concentration on hangar stowage rather than operation as a yardstick of carrier capability. A small flight deck, lower than the main one, was built over the forecastle to allow fighters to be launched rapidly out of the upper hangar if the main flight deck was full of aircraft, perhaps with a strike ranged aft. The concept was feasible with light fighters such as the Fairey Flycatcher of 1923, but later aircraft could not take off from such a small area and the space became used for the mounting of close-range armament.

The tactical dispositions of warships in 1930 were based on the movements of the battleships at the centre of a force. Thus if a carrier had to manoeuvre away from the battle line to turn into wind it could find itself alone and vulnerable, especially with the slow recovery rates accepted as normal. Because the carriers might be some distance from the battle line, all battleships and cruisers were fitted with catapults and hangars capable of operating up to four aircraft. All naval aircraft were specified to be capable of being catapulted and fitted with floats so that they could alight on the sea next to the parent ships and be recovered by crane. Thus, fighter aircraft could be embarked to protect the battle line, in the temporary absence of the carriers. Hawker Osprey fighters (a derivative of the RAF's Hart light bomber), which could double in the reconnaissance role, were embarked extensively in the 1930s. These tactics saw aircraft operations as secondary to the battle line.

By the early 1930s the 'creeping paralysis' of divided control began to be felt in aircraft procurement. Although it cannot be said that the RAF deliberately specified second-rate aircraft for naval use. Its perception that sea warfare was of secondary importance to the 'bomber offensive' against a potential enemy was not conducive to obtaining the best equipment. Statements to the effect that the equipment required in aircraft by the Admiralty impaired their efficiency inculcated a belief in British industry that carrier-borne aircraft had always to be inferior to their land-based contemporaries. In the United States and Japan, where navies were responsible for their own procurement, no such misapprehension existed and magnificent aircraft such as the Hellcat and Zero were the results. Split control also affected carrier design in that joint committees had to be formed to bring together air and ship technology. The lack of Air Ministry interest in seeing another department's point of view was hardly conducive to the quick and innovative design processes that would be required in the period of rearmament in the late 1930s.

In 1918 the Grand Fleet had had an Admiral Commanding Aircraft (ACA), Rear-Admiral R.F. Phillimore, responsible to the Commander-in-Chief for all air matters. No such appointment was made after the creation of the RAF until 1931, when Rear-Admiral R.G.H. Henderson was appointed as the first Rear-Admiral Aircraft Carriers (RAAC). Although not a pilot, he was alive to the potential of aviation and was a former captain of *Furious*. He believed that carriers had proved themselves as an important weapons system and was not prepared to let the status quo continue. His driving force was to set in train many new tactics which, in turn, required new enabling technologies making this a period in which tactics would dictate technology. To survive, a fleet at sea was believed to need the largest and most efficient embarked air force possible and in RAAC and his staff the Royal Navy obtained the institutional focus to demand change.

The most obvious need for improvement lay in the operation of aircraft from the deck. The US Navy's lead in this area was marked and naval attachés had reported on the pioneering work of men such as Commodore J. Reeves, USN, in the prototype carrier *Langley* to the Admiralty. The most obvious improvement was to cut down the landing interval and this was achieved by fitting carriers with a system of athwartship arrester wires. These connected with hydraulic pistons in a machinery room below the flight deck and their fitting in existing ships involved extensive dockyard work. The wire pennants across the flight deck were easily removable so that they could be replaced quickly when worn. *Courageous* and *Glorious* were fitted with four arrester wires, each capable of stopping an 11,000 lb aircraft travelling at 53 knots relative to the deck. The aircraft themselves had to be fitted with a retractable arrester hook and stressed to absorb its regular use. The Air Ministry was quick to criticise the difficulties of arrested landing, but it soon became the normal method of recovery for all carrier-borne aircraft.

The result of this innovation was that the interval between aircraft landing could be reduced by several seconds, but the flight deck still had to be cleared between landings and a deck park of aircraft was not practical. The next step was to modify and adopt practices pioneered by the US Navy using barriers and Deck Landing Control Officers (DLCOs). The former comprised a steel wire barrier across the flight deck, forward of the arrester wires. It was raised and lowered by hydraulic stanchions at either side of the deck and its use revolutionised deck landing. It was raised when aircraft landed into the wires and lowered so that they could taxi quickly over it into a deck park on the forward part of the flight deck. Once the aircraft was over it, it could be raised again so that should the next aircraft miss the wires, it would be stopped by the barrier rather than crash into the deck park. Aircraft no longer needed to be struck down after landing and could remain parked on the flight deck. Consequently the landing interval was reduced from over a minute to as little as 15 seconds for a worked-up squadron. The time spent 'into wind' was dramatically reduced and aircraft complements could be increased with a permanent deck park of aircraft in addition to those in the hangar. Other advantages followed and it was possible to make the forward flight deck area, known as 'Fly One', into a 'pit-stop' where aircraft could be refuelled and rearmed quickly during intensive flying operations.

The risk that some aircraft would miss all the arrester wires and crash into the barrier led directly to the second innovation. To achieve the best landing interval and a safe 'arrival' for every pilot, it was essential that all flew the optimum approach path using an identical, standardised technique. The DLCO, or 'batsman', was an experienced pilot, positioned on the port after edge of the flight deck, who used coloured bats and standard signals to indicate to pilots their position relative to the optimum glide slope, and his signal to 'cut' the throttle and take the landing was mandatory. Between them, all these innovations made the operation of large air groups a practical proposition; without them the scale of operations achieved in the Second World War could not have been achieved. They were made possible by the increasing number of experienced naval pilots available to make progress in the operation of their own service. The RAF pilots who had passed through the Fleet Air Arm before returning to 'normal' appointments in the metropolitan air force made little contribution to the development of naval flying. Compared to naval pilots who returned to operational squadrons over many appointments and gave a return on their expensive training, RAF pilots seldom carried out more than a single operational tour at sea and, in purely naval terms, they represented a high wastage rate.

From 1936 onwards, aircraft carriers were fitted with hydraulic catapults, initially known as aircraft accelerators. These were similar in design to those fitted in battleships and cruisers and required the aircraft to be fitted into a cradle before launch so that it left the deck in a flying attitude. They were intended at first to allow aircraft fitted with floats to be launched from the carrier but they soon proved to have other, more practical uses. Single aircraft could be catapulted rather than having to clear a take-off path on a crowded deck. Later, as carrier air groups increased in size, they allowed the first few aircraft from a deck load strike to be catapulted until sufficient space was cleared for the aircraft behind it to carry out free take-offs.

Ark Royal III, laid down in 1935 and completed in 1938, incorporated all this new technology and was the first really successful British carrier. She had eight wires similar to those in *Courageous* and *Glorious*. A single barrier capable of stopping an aircraft weighing 11,000 lb at 45 knots, relative to the deck, within 40 feet was fitted and she had two BH3 hydraulic catapults capable of launching a 12,000 lb aircraft at 56 knots end speed relative to the deck. She could operate up to 72 aircraft but normally operated 60 and had the most extensive workshops and bomb rooms yet fitted in a British carrier. Like the earlier conversions, she had two hangars, one on top of the other, a concept intended to provide the largest hangar area within the smallest hull. The three lifts were of an unusual design, each having two platforms. Thus to move an aircraft from the lower hangar to the flight deck, it would have to be pushed onto the lower platform, taken up to the upper hangar and pushed off. The lower platform would then be taken back down to the lower hangar deck and the upper platform lowered from the flight deck, the aircraft would be pushed onto it and raised to the flight deck. This cumbersome arrangement was never repeated. Lift wells were kept as small as possible to minimise the size of the openings in the flight deck and this had the effect of severely limiting the size of aircraft that could be operated. Whilst this had little effect on the Swordfish/Skua generation, it had a critical effect on the design of the high-performance aircraft that were to replace them.

In machinery terms, the ship was comparable with contemporary cruiser design. High speed was considered essential to regain station on the battle fleet after manoeuvring to operate aircraft and this in turn dictated a high fuel capacity. Armour and watertight sub-division also followed contemporary cruiser practice, but the British policy on the stowage of aircraft fuel was unique. The first seaplane carrier to be lost in the Great War was *Ben-my-Chree*. She was sunk by a petrol vapour explosion caused by enemy shellfire, and Admiralty designers were subsequently acutely aware of the danger of stowing large quantities of aviation gasoline (Avgas) in aircraft-carrying ships. Avgas was stowed in cylinders built into water-filled compartments. This removed much of the risk but drastically reduced the amount of fuel that could be carried. The US and Japanese designers were not as sensitive and stowed Avgas in ordinary hull tanks, like the furnace fuel oil with its much higher flashpoint. They lost a number of ships to fuel vapour explosions in consequence.

Ark Royal III was a 'watershed' design, arguably the first British carrier to be designed with a full knowledge of air group capability but the last to be designed against the perception that the ship was more complicated than its aircraft.

During the period of rearmament in the late 1930s, most carrier design effort went into fleet carriers but consideration was given, before 1939, to the construction of trade protection carriers intended to perform many of the traditional wartime functions of cruisers. Warship hulls were soon found to be unsuitable for this task because they lacked the large internal volume needed for hangars and workshops. Such ships would require a large cruising range and a minimal gun armament for close-range self-defence, mainly against aircraft. Flight decks and hangars built onto mercantile hulls were considered to be ideal, and two such conversions based on *Winchester Castle* of 20,000 tons and *Waipawa* of 12,500 tons were actually prepared. They were not proceeded with for a number of reasons, among them an under-appreciation of the U-boats' ability to range out of coastal waters into the mid-Atlantic and an over-appreciation of the detection capability of the Asdic sonar equipment fitted in the surface escort force. Other factors included hostility from the Ministry of Transport, which saw such conversions as a 'misuse' of large mercantile hulls that would be in short supply in war, and the practical inability of the British shipbuilding industry to do the work given the scale of rearmament work being contracted.

The development of naval aircraft

Despite its obsolete equipment, the Royal Navy made significant progress in some areas of naval aviation before 1939, most notably in the areas of multiple carrier operation and night strike operations with torpedo bomber aircraft. These required the exploitation of existing technology to its limits rather than anything new, but the increased requirement for unique items such as flight deck lighting and shore training aids encouraged a number of firms with no defence background to come forward and bid for work. These were to be of great value in the move to a war economy that characterised Britain in 1939. Despite the 'dead hand' of the RAF, some progress was also made with aircraft, their engines and weapons. The rapid world-wide progress in aircraft and engine design during the period worked against the Admiralty because the Air Ministry concentrated its research effort on land-based machines with liquid-cooled engines. In the main these were 'level' bombers and 'point defence' fighters with large batteries of light machine guns. Because the Admiralty lacked a sufficiently loud institutional 'voice' for its air arm's procurement strategy, it tended to be relegated to 'second user' status in the queue for development funding with designs intended for RAF use. These were not always robust enough or desirable for sea service and the impact of this non-focused development was to have a major effect on the war at sea. To be fair, many of the RAF's own rearmament projects proved to be failures, the Fairey Battle light bomber and the Short Stirling heavy bomber to give but two examples.

Experience in the operation of aircraft within new task forces led to a number of changes before 1939. The old Flight system was replaced by a new system of squadrons at the behest of RAAC in 1933. This used three-digit numbers in the 700 and 800 series and is still in use today in much the same way as the original concept intended. The larger squadrons reflected an ever-growing need for aircraft to fulfil tactical tasks with the fleet at sea. Increasing aircraft complexity and the need to get the most out of such aircraft as were embarked led to the design of multi-role aircraft and of these, the best example was the immortal Fairey Swordfish. It was designed to fulfil the three functions of Torpedo attack, Spotting the 'fall-of-shot' of battleships' guns and Reconnaissance (TSR). It was robust, easy to deck land and able to carry up to a ton of weapons on external pylons. It had a crew of three – pilot, observer and telegraphist air gunner – and was one of the few types to see service throughout the Second World War virtually unchanged. In service it took on many new roles, including anti-submarine search and strike and dive-bombing. Its multi-purpose partner in 1939 was the Blackburn Skua dive-bomber/fighter. It was an underpowered and relatively undistinguished aircraft but it had the distinction of shooting down the first Axis aircraft of the Second World War in 1939 and sinking the cruiser *Königsberg*, the first major warship to be sunk by air attack in 1940. It also achieved an impressive kill to loss ratio during the Norwegian campaign. Both aircraft had Bristol radial, air-cooled engines, the Pegasus and the Perseus delivering 750 and 900 horsepower respectively. These were robust, straightforward engines that were easy to maintain and less vulnerable to action damage than the complicated liquid-cooled engines, such as the Merlin, developed for the RAF. The Admiralty was fortunate that the UK aero-engine industry was sufficiently broadly based to accommodate small production runs of these engines alongside the vast orders for the RAF. The creation of the Ministry of Aircraft Production in 1940, however, led to a decision to concentrate production on a small number of proven engines and to abandon development work, for the time being, on new types. This led to the abandonment of the Rolls Royce Exe 24-cylinder, air-cooled engine intended for the Fairey Barracuda strike aircraft, condemning the aircraft to a mediocre performance and a lengthy redesign progress that proved another adverse influence on the Royal Navy's ability to fight. Both the US and Japanese navies were able to sponsor the development of powerful radial engines for their carrier-borne aircraft and the Royal Navy was able to benefit from the former under the Lend-Lease programme.

Practice strikes on warships revealed that the torpedo was the most effective 'ship killing' weapon. It placed a large explosion low down on an enemy hull and let in water, destroying the reserve of buoyancy and sinking it. Peacetime training revealed a probability that one weapon in four would hit the target, a far greater accuracy than that achieved with bombs, even when released from a steep dive. In any case, bombs damaged compartments above the waterline and let in air. Multiple hits would be needed to sink a target. Multiple hits required a large attacking force, which the navy did not have. Developments in fusing and detonators produced constant improvements in torpedo 'pistols' that exploded on contact with a ship's side and, in 1939, a magnetic pistol that exploded the warhead under the keel in the influence of the ship's magnetic signature. This was an area with no armour and where water pressure provided the greatest tamping effect, and even the largest ships were vulnerable to having their backs broken. Level bombing proved ineffective in hitting manoeuvring warships, as the Italian Air Force was to discover in the Mediterranean. After careful evaluation, the Royal Navy made no use of the technique. Dive-bombing was more accurate and the technique was adopted in Britain, the United States, Japan and Germany. Because it had no practical application to strategic bombing, however, the RAF had no interest in dive-bombing and constant Admiralty requests for a suitable sight were ignored.

Depth charges for aircraft came from RAF stock and followed that service's precept that a large number of small weapons were more effective than a smaller number of well-aimed large weapons. The 100 lb depth bomb proved a complete failure and wartime development led to a derivative of the depth charges used by surface escorts. Torpedoes remained under Admiralty control and their development for use as a strike weapon continued until well after the Second World War. Other weapons such as machine guns and bombs came from RAF stock until the advent of Lend-Lease when US Navy weapons such as the superb 0.5 inch heavy machine gun were made available in aircraft such as the Corsair and Avenger.

Rearmament forced the Admiralty to face a number of difficult decisions across the range of technology. The Swordfish aircraft represented the 'state of the art' and was a safe bet for mass production, but by 1939 it was already obsolete. Was it best to replace it with a modestly improved 'safe bet' or to embrace the new monoplane technology and take a risk in the hope gaining a much improved capability? The Admiralty adopted both paths and ordered the pedestrian Fairey Albacore into production 'off the drawing board' and the development of the very advanced Fairey Barracuda to replace it. The latter might well have been a very good aircraft, but the cancellation of its advanced engine and the higher priority given to production for the RAF blighted it and delayed its entry into service for three years, half the duration of the war in which it should have played a major part.

Another dilemma concerned the construction of a new generation of carriers to replace the aged collection of prototypes that were a legacy from the early years of aviation. The easy course of action would have been to build repeat *Ark Royal*s, but Admiral Henderson, the former RAAC and later Third Sea Lord and Controller, would not countenance this. He expected carriers to operate with battle fleets in the North Sea and Mediterranean where they were within range of land-based bombers. With the increasing speed of bombers and reliance on visual detection, he believed that they could not carry enough fighters to defend the fleet from every direction with standing air patrols. His solution was to rely on gunfire and to carry only enough fighters to escort torpedo strikes on enemy forces. He ordered a new class to be designed in the shortest time scale with armoured flight decks and hangar sides and equipped with heavy batteries of medium- and light-calibre anti-aircraft guns with sophisticated fire control systems. These were the six armoured carriers of the *Illustrious* class. They were complicated and expensive ships to build and with the weight of armour so high in the hull, the early ships had only one hangar and could carry only 36 aircraft, half the number in *Ark Royal.* They represented the limit of Britain's wartime shipbuilding capacity, and the last two ships, heavily modified with four rather than three shafts and double hangars, could only be worked on intermittently and did not complete until 1944.

It is ironic that the problem of interception was solved as the name ship came into service. Radar enabled an air plot to be developed in the carrier's operations room. Using this, fighter controllers could employ a small number of fighters on Combat Air Patrol (CAP) to maximum effect, using them to intercept enemy aircraft at long range, before they could release their weapons. Techniques were perfected in the Mediterranean and made available to the US Navy when *Victorious* was lent to the US Pacific Fleet in 1943. Early fears that high-performance, single-seat fighters would not be able to find their carriers after an interception beyond visual range were resolved by the introduction of coded homing beacons such as the Type 72 and later the YE beacon. These 'black boxes' in the cockpit allowed pilots to follow a 'course to steer' that would get them back to the deck. Later in the war, blind landing devices added to the ability of pilots to recover to their carriers at night or in adverse weather. An 'explosion' of technology produced a wide range of equipments that had a major impact on naval air warfare. These included Identification Friend or Foe (IFF) and VHF 'voice' radio-telephones that made it possible for fighter controllers to maintain practical two-way communication with the aircraft under their control.

As manufacturing industry made more of the new technology available, its use was widened and anti-submarine plots were set up in operations rooms in the new escort carriers. By fusing U-boat and aircraft position data on a single plot, controllers were able to direct strike aircraft accurately onto a contact even at night or in bad weather.

Development of naval aviation, 1939–1945

Progress in the war years was rapid. Much of this was due to the stimulus of war, but the resumption of full Admiralty control over the Fleet Air Arm, after the decision by Lord Inskip, the Minister for Defence Co-ordination in 1937, was the major factor. Procurement was now the responsibility of naval officers, expert in naval air warfare. It was no longer the domain of personnel from a separate service looking to make use of equipment for a 'second customer' who had little say in its design. The change took time, as evidenced by the emaciation of the Barracuda in 1940, but it happened. By 1945, every new tactical aircraft project was judged by its ability to perform against both RAF and Royal Navy requirements, a major achievement for the handful of officers at the Admiralty responsible for procurement.

Before 1939, the Admiralty's Fighting Instructions expected naval air to Find, Fix and Strike the enemy; in other words, to locate the enemy fleet, to plot it accurately, shadow it, and to slow it down with a torpedo attack to facilitate a surface attack by battleships. It soon showed the capability to do much more than that and it became imperative to get as many aircraft as possible to sea. Modifications to the flight deck of *Illustrious* and the adoption of US Navy-style deck parks gradually increased the number of aircraft the fleet carriers could embark. By 1945, *Illustrious* herself was able to operate 54 aircraft instead of the 36 she was designed to carry. The downside of this was the need to carry twice the number of maintenance ratings, which placed a great strain on messdeck accommodation and workshops. *Implacable*, the last of the class to complete, was able to carry over 80 aircraft in 1945.

The attack on the Italian fleet at Taranto in November 1940 showed what a carrier strike force could achieve. The idea stemmed from plans drawn up during the Abyssinian crisis which, in turn, had originated from plans drawn up by Admiral Beatty's staff to use carrier-borne aircraft to attack the German High Sea Fleet in its harbours in 1918. The attack was particularly successful when compared with Bomber Command's attempts to attack the German fleet in 1939. These had resulted in heavy losses for no damage to the enemy and were instrumental in the Command's decision to abandon daylight operations over enemy-held territory. Pearl Harbor and the loss of *Repulse* and *Prince of Wales* to air attack whilst under RAF fighter protection made it obvious to all that the size and composition of the fleet needed radical change. To recommend how best to achieve this, the Admiralty set up a 'Future Building Committee' in early 1942. This rapidly came to the conclusion that many more aircraft carriers were needed and this led to one of the biggest construction programmes in British history. Seven fleet carriers and no fewer than twenty-four light fleet carriers were ordered as a result. The latter were a new and remarkable type that achieved build times of as little as two years, less than that required for Battle-class destroyers.

These were to become known as 'light fleet carriers', a name that described them perfectly. Somewhat smaller than *Illustrious*, the design centred on the operation of the largest possible air group and *Colossus*, the name ship, was able to embark a mix of 42 Barracudas and Corsairs in 1945. The Director of Naval Construction's Department (DNC) was overloaded with work and the design was passed to Vickers. The brief stated that complicated systems were to be sacrificed to speed construction time and that the hulls should be expected to last for three years or the duration of the war, whichever was less! The last of the ships of the first, or 1942, batch, the former *Vengeance*, was not discarded by the Brazilian Navy until 2001, so that aspect of the ships can be said to have exceeded expectation. Mercantile hull materials and techniques were employed both to speed construction and to allow shipyards that usually only worked on merchant ships to participate. The aircraft were seen as the 'main armament' for the first time in a British carrier and guns were limited to close-range weapons that were visually sighted, obviating the need for complicated fire control systems. These ships can be regarded as a fusion of wartime experience in which the carrier had become the central unit of a task force, thus the high speed to regain position on the battle line was no longer an issue. The 1942 light fleets were therefore fitted with standard boilers and turbines identical to those fitted to destroyers and half those fitted to cruisers. Indeed, with the halting of cruiser construction in the late war years, many of the turbines actually came from cruiser projects that were cancelled, facilitating some of the rapid build times still further. The resulting two-shaft design delivered 40,000 shaft horsepower which gave a speed of just over 24 knots when installed in the 18,000-ton ships on build.

The light fleets were ordered in three distinct groups. The first were ordered in 1942, with four reaching operational status in the British Pacific Fleet's 11th Aircraft Carrier squadron by VJ Day, but none saw operational service. The second group incorporated a number of detail improvements including larger lifts and a strengthened flight deck whilst following the basic 1942 design. None of these saw service with the Royal Navy but, after sale, saw extensive post-war service with a number of Commonwealth navies, including Australia, Canada and India. The third, or 1943, group was extensively modified to have the higher speed necessary to operate with a fleet task group and to operate the larger aircraft foreseen by the Future Building Committee. Double the shaft horsepower gave the necessary 4-knot increase in speed to 28 knots. Slightly larger than the first two groups, these ships were ideal platforms for the first jet and helicopter generations in the post-war fleet and the four ships completed saw extensive service with the Royal Navy.

War experience made the planners look inexorably towards larger carrier designs. The Board were impressed by the magnificent *Essex*-class carriers of the US Navy and were aware of the move towards the even bigger 'battle carriers' of the *Midway* class with a projected air group of over 130 aircraft. Limits were imposed by the available British slipways and dry-dock facilities, but the *Malta* class of four ships, ordered in 1945, represented the zenith of British wartime carrier design. Had they been built they would have been approximately 55,000 tons, 915 feet long and would have operated over 90 aircraft. There would have been sixteen arrester wires, each capable of stopping a 20,000 lb aircraft at an entry speed of 75 knots. There would have been three barriers and two hydraulic catapults capable of launching a 30,000 lb aircraft at 130 knots end speed. These represented the extreme limit of what a hydraulic catapult could achieve and the figures make a fascinating comparison with *Ark Royal III*, completed only seven years earlier. All four ships were cancelled at the end of hostilities and it is probable that only *Malta* herself was laid down, but it is interesting to speculate how much better two of these ships would have been than *Eagle* and *Ark Royal IV*, which were completed to an earlier design as improved *Implacables*. Despite the intensity of design effort put into these ships, it is difficult to imagine that the wartime shipbuilding industry in Britain could have built them in a meaningful time scale.

Despite the pre-war doubts, escort carriers proved to be one of the key weapons systems of the Second World War. The first, *Audacity*, was converted in Britain from a captured German merchant ship. She proved so successful that massive programmes of conversion and construction were put in train in both Britain and the United States. Only a handful were converted in British yards but literally hundreds were built from scratch in the United States. The latter took advantage of production line techniques in new shipyards created to manufacture 'Liberty' ships against large orders by the British Purchasing Commission. These ships had a large internal volume, steam turbine engines and a single shaft capable of giving 18 knots. They had bunkerage for 3,000 tons of furnace fuel oil, which gave them a range of 27,000 miles at 11 knots or the capability to act as a tanker for escort destroyers in company. Nine arrester wires capable of stopping 19,800 lb at 55 knots, three barriers and a hydraulic catapult capable of launching 16,000 lb at 74 knots made them potent carriers capable of operating any naval aircraft in service. Over forty, of which twenty-three comprised the *Ruler* class and others the similar *Archer* and *Avenger* classes, were supplied to the Royal Navy under Lend-Lease arrangements by the US Navy. They were capable of operating up to 30 aircraft and, almost as important, ferrying up to 90 tightly packed in the hangar and on the flight deck.

After the loss of *Dasher* to a fuel vapour explosion in the Clyde and *Avenger* to a torpedo hit, all subsequent US escort carriers were extensively modified before entering Royal Navy service. This included the modification of the Avgas system to British standards and the fitting of protection around the bomb rooms. The resulting ships were robust and successful, with the survival of *Nabob* after a hit aft by a homing torpedo giving evidence of how resilient they could be. Despite being well down by the stern, she even managed to launch her Avenger aircraft for a night anti-submarine patrol. The opportunity was taken during 'Anglicisation' to install British radar, communications and operations rooms, making some ships into capable fighter and assault carriers capable of a wide variety of tasks considerably beyond the original concept of a simple auxiliary escort.

This additional capability allowed the Royal Navy to fill some of the gaps left by its lack of fleet carriers. Aircraft embarked in escort carriers provided fighter cover for the amphibious landings in North Africa, Sicily, Salerno and Burma. The same ships went on to strike at Axis forces in the Aegean Sea and their sisters operated in a series of strikes by the Home Fleet against German warships and installations on the Norwegian coast. All these in addition to the escort carriers giving valuable service with escort and hunter-killer groups on the convoy routes. After the war a number of these ships were converted for use as troop ships, moving British forces all over the world, before being returned to the US Navy at Norfolk navy yard.

The smallest carriers used in the Second World War were the British Merchant Aircraft Carriers, or MAC-ships. These were evolved at a time when it was feared that there would be a shortage of escort carriers and it was originally planned to build them in the United States as well as in

Britain. In the event, escort carrier production exceeded requirement and only eighteen British MAC-ships were completed. These were merchant ships with a crude flight deck, which formed part of a convoy and carried their normal cargo. They were manned by the Merchant Navy but carried a Royal Navy detachment to operate the three or four Swordfish aircraft embarked. The Royal Navy personnel had to 'sign on' the ships and some so took to the Merchant Navy ethos that they painted out the words 'Royal Navy' on their aircraft and replaced them with 'Merchant Navy'. The ships formed two distinct sub-groups. These were grain ships, which had a small hangar and could operate four Swordfish, and tankers without a hangar, which could operate only three. These had to remain on deck throughout the voyage. Flight decks were only 400 feet long and there was no catapult. One of the MAC-ships had the distinction of launching the last operational Swordfish sortie in 1945.

Since the build-up of the Mediterranean Fleet at the time of the Abyssinian crisis in 1935, it had been appreciated that carrier air groups would need support in the same way that submarines and destroyers required depot ships to maintain them. The aircraft repair ship *Unicorn* was laid down in 1939 to fulfil this role and completed in 1943. She was capable of being used as an operational carrier and was throughout 1943 seeing service as a convoy escort and in providing fighter cover for the Salerno landings. From 1944, she was used in her true role in the Eastern and British Pacific Fleets and again during the Korean War from 1950 to 1953. She had two hangars and had extensive workshops capable of repairing airframes, engines, instruments and avionics. A large lighter was stowed under the after end of the flight deck, used to move aircraft to and from operational carriers. Despite her extensive facilities, *Unicorn* alone was not big enough and two light fleets, renamed *Perseus* and *Pioneer*, were modified into the aircraft repair role. These each had half the workshop capacity of *Unicorn* but could not operate aircraft as workshops were built onto the former flight deck. There was still a shortage of capacity and a number of merchant ships were converted to act as engine and instrument repair ships for service with the British Pacific Fleet.

In addition to these maintenance facilities, 1945 saw a massive expansion of the Fleet Train to support the British Pacific Fleet (BPF) at sea. Within this was an Air Train charged with supplying operational aircraft, aircrew and components to the fleet carriers. At any one time the BPF had 250 aircraft embarked in four fleet carriers. To keep this number operational, over 2,000 aircraft were in transit from Britain and the United States to main bases in India and Australia. Once tested and tuned there, they were taken forward in escort carriers employed as replenishment ships to the fleet-operating areas off Okinawa and Japan. Other escort carriers acted as ferry ships moving aircraft across the oceans. By 1945, the BPF used sixteen escort carriers on ferry and replenishment duties. The US

Navy operated a force that was more than ten times larger and frequently 'borrowed back' British escort carriers to ferry US Navy aircraft across the Pacific.

From a handful of Royal Navy air stations ashore in 1939, the war saw an expansion to more than one hundred air stations and facilities throughout the world by 1945. These included vast 'hutted camps' such as the Air Yard at Cochin in India and even Mobile Operational Naval Air Bases (MONABs) capable of 'following the fleet'. These took equipment, vehicles and personnel in merchant ships to suitable locations where an airfield could be taken over to provide shore training, maintenance and engineering support for naval air squadrons whilst their parent carrier underwent maintenance in a dockyard. They also provided continuation flying for the constant stream of new aircrew on their way to join the embarked squadrons. Similar organisations set up Temporary Air Maintenance Yards (TAMYs) and mobile Receipt and Dispatch Units. Eight MONABs and two TAMYs were operational in Australia by August 1945 and others were established in the Admiralty Islands and Hong Kong. The Fleet Air Arm training organisation in Britain was capable of manning and training one MONAB per month. After the war, equipment and a skeleton staff for an expeditionary MONAB were maintained at readiness and not finally discarded until after the 1957 Defence Review.

These support measures were made necessary by the massive expansion of naval aviation during the Second World War. In 1939, the Royal Navy had held about 500 aircraft on charge. During the next six years, it took delivery of over 17,000 aircraft and many of these were far more complicated than the simple biplanes of the Swordfish era. The evolution and widespread fitting of radar, IFF, VHF radio and homing beacons made aircraft maintenance and support a complex logistical and engineering issue. Such was the complexity of day-to-day maintenance that serious consideration was given to using escort carriers as 'overnight maintenance ships' to support the fleet carriers off Japan in 1945. The scheme introduced almost as many issues as it solved, however, and was not proceeded with before the end of hostilities. One further logistic issue was the increasing size of naval aircraft. In 1939 a Swordfish needed 110 gallons of Avgas to fill its tank; by 1945 its replacement the Avenger needed 278. The number of sorties a fleet carrier could fuel was reduced and the number of tankers needed to support the carrier in the operating area was nearly trebled.

It can be argued that by bringing together logistic techniques that are still in use today and 'freeing' the fleet from the 'shackles' that tied it to dockyards and bases, the BPF laid the foundation of the modern, versatile Royal Navy, capable of deploying task forces throughout the world. Every aspect of that fleet is a fascinating study in its own right.

The impact of British industry deserves further mention. The bulk of the aircraft manufacturing industry was geared to the massive production of designs specified by the RAF. Variations of these to produce aircraft such as the Sea Hurricane and Seafire met with varying degrees of success, but it did not prove possible to 'break out' with a wholly new design for the navy until late in the war. Naval officers with the Ministry of Aircraft Production deserve much credit, however, for sponsoring standard tactical designs, capable of being built in both naval and the more limited land form. Examples include the Vampire, Hornet, Fury (cancelled by the RAF but became the Sea Fury) and Hawk (also cancelled by the RAF but became the Sea Hawk).

Mention has been made of small firms that discovered niche markets in war work. An interesting example of these was a stage lighting firm that created a Torpedo Attack Simulator at RNAS Crail to an Admiralty specification. This allowed a pilot seated in a Link trainer cockpit to 'fly' an attack against 'warships' projected onto a 350°, circular concrete wall. Clever lighting provided cloud, rain and night effects. Similar equipment was used to train fighter pilots and a number of pilots in blind carrier landing techniques for night operations.

The post-war world, 1945–1990

With the end of the war many major projects, including the big carriers and the aircraft intended to operate from them, were cancelled. Thousands of Lend-Lease aircraft were literally pushed over the side into the sea off Australia and Ceylon. The landing of a Sea Vampire jet fighter on *Ocean* in December 1945, the first jet deck landing in history, was thus something of a new beginning. The changes found necessary to take the new generation to sea proved to be the most radical in the innovative history of naval aviation.

The Admiralty viewed the new jet fighters with some misgiving. On the one hand, they offered a level of performance that was clearly beyond that of piston-engined aircraft, but on the other they used a fuel that was not yet refined in Britain and had to be bought with scarce dollars. On launch, the slow acceleration of the early jet engines meant that full power was barely reached by the time of take-off and on recovery, landing speed was so fast that the DLCO barely had time to 'gather the aircraft into the groove' before the 'cut' signal was given. Even here, that slow acceleration was a problem as once the pilot closed the throttle, he could not open it again in time to overshoot. If carrier aviation was to have a future, solutions needed to be found, and in the meantime the last generation of piston-engined aircraft remained in service throughout the Korean War while Sea Vampires were used in second-line squadrons to build up a core of jet experience.

The Royal Navy achieved a far-reaching series of new inventions, which made future carrier operations possible, from trials that were based on a false assumption. At first it was assumed that if the aircraft were made lighter, their deck performance would be improved. A version of the Sea Vampire was produced that could land on a rubber 'mat' with its undercarriage retracted to test the validity of 'undercarriage-less' fighters that would be 15 per cent lighter than normal aircraft. The idea worked ashore and a rubber deck was built onto *Warrior* for sea trials during 1949. Whilst these worked, they exposed the operational weakness of the concept. Once stopped, the aircraft had to be craned onto a trolley before it could clear the landing area. It had to stay on the trolley whilst in the deck park and, on launch, had to be catapulted off the trolley. A number of solutions were attempted, including wire pulleys that dragged the aircraft clear of the landing area and down a chute into the hangar, then someone suggested 'skewing' or angling the rubber deck ten degrees to port to allow faster clearance. The concept of the angled deck, subsequently used by every carrier navy, was born. With hindsight, the rubber deck trials seem bizarre. Such decks could never have operated helicopters, turbo-prop aircraft or even jet fighters with external bombs, missiles or drop tanks. The angled deck revolutionised carrier flying, however, allowing aircraft that missed the wires or 'bolted' to go round again instead of hitting the barrier. It also had the effect of lengthening the runway and keeping it clear of the parking area on the forward deck.

The fast landing problem was solved in two ways. Large air brakes were fitted to new aircraft, such as the Buccaneer, so that the aircraft turned finals with a high power setting and retracted the brake to overshoot rather than wait for the engine to accelerate. The DLCO was replaced by a mirror sight, in which the pilot kept a light accurately aligned against a datum bar, giving him an instant indication if he departed from the ideal glideslope. The need to launch ever-heavier aircraft was solved by the introduction of the steam catapult, extensively tested in an experimental installation on the maintenance carrier *Perseus* between 1949 and 1951. The US Navy took a keen interest in all these developments, including the rubber deck. Although cushioned by the larger size of its carrier decks it had foreseen the same problems and rapidly adopted the angled deck, steam catapult and mirror landing aid. It continues to use them to this day.

Other technical advances made the aircraft themselves far more potent. The 1950s saw Skyraider Airborne Early Warning aircraft introduced which could data link radar pictures back to the carrier or use the two observers in the aircraft's crew to control interceptions by fighters or to guide strike aircraft onto their target. The early AN/APS 20 radar could detect a destroyer-sized contact at 180 miles and a bomber aircraft at 60. The innovative Gannet was a complete anti-submarine hunter-killer able to carry both sensors and weapons on a single sortie. The Sea Vixen all-weather fighter was the first British aircraft designed as a weapons system, although its development was so protracted that it was obsolescent by the time it was introduced into service in 1958. Helicopters made significant strides and the Whirlwind became a 'workhorse' capable of amphibious assault with Royal Marines and anti-submarine search with a dipping sonar system, although it could not carry a weapon as well. Many were used in the search and rescue role both on carriers and ashore.

Despite the capability demonstrated by the new aircraft carriers and their flexible air groups, the Cold War led successive British governments to build up nuclear exchange forces such as the V-bombers and the Thor missile and to reduce the size of the navy. Escort carriers had soon been discarded after 1945 and after 1957 the light fleet carriers were discarded despite being able to operate the new generation of aircraft, albeit in small numbers. The question of size was again an important consideration and it was clear that only large ships could operate the new aircraft in large numbers and mount the new radar and communications systems necessary to control them. At first the Admiralty sought to contain cost by 'modernising' old hulls such as *Victorious* and *Eagle*. These were expected to produce effective capability for half the cost of a new ship but, of course, they only offered half the life expectancy. In the event the former took eight years to convert and the latter six; both were over budget and both were discarded early after changes in Government defence policy. Attempts to build new large carriers, similar in size to *Malta*, were cancelled in 1952 and 1966. The 1966 ship, referred to as CVA01, was to have been named *Queen Elizabeth*.

Catapult aircraft had been removed from battleships and cruisers in 1943 when it was felt that such ships would never operate far from a carrier. The contraction of the carrier force by 1955, however, meant that many ships, especially destroyers and frigates, might well have to operate far from carrier air support. The need to attack high-speed submarines at distance led to a concept that weapon-carrying light helicopters could be embarked in escorts. Trials were carried out using platforms built over the quarterdecks of *Grenville* and *Undaunted* which proved successful and led to orders for a Saunders-Roe design that entered service as the Westland Wasp. The Tribal-class general-purpose frigates were designed to operate Wasps in the Medium Anti-submarine Torpedo Carrying Helicopter (MATCH) role with the first ship, *Ashanti*, completed in 1961. Since then, every British destroyer or frigate has been capable of operating a Wasp, the more sophisticated Lynx, or even Sea King and Merlin helicopters. The US Navy attempted a different line using pilotless drone helicopters, but when these failed, they followed a similar policy to the Royal Navy, as have most of the world's navies.

The Royal Navy first showed an interest in 'vertical take-off' (VTO) fighters in 1945 as a counter to the Kamikaze threat. A number of the 'paper' carriers designed around the rubber deck concept showed vertical launch ramps for the fighters as a complement to the landing mats. No practical aircraft design emerged, however, until the Hawker P1154 Joint Strike Fighter Project of 1961 The Admiralty eventually opposed this project and sought the US Navy Phantom, not because it was averse to VTOL but because the aircraft came nowhere near meeting the Naval Staff target for an air superiority fighter to replace the Sea Vixen. It also failed to meet the RAF target and that service also bought the Phantom.

The cancellation of the big carrier project in 1966 and the rundown of the carrier force led to the procurement of the *Invincible* class laid down from 1973. These were effectively a new class of light fleet carrier attempting to combine the roles of anti-air warfare (AAW) destroyer and anti-submarine (AS) frigate with that of a small carrier. The procurement of a navalised version of the RAF Harrier, known as the Sea Harrier, to operate from these ships was a wise move and proved very effective during the South Atlantic Campaign of 1982 and in a number of subsequent operations. The 'ski-jump' fitted to the *Invincibles* and *Hermes* allowed the Sea Harriers to take off at a greater all-up mass and had the effect of lengthening the take-off run. Spain, Italy, Russia and India adopted the concept but, surprisingly, not the US Navy despite extensive tests using both VSTOL and conventional aircraft from a jump fitted ashore.

Critics of the VTOL concept originally argued that weight growth during the operational life of such an aircraft would make the vertical landing difficult and impossible if any weapons were to be brought back to the deck, especially in hot weather such that found in the Middle East. This is precisely why the decision was taken to withdraw the Sea Harrier from service earlier than expected in 2006. The three *Invincible*-class ships have undergone a considerable reappraisal since the end of the Cold War and have had their AAW missiles and AS sonar removed to allow them to concentrate on aircraft operations. They were originally configured to specialise in anti-submarine helicopter operations but now concentrate on the embarkation of Harrier strike aircraft, the GR 9 version being intended for use by both naval and RAF squadrons from the deck as part of Joint Force Harrier. The helicopters tend to operate from the decks of ships in company, including both frigates and Royal Fleet Auxiliaries, in order to maximise the number of strike aircraft in the carriers.

It is interesting to note how closely the current plans mirror those of the 1960s for the use of carrier-borne aircraft to support a joint expeditionary warfare capability. There is even a big carrier project, the future carrier or CVF, similar in size to *Malta* and CVA01 It has been given the same name, *Queen Elizabeth*. It is complemented, as before, by a joint Royal Navy/RAF strike aircraft, although this time the UK is a partner in a massive US project to deliver aircraft to the US Air Force, Navy and Marine Corps and other export customers as well as the British. Present plans call for the procurement of a Short Take Off Vertical Landing (STOVL) version, but this is inferior in every respect to the US Navy's 'tailhook' version. If military rather than political logic prevails, it is very difficult to see why the latter version does not represent better value for money as well as being a better vehicle for the closest co-operation with our most significant ally.

The logic for building large carriers is inescapable. So too is the logic for sea basing on a planet that is largely covered by water and on which host nation support for a base on foreign soil cannot be taken for granted. Those who have sought alternatives have usually spent more money on less capability, just as studies in the 1960s predicted. Ships, aircraft and even weapons are being improved rapidly by technology, but the fundamental common sense that has underpinned carrier aviation since HMS *Argus*, the world's first true carrier went to sea in 1918, is obvious. Techniques may change, but the flying sailors of 1918 and 1939 would feel at home with the broad direction in which the Royal Navy's Fleet Air Arm of today is headed. They would probably express a few home truths about the detailed methods of implementation, however!

Notes

This chapter is based upon the following material held at the National Archives (Public Record Office), the Naval Historical Branch, and the Fleet Air Arm's Museum Archive, Yeovilton. Additional material can be found in the consolidated bibliography.

ADM 1/9211 *Hermes* outline design.
ADM 1/9259 *Courageous* legend 1925.
ADM 1/9406 *Illustrious* 1940.
ADM 1/9433 *Indomitable* re-design.
ADM 1/11845 MAC and CAM ships.
ADM 1/12058 Building programme 1942.
ADM 1/14798 Post delivery modifications to escort carriers 1943.
ADM 1/14842 Delays in escort carrier completion.
ADM 1/22421 Angled deck proposal.
ADM 116/3871 Air instructions to the Mediterranean Fleet 1934–1939.
ADM 234/383 Naval Staff History 'The Development of British Naval Aviation 1919–1945', Volume 1, 1954.
ADM 234/384 Naval Staff History 'The Development of British Naval Aviation 1919–1945', Volume 2, 1956.
CB 04484 Aircraft carrier and Commando Ship Handbook, 1970 (declassified).

Notes on 'The Development of British Naval Aviation 1919–1945', Volume 3, not completed.

Flight Deck Magazines 1944–2000.

4

WELDING AND THE BRITISH SHIPBUILDING INDUSTRY

A major constraint?

Lewis Johnman and Hugh Murphy

Major technological change of lasting value necessarily takes place over time, and has three more or less distinct phases, invention, innovation and diffusion. Invention is either based on new scientific knowledge or on less well-understood scientific principles and leads to a product or particular process being patented. Innovation occurs when an entrepreneur, firm, or cluster of firms commercially introduce an invention, which can lead to further patents extending the period of innovation. In this sense, innovation is a continuing process where incremental improvements are made over time, and this phase can be local, national or international in character. Last, diffusion occurs when firms across a particular industry or industries adopt a process as their main method of production, or as a necessary adjunct to it. The latter is often a matter of timing as some firms will definitely hold off, particularly those in mature industries such as shipbuilding and marine engineering, until a process has been truly diffused and therefore proven. Then the more widespread adoption of a particular process is incorporated into or replaces the extant mode of production, and in the latter case is often undertaken under the umbrella term of 'modernisation'. New entrants can of course adopt the process wholesale and steal a march on competitors, and it can also be argued that innovation and diffusion are sometimes blurred and as a result this can lead to a host of definitions and a circularity of argument.

It is with diffusion, however, and the institutional factors aiding or hampering the long-run adoption of the innovation of electric arc welding to replace riveting as the principal method of metal joining in the British shipbuilding industry, that we are primarily concerned here. A process that we shall argue exemplified technological conservatism in the industry, and which would definitely have taken even longer to achieve but for Admiralty encouragement of welding in warships from the 1930s onwards and government investigation and financial aid to the industry during the Second World War.[1]

Electric arc welding in British shipbuilding

Welded construction offers considerable savings in weight and space when compared with riveting and results in a more streamlined ship, and when undertaken with suitable facilities lends itself to prefabrication and assembly of ship structures and sections away from the berth.[2] In British shipbuilding up to the Second World War, however, the development, assimilation and diffusion of electric arc welding was a slow and frustrating process. Nevertheless, the shipyard employers had long known that welding, in terms of work organisation and attendant costs, had the potential to supplant riveting as the industry's main method of production. It was generally acknowledged that the potential to train welders in far less time than riveters existed, and that the process lent itself to automation, particularly on large flat sections of plate. Welding was less physically demanding and skilful than riveting, and did not require the squads of workmen associated with the latter process. Despite the slow progress of welding generally, as early as 1920 one firm in the British shipbuilding industry had taken an early world lead in all welded ship construction and it is to this development that we now turn.

The *Fullagar* experiment

Although the principles of electric arc welding, first by use of a bare wire and later by a covered electrode, were relatively well known in shipbuilding circles, the process was not introduced into a British shipyard until 1917. That year the Quasi Arc Company installed arc welding plant and equipment in the shipyard of the Birkenhead shipbuilders and engineers, Cammell Laird. The following year construction of the first all-welded ship built in the British Isles had begun, and consequently in 1920 the motor vessel *Fullagar*, also engined by Cammell Laird, was completed.[3] A coaster of 150 feet in length, *Fullagar* (later renamed *Caria*, *Shean* and *Cedros*) was built under the supervision of Lloyd's Register surveyors and given a special class of her own in the Annual Register of '100 A1 Electrically Welded; Subject to Biennial Survey Experimental'.[4] It was noted that *Fullagar's* hull did not have the flush appearance of later welded ships as her plates were joggled, giving her 'the appearance of a welded ship with straight lines'. The vessel was nevertheless a full-scale experiment in electric arc welding and in 1924, now renamed *Caria*, despite running aground and sustaining serious damage, she remained watertight before being repaired. Although classed as a coaster, its owners were given permission after repair for the vessel to cross the Atlantic Ocean, pass through the Panama Canal and make its way up the North Pacific coast to Victoria in British Columbia, where she was eventually renamed *Shean* and employed as a cement carrier. Subsequently, when fully loaded, *Shean* struck a rock, was seriously damaged, but was repaired and passed her tenth annual survey. Had similar damage been sustained by a riveted ship in the same circumstances it would have in all probability sunk.[5]

Despite this early world lead in all-welded construction, the British shipbuilding industry in the largely depressed 1920s on the whole failed to exploit welding's potential, and remained wedded to riveted ships. Welding was mainly confined to the ship repair industry as ships of riveted construction suited existing shipyard layouts and the organisation of work therein.[6] Shipyard plant and equipment also suited riveting and the process had long been technologically proven in ocean-going ships. The industry continued to build to order largely bespoke riveted vessels, and what little standardisation that existed was mainly in the tramp cargo steamer market. Reinforcing the generally low take-up of the new technology of welding in the industry was the incremental approach of the Admiralty on the naval side, and the reluctance of classification societies and insurers on the mercantile side to fully endorse the new method of construction because of fears over the particular stresses on metal joints that could lead to fractures in ocean-going vessels. On the mercantile side of the industry, only in 1932, when welding was being more widely used, did the classification societies publish amended rules and regulations regarding its use in ship construction.[7]

Riveting and labour organisation

From the age of iron and then steel shipbuilding, riveters occupied a pivotal place in shipyard organisation. Riveting was first undertaken by hand when plates were erected piece by piece at the berth and later during the inter-war period by pneumatic and hydraulic means, the latter introducing an element of prefabrication. Only those who had undertaken a five-year apprenticeship could call themselves riveters, and a riveting squad normally comprised one right-handed and one left-handed riveter, a holder on, a catcher and a rivet heater. Riveting was, in turn, linked to the other hull trades of drilling, plating and the much older trade of caulking in order to make the ship watertight. Apart from shipwrights, the organisation of the hull trades generally resided in the Praetorian Guard of the shipyard unions, the Boilermakers Society, which jealously guarded its hard-won status at the apex of the shipyard production process.[8]

British shipyards, most of which were spatially constrained, had been set up to take advantage of riveting and the physical allocation of work had been organised accordingly. Labour- rather than capital-intensive methods of work organisation predominated; and riveting squads were paid on a piecework basis after verification of the number of rivets deposited in a single shift. Payment, therefore, was directly related to effort expended and riveters were widely admired for their metronome skills and were easily heard for miles around a shipyard. Indeed the extant system of work organisation suited the employers; workers were casualised and were hired and fired on a regular basis by shipyard foremen. With the reliance on foremen and middle management, most of whom had risen through the ranks, the extent of higher management control at the yard level over work organisation of the strictly demarcated shipyard trades was limited. No interchangeability of trades existed and in the shipyard division of labour, all knew their place and function in the production process. Clearly, as McKinlay has noted, the employers saw the majority of their workforces as variable and not fixed costs of production.[9] Accordingly, security, or more correctly periodisation of employment, was directly related to work in hand.

Where higher management control was particularly evident, however, was in the field of setting wage rates and in dispute resolution. To this end, agreements between the employers and the myriad shipyard craft unions on rates of pay and payments for particular processes were negotiated at yard, district and national level under the aegis of the Shipbuilding Employers Federation (SEF), to which every major shipbuilding firm in the British Isles belonged. This often protracted co-operation apart, the shipyard trade unions, although affiliated for negotiating purposes to a federation, were inherently sectionalised and fought each other over the right to control particular processes. In reality, both management and workers were essentially polarised with the former obsessively reliant on procedure and the latter wedded to restrictive trade practices to preserve status and employment. This mirrored the institutional nature of the industry as a whole where conditions of work were governed by a National Rule Book to which the Boilermakers were not a signatory. Any widespread adoption, therefore, of a new industrial process such as electric arc welding, quite separate from the question of high start-up costs, was more than likely to be severely constrained by the extant system of demarcated industrial relations.[10]

With their casualised livelihood dependent on shipbuilding in areas where little alternative employment existed, particularly for the inelastic hull trades, organised labour had always clung tenaciously to hard-won trade practices and there was every reason to suspect that this would remain the case. This was evident in that the employers had failed to upset the status quo with the widespread introduction of pneumatic tools and less so of hydraulic riveting machines in the inter-war period, even though this ushered in a noticeable drop in skill content. According to Wrigley, hydraulic machines when used on the ground away from the berth facilitated riveted structures at between two and three times the rate achievable by the same number of men employed on either the manual or pneumatic method. Hydraulic machines were, however, considerable items of capital expenditure, and in a largely labour-intensive industry, hand and pneumatic riveting held sway. Thus, by 1935, only 12 per cent of riveting was carried out hydraulically.[11]

The potential for de-skilling trades by the increased use of mechanical aids in shipyard production generally was quickly recognised by the employers. When the post-war shipbuilding boom had turned to bust in 1921, the President of the SEF, the Port Glasgow shipbuilder James Lithgow, had publicly pointed out that the increased use of mechanical aids in shipbuilding had de-skilled many jobs without a corresponding decrease in wages.[12] Lithgow, the issue of wage reductions aside, was in effect acknowledging that what had suited the employers in the past, the sub-division of trades, such as that of boilermaking into different crafts, leading to a very high percentage of skilled workers in the industry, was no longer applicable in the light of increased foreign competition and reduced demand. Throughout the mainly depressed inter-war period, Lithgow consistently maintained this stance, and was active in policy matters in the industry's national organisations and elsewhere.[13] However, any attempt by the employers to impose a new system of work organisation on a national basis, in an atomistic industry with a preponderance of family-owned firms, and a significantly powerful group of public vertically integrated conglomerates, had necessarily to be a united one.[14]

The employers' situation in context

From a pre-First World War position of world market dominance when British shipbuilding held two-thirds of global output, the tremendous increase in world shipbuilding capacity consequent upon the war and the rise of economic nationalism overseas offered a portent of increased foreign competition to come. Continental countries in particular had built up their shipbuilding industries as a matter of national policy, and had resorted to subsidy, competitive devaluations, tariffs and flag discrimination as means of protection.[15] In contrast, the British shipbuilding industry on the whole remained wedded to the concept of free trade and for the most part, mail contracts and conference cartels aside, eschewed state subsidies. The British mercantile marine remained the world's largest fleet and British owners remained loyal to their domestic industry.

In tandem with mercantile work, highly profitable warship construction for the Royal Navy and, with Admiralty permission, foreign navies, formed an integral part of the business plans of all the largest firms in the industry, the mixed naval and mercantile builders. All of the mixed builders had bespoke linkages with shipping and liner firms and long associations with the Admiralty as a matter of business prudence, and none were willing to put all their eggs in the one basket. Apart from passenger liner work, naval work, in stark contrast to run-of-the-mill mercantile construction, was infinitely more skilled, the duration of contracts from design to completion was long and profitable, and in theory and sometimes in practice this provided a bulwark against a slump in mercantile demand. What the shipbuilders dreaded, however, was a simultaneous slump in demand in both sectors.

By 1918, British shipbuilding capacity, measured by the maximum productive capacity being fully utilised with no supply constraints impinging, stood at 40 per cent above that of 1914.[16] World tonnage had also grown dramatically with the United States, mainly through its war emergency shipbuilding programme, being responsible for 86 per cent of the increase in net world shipbuilding output between 1914 and 1921.[17] After the short speculative post-war boom based on the rapid replacement of lost tonnage, freight rates had fallen in 1920 and had plummeted by 1921.[18] This precipitated a slump in mercantile demand of hitherto unknown longevity, which was to last for almost the entire inter-war period. Prior to the First World War, although the Royal Dockyards were primarily but not exclusively involved in repair and maintenance of the fleet, the Admiralty's reliance on the private producers was clear. Buoyed by the various programmes of the Fisher era, the private builders had built nearly 60 per cent of Royal Navy warships, excluding foreign orders, between 1890 and 1914.[19] By 1920 the industry, which had been specifically skewed towards naval production during the First World War, employed over 300,000 workers and indirectly many more. Although the Two Power Standard had been abandoned in 1920, battlecruiser orders to three upper Clyde mixed builders, Beardmore, Fairfield and John Brown, and one on the Tyne, Swan Hunter, seemed to confirm that the Admiralty desired to retain the status of the Royal Navy. However, when Britain signed up to the Washington Naval Treaty in December 1921, which banned the construction of capital ships in excess of 10,000 standard displacement tons, or which carried guns with a calibre in excess of 8 inches, its impact was immediate, and the four battlecruiser contracts were cancelled, ushering in an almost equally enduring slump in naval demand.[20]

This combination of slump conditions in both the mercantile and naval markets left the better equipped mixed builders – many of whom, in particular Beardmore, had invested heavily with Admiralty encouragement on the expectation of continuing naval work – between a rock and a hard place.[21] Although accumulated profits and reserves from the war would provide some bulwark in slump conditions, the employers quickly moved to lay off their workforces in a situation where overblown mercantile world capacity was hugely in excess of likely future demand. From just under 12 per cent of the insured workforce unemployed in 1921, some 35 per cent were unemployed in 1922 and in 1923. Although the workforces were somewhat inured to periods of unemployment and did work along river centres, the portents for the long term were not good and unemployment in shipbuilding districts, peaking at 37 per cent in 1926, remained stubbornly high for the rest of the decade.[22]

Another impact of the Washington Treaty on the industry, cancellations aside, was that in 1922–3 the total value of naval construction work for the Admiralty plummeted from £11,816,000 to a derisory £721,000.[23] Faced with a shortage of both naval and mercantile orders and increased domestic and foreign competition, the industry forced wage reductions on its remaining workforces. 1923 was notable for an extended lock-out by the employers of members of the Boilermakers Society over the lack of an overtime and shift-work agreement in slump conditions that lasted seven months, and which was not resolved until July 1924.[24]

Comparative strife and stagnation persisted, and in this climate the industry's competitive position was brought into sharp focus when in 1925 Furness Withy ordered a series of vessels from a German shipyard on the grounds of price and delivery at a price which was £300,000 less than the lowest British tender. Predictably, this sparked public outrage and prompted a joint SEF and shipyard trade unions enquiry into foreign competition and conditions in the shipbuilding industry, which reported in 1926. Conducted in an atmosphere of collective pique, the conclusion of the enquiry had the effect of apportioning the blame for a lack of international competitiveness on factors outside the industry's control, although it did recognise that some form of interchangeability of labour was desirable if Britain were to remain competitive with continental Europe.[25]

Faced with the prospect of a continuing slump in mercantile and naval demand, yard closures were rife, and vertically integrated mixed naval and mercantile firms such as Armstrong Whitworth and Beardmore – the former had a dedicated naval yard on the Tyne and the latter a naval complex at Dalmuir, on the Clyde – were in deep financial trouble and were subject to Bank of England-inspired rationalisation schemes. In this climate, as Slaven has noted, the warship builders (his term) were the first to run for cover and meetings began in 1925 on current problems; soon after the participants, the largest firms in the industry, privately devised a rota scheme of three years' duration to share out work, which came into effect in November 1926. As these firms were in effect also mercantile builders and were concurrently involved in steam turbine and marine diesel building, this in turn prompted a series of meetings encompassing other mercantile-only firms. By April 1927, all interested shipbuilders had formed a committee, and a year later the twenty-seven largest firms in an industry that had hitherto been a bastion of rampant individualism and harsh domestic competition had moved towards mutual co-operation by forming a price-protective trade organisation, the Shipbuilding Conference.[26] From this point onwards a united response to the continuing problems of shipyard capacity exceeding likely future demand in both naval and mercantile sectors was possible.

National Shipbuilders Security Limited

The vehicle chosen to bring the over-capacity of the British shipbuilding industry more into line with likely future demand was National Shipbuilders Security Limited (NSS). Undertaken against a background of rationalisation generally, NSS was formed in co-operation with the Bank of England in February 1930 with the aim of voluntarily buying up redundant shipyards and sterilising them against any future return to shipbuilding by restrictive covenants.[27] Clearly there was a mutuality of interests between the Bank, whose vehicles Bankers Industrial Development and Securities Management Trust were involved in the rationalisation of cross-sector firms, including Armstrong Whitworth and Beardmore, and the shipbuilders. Moreover, there existed a pressing desire to keep government at bay in the rationalisation process generally and in shipbuilding in particular.[28]

NSS's first purchase, the specially constructed Dalmuir Naval Yard of the cross-sectoral firm of Sir William Beardmore, which had a scrap value of £30,000, was at £209,000 the most costly, but gave the Bank of England a good return for its interest. NSS consolidated its rationalisation scheme first on Clydeside, and then moved to the north-east coast of England, and by 1935 the company's most controversial purchase occurred at Palmer's of Jarrow and Hebburn on the Tyne, which at Jarrow alone left a local unemployment rate of 73 per cent, and sparked the Jarrow March.[29] The chairman of NSS, the ubiquitous Sir James Lithgow, firmly believed that over-capacity existed in relation to prospective demand and in this respect he was correct. However, the underlying aim of NSS, which remained a private company throughout, was to increase contract prices and therefore profits by collusion between member firms in a period of generally catastrophic economic conditions. There was no pretence whatsoever at concentrating the industry by a series of amalgamations or mergers. Demand in the early years of NSS operation had remained stubbornly low, and in 1933, at the nadir of the depression in British shipbuilding, Clyde builders launched only 56,000 gross registered tons of shipping, against a UK total of 133,000 gross tons.[30]

By this stage, the industry's insured workforce had more than halved since 1921 and now stood at 169,000 with 78,000 unemployed; and by 1935, the total labour force had fallen by a quarter since 1930. As Wrigley has noted, it could therefore be reasonably inferred that those workers remaining in shipbuilding treated it as a permanent occupation. This, in turn, impelled a greater degree of trade protectionism, and up to 1934 the intake of apprentices into shipbuilding was only one-tenth of the pre-war average.[31] To give a clear indication of the conditions world-wide, one firm, the Port Glasgow cargo tramp builder, Lithgows, had built on average over 5 per cent of world tonnage in the three years from 1932 to 1934, or to put it another way, one in every sixteen new vessels launched.[32] Lithgows aside, conditions for the mixed naval and mercantile builders, particularly with the signing of the London Naval Treaty of 1930, banning the construction of capital ships for another five years, remained parlous. Treaty conditions, especially weight restrictions, did however compel the Admiralty to reconsider its approach to the design and specifications of warships, and it is to Admiralty encouragement of electric arc welding of warships in the private shipyards that we now turn.

The Admiralty and electric arc welding

The early encouragement of electric arc welding in warships by the Admiralty to an extent mirrored the approach of the classification societies and insurers; it was both cautious and incremental. Nevertheless, Admiralty design of warships had its own internal standards of strength and capability and was not subject to outside approval by commercial interests. Design was often forged in the experience of war and practicality often overrode aesthetics. It was generally accepted that welded practice in ships offered savings in weight of between 10 and 15 per cent over similar riveted vessels, an important factor when building warships to treaty limitations on displacement. Indeed, the Admiralty, unlike commercial interests, could afford to be more experimental to gain experience, and by 1930 warship plans included specifications for welded parts. This acceptance that welding should be encouraged underpinned the fact that the Admiralty was the British shipbuilding industry's main customer for warships, had its own contracts, design and other technical departments within the Royal Corps of Naval Constructors (RCNC), and also had to give approval for foreign warship exports.[33] In short, although the Admiralty had always been quick to take up developments in the private sector – Parsons' marine turbine being an excellent example – the drive for technological innovation generally was firmly in its court. Producers basically built to Admiralty design specifications on the basis of tenders for individual contracts, agreed to a list of sub-contracted work and Admiralty Free Issues, and coped later with the frequent changes in design and equipment instigated by the Admiralty. This was, however, not a one-way relationship; and the balance of advantage shifted between the Admiralty and the private mixed builders – who all belonged to the secretive Warship Group – owing to external factors, notably war, where too rigid control of producers could prove to be counterproductive.

Internal factors were just as important, such as private firms in the Warship Group colluding on prices and profits in conditions of imperfect competition where only indigenous producers built for the Royal Navy.

Although the connection between a country's industrial capacity and seapower is an obvious one, less obvious is the internal dynamics and interdependence over time which holds sway between the state and private industry, which at some stage coalesce into the most efficient way to prosecute a country's potential for war. It was clearly in the Admiralty's interest to retain as much naval capacity and skills as possible and, as Gordon has pointed out, by the First World War 'a massive and intimate – perhaps too intimate – industrial complex had grown up around the Royal Navy'.[34] Despite this, however, no coherent policy for the maritime industries in general in Britain existed. Neither was there any question of an Admiralty-inspired rationalisation of the bloated private warship-building sector it had helped to create in the first place. Constrained by treaty restrictions, annual battles with the Treasury on Naval Estimates and various attempts to usurp its position on procuring its own warships and ordnance, it was obviously in the Admiralty's wider interests to share out as equitably as possible the small amount of naval work that it secured. In the wider deflationary climate, however, *ad hoc* and short-term solutions to particular problems and crises dominated the political landscape of shipbuilding in the inter-war period. A prime example of this tendency was the collapse of the huge Royal Mail Steam Packet Group of companies in 1930, which threatened the entire British maritime economy.[35]

Despite the backdrop of crisis in the shipbuilding industry, 1931 saw the first major application of Admiralty policy on welding when the mixed builder and Warship Group member, Cammell Laird, began to build the cruiser *Achilles* with welded main oil and watertight bulkheads, strengthened by tee-bar stiffeners. The welding of bulkheads, all of which were prefabricated on the ground in a covered shed with the aid of a 10-ton travelling crane, avoided the use of time-consuming overhead and vertical welding.[36] By 1933, however, C.S. Lillicrap of the RCNC admitted that although the Admiralty still had much to learn, it was nevertheless continuing with the extension of welding on lines that were generally sound given that experimental work had been continuous and had been supplemented by experience in construction. It was now general policy at the Admiralty to use electric arc welding extensively in place of or to supplement riveting, and by this stage, on minor work, welding had supplanted riveting entirely.[37] Moreover, on major construction work such as bulkheads, practically all were now being welded, and the policy continued to the extent that the aircraft carrier *Ark Royal* laid down in 1935 and launched in 1937 by Cammell Laird was over 75 per cent electrically arc welded.[38]

Despite the ongoing depression in both mercantile and naval demand, the denuding of mercantile and naval capacity by NSS, and continuing structural unemployment, the employers had retained their belief in the possibility that the introduction of welding on their terms could drive a coach and horses through the extant system of shipyard work organisation. Underpinning this was the dual knowledge that the Admiralty would again become the industry's major customer for warships when treaty restrictions abated, and that future warship work would accordingly extend the practice of welding. British shipbuilders successfully kept developments in welding solely within their own compass, and to this end were determined to introduce welding on their own terms. Standards institutions were therefore to be sidetracked and the industry's attitude to certification and examination by outside bodies was initially hostile from 1931, and remained so throughout the decade and beyond. No certificates were required of any trade in British shipbuilding, and the employers reserved the sole right to train and recognise tradesmen as they had done in the past.[39]

For the majority of the inter-war period the industry through the SEF and later by association with NSS and its attendant schemes did in general seek to cut costs by the easiest manner, wages, and by so doing increase its profitability. By association and in practice any extension of welding would take place in this context, and to control wage levels the employers' consistent stance was that no one group of workers, especially the Boilermakers Society, had an exclusive right to the process and to organise their members accordingly. In theory, welding offered the enticing option of changing rather than reinforcing the extant system of work organisation, and when fully taken up would displace the existing hull trades of drilling, caulking and riveting, and severely affect plating. This was, however, a distinctly long-term option, and in the short term the numbers of welders already employed in relation to platers and riveters were insignificant. For the employers, what was important in the short term was to establish the practice of welding on their terms as a semi-skilled, not a skilled occupation for the de-skilling faction, or at best for those employers who saw it as more skilful, a skilled occupation controlled by apprenticeship with no one trade union having exclusive rights to the process. If this were achieved, then wage cuts and reductions in numbers of established highly paid trades such as plating would be possible.

By September 1932, the SEF Electric Arc Welding Committee, after a number of initial studies, recommended that a special class of ship welders should be created for all ship construction work.[40] As McGoldrick has noted, the SEF finally presented their plans on welding to the shipyard unions in May 1933, which were to be implemented by October of that year.[41] A new trade was to be created termed 'Ship Welder'. Entry qualification would be the normal five-year apprenticeship for new boy recruits, but displaced trades could take up the new trade after two years' training. Crucially, unskilled shipyard workers such as labourers could also take up the new trade after two years' training as could time-served apprentices in other trades. Predictably, in a series of meetings the trade unions were unanimous in their opposition to the proposed scheme, seeing it as an attempt to introduce dilution, and thus change the extant system of demarcation of trades. Moreover, they viewed it as an attempt to cut wages and saw no need to create a special class of welder at all.[42]

After a series of predictably failed conferences, the SEF decided to introduce the scheme in any event, and did so formally in April 1934. Opposition to the scheme primarily from the Boilermakers Society continued, and as McGoldrick has presciently pointed out, they, like the employers, knew that despite its slow growth a rapid acceleration in the rate of welding was imminent.[43] The Society, by aggressive recruitment, unofficial strikes, and an overall coherent national strategy, albeit led at the district level, determined that it would see off the employers' plans. Unofficial strikes by boilermakers on Clydeside – where only seven major firms, six of whom were mixed builders, employed welders – began during the negotiating period, and this was followed by unofficial strikes by boilermakers on the Tyne, Mersey and at Barrow. These strikes obviously affected the competitive advantages of the larger firms involved in welding, and by extension adversely interfered with profitable naval work. Accordingly, the mixed builders, all of whom had sufficient production experience of welding in warships, attempted to modify the SEF scheme, which insisted on a national plain time rate for welding of £3 per week, and resolved that a system based on piecework on warships where a large volume of welding was to be done was essential.[44] This took away a central plank of the employers' hitherto united front that payments for Ship Welders should be held at a national uniform rate, and in tandem with the stance of the Boilermakers, the scheme, as McGoldrick noted, began to crumble, and shortly afterwards was dead in the water when some firms agreed to a payment by results system on welding and on the Boilermakers Society's right to control the process.[45]

What the entire process had shown thus far was that on the issue of welding the Boilermakers Society's membership, despite or because of the fact that over 40 per cent of their brethren were unemployed, were more united than the employers were over the long term. Short-term gain after the years of pain proved too powerful a lure for the mixed builders, and the likelihood of increased naval profits when rearmament had begun in earnest was a powerful disincentive to root and branch reform. Craft integrity and unity among boilermakers was paramount despite the erosion of skill in the inter-war years, and technical change, in the sense of the theoretical economies of scale and scope associated with welding, was successfully resisted in the short term in full knowledge that when fully introduced, welding would to all intents and purposes be demarcated in favour of the Society's members. Those members of the SEF who were in the de-skilling faction would have to wait nearly a decade to reinforce their point that welding was essentially an unskilled process, and could be learned in a matter of weeks.

Rearmament and the further extension of welding

It will be recalled that the Warship Group of mixed builders had privately devised a rota scheme to share out warship work between them in 1926, which continued into the 1930s. The existence of this Group had been kept secret because it could be seen as a price-protective cabal or, in the argot of the period, a 'ring'. This was precisely what it was and in consequence it had no direct relationship with the Admiralty, although the Admiralty's Contracts and Technical Departments had strong suspicions that a ring existed, yet no official investigation had taken place to confirm or deny this. Only in February 1935 was the existence of the Warship Group officially confirmed to the Government in a private memorandum to the Royal Commission on the Private Manufacture of and Trading in Arms. Fearing a full-scale investigation, the Warship Group finally admitted that it had indeed regulated both the distribution of warships in the industry and prices. In an appendix to the memorandum, the Group also explained the reasons for its formation, and that of NSS – clear evidence that the two were inextricably linked. Despite this belated candour, however, neither direct reference nor adverse comment was passed upon the Group in the body of the Commission's report and the appendix was unpublished. Thereafter, the Warship Group's existence was officially recognised by the Admiralty and meetings instituted by either party through the auspices of the Shipbuilding Conference commenced.[46]

With the prospect of rearmament commencing in the near future, it was obviously in the interests of both employers and the Admiralty to retain the *status quo ante*. Moreover, the Admiralty now had a suitable conduit in the Warship Group to advance its future plans, and in light of the already declared policy on the extension of welding, the return to capital ship construction strengthened the hand of the Boilermakers Society in attempting to monopolise control of the process. Prior to rearmament which properly began in 1936, Warship Group rotas, the loss of naval capacity through NSS of two large mixed builders, and Admiralty policy in spreading around the small amount of orders, albeit mainly on destroyer, cruiser and submarine work, had kept the bulk of the larger firms in business. It must be stressed, however, that during the inter-war period such was the collapse in demand, that both mixed builders and mercantile firms resorted to temporarily and permanently closing their facilities without the aid of NSS.

Rearmament gave the prospect of, if not virtually guaranteeing, an overall return to profitability. So it proved, and firms on the Clyde, the river with the largest amount of mixed builders, all returned to profit by 1939.[47] One Clyde firm, Scott's, was exceptional in returning an ordinary dividend in 1934 for the first time since 1926, and posted a trading profit before depreciation of £105,383 on the back of net profits on two destroyers and an appropriation against work in progress on a cruiser. Earlier in 1933, the firm had inaugurated a welding school on the back of existing and future naval contracts.[48]

The Admiralty, however, clearly remained – with certain obvious exceptions – sceptical concerning the commitment and probably the ability of the private shipbuilders to deliver decent welded structure. For example, the cruiser HMS *Leander* was built at Devonport Dockyard and was launched in 1931, and was deliberately viewed as an experiment in the value (or otherwise) of welded structure. All of the other ships in the class – HMS *Achilles* built by Cammell Laird and launched in 1932, HMS *Orion* built by Devonport Dockyard and launched in 1932, HMS *Neptune* built by Portsmouth Dockyard and launched in 1933, and finally HMS *Ajax* built by Vickers-Armstrong at Barrow and launched in 1934 – contained significant amounts of welding. *Achilles* had all of her main bulkheads welded and for the Leander's sister class, the Arethusa, HMS *Arethusa* herself, built in Chatham Dockyard, had all internal decks, superstructure, framing in the double bottom, bulkheads, some of the shell and strength deck and a considerable amount of minor work done by welding. The distribution of orders, which were allocated to the Royal Dockyards and two of the private firms that had experience in welding, was complicated by the qualities of steel being used by the Royal Navy. A new, strong steel had been introduced in 1922 known as 'D' quality and although it saved weight, its high carbon content was inimical to welding and during the Second World War a lower carbon steel, known as 'DW', was developed. A special steel for submarine pressure hulls, known as 'S', was also developed.[49]

For the larger mixed builders the prospect of treaty restrictions being lifted on capital ship construction from 1 January 1937 was enticing. Given this, the need to retain highly skilled warship workers, especially those involved in the fitting-out trades, to advance the rearmament programme was obvious. Despite this, however, given the experience of the 1920s the mixed builders were understandably cautious as to the duration and extent of the programme, which if past performance was any guide would likely result in a slump after completion – a position reinforced by the dire state of the mercantile market, which by 1938 was bleak, and compounded by the fact that many of the industry's skilled workers had left it for good in the intervening years. By September 1939 there was 50 per cent fewer men available than there had been in 1921 and on the mercantile side only 26,000 men remained at the outbreak of the Second World War.[50] This obviously impacted on the industry's ability to produce to its maximum output level, and despite NSS taking out a third of its berths, 30–40 per cent of the industry's capacity remained unused. Even at the peak of demand in 1937, the industry could work at only 64 per cent of its available capacity.[51]

The overall situation regarding welding and its further extension were also held back by the industry's lack of capital expenditure in the intervening years. As Peebles has noted in relation to three Clyde mixed builders, John Brown, Fairfield and Scott's, whilst capital expenditure in the five years to 1938–9 was higher than at any period since 1920, total expenditure on net additions to fixed assets 'in the decade preceding the outbreak of the Second World War was markedly lower than it had been in the decade preceding the First World War'. Peebles attributes this in part to the absence of any technical stimulus comparable to the introduction of the steam turbine and the advent of the dreadnought in the decade prior to the Great War. Moreover, expenditures on net additions to plant and machinery at the three firms was no greater than it had been years earlier when costs were much lower.[52]

There is little reason to doubt that Peebles' assertions were representative of the mixed builders in general. The technical stimulus of welding in warships during the 1930s was, despite the avowed intention of the Admiralty to promote it, stunted by the employers' reluctance to embrace it in terms of re-equipment and layout of yards to take advantage of its potential. Their main concern remained in reducing costs and not in adding to them. Bitter experience had shown that shipbuilding was by its very nature cyclical and the next slump almost inevitably lurked around the corner. Vision in the sense of one firm biting the financial bullet and leading the way on welding was distinctly lacking. With the likelihood of war increasing, it was doubtful in the extreme that a spatially constrained industry, where on the whole, plant and equipment was old, investment was lacking, and where management and men were polarised, could find the internal resources to maximise fully its productive potential. It remained to be seen whether or not the one actor capable of providing these resources, the state, would at some point intervene.

It was not however, as we have seen, for the want of trying, but perhaps Cammell Laird and Vickers-Armstrong remained anomalies rather that the norm. Although *Ark Royal* and other vessels were clearly the face of the future, the Admiralty decided to conduct its own trial tests by constructing two sister ship minesweepers, *Seagull* to be all welded and *Leda* to be all riveted (although in fact her bulkheads were welded, which rather distorted the comparison), in the late 1930s. This somewhat mirrored *Ark Royal* where a welding shop, which included a training school, was established at the head of the slipway, with craneage to lift prefabricated sections and some two hundred welders employed. The work was subjected to rigorous scrutiny. *Seagull*, however, was designed as an all-welded ship with a flush welded skin and longitudinal framing. As D.K. Brown has observed, 'The number of welders employed averaged twenty with a peak of forty-one. Great attention was paid to the selection and training of the welders and, even more important, their supervisors, and careful records were kept of each individual's performance.' Indeed to maximize the use of downhand welding the bottom units were fabricated upside down and away from the berth. Welding also implied, if it did not exactly mean, a substantial reduction in the costs of water testing and rectification. The conclusions may not have been exactly stark but they were certainly revealing, as Table 4.1 shows. Whilst not immediately obvious, the advantages, however, of what was still a new technology were clear. The question remained, could they be taken across the industry and across all ship forms?[53]

The extension of welding in the Second World War

By February 1940 the British shipbuilding industry had been brought under direct Admiralty control and its leading figures in the inter-war period, Sir James Lithgow and Sir Amos Ayre, were appointed to the Board of Admiralty as Controller of Merchant Shipbuilding and Repair, and Director of Merchant Shipbuilding, respectively.[54] From the outset in an industry that was both quantitatively and qualitatively weaker than it had been in the First World War, the shipbuilders had been determined to keep other departments at bay on the basis that it was better to deal with the devil they knew in order to keep the problems of the industry in house. Lithgow and Ayre, both of whom had played leading roles in NSS in denuding the industry of a third of its capacity, were now in charge of a situation where capacity constraints and shortages of skilled labour threatened production. It was also richly ironic that a greater degree of co-operation by the employers with organised labour was necessary as

Table 4.1 Comparative details of minesweepers *Seagull* and *Leda*

	Seagull	*Leda*
Time building to launch (weeks)	37	30
Weight of structure (tons)	311	345
Direct labour cost	13,998	14,248
Cost per ton (£)	45	41

Source: D.K. Brown, *Nelson to Vanguard*, p. 124.

opposed to confronting it in their own interests if Lithgow and Ayre were to ensure that what productive capacity remained was fully utilised.

Capacity constraints, with the larger mixed builders all engaged on the construction of capital ships and the smaller ones on cruisers, destroyers and submarines, all of which required large quantities of welding, were immediately obvious. To combat this, orders for the smaller classes of warships such as corvettes and – of more pressing importance – minesweepers, were placed in the mercantile sector, in which three major firms, Doxford, Gray and Lithgows, concentrated on cargo tramp production for the duration of the war. The increased concentration on the provision of escort vessels obviously impacted on the capacity of the mercantile sector in general and it was soon decided to order sixty additional cargo vessels to a modified British design and specification from the United States. The design of these Ocean-class vessels, the progenitors of the huge American Liberty Ship programme, was based on a Wear cargo tramp ship and thirty each were built in two specially constructed yards in Richmond, California, and Portland, Maine, with the keel of the first, the mainly welded *Ocean Vanguard*, being laid in April 1941.[55]

The American orders were also confirmation that in Britain a more widespread development of welding in the initial stages of the war was hardly a priority, production and the speedy repair of existing tonnage by extant methods being paramount. Dilution, with its potential for interchangeability, first of the existing shipbuilding workforce with its high per centage of skilled workers, and then from without to boost manpower was, given the urgent need to produce and the trade unions' innate hostility to the de-skilling of work, virtually a non-runner. Throughout the war the proportion of skilled workers employed in the industry hardly changed at all irrespective of later national dilution agreements and the increased use from 1942 onwards of unskilled labour, particularly women.[56]

In this climate, Admiralty encouragement of welding continued on its incremental way; the first all-welded minesweeper, HMS *Seagull*, had been launched at Devonport in 1938, but it was not until late in 1942 after extensive discussions that the Admiralty decided that the Cowes shipbuilder and Warship Group member, J. Samuel White, whose yard had already been bombed, should investigate the possibilities of successfully building a series of all-welded destroyers. Like all other yards, White's had been set up for riveting, and to gain the necessary personnel and accumulate experience a hybrid system of building combining welding and riveting was commenced for the first two destroyers. This of itself increased the percentage of structural welding undertaken over previous destroyers by at least 500 per cent. The initial problem of whether to construct the vessels at the berth in the traditional manner or prefabricate away from the berth was resolved in favour of the latter. The bulk of production could be carried out under cover irrespective of weather and blackout considerations and output increased accordingly. Output could also be increased by prefabrication methods ensuring downhand manual and continuous automatic welding. This method of production also minimised locked-up stress in structures and indoor work generally showed less distortion, and entailed a thorough reorganisation of the shipyard plant, equipment and facilities. Fabricated units were to be as complete as possible and were to weigh between 8 and 10 tons and not exceed 40 feet in length. The bulk of the additional welders required, including females, were trained in the firm's own establishment and in the case of the men were recruited from existing trades, mainly from riveting. This was further facilitated by the construction of new fabrication shops to replace bomb-damaged units destroyed by the Luftwaffe earlier in 1942. White's went on to successfully complete a series of all-welded destroyers and in the process built up considerable experience in this form of construction, and by the end of the war were fully convinced of the advantages of welding over riveting.[57]

This somewhat belated conversion to welding was representative of the industry as a whole, and another south coast firm, Thornycroft, had to be literally forced by the Admiralty through the prospect of a cessation in naval orders into embracing the process.[58] With the Battle of Atlantic at its height, the Admiralty quest for a greater extension of welding had been given added impetus by two highly critical government reports on the industry published in July and September of 1942 respectively. First, the Barlow Report into conditions of labour in the shipyards recommended increased dilution, interchangeability and modernisation of facilities as a matter of urgency. The second, a report to the Machine Tool Controller by Cecil Bentham, who toured the shipyards and reported his conclusions on a yard-by-yard basis, recommended a series of improvements in plant and equipment, and an increase in welding. These conclusions were hardly surprising given the effects of the prolonged inter-war depression and consequent lack of investment, and both reports explicitly recognised that financial assistance from the state was necessary. During his tour Bentham had noted that the percentage of modern plant on Clydeside, with its greater concentration of warship builders, was around 50 per cent and half that on the north-east coast of England. He also noted that the planning of work in shipyards had made very little progress in the inter-war period, the methodical handling of material was rare, and that construction tended to proceed with the maximum rather than the minimum of effort.[59]

The immediate effect of the two reports was the establishment of a Shipyard Development Committee (SDC) with a wide-ranging but detailed remit which had began to meet in November 1942. The SDC, with Bentham in an advisory capacity, was chaired by Sir James Lithgow and consisted of representatives of the Admiralty, shipbuilding firms and organised labour.[60] From the outset the SDC identified three linked schemes of shipyard modernisation that it deemed to be absolutely necessary: an extension of welding schemes, the provision of new machine tools, and schemes for yard development including new craneage with greater lifting capacity. Although welding was in part subsumed into the general development schemes that followed, the Admiralty's financial contribution to naval yards' general development was £2,490,482 out of a total of £3,084,618 expended, and in the case of mercantile yards, of the £776,866 specifically spent on welding the Admiralty contributed £451,781. The total value of SDC schemes was almost £7 million of which the Admiralty provided just over £5 million. This was far more than the 50 per cent Admiralty contribution initially envisaged and confirmation that the industry was in a sorry state overall.[61] When the schemes of general development were fully implemented, as Barnett has pointed out, this was 'a remarkable feat of re-equipment in the middle of a world war'.[62] This was undoubtedly the case, but in terms of historical significance, 'the extension of welding in British shipbuilding was the major and ultimately the most far-reaching change to the industry in wartime'.[63]

By September 1943, 90 per cent of the welding schemes initiated by the SDC had been completed and for the first time by the end of the year the numbers of welders employed in the main shipbuilding firms exceeded that of riveters, excluding holders on, catchers and heaters.[64] A government training establishment set up in Tyneside in 1943 to train more riveters had failed to attract potential recruits and was confirmation of a trend away from the trade as welding gained ground. Previously there had definitely been a move away from riveting to welding, particularly among younger men as pay and conditions in the latter occupation improved and its more widespread use became apparent. A Ministry of Labour riveting school set up in a disused shipyard at Jordanvale on Clydeside, which opened in April 1942, had the capacity to train 700 apprentice riveters per annum, but difficulties in recruitment and retention were experienced and after two years only 460 boys had passed out and little more than half remained in the industry. Riveting in stark contrast to welding was not easily learnt and the output of a newly trained squad was only a quarter of that of more experienced workers.[65]

During 1942 the need for escort and anti-submarine vessels was urgent, some 75 destroyers were completed, and the bulk of the larger mixed builders were engaged on capital ship production. Escort vessels were given the highest priority at the height of the Battle of the Atlantic and the need for simpler vessels such as corvettes was apparent. Given this, the Admiralty embarked upon its first venture into large-scale schemes of prefabrication and reorganisation of production in inland constructional engineering firms, particularly on the corvette programme, and this capacity was later utilised for landing craft production. Large prefabricated sections were then delivered to shipyards for assembly. To engineers used to detailed drawings, shipyard draught plans proved problematic, and in the case of 18 drawings supplied for a midship section from a shipyard, this had to be elaborated to 333 drawings before the first plates could be assembled.[66]

Automatic welding machines were, from 1942 onwards, obtained under Lend-Lease provisions from the United States where they were used extensively and contributed enormously to the speed of production in specially laid-out yards. With no labour shortages impinging, facilities tailored to techniques of multiple production, minimal union organisation, and little regard to cost, American output figures on Liberty Ship production were spectacular.[67] It did not necessarily follow, however, that welding was any quicker in itself than riveting. By 1943, automatic welding in British shipyards had increased in tandem with the schemes of general yard development initiated by the SDC. However, according to Wrigley, these machines were regarded by the shipbuilders as being entirely uneconomical except when speed of production was paramount. By this stage some spectacular failures in welded merchant ships built in the United States had come to light, notably that of an all-welded tanker, *Schenectady*, which broke in two at an outfitting quay in Portland, Oregon, in January 1943. Although experience of welding in Britain had not led to similar trouble, it was decided by the First Lord of the Admiralty in light of the declared policy of the extension of welding that a committee be set up to look at problems associated with welding in ships' structures and to advise upon their solution. From June 1943 an Admiralty Ship Welding Committee (ASWC) was formed, consisting of senior representatives of the Admiralty, private industry and various research organisations.[68]

Contemporaneously, profiteering by the Warship Group of private shipbuilders had finally been brought to light through a parliamentary investigation, which was critical over lax Admiralty financial controls over contracts. With profit rates exceeding 70 per cent on submarines, and the median profit rate on all warships at 27–28 per cent, the then Director of Naval Construction, Sir Stanley Goodall, had an uncomfortable time under the spotlight of parliamentary scrutiny.[69] Earlier in August 1942 as a consequence of the Barlow Report, an incensed Warship Group had met the Controller of the Navy, Wake Walker, to voice their criticism over Barlow's use of the phrase 'a degree of complacency permeates the whole field of production'. Accordingly, the Controller told the meeting that he did not want a situation to arise that caused other ministries to throw bricks at the Admiralty and would welcome anything that came direct from the industry to improve production. Previously, the Warship Group had agreed that all problems must be resolved within the industry and that other ministries must be kept out at all costs. Moreover, it was a cardinal principle that the Group's standard profit was sacrosanct, and in due course the Group formed four zonal committees in an attempt to co-ordinate production.[70] Once again, with Admiralty encouragement, the shipbuilders had succeeded in keeping the problems of the industry in house.

The industry looks to the future

Consequent upon the Allied invasion of Europe, the industry through its organisations met in August 1944 to consider the post-war competitive position of the industry. Although the prospects for future demand were certainly better than had been the case in the inter-war period, the need to restore the industry's competitive strength after its steady decline before the war was seen as paramount by the president of the SEF, Tristram Edwards, in whose view the reduction of costs was at the heart of the competitive position. Edwards also believed that competitiveness could be restored by a greater degree of co-operation between higher management and unions. In stark contrast, Sir Amos Ayre's view was that war output had been limited to what the Boilermakers Society's members were prepared to produce, but even he thought that at some stage the industry must talk to the unions. John Boyd, for the SEF, got to the heart of the problem by stating that in the long run it was what the industry, not the unions, was prepared to do that mattered. Having conceded *de facto* control of welding to the Boilermakers from 1934 and with the prospect, certainly as a result of shipyard development money, of a post-war increase in the process in the rest of the industry, the ball was firmly in the employers' court. After a further series of meetings a Committee on Improved Shipbuilding Practice was formed, which in turn spawned four sub-committees on methods of shipbuilding production, one of which was concerned with welding. Before any of these sub-committees could report, however, an interim report of the main committee was issued in March 1945. The report repeated many of the assertions of the past, and in a climate that promised far better times, at least until international competition inevitably resurfaced, the four sub-committees were subsequently allowed to wither on the vine.[71]

Although welding had made great strides in the mixed yards, many other shipbuilders remained to be convinced. Mixed yards were just that and after the cessation of hostilities and reconversion of tonnage they would return to their previous product mix and restore bespoke linkages with shipping firms. The basic dichotomy between on the one hand firms producing mainly welded warships for the Admiralty and riveted ones for civilian customers on the same premises was not addressed. Although some areas of crossover were apparent, particularly on all-welded tankers, the industry's largest firms remained reluctant to commit fully either way.

Earlier in 1944, the First Lord, A.V. Alexander, in the context of creating a post-war Shipbuilding Advisory Committee (SAC) embracing Admiralty, industry and union representatives, had warned against any return to 'the chaotic conditions of the past'. By March 1945, the Under-Secretary at the Admiralty, A.E. Seal, who had experience of American shipbuilding methods during the war, in a letter to the Director of Naval Construction, Charles Lillicrap, was far more critical.

Seal believed that despite the SDC schemes, the industry remained in an unhealthy position owing to a distinct lack of modern equipment. Moreover, management generally had never faced up to their deficiencies in this respect or attempted to remedy them. The real point was to face up to the future of the industry, but Seal believed that the industry consisted of a good deal of 'small minded pettifoggers simply worrying about a minor and insignificant detail and using their alleged lack of capital as an excuse'. Presciently, Seal foresaw that the practices based upon multiple production techniques in shipbuilding pioneered in the United States, with the emphasis on welding and prefabrication, would be widely copied elsewhere, and that this in turn would presage intense international competition. In this respect he understood the nature of diffusion of technology better than British shipbuilders did, as more capital-intensive rather than craft-dominated continental producers would be more inclined to adopt welding. Seal urged Lillicrap to convene a meeting with the shipbuilders in order to voice his deeply held convictions on the industry and also to instigate a full-scale enquiry on whether or not it was adequately equipped financially, managerially, and in terms of plant and machinery for post-war competition. On Seal's memorandum, Lillicrap, whilst generally agreeing, also bolstered his argument by observing that the innately conservative shipbuilders were reluctant to face up to the fact that the old methods were outmoded, and that welding was here to stay. Lillicrap, whilst agreeing with Seal's diagnosis, was however unable to agree to his proposal for an enquiry as opposition among shipbuilders to it would be total.[72] Confidence in the shipbuilders' ability to put their own house in order in the post-war period was also lacking at the political level, and both A.V. Alexander and the Minister of War Transport, Lord Leathers, believed that there was no future in letting the industry carry on as it had before. In Alexander's opinion, 'the attitudes of the shipbuilders were proving to be even more intractable in 1944 than they had been in 1917'.[73]

Although these criticisms were deeply held, short of creating an SAC in the post-war period, which rapidly became a talking shop for vested interests, the fear of upsetting the innately conservative shipbuilders, who after all would take some years to restore the mercantile marine and reconvert naval ships to civilian use, was high. On the technical side, however, the Admiralty, research associations and the industry had made great strides in their knowledge of the particular stresses associated with welding though the work of the ASWC. Indeed, the weight of accumulated knowledge on the structural integrity of welded ships had at last placed Britain in the forefront of welding developments – a point not lost on the President of the British Welding Association, Sir William Larke, who believed that welding was in general the method of metal construction for the immediate future. He stated in December 1946 that 'If we [Britain] took advantage of our superiority in scientific discovery and technological advance and applied it more rapidly than other countries, then we would repeat the advantages which the industrial revolution gave us in the export markets of the world.'[74]

Larke's pronouncement was no doubt a deeply held conviction, but in terms of the British shipbuilding industry it was nearer the level of wish fulfilment. The SEF Works and Conference Board noted in May 1945 that there was still a definite future for riveting and that recruitment should be by means of apprenticeship.[75] Swan Hunter, a mixed builder and Warship Group member, built a new hydraulic riveting shed with suitable craneage in 1948.[76] Another mixed builder and Warship Group member, Scott's of Greenock, did not build its first all-welded tanker until 1956 and yet another, Harland & Wolff, was still building mainly riveted passenger liners up to 1960.[77]

In Britain the process of electric arc welding in shipbuilding had been entirely vindicated by the experience gained during the Second World War. Nevertheless, the bulk of the industry was playing catch-up as it was in no fit state to promote it during the inter-war years. In this respect the Admiralty's incremental approach to welding had taken account of financial realities in the industry, and its extension in wartime was a logical step in a continuing process of technological change. However, only one actor, the state, could and did intervene to promote its more widespread use. The industry as a whole, however, including the bulk of the mixed builders, failed to grasp the baton of new technology in a market that was entirely different from that of the barren inter-war years. Technological conservatism won out as the lure of increased prices and profits on mercantile construction, and the retention of previous bespoke linkages with shipping firms, were just too great to facilitate root and branch reform in a period of hitherto unknown longevity of demand and concomitant explosion in the volume of world trade. The large-scale move towards all-welded construction, and crucially in the attendant facilities, plant and equipment to ensure its success in the industry as a whole, did not occur until the late 1950s and early 1960s. By that stage, the British shipbuilding industry, which had led the world in all-welded construction as far back as 1920, had failed to increase its capacity and facilities in the boom years and had accordingly suffered badly in comparison to international competition.[78]

Notes

1 On innovation, cf. B. Ranft (ed.), *Technical Change and British Naval Policy 1860–1939* (London: Hodder & Stoughton, 1977). In the much wider context of innovation, see K. Poolman, *The Winning Edge: Naval Technology in Action, 1939–1945* (Stroud: Sutton, 1977), F.A. Kingsley (ed.), *The Application of Radar and Other Electronic Systems in the Royal Navy in World War 2* (London: Macmillan, 1995) and W. Murray and A.R. Millett, *Military Innovation in the Interwar Period* (Cambridge: Cambridge University Press, 1996). On naval shipbuilding in general, cf. D.K. Brown, *Nelson to Vanguard: Warship Design and Development 1923–1945* (London: Chatham Publishing, 2000), *Conway's All the World's Fighting Ships 1922–1946* (London: Conway, 1980) and I.K. Buxton, *Warship Building and Repair During the Second World War* (Glasgow: University of Glasgow Business History Unit, 1977).

2 Electric arc welding is a fusion process where the arc, a very short conductor with a very high resistance, is used to heat two pieces of metal to be joined together by molten heat by means of a covered electrode or welding rod. The rod, held by an insulated holder, conveys the electrical energy to the arc for conversion into essential heat and also supplies the filler metal to complete the weld, which on cooling presents a very strong bond. The fundamental principles of electric arc welding and metallurgical considerations are fully explained in technical detail by various authors in *Electric Arc Welding in British Shipbuilding: A Series of Lectures given at Stow College Glasgow by authority of the Lords Commissioners of the Admiralty* (London: HMSO, 1943).

3 G. Simpson, 'Early Developments in Shipyard Welding', in *Electric Welding in British Shipbuilding*, 282.

4 G. Blake, *Lloyd's Register of Shipping 1760–1960* (London: Lloyd's, 1960), 106.

5 Simpson, 'Early Developments in Shipyard Welding', 282–4.

6 'Welding in Ship Repairs', *Shipbuilding & Shipping Record*, 9 July 1925.

7 These were the British Corporation Register of Shipping and Aircraft, Lloyd's Register and Bureau Veritas. 'Welding and the Classification Societies', *Shipbuilding & Shipping Record*, 22 Sept. 1932.

8 For a history of the Society, see J.E. Mortimer, *History of the Boilermakers Society*, 3 vols (London: Verso, 1973, 1981, 1994).

9 A. McKinlay, 'The Interwar Depression and the Effort Bargain: Shipyard Riveters and the Workman's Foreman, 1919–1939', *Scottish Economic & Social History*, 9 (1989).

10 The records of the SEF and those of the Shipbuilding Conference, the industry's trade association, are contained in the Shipbuilders and Repairers National Association papers held by the National Maritime Museum, Greenwich (hereafter referred to as NMM SRNA). A long series of Minute Books held within the SEF collections is an invaluable source to understanding the labour negotiating process in the industry.

11 The National Archives: Public Record Office, Kew (hereafter, TNA: PRO), CAB 102/440, 'Merchant Shipbuilding and Repairs in the Second World War by C.C. Wrigley', unpaginated draft.

12 *Glasgow Herald Annual Trade Review*, 1921.

13 See, for example, James Lithgow, 'The Economic Position of the Shipbuilding Industry', *Proceedings of the Royal Philosophical Society of Glasgow*, 126th Session, 1927–8, and presidential addresses to the Institute of Engineers and Shipbuilders in Scotland, *Proceedings*, 1929–30, and to the Institute of Welding

Scottish Branch, 'Labour Grading in British Shipbuilding', reprinted in *Journal of Commerce*, Shipbuilding and Engineering Edition, Feb. 1939.

14 For the life and work of Sir James Lithgow, see J.M. Reid, *James Lithgow, Master of Work* (London: Hutchinson, 1964).

15 These measures are discussed in some detail by L. Jones, *Shipbuilding in Britain, Mainly Between the Two World Wars* (Cardiff: University of Wales Press, 1957).

16 Great Britain, Parliamentary Papers, Committee on Industry and Trade: Survey of the Metal Industries (1928), Appendix III, 404.

17 Jones, *Shipbuilding in Britain*, 28.

18 A. Slaven, 'Self Liquidation: The National Shipbuilders Security Limited and British Shipbuilding in the 1930s', in S. Palmer and G. Williams, *Charted and Uncharted Waters: Proceedings of a Conference on British Maritime History* (London: National Maritime Museum, 1982), 128. Slaven notes that tramp ship freight rates, from a base of 100 in 1913, peaked at 439 in 1920 before collapsing to 158 in 1921

19 L. Johnman and H. Murphy, *British Shipbuilding and the State since 1918: A Political Economy of Decline* (Exeter: University of Exeter Press, 2002), 7.

20 For naval policy in the inter-war period, see S. Roskill, *Naval Policy Between the Wars*, 2 vols (London, 1968, 1976).

21 For Beardmore, see J.R. Hume and M.S. Moss, *Beardmore: The History of a Scottish Industrial Giant* (London: Hutchinson, 1979) and I. Johnston, *Beardmore Built* (Clydebank: Clydebank District Libraries, 1993).

22 NMM SRNA, SEF Employment Statistics, various years.

23 Johnman and Murphy, *British Shipbuilding and the State*, 19.

24 Mortimer, *History of the Boilermakers Society*, vol. 2, 139–44.

25 NMM SRNA, F1-Foreign Competition, Report of a Joint Enquiry into Foreign Competition in the Shipbuilding Industry, June 1926.

26 Slaven, 'Self Liquidation', 128.

27 NSS raised a nominal capital of £10,000 in the first instance and had borrowing powers of up to £3 million. In addition, a levy of 1 per cent from member firms on contract prices was agreed to repay debenture loans, and firms covenanted not to increase the capacity of their yards for a period of ten years. For the rationalisation movement generally, see L. Hannah, *The Rise of the Corporate Economy* (London: Methuen, 1983), 27–40.

28 Bank of England Archives, Securities Management Trust Papers, SMT 2/280 NSS, Apr. 1929. For the general attempts at rationalisation in the 'staple' industries, see Hannah, *The Rise of the Corporate Economy*, and in the Scottish context, R.H. Campbell, *The Rise and Fall of Scottish Industry, 1707–1939* (Edinburgh: John Donald, 1980).

29 E.C. Wilkinson, *The Town that was Murdered: The Life Story of Jarrow* (London: Gollanz, 1939), 259.

30 *Glasgow Herald Annual Trade Review*, 1933.

31 Wrigley, 'Merchant Shipbuilding and Repairs'.

32 Reid, *James Lithgow*, 142.

33 For the history of the RCNC, see D.K. Brown, *A Century of Naval Construction* (London: Conway, 1983).

34 G.A.H. Gordon, *British Seapower and Procurement Between the Wars: A Reappraisal of Rearmament* (London: Macmillan, 1988), 7.

35 For the Royal Mail Group, see E. Green and M. Moss, *A Business of National Importance: The Royal Mail Shipping Group 1902–1937* (London: Methuen,

1982). For the collapse and its ramifications, see Johnman and Murphy, *British Shipbuilding and the State,* 37–47.

36 Simpson, 'Early Developments in Shipyard Welding', 284.

37 C.S. Lillicrap, 'The Use of Electric Arc Welding in Warship Construction', *Proceedings of the Institute of Naval Architects*, Apr. 1933.

38 Simpson, 'Early Developments in Shipyard Welding', 286; cf. also S.V. Goddall, 'HMS *Ark Royal*', *Transactions of the Institute of Naval Architects,* 1939.

39 NMM SRNA, SEF 1/4360, letter from J.T. Batey, Hebburn Shipyard, to R.W. Dana, Institute of Naval Architects, 19 Mar. 1932; memorandum from A. Belch, Shipbuilding Conference, 4 Mar. 1937; letter from George Parker, Lithgows, to William Watson, SEF, 13 June 1938.

40 NMM SRNA, SEF London Minute Book 1932, Report of SEF Committee on Electric Arc Welding, 28 Sept. 1932.

41 The initial schemes and investigations are fully analysed through SEF Circular letters to its membership by J. McGoldrick, 'Crisis and the Division of Labour: Clydeside Shipbuilding in the Inter-War Period', in T. Dickson (ed.), *Capital and Class in Scotland* (Edinburgh: John Donald, 1983), 143–85.

42 NMM SRNA, SEF London Minute Book 1933, Proceedings in Conference between the SEF and the Federation of Engineering and Shipbuilding Unions, Edinburgh, 27 July 1933, and further Conference SEF Executive Committee, Meeting of SEF Welding Committee and Federation of Engineering Unions, Edinburgh, 23 Aug. 1933.

43 McGoldrick, 'Crisis and the Division of Labour', 177.

44 NMM SRNA, SEF London Minute Book 1934, Meeting of Electric Arc Welding Committee, Carlisle, 22 Jan. 1934.

45 McGoldrick, 'Crisis and the Division of Labour', 179.

46 The above information on the Warship Group is taken from a memorandum to all Warship Group firms, by Captain T.E. Crease, Acting Chairman of the Shipbuilding Conference and Representative of the Warship Group, 18 July 1940, located in the papers of Scott's Shipbuilding and Engineering Company, GD319/12/1/6, held at the Scottish Business Archive (hereafter SBA), University of Glasgow.

47 H. Peebles, *Warshipbuilding on the Clyde* (Edinburgh: John Donald, 1986), 151.

48 SBA, GD319/1/1/2, Scott's Minute Book, Balance Sheet for year ended 31 Dec. 1934.

49 On this issue see C.E. Sherwin, 'Electric Welding in Cruiser Construction'. *Transactions of the Institute of Naval Architects*, 1939. See also Brown, *Nelson to Vanguard*, 72–5 and *Conway's All the World's Fighting Ships*, 30–1.

50 NMM SRNA, SEF Employment Statistics, various years.

51 NMM SRNA, SEF Shipbuilding Conference General Meeting Reports, Minutes of AGM, 4 Nov. 1937.

52 Peebles, *Warshipbuilding on the Clyde*, 152.

53 D.K. Brown, *Nelson to Vanguard*, 48, 123–4. See also A. Nichols, 'The All-Welded Hull Construction of HMS *Seagull*', *Transactions of the Institute of Naval Architects*, 1939.

54 SBA, DC 35/27, Sir James Lithgow Papers. Lithgow characteristically refused to take a salary for his efforts.

55 For an analysis of this episode and mercantile building in the war generally, see L. Johnman and H. Murphy, 'The British Merchant Shipping Mission to the United States and British Merchant Shipbuilding in the Second World War', *The Northern Mariner/Le marin du nord*, 12(3), July 2002. See also R.C.

Thompson and H. Hunter, 'The British Merchant Shipbuilding Programme in North America, 1940–42', *Transactions of the North East Coast Institution of Engineers and Shipbuilders*, 1942.

56 Peggy Inman, the official historian of the munitions industries, noted that the percentage of skilled men in relation to other workers in the industry dropped from 50 per cent in 1940 to 47 per cent in 1942–3 and then rose again to 48 per cent for the remainder of the war. P. Inman, *Labour in the Munitions Industries* (London: HMSO, 1957), 141. The role of dilution and women in shipbuilding is analysed in H. Murphy, 'From the Crinoline to the Boilersuit: Women Workers in British Shipbuilding during the Second World War', in *Contemporary British History*, 13(4), Winter 1999.

57 'All-Welded Destroyers Built by J. Samuel White & Co., Ltd.', first published in *The Welder*, Jan.–Mar. 1946. See L. Johnman, 'Old Attitudes and Technology', in P.C. van Royen, L.R. Fischer and D.M. Williams (eds.), *Frutta di Mare: Evolution and Revolution in the Maritime World in the 19th and 20th Centuries* (Amsterdam: Batavian Lion International, 1998), 138. On the same page Johnman also quotes a representative of the Director of Naval Construction as stating that 'it is the DNC's policy to increase welding as much as we would like... firms should be encouraged to weld rather than rivet'. NMM, Ship's Box 666, Intermediate Aircraft Carrier 1942, 'Note of a controllers' meeting held at the Grand Pump Room Hotel, Bath', 11 Mar. 1942.

58 TNA: PRO, ADM 116/5555, Letter from Charles Lillicrap DNC to E.A. Seal, Under-Secretary Admiralty, 23 Mar. 1945.

59 TNA: PRO, ADM 116/5555, Report to the Minister of Production of the Committee set up by him to Enquire into Conditions of Labour in the Shipyards, 24 July 1942; PRO BT 28/319, Report to the Machine Tool Controller on the Equipment of Shipyards and Marine Engineering Shops, 30 Sept. 1942; and PRO CAB 102/441, Notes by Mr Bentham on his visits to Shipbuilding and Marine Engineering Firms, Aug. to Sept. 1942.

60 TNA: PRO, ADM 118/5052, Memorandum by Sir James Lithgow on the SDC, July 1942. The SDC terms of reference were 'to consider proposals and where necessary initiate action for the improved equipment, re-equipment and/or extension of shipyards and marine engineering works with a view to achieving maximum economic production and to ensure that such proposals are consistent with the most economical use of manpower'.

61 TNA: PRO, CAB 102/444, Merchant Shipbuilding and Repair. See Johnman and Murphy, 'The British Merchant Shipping Mission', 10–11.

62 C. Barnett, *The Audit of War* (London: Macmillan, 1996), 119.

63 Johnman and Murphy, *British Shipbuilding and The State*, 82.

64 NMM SRNA, SEF Labour Statistics, 1943.

65 Inman, *Labour in the Munitions Industries*, 122–5.

66 J. Lenaghan, 'Shipbuilding and the War', *Transactions of the Institute of Engineers and Shipbuilders in Scotland*, 18 Mar. 1947.

67 For the emergency shipbuilding programme in the USA in general, see F.C. Lane, *Ships for Victory: A History of Shipbuilding under the US Maritime Commission in World War II* (Baltimore, MD: Johns Hopkins, 1951).

68 For the ASWC see A. Ayre, 'The Work of the Admiralty Ship Welding Committee', *Transactions of the Institute of Naval Architects*, 1946.

69 Parliamentary Papers 1942–43, vol. 2, Public Accounts Committee, Minutes of Evidence, Navy Appropriation Account, 9 June 1943, para. 4066.

70 SBA, GD319/12/1/10, Admiralty Correspondence, Shipbuilding Inquiry Report July 1942, preliminary meeting held by Warship Group before meeting with

Controller, 20 Aug. 1942, and meeting of the Warship Group, Carlisle, 25 Aug. 1943. These episodes are discussed in more detail in Johnman and Murphy, *British Shipbuilding and the State*, 75–80.

71 NMM SRNA, 4 PII/1, Improved Shipbuilding Practice. Future of the Shipbuilding Industries after the War. Notes of a Joint Meeting of Office Bearers and Past Presidents of the Shipbuilding Conference and SEF, Edinburgh, 29 Aug. 1944. Committee on Improved Shipbuilding Practice, Interim Report, Mar. 1945.

72 TNA: PRO, ADM 116/5555, letter from Seal to Lillicrap and reply from Lillicrap to Seal, 22 and 23 Mar. 1945 respectively. Discussed in L. Johnman and H. Murphy, 'The British Merchant Shipping Mission', 13–15.

73 TNA: PRO, MT9/33595, Notes of a Meeting held at the Admiralty to discuss the Government's scheme for the Shipbuilding Industry, 16 Nov. 1944.

74 *Lloyd's List*, 4 Dec. 1946.

75 NMM SRNA, 7 SEF 4/101, Conclusions reached by a Conference and Works Board Meeting, 25 May 1945.

76 *Lloyd's List*, 29 Aug. 1951.

77 *Scott's of Greenock, Two Hundred and Fifty Years of Shipbuilding* (Greenock: privately published, 1961), 167; M. Moss and J. Hume, *Shipbuilders to the World: 125 Years of Harland & Wolff, Belfast 1861–1986* (Belfast: Black Staff Press, 1986), 378–81.

78 Many of the factors underpinning the lack of international competitiveness of the industry during the long post-war boom are analysed by Johnman and Murphy, *British Shipbuilding and the State*, 94–132. The debate on welding raged on in the post-war period. Lest anyone be convinced that diffusion flowed in an easy way from the naval to the mercantile sectors, the following papers are instructive: W.A. Stewart, 'The All-Welded Tanker, *Phoenix*', *Transactions of the North East Coast Institute of Engineers and Shipbuilders* (1945–6); F.A.J. Hodges, 'The Application of Modern Management Methods to the Shipbuilding Industry', *Transactions of the North East Coast Institute of Engineers and Shipbuilders*, 1946–7; and E. Ringstead, 'From Riveting to Welding in a Merchant Shipyard', *Royal Institute of Naval Architects*, 1950.

5

ANTI-SUBMARINE WARFARE, 1939–1945

W.J.R. Gardner

A retrospective from 1945

In a sense the best starting point for consideration of the innovation in anti-submarine warfare that took place is not, as might be expected, 1939 but rather 1945. Not only is it the point that was reached but, in a curious way, it echoes the era of 1939 to some extent. This somewhat paradoxical and even gnomic statement needs some explanation, as also does the intention to begin with a brief review of submarine warfare, as it is only by way of understanding the submarine problem that anti-submarine warfare's progress – or lack of it – can be assessed with any degree of soundness.

Here the perspective of 1945 indicates something immediately, that the 1945 submarine – if only in terms of its potential – had taken a giant step forward from its earlier brother of the late 1930s. It is true that only one nation, Germany, had managed to reach this position, but nevertheless this was sufficient to give great concern to the Allies, especially the British. The story of how this challenge was dealt with after 1945 belongs elsewhere in this book, but the matter of how it was faced up to before the end of the war in Europe in May 1945 does belong here and fits very well into the main section of this chapter.

So what was the revolutionary nature of the submarines that the Germans were able to deploy by the end of the war? The Germans, having started the war with submarines that were qualitatively little different from those with which they had finished the First World War, became well aware as time progressed of the inadequacy of such vessels. Although their mainstays, the Type VII and IX submarines, were competent enough in doing what they were designed to do, and somewhat more besides, they were not suited to an intense anti-submarine warfare (ASW) environment.[1] What had been perfectly adequate in 1939–40 was totally out-fought and out-thought by the Allies by the middle of 1943. But it should not be thought that it was only then that the Germans turned their minds towards producing an improved submarine; they had been working to this end for some time. Their clearly perceived aim was to produce a true submarine as opposed to the submersible torpedo boat which in many important particulars the earlier boats were. They saw underwater endurance and speed as their goals, implemented through the revolutionary nature of the Walter turbine system of propulsion. But this had significant drawbacks. First, it was complex and this often had the corollary effect of unreliability. Second, and perhaps just as importantly, it relied on the fuel hydrogen peroxide which was difficult to handle, unstable and dangerous.[2] Although Walter was able to give convincing demonstrations of his technology, no submarine using this method of propulsion ever saw operational service.

But the development was far from being a totally wasted effort for the Germans. For as well as intending to have a submarine with advanced underwater propulsion, the same hull had other developments too. Its underwater shape was designed primarily for the underwater environment incorporating advanced hydrodynamic measures making it capable of greater underwater speed for the application of the same amount of power. Further, advanced battery technology was deployed together with more powerful electric motors giving a step increase in both submerged speed and underwater endurance over the Type VII and IX boats. All these innovations were realised in the Type XXI and XXIII submarines, a number of which were completed and a few deployed by the last months of the war.

It really did not signify for the war effort when looked at holistically as these submarines were never able to demonstrate anything like their true potential. Had they done so, then the Allies might have been back where they started, working uphill against a difficult opponent and before such longer-term assets such as the economy, industrial capacity and, especially, innovation could start to count in the struggle against the submarine.

The essence of anti-submarine warfare

So back to 1939. What was the nature of submarine warfare and what were the methods of dealing with it? Without reiterating the whole story of that magnificent misnomer – the Battle of the Atlantic – which is better understood as a series of large-scale campaigns, there were fundamentally two types of offensive action by submarines: attack on single merchant ships and attacks on convoys. Although not unimportant, attack on warships could be regarded as a more specialised case of the assault on merchant shipping. To be sure, it called for more skill, luck and even sometimes weaponry but, despite the obvious dramatic attraction of such incidents as the sinking of *Royal Oak* in Scapa Flow, it was the war on shipping that was of more significance.

Submarine attack on individual ships could be carried out in a variety of ways. In the end it came down to a surface attack by gun or a submerged one by torpedo. There was little really that could be done initially to prevent the subsequent sinking. Merchant ships often had guns, sometimes of similar calibres to that of the submarines they were up against, but they rarely prevailed against a submarine. The latter could, in any case, submerge and use the torpedo. There was not a great deal tactically or by way of technical innovation that was likely to alter the eventual outcome. What did work, although it could hardly be regarded as novel, was the ever-growing Allied convoy system. This had a history extending back over centuries and had it not been for a gap, from about the middle of the nineteenth century to the first decades of the twentieth, would have had a continuous record of good service. The Admiralty in 1939 needed little persuasion to establish a convoy system, although its limited assets and the many calls made on those from dealing with German surface raiders to the invasion of Norway, followed by the fall of France, did nothing to make such assets free. Consequently the convoy system was limited in the routes to which it applied and the extent of escort. For example, it took quite a long time to have escorts organised to take convoys all the way across the Atlantic and with escorts – no matter how weak – allocated for the entire route.

However, by the middle of 1941 a pattern of warfare had been established in which groups of submarines took on convoys, largely in mid-Atlantic. This general theme was to be maintained until the middle of 1943 with only one important excursion during the few months after the entry into the war of the United States in December 1941. These two important years saw a number of innovatory progressions at work. Some of this was evolutionary and tactical, refining the ways in which convoys were regulated and fought through against large submarine groups. For example, command and control of convoys, together with the method of communicating both within and beyond convoys, was a relatively low-level activity subject to gradual improvement and not something that suddenly jumped forward, resulting in enormous gains. Much of this could and should be regarded as the application of experience rather than innovation. Some idea of the finer-grain aspects of convoys can be gained from Arnold Hague.[3]

Developing tactics, of course, tend to be innovatory but they also tend to be limited by the platforms, sensors and weapons involved and so some flavour of this aspect belongs after discussion not only of these three subjects but also of some of the less visible, but nevertheless important measures that supported them.

Platforms

Platform is a term that may be felt to be too modern for this period, but it conveniently describes any unit – surface or air – used for ASW without the ambiguity of 'unit' also referring to groups or formations. There were many different aspects of development of the platforms involved in anti-submarine warfare during the Second World War. It can clearly be seen that not only did they develop in depth and detail but also – and quite crucially – in breadth too. During the First World War, there had been very little in the way of ships produced specifically for ASW. However, the Second World War saw much more of this despite the retention of many general-purpose features to allow for the ship being used in a wide variety of roles. What was also especially marked was the extent of size and function. In general, such ships could be classified as close escorts and others. Indeed it could be suggested that all ships had ASW potential, at least all those below cruisers and capital ships. Among close escorts could be found such diverse ships as destroyers, frigates, sloops and corvettes. Little except detail distinguished these as far as fits of ASW sensors and weapons were concerned. Perhaps their greatest differences lay in the field of speed and endurance, with the slim, elegant destroyers winning on speed against the much smaller, stubbier corvettes which nevertheless boasted impressive endurance. Frigates and sloops tended to inhabit a middle ground between these two extremes. Their crews, too, might draw distinctions in living conditions, with destroyers sometimes having better conditions than the smaller ships, although none of these ships were comfortable by modern standards. Corvettes, especially, were renowned for their tendency to 'roll on wet grass'.[4]

The generic characteristics of these ships is that they were all fitted with radar, asdic (sonar) and, latterly, high-frequency direction-finding. The significance of these sensors (together with the weapons about to be described) is discussed later. Weapons consisted of the ubiquitous depth charge, either rolled off the ship or else fired a few hundred feet laterally. A later development was to be ahead-thrown weapons, such as Hedgehog and Squid. An important general point to bear in mind is that not all of these were available at the outset of the war and progress in fitting together with improvements in performance and – just as importantly – reliability was a relatively slow incremental business.

What was new was the innovation of escort carriers. These were cheaply constructed on the basis of merchant ship hulls and built on the west coast of the United States, largely on green-field sites rather than in established shipyards. They were lightly built, had only limited facilities and could carry a relatively small number of aircraft compared to their much larger sisters, the fleet carriers.[5] What this meant was that they tended to carry only one type of aircraft. This was of little importance for ASW as it was only really in very few areas such as the North Russian convoys where significant threats were encountered from anything other than submarines. However, the very ability to put aircraft to sea ensured the attractiveness of the escort carrier for all manners of campaigns; these included the northern convoys just alluded to and the landings in north-west Africa in late 1942. As a result it was not until mid-1943 that these ships saw significant service in the mid-Atlantic for ASW, possibly after the main demand for their usefulness in plugging the air gap had passed.

This also serves to introduce the other very important platform, the land-based aircraft. Initially these were often improvised and relatively short-ranged aircraft such as Ansons and Hudsons. Further, these were fundamentally adaptations of aircraft designed for other, land-oriented purposes. It was only the relatively small number of types designed for maritime use, such as the American Catalina and British Sunderland, that were exceptions to this general rule. But with the passage of time, longer-legged aircraft began to be employed, nearly always bombers that had in some way had been found wanting in the hard campaigns over Germany. Thus the medium Wellington, outclassed by four-engined aircraft, and the Halifax, less good than the contemporaneous Lancaster, did satisfactory service in the Bay of Biscay and elsewhere. Similarly, the most outstanding Very Long Range (VLR) B-24 Liberator only began to appear in significant numbers once it was appreciated that its relatively limited ceiling made it more vulnerable over Germany. Over the Atlantic this drawback was, of course, irrelevant.

These in outline were the main ASW participants at sea and in the air of the Battle of the Atlantic. Aspects of them will be referred to later as they interact with the sensors, weapons, tactics, technologies and other factors that form the main part of the story of innovation in and surrounding the war at sea.

Sensors

Underwater

For underwater detection there was essentially one sensor, called asdic (as it was known to the British) or sonar.[6] The principle on which this operated was by sending out a narrow beam of sound energy that would be reflected off a solid object (a submarine) and would then be received back by the transmitting ship, which would now know the target's bearing from the transmitted bearing and its range from the time between transmission and reception of the pulse. The latter depended on the speed of sound in water being pretty well constant.

This active sonar method of underwater detection is delightfully simple in theory but rather more complicated in practice, and this was the reason for much of the work that still had to be carried out to make sonar a better-performing sensor in every sense: range and probability of detection, equipment reliability, ability to distinguish true targets from false ones and, ever more importantly, the connection with any associated weapon system. When active sonar was first developed during the First World War it could rightly be regarded as one of the cutting-edge technological applications of its time. There were many problems to be solved such as putting sufficient acoustic power into the water at the desired frequency, the considerable difficulties of trying to deal with the acoustic difficulties of the ship to which it was attached creating all sorts of unwanted noise through propulsion and its own progress through the water and, not least, the sheer problems of producing equipment capable of operating for days at a time in the hostile environment of salt water.

The range and probability of detection problems are closely bound together, being intimately related to the physical characteristics of the sea. There is not space here to deal with this subject fully; that belongs elsewhere.[7] It is important to note, however, that the characteristics of the sea limit the maximum detection range of the sonars deployed in the Second World War to a few thousand yards at most. This is a function of physical characteristics and the only real way round this lies in producing relatively large sonar equipments that deal in lower-frequency sound, a technology not practically available in 1939–45. But the problems do not end there. The thermal structure of the sea can have a marked effect on sonar beams. In outline, where temperatures change relatively suddenly, the sound beam may be bent either upwards or downwards. If upwards, this may actually have the possibly beneficial effect of channelling the sound into what is known as the surface duct and extending ranges in that zone. As German submarines of the period often operated in or near the surface, this was exploitable but also led to reduced performance against any submarine that was operating at greater depths.

More probably the beam would be bent downwards resulting in reduced detection ranges. There was little or anything that could be done about this and sonar was thus, in a sense, a sensor more associated with attacking submerged submarines rather than finding them.

Even if the physics of the ocean did not militate against detection at reasonable ranges, there were still problems in conveying the information to the operator. This was done in two media: aural and visual. The aural was effected by an operator listening to the returning sound. This required physical capacity (not present in all sailors), an ability to discriminate from the echoes of the surrounding sea (known technically as reverberations) and a degree of skill and experience. It was the function of the scientists and engineers who developed and built sonars to present this information to operators in the best form possible, but a good operator could add much, first in detecting a weak returning signal against a noisy background and then in often providing added value by being able to detect changes in target behaviour by relatively small changes in echo quality. Natural skills could often be honed by experience, but very few operators had sufficient regular experience to really build this up. Much of the skill deficit was made up by the innovation of reasonably realistic shore training equipment. Initially this was to be found only in the main training establishments. Not only could operators be exposed to some idea of what a submarine could sound like on sonar, but a number of conditions could be simulated that would be difficult or expensive (in time rather than money) to replicate in sea training. Such facilities were eventually extended to the bases in which escort forces were based and even became semi-mobile, being built into buses or vans.[8]

But sonar was not only used to detect submarines, but also to track, then attack them, and the equipment played an important role in providing the information for this. In essence, bearing and range information was collated in order to provide a plot of submarine movements with the aim of delivering a weapon onto the target. The sonar operator's part was to keep the beam on the target's centre whilst also producing accurate ranges marked up on an electrostatic recorder. Often a beam of light could be aligned with the identified target echo on a range recorder producing information for weapon release.[9] Further the information was also used to generate relatively crude plots of target movement in order to optimise tactical manoeuvring for one or more escorts to best deal with the submarine. A further innovation dealing with determination of submarine depth will be described in the section on weapons (page 127).

There were two other significant ways of detecting a fully submerged submarine, both largely developed by the United States. The first was Magnetic Anomaly Detection (MAD). This relied on the fact that a submarine was a sufficiently large mass of metal to be noted against the relatively low magnetic signature of the earth. Because of the metallic nature of all ASW platforms, it was only practical to deploy this from an aircraft and the sensor had to be towed some distance behind the parent aircraft. The aircraft had to fly low to allow a reasonable chance of detection and it was only effective up to a few hundred feet either side of its path. It was also liable to register detections caused by surface ships (which were reasonably easy to correlate with a MAD contact) and terrestrial anomalies and wrecks (especially in shallow water). It therefore tended to be used as a confirmatory sensor prior to attack, although in certain constricted areas it could be used as for search, notably in the Straits of Gibraltar.

The other sensor was also associated with aerial platforms and was the sonobuoy. In the late twentieth century this has become a very familiar device, but this was quite revolutionary when introduced in the latter part of the Second World war, again by the United States. It had three main components. Firstly a hydrophone, or underwater microphone. This could only detect a submarine which was cavitating, that is, making a significant amount of propulsive noise. Further it was incapable of determining the direction of the noise source. But this mattered little in reality as the relatively limited range of this sensor was sufficiently good for the release of another innovation (described later) of the homing torpedo. This was attached by cable to a surface buoy. The buoy also had a small low-powered radio link to its parent aircraft on board allowing the transmission of the acoustic data from the hydrophone.[10]

Above water

Finding a submarine on the surface was, in theory at least, a lot easier than trying to detect it underwater. However, as in many things, theory and practice were often separated. Obviously in conditions of good light and visibility a surface submarine can be seen several miles distant. That said, the relative ranges at which a submarine, a single escort and a group of ships such as a convoy can be seen works very much to the advantage of the submarine. It would be a foolish submarine commander indeed who would persist in using the surface once he had self-evidently become visible to his enemy. It is only when aircraft enter the equation that the submarine's visual advantage is reversed. Not only does the former have a comparably small silhouette but it is faster and may be able to make use of cloud to convert a longer-range sighting into a close-range surprise attack. All this discussion makes the point of the continuing importance of the eye as a prime sensor for ASW in this period. There was little that technology or innovation could do to alter this: it is probable that, for the moment, optical technology had reached its peak with the excellent Zeiss binoculars with which the U-boats were equipped.

At the outset of the Battle of the Atlantic the eye was just about the only above-water sensor available to either side. It is also important to understand the limitations of visual detection, especially because of the way in which the new sensors overcame these problems. The obvious restriction was by night where a trimmed-down submarine, the desired condition for attacking a convoy, presented even less of a silhouette than it did by day. Moonlight might provide some assistance to the defender, but that too could be taken into account by the submarine commander, the preferred approach position being down-moon from the convoy.[11] Poor conditions of visibility too would reduce the efficacy of visual observation, although this might be as much, if not more, to the advantage of the convoy.

When the generally disadvantageous nature of visual detection for ASW is combined with the considerable use made of the surface by U-boats in the first four years of the Battle of the Atlantic, the value of radar is obvious. What this sensor did was to make the night light and roll away the fog in metaphorical terms. Submarines could no longer use the surface with the impunity and immunity previously enjoyed. That said, the impact of radar was not instant. This was because of qualitative and quantitative factors.[12] Early radars would hardly be recognised as such today or even by those who became familiar with them in the decades after the Second World War. They were cumbersome and temperamental. Further they operated in such a frequency range that they suffered from a considerable risk of generating false targets, especially in the presence of other non-enemy ships – precisely the situation of a convoy escort. Their displays were crude, difficult to read and not amenable to long attention under any conditions, particularly realistic ones in the Atlantic.

The other problem was that this was a technology much in demand – it was not just applicable or needed for ASW. It had applications for surface search, gunnery fire control and perhaps most importantly air warning, to mention only the surface-ship mounted applications.[13] The net result of this was that radar was slow to spread to Atlantic escorts. However, once it was in place the surface became a prohibited area for German submarines, effectively neutralising them. But even as late as March 1943, qualitative problems could have an adverse effect on convoy defence.[14]

Fitting radar into aircraft was, if anything, even more technically challenging than equipping surface ships. Initially only capable of deploying relatively crude metric wavelength (relatively low frequency) sets, their performance was limited but sufficient to indicate the potential of the sensor. Early sets could only look directly ahead of the aircraft but later ones allowed a degree of scanning. Sea returns (radar echoes from the sea) were a considerable problem, as was rough sea. However, radar gave aircraft an enormous potential search capability combining a reasonable swept path with a much greater sweep speed than surface forces. Further, aircraft were now capable of detecting submarines by night, a capability rarely available previously. It is true that a further sensor was needed to convert a detection into an attack and that was provided, after several false starts, with the Leigh Light.

Tactically, too, radar allowed detection, then tracking, of a submarine whilst retaining the benefits of cloud cover if available. This then allowed a sudden descent on the submarine, hopefully catching it on the surface and thus maximising the chance of a successful attack. Despite an early dismissing of aircraft as ineffective by Admiral Karl Dönitz, it is clear that the Germans took the problem very seriously indeed. The drive to have successful radar detectors on submarines was driven not by surface but by air radars. Even here, the German innovation was to a large extent outflanked by the development of centimetric (higher frequency) air radars. Not only were these qualitatively superior to their predecessors, but it took the Germans some time to appreciate that they had been deployed and then to develop a working radar detector against the new sensor.

There is one other important sensor to mention, which receives very little mention in the literature: high-frequency direction-finding (HF DF) deployed at sea. This radio interception technique had long been used on shore and it formed an important part of the Sigint tapestry. But putting this on a ship was fraught with technical difficulty and its successful development was beset with many problems. By the middle of the Battle of the Atlantic, however, it had been developed simultaneously in both Britain and the United States, the latter with some French help.[15] Although critically dependent on a co-operating submarine, this sensor, which at best produced a cross-fix, or at least a bearing, usually outranged radar by a considerable amount, providing warning, identification and an opportunity to attack a submarine or at least submerge it. The latter was, in practical convoy warfare at least, as important as being able to make an attack.

Weapons

Surface ship

Provided that it could be seen, either visually or by radar, attacking a surfaced submarine presented few difficult technical problems for warship gunnery systems. Seeing the target was the key condition and under the conditions of night surface attack by submarine this was often difficult. It was not uncommon for the first notice for a convoy escort of the close presence of a submarine to be when one of the convoy was attacked by torpedo. If the attacking U-boat had not previously been seen, then illuminants provided the only help. These were usually gun-fired and progressed slowly during the war. The advent of widely available, good-quality radar to some extent did away with their value. In close proximity of a surfaced submarine when a gun could not be brought to bear, ramming was sometimes resorted to. A crude tactic but an effective one, it accounted for several submarines, often at the expense of damage (sometimes to sonar underwater fittings) to the ramming escort.

Underwater, attacking a submarine was full of uncertainties and low probabilities. The classical attack using a number of depth charges presented many problems.[16] Assuming the case of a single ship attacking, the first problem was one of accuracy in the lateral plane. The nature of sonar was such that the surface ship almost certainly had to over-run the target, thus losing sonar contact. A perceptive submarine captain would appreciate that this had happened and usually initiate a radical manoeuvre, degrading the attack accuracy still further. There was no immediate solution to this problem. The palliative normally adopted was to use several depth charges, some projected outwards from the firing ship, some being rolled off the stern. Even then the lethal radius of any one depth charge was measurable in feet and one attack rarely sufficed. Thus multiple attacks were often necessary, although the disturbance in the water caused by the first attack often made regaining sonar contact problematical. Nevertheless repeated attacks were often effective.

There were several possible solutions to the lost contact problem. One was tactical, using two ships rather than one. In this, known as the Deep Creep attack, pioneered by the famous Captain Walker, one escort held contact and directed the second ship, which did not use its sonar to a firing position, where the first ship ordered the firing. The other solution was to develop ahead-thrown weapons that allowed a single ship to fire before contact was lost. These will be described shortly.

One problem affecting all depth charge attacks and creating a further dimension of inaccuracy was that of determining target depth. Sonar as initially fitted to escorts could do no more than estimate target depth and then only by doing so when contact was lost. A further factor compounding the problem was that initially the operational diving depth of German submarines was underestimated. A setting could be applied to depth charges prior to release and some account could be taken of uncertainty by setting different charges in the pattern to different depths, but there were remaining elements of the unknown. Eventually depth-determining sonars were produced making the attack more deadly.

Another measure to try and deal with the depth determination problem lay in the radical approach of the weapon Hedgehog. This was an ahead-thrown weapon, consisting of 24 spigot mortar bombs mounted on a matrix launcher. These were launched so that they fell in a circular pattern. Their charges were very much smaller than depth charges and no attempt was made to explode them at a specific depth. Rather they operated by contact fusing. Thus they would not explode unless they hit an underwater target. The small charge was nevertheless effective against a submarine pressure hull. Initially this was not a popular weapon at sea, largely because it was felt that depth charges, even when they missed, created a lot of explosive energy in the water, which might affect submariners' morale. Once Hedgehog started obtaining kills, it became a well-liked and very effective weapon.

A further development of the ahead-thrown weapon was Squid, a triple-barrelled mortar firing ahead of the escort but a little further than Hedgehog. Although there were only three barrels, each contained a substantial charge whose depth of explosion could be set and these were generally fitted in pairs.

Aircraft

For aircraft, too, the depth charge was the staple weapon against the submarine. However, the limited capacity of an aircraft militated against the repeated attack with many weapons, in which the surface escort could indulge. This was to a large extent offset by the fact that it was not until the advent of the sonobuoys – never widely available – that aircraft were in a position to attack anything other than a submarine either on the surface or having only just submerged. The ability to visually aim the weapon obviated many of the errors associated with sonar attack, always provided that the aircrew were sufficiently skilled.

But another problem arose because aircraft-launched depth charges could only have their actuation depth preset before take-off. Initially doctrine suggested that the charges should explode at about 150 feet, midway between the surface and the expected maximum submarine depth. A new innovation was the science of operations (or operational) research (OR). Its practitioners, drawn from a variety of mathematical and scientific academics, examined the problem of aircraft attacks almost never sinking submarines and rarely damaging them, and compared this information with the nature of attacks. They discovered, perhaps unsurprisingly with the benefit of perfect hindsight, that most attacks were carried out against submarines either on the surface or having just submerged. Clearly the U-boats could not reach anything like the depth at which the charges exploded. Settings were immediately set shallower and the effectiveness of aircraft attacks improved immediately.[17]

There were three other important air weapons. The first was one designed to compensate for one of the drawbacks of the British carrier aircraft, the Swordfish. This biplane was originally designed for reconnaissance and torpedo attack of surface ships, but by the latter part of the war it had metamorphosed into an ASW aircraft fitted with radar and depth charges. But it had one significant defect: it was very slow. Thus many a promising attack was thwarted by the submarine being at a safe depth before the aircraft arrived. The answer lay in a faster weapon, the visually aimed rocket, which was designed to hit the submarine underwater, rupturing the pressure hull. This proved very effective.

The sensor MAD (see above) was capable of detecting a submerged submarine, noting its position and by means of consecutive overflights establishing its track. The problem lay in attacking the submarine. If a depth charge was released on receiving a MAD mark on the equipment, the aircraft's speed would ensure that the weapon fell well ahead of the target, considerably beyond damage range. The solution to the problem lay in an ingenious innovation, retro-bombs, which were fired backwards in patterns, thus negating the forward throw of the aircraft. These, too, were effective.

The last aircraft weapon was probably the most ingenious of all and demonstrated the way forward for ASW weapons into the second half of the twentieth century and the Cold War. It was designed to exploit sonobuoys (see above). The problem with attacking sonobuoy contacts was that a submarine's exact location was not known, only the area around the buoy in contact. Depth charges would have been far too inaccurate, so an acoustic homing torpedo was developed homing on the noise made by the submarine's propulsion system as it moved through the water. This was especially effective against submarines using their diesel engines together with snorkel masts as they made considerable noise.

Other innovations

Although ample evidence of Allied ASW innovation in the fields of platforms, sensors and weapons has already been demonstrated, it would be wrong to see these as the only areas in which ingenuity and resource was evident; in other words we should be innovative about our concepts of innovation. The remainder of this chapter does just this by proposing some subjects that are not always considered as part of the ASW picture. In doing so it is perhaps a good idea to consider a broad definition of ASW: any and all measures that contribute to the ineffectiveness of an enemy's submarines.

However, the first item is one that was used at sea but never damaged, far less sank, a single submarine. The Germans introduced an acoustic homing torpedo in 1943, specifically designed for use against escorts. Fortunately the Allies were aware of the impending deployment and had countermeasures ready to use. These consisted of various forms of simple mechanical noise-makers towed behind escorts. Although these caused some acoustic degradation to the towing ship's sonar, they were good enough to decoy torpedoes and saved several ships.

After mid-1944, German submarines switched to an inshore campaign, operating submarines singly around the coasts of the UK and Ireland, as opposed to groups operating in oceanic waters. Submerged most of the time and making use of the snorkel, they were difficult to detect by radar or sonar. Often the first intimation of a submarine's presence was when a ship was torpedoed. If escorts or aircraft were close (and they often were), the submarine was counter-attacked and often sunk. But even the relatively low loss rate and favourable exchange was not sufficiently good for the Allies and other measures were adopted. Largely these consisted of the sowing of Deep Trap minefields. These were mines specifically designed to be actuated against submerged submarines and nothing else. The drawback to these was that it was nearly always impossible to know what results had been obtained. Nevertheless they were effective.

A brief mention has already been made of the subject of operational research (OR) in the context of air-dropped depth charge settings. This bringing to ASW of people with no previous knowledge or preconceptions allowed many of the problems, across a broad range, to be considered and solutions to them optimised without necessarily having recourse to new equipment. This was an enormous force multiplier and gave the Allies a very considerable advantage in the Battle of the Atlantic.[18]

Two brief examples will suffice to illustrate the worth of this new discipline. OR practitioners established that larger convoys did not mean larger losses and that, in fact, the opposite was the case, larger convoys suffering proportionally lower losses and effecting economy of escorts. The only remaining problem that remained was that of convoy management, both at sea and in terminal ports – relatively easy problems to solve. Another subject of study was the optimal way in which to service maritime patrol aircraft to ensure their greatest availability for operations.[19]

Another way in which the Allies held an advantage over the German offensive was in its bureaucratic efficiency. Obviously this is a judgement that is both comparative and, to some extent, subjective. A comparison could well be drawn with Third Reich Germany where organisational inefficiency was deeply rooted. Bodies had greatly overlapping spheres of responsibility, enormous efforts were put into turf battles rather than tackling the military enemy, co-operation with other entities was positively discouraged, and equipment projects were persisted with, despite evidence that they were unlikely to benefit the war effort. Further, most matters of high policy were dealt with in successive bilateral meetings between the Führer, and the relevant organisation, such as the Kriegsmarine.[20] This had two bad consequences. First, complex matters were not attended to in one place at one time by all the concerned parties. Second, unrealistic promises tended to be made, especially those by the Führer himself.

In Britain, particularly, this was not the case and although collaboration between all entities was not perfect all of the time on all matters, it was very much better generally. A good example of this was the Anti-U-boat Warfare Committee, a British Cabinet Committee, which brought together representatives of government (both political and officials), the Royal Navy and Royal Air Force together with scientists and delegates from the United States.[21] It considered few relevant subjects about the prosecution of the Battle of the Atlantic to be outside its purview and most matters brought to it were resolved. It is quite impossible to envisage such a group in Hitlerian Germany.

But it was not just in high policy that there was an Allied superiority. Whilst it has been contended that it was the predominance of Allied matériel, especially in quantity, that won the war in general and the Battle of the Atlantic in particular, there are aspects of how that position may have been reached that are important.[22] In the field of production engineering alone, there are two aspects of importance. The first is that the Allies, once they had decided on putting a piece of equipment, be it a radar set or a ship, into production, managed to do this, to do it well and to do it quickly, in general. The second is the sheer scale and innovation of how this was done, especially in the United States. The escort carriers, for example, were produced based on merchant ship hulls and were built on green-field sites on the US Pacific coast. Further, merchant shipbuilding was carried out virtually on a production line basis. This alone was an important war-winning factor, and one little considered by historians.

One aspect of the Second World War and ASW that has received much attention in the last few decades is that of intelligence. However, care has to be taken that its true merits are not obscured by much of the hyperbole that surrounds it, most of all concerning Ultra.[23] In general the Allies enjoyed a significant intelligence advantage, although there were periods when that was not the case. That advantage has as much to do with the ways in which the many sources of intelligence were brought together to produce a single comprehensive picture of the enemy, his methods and aspirations rather than the almost mystical qualities of any one source.[24] Further there was an inbuilt tendency to question judgements, a process that did much to strengthen the product. Unlike German naval intelligence, many of the people in the Admiralty's Naval Intelligence Division (NID) were not seasoned naval officers but rather talented civilians. This was very obviously the case with the Submarine Tracking Room of the Operational Intelligence Centre, whose head was a talented barrister.

One of the best ASW campaigns of the war is also one of the least known. The revolutionary Type XXI and XXIII submarines mentioned at the outset were strong on potential but low in achieved operational performance. This was not because they were flawed but because the Allies took positive action against them. Based on good intelligence, obtained by Ultra, the nature of the new submarines was well known, as was their revolutionary construction (they were built inland in prefabricated units, then transported to Baltic shipyards for construction). All parts of this chain were attacked by air and this certainly slowed the production rate.

However, a significant number of submarines were still built. What was to be done? The answer lay in a long-term but hitherto low-key campaign that had been taking place in the Baltic. This was used by the Germans for submarine trials and training, a process that they never skimped. For a long time the British had known a great deal, through intelligence, about the German *modus operandi*. Part of this included the German perception of British mining in the Baltic. Most importantly the German system of mine-free routes was known. This was a very valuable piece of information as it enabled the economical laying of mines, in areas the Germans thought to be clear, thus vastly amplifying the effects of a very small number of mines.

It was not so much that these mines resulted in loss or damage to a large number of these new submarines – very few were so affected. The more important outcome was that the German activities were severely disrupted as they laboured to clear the areas to allow safe trials and training. Until this happened activities were suspended, or at least considerably curtailed. This, too, was ASW – and it was innovative ASW.

Conclusion

What this chapter ought to have made clear is that ASW is not a narrow subject but a very broad one. It is, of course, perfectly true that a nation or alliance is unlikely to succumb to submarines alone, even a state as peculiarly vulnerable to this potent weapon as the United Kingdom. It is arguable that the Germans put too little stress on the submarine early in the war and too much later on. It is also the case that war at sea can never be divorced from conflict on land. Perhaps the greatest blow that ASW took was not at sea at all but by the German success wrought on land – and in the air – that resulted in the fall of France in 1940. Not only were significant destroyer casualties incurred during the Dunkirk operation, not only did a large part of the remaining surface fleet have to be kept as an anti-invasion force but, most importantly, the Biscay ports fell into German hands facilitating, at a stroke, submarine operations in the Atlantic. Similarly, Britain gained in the Battle of the Atlantic by Hitler's invasion of Russia in June 1941 as this removed any realistic threat of cross-Channel invasion, releasing warships for convoy escort.

The scale of the Battle of the Atlantic, both in terms of space and time, together with the intensity of its more exciting moments, has often concealed many of its more interesting and innovative technologies and ideas. Some of these have been brought out in this chapter but it cannot possibly cover all of them. For example, such clearly innovatory factors as the Western Approaches Tactical Unit under Captain Gilbert Roberts deserve recording, as does the training organisation at Tobermory under Commodore Gilbert Stephenson.[25] Other areas of importance and merit, too, such as the economics and control of wartime shipping, produce examples of problems and the methods, often novel, to deal with them.[26]

What is illustrated by this and the other parts of this chapter is that innovation played a very important part in Allied ASW during the Second World War. What should never be forgotten, however, is that all this resourcefulness would have been of little use without the physical matériel of ships and aircraft and, most of all, the efforts of many men and women, not all of whom survived the conflict.

Notes

1 See Eberhard Rössler; *The U-Boat: The Evolution and Technical History of German Submarines* (London: Arms and Armour, 1981) for all classes and

Robert C. Stern, *Type VII U-Boats* (London: Arms and Armour, 1991) for a monograph on the most numerous type.

2 It is interesting to note that although several nations attempted to make Walter technology work post-war, none really succeeded and the problems with hydrogen peroxide have caused loss of life and submarines, probably down to the loss of the Russian submarine *Kursk* in the year 2000.

3 Arnold Hague, *The Allied Convoy System: Its Organization, Defence and Operation* (London: Chatham Publishing, 2000).

4 Chris Howard Bailey, *The Royal Naval Museum Book of the Battle of the Atlantic: The Corvettes and Their Crews: An Oral History* (Stroud: Alan Sutton, 1994); J.P.W. Mallalieu, *Very Ordinary Seaman* (London: Gollancz, 1944).

5 Kenneth Poolman, *Allied Escort Carriers of World War Two in Action* (London: Blandford Press, 1988).

6 Willem Hackmann, *Seek and Strike: Sonar, Anti-Submarine Warfare and the Royal Navy 1914–1954* (London: HMSO, 1984), xxv, casts considerable doubt on the normal acronymic derivation of asdic.

7 See, for example, Robert J. Urick, *Principles of Underwater Sound* (New York: McGraw-Hill, 1983) and W.J.R. Gardner, *Anti-Submarine Warfare* (London: Brassey's, 1996).

8 Hackmann, *Seek and Strike*, 278.

9 Ibid., 187.

10 Alfred Price, *Aircraft versus Submarine: The Evolution of the Anti-Submarine Aircraft, 1912 to 1980* (London: Jane's Publishing, 1980), 108–9.

11 Anon., *The U-Boat Commander's Handbook* (English translation; Gettysburg, PA: Thomas Publications, 1989), Article 203.

12 Derek Howse, *Radar at Sea: The Royal Navy in World War Two* (Basingstoke: Macmillan, 1993).

13 There could be other problems too, of technological capacity and bureaucratic friction. See David Zimmermann, *The Great Naval Battle of Ottawa* (Toronto: University of Toronto Press, 1989).

14 The problems associated with convoys SC122 and HX229 are in part attributable to radar problems.

15 Kathleen Broome Williams, *Secret Weapon: US High-Frequency Direction Finding in the Battle of the Atlantic* (Annapolis, MD: Naval Institute Press, 1996) and chapter by Redgement in F.A. Kingsley, *The Development of Radar Equipments for the Royal Navy, 1935–1945* (London: Macmillan, 1995), 235–47.

16 Details of depth charges and other underwater weapons are described in John Campbell, *Naval Weapons of World War Two* (London: Conway Maritime Press, 1985), 89–94.

17 C.H. Waddington, *OR in World War 2: Operational Research against the U-Boat* (London: Paul Elek, 1973), 172–205.

18 Waddington and chapters by Llewellyn-Jones and Gardner in Peter Hore, *Patrick Blackett: Sailor, Scientist, Socialist* (London: Frank Cass, 2003).

19 Waddington, *OR in World War 2*, chap. 3.

20 Anon., *Fuehrer Conferences on Naval Affairs* (London: Greenhill Books, 1990).

21 Stephen Howarth and Derek Law, *The Battle of the Atlantic 1939–1945: The 50th Anniversary International Naval Conference* (London: Greenhill Books, 1994), 522–8.

22 John Ellis, *Brute Force: Allied Strategy and Tactics in the Second World War* (London: André Deutsch, 1990).

23 W.J.R. Gardner, *Decoding History: The Battle of the Atlantic and Ultra* (Basingstoke: Macmillan, 1999).
24 Donald McLachlan, *Room 39: Naval Intelligence in Action 1939–1945* (London: Weidenfeld & Nicolson, 1968) lists 17 sources.
25 Mark Williams, *Captain Gilbert Roberts R.N. and the Anti-U-Boat School* (London: Cassell, 1979) describes WATU, and Richard Baker, *The Terror of Tobermory: Vice-Admiral Sir Gilbert Stephenson, KBE, CBE, CMG* (London: W.H. Allen, 1972) gives an account of Tobermory.
26 C.B.A. Behrens, *Merchant Shipping and the Demands of War* (London: HMSO, 1955); Kevin Smith, *Conflict over Convoys: Anglo-American Logistics Diplomacy in the Second World War* (Cambridge: Cambridge University Press, 1996).

6

THE ROYAL NAVY AND THE CHALLENGE OF THE FAST SUBMARINE, 1944–1954

Innovation or evolution?

Malcolm Llewellyn-Jones

Beginnings

This chapter charts the innovation of British anti-submarine (A/S) tactics and technology used by destroyers and frigates in the early 1950s to attack fast submarines, at the dawn of modern anti-submarine warfare. The innovation process shows a strong filial connection to the tactics and technology developed since the early 1940s, which could not have occurred without a strong organisation in the Admiralty to prompt and support them. For reasons of space, however, this chapter eschews the developments applied to the problem of locating the submarine, and of attacking them from A/S aircraft and A/S submarines.[1] The key technology used for the detection and tracking of a U-boat once it had submerged was the 'asdic' acoustic echo-location of submarines. This later became known by the American name of sonar, though to preserve an idea of the essential differences between modern sonar and the equipment used in the Second World War and the immediate aftermath, the term asdic will be retained here.

The wartime asdic transmitter consisted of a 15 inches in diameter circular oscillator, operating at an acoustic frequency between 14 and 22 kHz. In its primary mode, the asdic transmitted sound pulses and listened for echoes within a 16–20° conical (searchlight) beam. The set could also be used in a purely passive mode listening for submarine noises (known as hydrophone effect, or HE). The asdic could be rotated to any compass bearing but could not be depressed from the horizontal.[2] Attacks were made with patterns of depth-charges dropped from the stern of the ship and projected a short distance on either beam. The first requirement was to establish the centre bearing of the U-boat as accurately as possible.

However, with a single beam it was not possible to measure the bearing directly. The asdic was trained off to one side of the target until contact was lost and then stepped back in $2\frac{1}{2}^{\circ}$ steps until contact was regained. The bearing of the oscillator was noted, and the procedure repeated on the other side of the echo. This gave two 'cut-on' bearings, though neither was accurate because the boundaries of the target echo were not sharply defined, especially when wake echoes were strong. For practical purposes the 'cut-ons' could be measured to within $\pm 5^{\circ}$.[3] A further error was induced by the target's movements during the time the procedure took, though this was not significant against slow-moving U-boats.

As the escort ran in to attack, echoes from the submarine were displayed by a range-recorder and from the rate of decrease of range, the time to fire the depth-charges could be estimated. The attack was complicated by the need to drop the depth-charge pattern some way ahead of the U-boat's position at the moment of attack to allow for the time taken by the depth-charges to sink to the required depth. The A/S ship had therefore to be steered to a drop point some distance ahead of the target. The throw-off angle could be as large as 45° against a deep U-boat travelling at 6 knots, but the asdic instruments could not calculate an accurate deflection, which was in practice derived from inspired guesswork and honed by practice.[4] Moreover, because the asdic beam could not be depressed, a deep U-boat would pass out of the asdic beam at close range resulting in the loss of contact. During this 'dead time' the accuracy of the U-boat's assumed azimuth position would degrade about five-fold during the final stages of an attack. Nor was it possible directly to measure the U-boat's depth, although a rough estimate could be obtained by noting the range when contact was lost by the U-boat passing below the asdic beam. The practical results were very rough with estimation varying by up to 200 feet.[5] In an attempt to compensate for the azimuth and depth uncertainty, the original 5-charge attack pattern was increased to 10 or 14 charges with additional beam-firing throwers and a proportion of faster sinking depth-charges, so that the full pattern was formed of 2 or 3 layers each of 4–5 charges.

It had long been recognised that if the A/S weapon were projected some distance from the escort, then the effectiveness of attacks could be greatly improved. The idea was not new. Various howitzers and bomb-throwers were widely fitted to A/S ships during the First World War and were used to throw impact or depth-fused bombs out to about 800 yards at U-boats that were still visible or very recently submerged.[6] The idea was to get a weapon into the close vicinity of a U-boat more rapidly than could be achieved by steaming the ship over the last-known position and dropping a barrage of depth-charges when the uncertainty of the U-boat's position would have increased markedly. However, the relatively small charge of these single howitzer and thrower projectiles and the inherent inaccuracy of manually aimed weapons fired from a rolling and pitching deck did not lead to any success.[7] Spasmodic development had continued during the inter-war years and just before the Second World War HM Anti-Submarine Experimental Establishment (HMA/SEE) had been exploring the idea of projecting small contact weapons in the place of depth-charges.[8] By 1940 the Director of the Miscellaneous Weapons Department (MWD) together with other departments had been exploring the possibility of using rockets to propel projectiles as had already been proposed for an anti-tank bombardment weapon. These several ideas were brought together the following year as the first successful anti-U-boat 'ahead throwing weapon' (or ATW), known as 'Hedgehog'. After a long period of teething troubles, both technical and operational, this weapon achieved its forecast potential and became almost five times more effective than the standard 10-charge depth-charge pattern.[9]

By mid-1942 a new asdic set followed on the heels of Hedgehog. This was the Type 144, which still used the earlier searchlight oscillator, 'but the remainder was completely redesigned to enable the last ounce of information and efficiency to be squeezed out of the underwater sound'.[10] This included much improved displays and automated training controls, though obtaining the centre bearing of the U-boat was still reliant on the cumbersome cut-on procedure. The Type 144 could also provide the means to automatically fire the ATW. The question was: what could be done to improve attack performance, especially as U-boats were now evading by going very deep? This meant that the accurate measurement of the U-boat's centre bearing and the lack of depth determination made attacks even more inaccurate (including even those with Hedgehog). Professor P.M.S. Blackett, Director of Naval Operational Research (DNOR), noted that a 'promising line of "thin beam" [asdic] is being developed to give accurate bearings during the late stages of attack'.[11]

HMA/SEE had been experimenting for some time with a horizontal strip oscillator operating at about 38.5 kHz which transmitted a vertical fan-shaped beam about 3–5° wide. This was known as the 'Q' Attachment, which was fixed to the bottom of the main Type 144 oscillator (which thus became Type 144Q), so that its beam extended vertically from the lower edge of the main beam down to 45° (later to 60°).[12] The 'Q' Attachment had a maximum range of only 1,200 yards but could maintain contact on a U-boat down to about 700 feet. It was introduced into service in July 1943. Of course, the fitting programme took some time, so, for those ships not equipped with the 'Q' Attachment, an attack using a barrage of depth-charges was introduced in the autumn of 1943.[13] In this tactic, known as the 'Creeping Attack', one ship held contact on the deep U-boat with the main Type 144 asdic at a range of about 1,500–2,000 yards. One or more attacking ships were then guided by radio over the U-boat where they laid a barrage of 22 or more depth-charges.[14] This tactic initially achieved a high success rate against U-boats that were quiescent at the moment of attack. Eventually, however, the method 'was "rumbled" by the enemy and his U-boats were able to evade it by frequent alterations of course'.[15]

In parallel with the 'Q' Attachment, HMA/SEE had been experimenting since early 1942 with a vertically mounted strip oscillator operating at 50 kHz which produced a 60° horizontal and $2\frac{1}{2}°$ vertical fan-shaped beam with a range of about 1,000 yards.[16] In its final form, this set, designated the Type 147B (often known as the 'Sword'), was fixed on the ship's head but could be depressed to a maximum angle of 45°. By noting the angle of depression needed to achieve the maximum echo strength from the U-boat, the Type 147B was able to determine U-boat depths down to about 800 feet. The Type 144Q, which incorporated a number of incremental modifications, and Type 147B produced the ultimate wartime asdic system. By the autumn of 1943, the combined system produced the most accurate bearing measurement and depth determination to date. This was aided by improvements in operating procedures, including the alternative 'step-across' bearing procedure that had been explored at HMA/SEE. This revised procedure was intended to produce a more complete range record by keeping the asdic in contact for a greater proportion of the approach run. It seems to have been the preferred method when the 'Q' Attachment was used during the final stages of an attack.[17] With these improvements, work was hurriedly put in hand in mid-1943 to increase the maximum depth-charge depth setting from 500 feet to 700 feet or more and although a modified pistol was produced, the rate of failures at extreme depths was not resolved until the end of the war.[18]

While these developments were in train, a meeting was held at the Admiralty in February 1942 where it was decided to develop a more sophisticated ATW capable of firing 'a pattern of six projectiles each weighing 390 lb (in air) to sink to two layers 60 feet apart in depth (three projectiles in each layer) and with a sinking speed of about 40 feet per second'. The pattern was to be 140 feet in diameter with the centre 250 yards (later increased to 275 yards) ahead of the firing ship. The weapon, known as 'Squid', was to be stabilised against ship's yaw and roll to ±40°, with the projectiles set to explode at the target's depth from the Type 147B. The ship's helmsman was also provided with the course to steer to intercept the firing point, at which time the weapon was automatically set with the necessary deflection (if required) and fired by signals from the asdic range recorder. The first complete Type 144Q with Type 147B and Squid operational system was installed in early September 1943.[19] This integrated, semi-automated precision system represented 'the high-water mark of British wartime A/S technology'.[20] Attacks against slow wartime U-boats were comparatively academic affairs and by the end of the Second World War the Squid was achieving a 60 per cent success rate against the conventional (slow) U-boats.[21] These attacks demanded a different philosophical approach from the A/S teams because they emphasised attention to detail, accuracy and the deliberate stalking of the U-boat up to the moment of firing. Gone was the 'artistry' of the depth-charge attack, as A/S warfare became more remote and scientific.

The fast submarine

By mid-1942, the ubiquity and increasing effectiveness of Allied anti-submarine measures had impelled the German Commander-in-Chief, Admiral Dönitz, to press for innovative solutions to continue the U-boat war with some prospect of success for the remainder of the war. Conversion of existing types with the schnorkel breathing-tube, which allowed U-boats to operate continuously submerged, was only a short-term palliative because of their resultant low underwater mobility. The schnorkel device was a step forward but needed to be combined with a U-boat also capable of high underwater speed and endurance. This, it seemed, could be achieved by accelerating the development of the novel Type XXVI U-boat driven by the Walter turbine. This engine was powered by the combustion of specially refined diesel with oxygen and heat produced by the decomposition of hydrogen peroxide (or HTP) fuel.[22] Continuous high-speed submerged performance was achieved while the limited cargo of HTP lasted.[23] Experimental work had been underway in Germany since before the Second World War. However, designs for operational boats were 'not responding to full scale application' of the Walter design and only three experimental Type XVII Walter-boats were completed. The Germans therefore embarked on an intermediate hybrid design U-boat, which retained the streamlined hull of the Walter-boats but was fitted with a conventional drive and much greater battery capacity. This was the Type XXI, which had a maximum underwater speed of 15–17 knots for about an hour.[24] In the event, only one Type XXI, *U-2511*, started a war patrol in the last weeks of the Second World War under the command of Korvettenkapitän Adalbert Schnee, during which she encountered a British force.[25] Whatever the actual events, this incident has entered the folklore of the Battle of the Atlantic as an exemplar of the power of these new U-boats and the impending danger they posed to British trade. Such views have been amplified by the assumption that after the war the Soviet Union had rapidly adopted the Type XXI technology from captured examples. In 1945, however, the Schnee incident made little impact on the Admiralty, for by the end of the war the British had a firm grasp of the nature of this threat and had evolved anti-submarine measures to deal with it.[26]

During the winter of 1943–4 the Naval Intelligence Division (NID), from disparate elements of intelligence, realised that the Germans were developing new U-boat types, although their exact nature remained obscure until spring 1944 when the Type XXI U-boat was identified.[27] The British Command machine rapidly swung into action and Captain N.A. Prichard, in the Admiralty's Directorate of Anti-Submarine Warfare (DASW), rapidly drew together the measures necessary to counter this threat.[28] The new German U-boat was assessed to have an extreme diving depth, long endurance and high underwater speed. Attacking such a U-boat, Prichard reasoned, would be difficult, especially if only one escort was present. Even when a consort joined the close action, attacks would be difficult, given the U-boat's high manoeuvrability. Engagements were likely to be highly dynamic, and depth-charges would be rendered wholly ineffective. Consequently, Prichard saw that ATWs offered the best chance of success. Even so, the rate of change in the target's bearing would be close to the maximum turning rate of the attacking ship, which at the ATW's short firing range would make accurate aiming difficult. During the action, A/S ships would have to be constantly wary of counter-attacks by the U-boat with a Gnat anti-escort homing torpedo.[29]

By the autumn of 1944, as the British were busily relearning the A/S techniques necessary to combat the schnorkel-fitted conventional U-boats in shallow coastal waters, the Admiralty was also able to flesh out its assessment of the Type XXI threat. Captain C.D. Howard-Johnston, Director of the Anti-U-Boat Division (DAUD), provided a précis of the U-boat's capability in the Monthly Anti-Submarine Report, based on the detailed analysis by Professor E.J. Williams from DNOR and one of the Special Intelligence confidants. It was known, therefore, that these U-boats could maintain about 17 knots for an hour before exhausting their batteries.[30] By this time the British plans were well advanced for sea trials with the specially streamlined submarine HM *Seraph*. Although capable of only 12 knots, *Seraph*, nevertheless, was able to mimic the Type XXI sufficiently well for the trials to confirm with reasonable certainty the Admiralty's and research establishment's theoretical assessments. The attack trials were conducted in the Irish Sea by the 19th Escort Group (EG19) under the direction of Lieutenant-Commander D.R. Mitchell, DSO, DSC, from the Western Approaches Command, supported by Professor W.M. McCrea from DNOR and J.A. Hakes, a scientist from HMA/SEE, who collated and analysed the technical data.[31] When Mitchell reviewed the results, he concluded that 'the difficulty in attacking is primarily due, not to the unsuitability of ships or instruments... but to the very reduced margin of error which [*Seraph's*] high speed permits the hunting ships'.[32]

Further exercises 'proved that training in attacks on a fast submarine was 90 per cent of the battle'.[33] They also confirmed that the ships that did best were those fitted with the latest semi-automated A/S attack systems, thereby removing as much opportunity for human error as possible. Thus, when *Seraph* took modest avoiding action at 12 knots, ATW attacks were possible, provided recordable echoes were received (though this was not always possible when the submarine's HE from its propellers drowned out the asdic echo) and the A/S instruments were accurately aligned. Equipment maintenance was, therefore, assuming growing importance in operational effectiveness. Yet there was one ominous note in this otherwise optimistic view. Echoing Prichard's earlier warning, Professor McCrea wondered if the Type XXI U-boat's higher speed of some 15–17 knots might be enough to tip the dynamic tactical balance in favour of the submarine.[34] The trouble was that during the last stages of an attack, the Squid system relied on accurate target bearings. At ship and target speed of 15 knots, the target's bearing could alter by as much as 2° between successive asdic transmissions. It could be difficult to keep 'Q' on the target and without an adequate echo trace the firing deflection and time to fire could not be accurately calculated by the system. The dynamics could be so great that contact was lost altogether.[35]

The thrall of the Walter-boat

By March 1945 DNI reported that the Germans had 'developed two new fast U-boats'.[36] These were the small Type XVIIB and the large Type XXVI U-boats, both incorporating the Walter gas turbine propulsion unit for very high speed submerged. It appeared that the Germans had completed three Type XVIIBs and were building more, but that production of the Type XXVI had not yet started. DNI also thought that the Germans would shortly start producing the Type XXVI, which it was soon learned were capable of at least 23 knots.[37] As more knowledge emerged by mid-1945, the Assistant Chief of Naval Staff (Warfare) found himself 'not satisfied that the Squid is an adequate weapon for dealing with a 25-knot submarine'.[38] He wanted an appreciation of the situation. Prichard thereupon drafted a paper to prompt discussion within the Admiralty, and the Training and Experimental Establishments. The problem, Prichard suggested, was a complex one, because the analysis would have to consider the 'efficiency of the asdic set and the manoeuvring qualities of the ship' in order to arrive at an estimate of the effectiveness of the weapon.[39] It was also necessary to consider the modifications already planned to weapons and asdics which would be forthcoming in about five years' time.

Squid, Prichard noted, had been designed to destroy 'a slow-moving U-boat whose maximum diving depth was about 800 ft'.[40] Because of the high sink rate of the Squid bombs, it was unlikely that a U-boat, even at great depth, would be able to avoid the pattern by an alteration of course, unless he used speeds in excess of 3 knots, or had ample warning of the moment of firing by the A/S ship. Wartime experience suggested that conventional U-boats achieved neither of these criteria. Consequently, during the last months of the war, Squid-fitted ships were achieving a 60 per cent kill rate, double that of Hedgehog and 12 times higher than depth-charges. However, against a submarine capable of up to 25 knots the probability of success would be 'wholly different'.[41] Prichard cited several reasons for this. In any deliberate hunt against a fast submarine, attacks tended to be delivered from the stern of the submarine, as the trials with *Seraph* had shown. At this aspect, accurate asdic ranging on the target would be made more difficult by the interference caused by the submarine's wake. Errors would therefore be introduced in the calculation of the moment to fire, and this, in turn, would degrade the accuracy of the attack. It was also possible that the HE from the target would be so loud as to obliterate the echoes in the operator's headphones and on the asdic recorder, making it impossible to fire at all. Even if contact could be maintained, the submarine could make much greater use of the weapon's dead time, that is, the time between the moment of firing and the arrival of the bombs at the preset target depth, to avoid damage from the pattern. The situation was equivalent to attacks with depth-charges against slow submersibles.

It might not be possible to set sufficient deflection on the Squid mounting to hit a submarine on a crossing course when it was taking avoiding action. The firing bearing would therefore have to be estimated by the ship's team. Similarly, in a counter-attack, when the submarine might be closing the A/S ship at high speed, the accuracy of the attack could be compromised by the high dynamics. 'In fact', Prichard concluded, 'the difficulties of attack with present asdic and Squid gear are so numerous that nothing other than a "snap" attack could reasonably be attempted against a U-boat travelling at 25 knots'.[42] At 25 knots, however, the HE from a submarine, Prichard thought, would be very loud, making it possible for the A/S ships to hold contact fairly easily, as least for a time. However, this presupposed that the asdic would function as a hydrophone at the high speeds necessary for the escorts to remain close to the target. This might be a particular problem if the submarine chose to evade at high speed and up sea. A/S ships might not be able to keep up and 'loss of contact might well be the rule'. Prichard observed that a new dome to house the asdic was being produced at the highest priority, which, he hoped, would allow asdics to be operated at 25–30 knots by reducing effects of flow noise round the dome. In all this he was ignoring the possibility that, if the submarine were able to evade at great depth, then the HE from its propellers might be much reduced, as DNOR and ASWORG had noted in earlier analyses.[43]

Beyond the next five years, Prichard hoped that certain modifications would improve the situation. Squid, as had been foreseen a year earlier, needed to be 'adapted ... for use as an A/S gun'. In such a form the weapon would be used to fire salvoes of bombs 'with a fair degree of accuracy', either in a counter-attack or in a series of firings to achieve a kill. But this could only be attained 'in conjunction with improvements to the asdic gear'. These improvements were the adoption of the asdic split-beam technique (which eliminated the need for the 'cut-on' procedure) and PPI displays, which would allow a high-speed contact to be held accurately. To hold contact, the asdic domes would have to be modified to allow operation 'in any seaway in which high speed is possible'. The asdic amplifiers, too, had to be modified 'to overcome the heavy masking of the echo by the HE of the target, thus enabling a succession of attacks to be delivered on a fast moving target'.[44] In this paper, Prichard had not quite defined the ultimate requirement for this type of weapon: the capability to fire on any bearing and at a variable range. Prichard had already suggested that even against a U-boat travelling at only 12 knots, 'some form of homing torpedo to be fired from surface craft ... might be a most suitable weapon'.[45] However, he did think that a weapon of the A/S gun type held one major advantage over a homing torpedo, which could only hit or miss, and therefore was of little use in a counter-attack and could not contribute to the destruction of a submarine by cumulative damage (as had frequently been the case with depth-charge attacks).

Trials and tribulations

While the trials with *Seraph* were still underway in the autumn of 1944, Rear Admiral G.E. Creasy, Flag Officer (Submarines), proposed that some U-boats should be taken over at the German surrender for technical investigation and sea trials.[46] Both Creasy and DNI initially thought that trials with the Type XXI were of 'the greatest importance'.[47] With the later knowledge of the Walter-boats, these too were to be included. Immediately after the German surrender a number of Type XXIs came into British hands. Captain Ashbourne, the Captain (S/M), Third Submarine Flotilla, conceded that the Germans were 'streets ahead of [the British] ... in hull forms both as regards surface and dived speeds and deep diving depths'. But on closer inspection the 'general impression is one of admiral [*sic*] conception, but poor execution'. Overall, he added, 'these German submarines [were] ... a queer mixture of very good and very bad points'.[48] Following a series of major defects the Admiralty decided to abandon the planned trials with the Type XXIs.[49]

It was also apparent that the technical difficulties with the captured Walter-boat, *U-1407*, meant that she would not be available for weapons trials for several years. The decision, sound though it seemed at the time, provoked considerable concern among many departments. The wide interest in the planned trials of the Type XXI highlighted the importance attached to investigations with a submarine capable of speeds in the order of 15 knots, both to test existing A/S equipment and tactics, and also to provide data from which new weapons and tactics could be developed. The cancellation of the trials with the Type XXI was therefore a serious blow to these development programmes. Leon Solomon, of DNOR, suggested that the Americans should be asked to confirm their intention to continue with the trials, for if they too were to cancel it would leave both nations with a lack of information on fast submarines, until data was available from the captured Walter-boat, *U-1407*.[50] The Director of the Operations Division replied that he had ascertained, unofficially, from a submarine officer on the US Navy staff in London that the Type XXIs in America were being refitted, after which it appeared that the Americans planned to continue with sea trials.[51] The American results, however, did not begin to filter through to the British until the spring of 1947, and even then were limited to mainly hydrodynamic data.[52] The Americans were hardly better informed, for as late as spring 1948 one American submarine squadron commander complained that there was insufficient data on the Type XXI 'upon which to base even a preliminary analysis of its full potentialities or weaknesses'.[53]

Within a month of the end of the war the Admiralty began to streamline its wartime organisation. The several divisions concerned wholly or partly with A/S warfare were amalgamated into a single Directorate of Torpedo, Anti-Submarine and Mine Warfare (DTASW), with a legion of responsibilities.[54] The first Director of the Division was Captain Lord Ashbourne, DSO, RN, and in his A/S section was a trio of specialist A/S officers under Captain P.W. Burnett, DSO, DSC, RN, each of whom had a distinguished wartime career in the anti-U-boat campaigns. These men began to develop the doctrine and operational requirements necessary to meet the future threat from the fast submarine. However, the absence of a fast submarine target for trials, Ashbourne complained, 'will greatly handicap long-term development work on a weapon to counter 20 knot or faster U-boats'.[55] Heads of other divisions supported his view, including the Director of Naval Construction who added that investigations were in hand into the possibility of modifications to further increase the speed of the streamlined 'S'-Class.[56] The Admiralty also had to hand all the studies done on the implications of the fast submarine threat, as well as information gleaned from the interrogation of German U-boat officers and some captured documents.[57] Of course, the way in which these submarines might be used would depend on the methods employed by the new enemy, the Soviet Union.

Assessments of the Russian threat

During the Second World War the submarine threat had been obvious and immediate and had a direct impact on the direction of A/S development. That had not always been so in the inter-war period, which 'was initially driven by a general awareness of the potential threat posed by submarines'.[58] In the same way, after the Second World War A/S measures were directed towards countering a generic threat imprinted on the Naval Staff's consciousness by six years of war experience, and because a Russian submarine threat against our trade or military operations was largely discounted in 1945.[59] Of course, account was taken of Russia as the only possible enemy, assuming that there would not be a resurgence of the threat from Germany. In spring 1946, the Joint Intelligence Committee (JIC) calculated that Russia possessed

> about 210 submarines, including 10 ex-German. She takes a great interest in submarine warfare and in this particular arm of the Naval Service she has shown herself to be more proficient than in any other. She is, however, still inexperienced in attack tactics. So far as the building of submarines is concerned, Soviet Russia has already carried out one large programme with success. German assistance and methods, particularly in connection with pre-fabricated [Type XXIs and the like] submarines, would enable her to construct a formidable Submarine Force in a comparatively short time.[60]

These assessments were reflected in the departmental calculations. Numbers alone, however, did not tell the complete story. Many of the Russian boats were obsolete submersibles and most of the ocean-going submarines were similar to the wartime German Type VII but without the schnorkel. The Russians had captured the plans of the later German Type XXIs and the Type XXVI Walter-boats, though it was thought unlikely that they could produce a home-grown version of this latter type until 1949 at the earliest. In fact, the Russians used their three allocated Type XXI boats for trials until 1958, though the Type XXIs which they captured in varying states of completion were all scrapped or scuttled by early 1948. In general the Soviet Navy was critical of the Type XXI's technology, though the German concepts influenced Russian 'Zulu' and 'Whiskey' submarine designs which became operational in the latter part of the 1950s.[61] A Soviet version of the Type XXVI was completed in 1955 and was tested in the Baltic between 1956 and 1959. Fewer than 5 per cent of the trials were carried out submerged and, after an explosion on one of these runs, the project was abandoned in favour of a nuclear propulsion system.[62]

This detail was largely unknown to the British at the time. Nevertheless, in late 1946, NID assessed that:

> The Russians are far from being a nation of seamen, and this weakness is reflected in the operation of their submarines, however technically good these boats may be. Their attack technique is amateurish to a degree.... The submarines themselves

> are probably capable of carrying heavy armament a long way with reliability, but are by no means certain of hitting the target when they get there.

Crucially, NID concluded that:

> Unless their evasive tactics have been much improved in the last year or so, they would stand little chance against our escort groups, and we have no information that attack-training has been carried out by them to any degree. This particularly applies to the large Russian submarines.[63]

This was a common theme for most of the immediate post-war period. Similar assessments appear in many of the JIC papers. They did not believe

> that by 1957 ... [the Russians] will think themselves capable of co-ordinated pack attacks on escorted convoys; we consider that their methods are far more likely to be comparable to those used by the Germans in World War I; but they may hope that such devices as homing torpedoes will at least partially offset their tactical shortcomings.[64]

When DNI circulated its paper in October 1946 on 'Russian Naval Tactics' round the Naval Staff, DCNS 'directed that an argument was to be developed as to the number of escort vessels we would require to meet this threat'.[65] The detail of this debate is not covered here, but the way in which these vessels were to be used is. No very great opinion was entertained of the Russian submarine operational capability, which was drawn together from the experiences of British and American liaison officers during the war, and information from the interrogation of German prisoners who had operated against the Russians. Captain Mackenzie, who made at least one war patrol in a Soviet submarine, later echoed the general impression, that since 'their A/S training is so backward is it not likely that their submarine tactics, particularly in attacks may be backward also?' His belief was that Russian submarine commanding officers' attacks were, at best, amateurish.[66] These views, the Historical Section later pointed out, had to be considered in the context of the difficult environmental conditions in which many Russian submarines had operated.[67]

Within the Admiralty, then, there seems to have been no direct pressure from an impending threat to drive A/S development, because the Russian threat was not yet well developed and would not be so until, say, 1955–60.[68] There was, as the Chiefs of Staff noted in May 1947, a need for a state of preparedness.[69] The wise counsel of staff officers, like Ashbourne and Burnett, was that unless work was done now and the issue kept in the forefront of the naval agenda, it would be too late to improvise counters to the fast submarine, when the Russians finally realised their potential. Over the next two years the Admiralty repeatedly asked the JIC to assess 'the capabilities and intention of the Russians and to forecast the probable scale and nature of attack in various possible theatres of war both in the near future and in some years ahead'. The appreciations were, generally, accurate in terms of actual strength of the Russian forces, but the Admiralty were concerned that the JIC 'tended to exaggerate Russian potentialities'. This was serious, because, the Admiralty pointed out, 'not only our present plans but also the future disposition of forces and the build up of military strength depends so greatly on what we estimate to be the Russian plans'.[70]

Financial considerations would heavily influence the outcome of these deliberations, but at least a start was being made on the development of the doctrine for how these forces were to be operated. These implicitly assumed the ultimate state of British strength which could be achieved some years into another World War. These were the conditions to which officers like Ashbourne and Burnett had been accustomed for much of their seagoing wartime experience. Compromises would have to be made at the beginning of a future war, as had been the case at the start of the Second World War. However, to keep a firm focus on the A/S threat and the necessary counter-measures would be a challenge, for

> in spite of all that has been done and is being said to the contrary, there remains a very grave danger of our sliding back once more in the coming 'peace' into errors in Naval training similar to those of the last one. The temptation to concentrate on the more amusing and spectacular attack on the Fleet rather than the dull and difficult (but much more important) defence of trade is desperately strong.[71]

Captain G. French, RN, Deputy Director of Plans, went further when he observed that:

> the root of this matter is a question of outlook and of the importance... attached to the adequacy of our A/S training and of trade protection exercises.... It is improbable that these will be given full weight unless there is a sufficiently powerful body of thought in the Admiralty organisation to insist upon it.[72]

Ashbourne agreed and proposed the establishment of a Joint Sea/Air Warfare Committee (SAWC) with both Royal Navy and RAF membership and chaired at the Vice Chief of the Naval and Air Staff level. The Committee, and eventually its sub-committees, would hammer out joint policy on all matters connected with A/S warfare and make policy recommendations to the Board of Admiralty and Air Council. This was to be done via the normal working of the relevant staffs of the Admiralty and Air Ministry. At their first meeting in May 1946 the committee discussed Ashbourne's paper on the implications of the schnorkel-fitted, fast U-boat. Thereafter a steady stream of papers were presented to the SAWC for approval. Furthermore, the Admiralty set up a series of 'TAS Liaison Meetings' at which several hundred officers of the A/S community were present, and including representatives from the 'old' Commonwealth and the United States.[73]

The assessment of limited Russian capability up to 1950 and a gradual increase in the severity of the threat thereafter up to about 1957 fitted neatly with the British plans for A/S development, which Ashbourne and his team had split into two phases – the 'Short-Term Problem' up to 1950, and the 'Long-Term Problem' after 1950 – a categorisation that was sanctioned by the SAWC.[74] For the short term, reliance was to be placed on existing A/S material with minimal modifications, which would be adequate for dealing with the equivalent of the Type XXI. To meet the long-term problem, research was needed to develop improved equipment to counter the 25-knot submarine, based on the German Walter-boats.[75] To improve the search rate of asdic an 'all-round scanning' set was being developed. Initial detection would be made easier if ship's self noise, particularly from its propellers, could be reduced. Searching would then be possible at higher speeds, and the A/S ship would be less vulnerable to anti-escort homing torpedoes. To increase the accuracy of weapon aiming against fast submarines, a new attack asdic, the Type 170, was well advanced. This was based on the 'split-beam' principle, which had been under development since 1941[76] It allowed both azimuth and depth data to be measured instantaneously, thus avoiding the laborious 'cut-on' procedure of the searchlight asdics. The resultant fire control solution could be applied to a relatively short-range 'A/S Gun', the three-barrelled 'Limbo' mortar, firing Squid-type projectiles all-round and at infinitely variable ranges from 300 to 1,000 yards which was also under development.[77] To extend the firing range further, it would be necessary to use a rocket projectile (as was being explored in America), owing to weight considerations of the mounting.[78] However, it was difficult to find an accurate method of controlling the propellant (and therefore the range), and it seemed that the 'gun' method was likely to be the more promising of the two. Simultaneously, investigation was underway into a proximity doppler fuse for the weapon. Research was also in hand into a homing weapon, called 'Zeta', which would benefit from data from the trials on the interim 'Bidder' and 'Dealer' weapons, which could be fired on the longer-range data from the new asdics.[79] The testing and refining of these weapons was hampered by the lack of a 15-knot target.

Trials against fast submarines

Post-war thinking recognised that the most difficult part of an A/S hunt was gaining initial contact, its classification, and maintaining contact with a fast submarine. By 1947 it was felt that the more ships that could be brought into asdic range, the greater chance there was of at least one ship holding contact. The wartime two-ship close A/S action tactic, however, meant that 'the additional ships are not employed to the best advantage' because they were held clear of the submarine and could not contribute to maintaining asdic contact.[80] It was with this idea in mind that the 'Ring' formation of four or more A/S ships around a submarine had been developed by the Fourth Escort Flotilla (4EF) in early 1947, presumably using the 12-knot 'S'-Class conversions as targets.[81] The first ship to gain contact was designated the 'Attacking Ship' and attacked immediately. As other supporting ships arrived, they were disposed 'equidistantly apart on the perimeter of an imaginary circle, the centre of which is the submarine', and whose diameter was between one and two miles, depending on the prevailing asdic conditions. The ships were then manoeuvred by the Senior Officer to conform with the course and speed of the submarine which was, ideally, kept in the centre of the ring. During the latter part of 1947 the Third Escort Flotilla (3EF), based at Portland and responsible for tactical investigations, also worked on the idea, but were hampered by inferior Action Information Organization (AIO) facilities in the ships, which made it difficult for the Senior Officer to control the dynamic tactical engagements.[82] Stationing of ships was also a problem because of the conflict between simultaneously maintaining a ring formation and manoeuvring individual ships so that they could make attacks with their ATWs (which could only be fired over limited arcs ahead of the ship). Any A/S ship ahead of the submarine if it wished to attack would have to turn by as much as 180° and might then be faced with a rapidly closing target at close range. In these circumstances an ATW attack would probably be inaccurate.

In the late spring of 1948, USS *Trumpetfish* visited Britain at the invitation of the Admiralty.[83] She was one of the early 'Greater Underwater Propulsive Power', or 'Guppy' wartime fleet submarine conversions which, by streamlining, was capable of submerged speeds of about 17 knots for an hour.[84] *Trumpetfish* was thus equivalent to the Type XXI. In the waters off Londonderry she carried out a series of exercises with the 4EF under its Senior Officer, Captain E.A. Gibbs, DSO***, RN, an officer with considerable wartime experience of actions against U-boats.

It had been Gibbs's intention to use the 'Ring' tactic to contain and attack *Trumpetfish*. But even in the more stereotyped serials he found that the manoeuvring of the 'Ring' in strict formation was difficult. As a result the direct tactical co-ordination of the 'Ring' was relaxed. The first ship to gain a firm detection of the submarine was designated as the 'Contact Ship', and was given total freedom of manoeuvre as necessary to maintain contact. The rest of the flotilla would then

> conform by eye and plot to the contact ship's movements, except in rare conditions when the SO found it was necessary to initiate a drastic alteration of course or speed by signal. Attacking ships were detailed by the SO, the choice falling upon the most suitably placed ship. The hunt was in the main conducted from the Bridge, which has the great advantage of immediate realisation of one's consorts angle of inclination. The flow of information from the Plot to the Bridge was satisfactory and this coupled with the view of plots necessitated only infrequent visits to the AIC [or Action Information Centre]. The handling of the consorts presented no difficulty and this form of loose 'Ring' has the great advantage of being not in the least tiring, and the hunt could, ... [Gibbs thought], be continued almost indefinitely without undue fatigue.[85]

During the more tactical serials 4EF quickly appreciated a more dramatic problem. With the submarine with a full battery and travelling at 14 knots or more, the frigates of the hunting force had insufficient speed to overhaul *Trumpetfish* and form a 'Ring' around her unless she made a tactical mistake. So the serials degenerated into a stern chase, not dissimilar to those experienced during the *Seraph* trials four years earlier, with the frigates clinging onto the submarine's HE bearings. Unable to fix the position of *Trumpetfish*, Gibbs's ships became scattered and vulnerable to counter-attack by the aggressive submarine not distracted while trying to attack a convoy. In one serial, assisted by very poor asdic conditions, *Trumpetfish* probably succeeded in sinking each of the 4EF ships in turn. The A/S ships achieved little recompense and Gibbs found the experience 'disastrous and profoundly depressing'. Nevertheless, he was able to salvage a modification to the 'Ring' tactic, which he termed Operation 'Umbrella', as a general chase, in which:

> The ship in contact represents the handle of an opened 'umbrella', and the consorts spread evenly in loose formation around the perifory [*sic*] of the 'umbrella' astern of the contact ship, the shaft of the 'umbrella' pointing through the contact ship towards the submarine. Once formed there is no need to signal a new shaft

> and escorts conform to the movements of the contact ship. Wing escorts are well placed to intercept if the submarine breaks out to a flank; rear escorts are well place if the submarine doubles back under the contact ship and contact is lost; and all rear escorts are well placed to form a line abreast search for echo contact if the submarine slows down and HE contact is lost.[86]

While the 4EF was working with *Trumpetfish*, Captain Sir Charles E. Madden's Sixth Destroyer Flotilla (6DF) started working-up for a year-long set of trials and exercises against fast submarines. These practices were intended to prepare them for exercises with another Guppy, USS *Amberjack*, off Key West in the Straits of Florida in July and August. These were to be followed by serials with HMS *Scotsman* and a third Guppy, USS *Dogfish*, in the waters off Northern Ireland between November 1948 and March 1949. During these later exercises Madden would be joined by two more ships of his flotilla, *Scorpion* and *Broadsword*.[87] Madden also discovered that the formal 'Ring' tactic could not be put into practice, 'because each A/S action very soon became a stern chase with the submarine doing 18 knots having had a few minutes start, and the two surface ships pursuing at 21 knots'.[88] As a result he used a form of Gibbs's 'Umbrella' formation. The overall results illustrate the complexity of the interactions between these factors:

Submarine	*Chance of 'surfacing damage' or a 'kill'*[89]
Selene	25.7%
Amberjack	15.4%
Scotsman	13.0%
Dogfish	32.3%

These figures also have to be taken in the context of peacetime safety rules. In wartime the submarine would be able to shoot back with anti-escort homing torpedoes. The exercises with *Trumpetfish* had demonstrated how an aggressively minded submarine could behave, but, on the other hand, the peacetime submarine could afford to behave more liberally, when 'the penalty for being detected was one hand grenade as opposed to a full pattern of depth-charges [or Squid projectiles]. The thought doth make the submariner prudent!'[90] The Admiralty pointed out, that during the trials off Key West, *Amberjack*'s battery had been in the fully charged state at the beginning of each A/S action, 'a state most unlikely to be met with in war'.[91] Nevertheless, while these results gave apparently conflicting values, one fact stood out clearly. With existing wartime asdic Type 144 and Squid, in favourable conditions existing British asdic equipment and weapons in the hands of a worked-up escort group were able to achieve a killing rate of at best 30 per cent, '*provided the target's speed [was] less than 12 knots*'.[92] At higher submarine speeds the killing rate fell off to practically zero, perhaps exacerbated by the reputed poor handling qualities of the 6DF ships.[93]

Technological answers?

While the tactical adaptation evident from the trials with *Seraph* in 1944 through to the exercises by Gibbs and Madden in 1948–9 was able to exploit the potential of existing asdic and ATWs, a more effective solution to attacking the fast submarine was not found until new technology was introduced into the equation. This technological development culminated in the Asdic Type 170 and the Mortar Mk 10 (or 'Limbo') which, as a complete system, had a high probability of causing surfacing damage to a fast submarine. However, the origins of this technology were not founded on the requirement to defeat a fast submarine. It is necessary to retrace the steps by which this system came into operation. It will be remembered that Blackett had referred to the application of radar methods to asdic. At some stage in the summer of 1942, R.D. Keynes at HMA/SEE suggested that the split-beam technique might be applied to asdic to improve direction-finding.[94] For some time the bureaucracy stifled progress, but this was eventually overcome by powerful scientific support in the Admiralty.[95] However, Blackett had observed that while the early split-beam asdic 'offered possibilities of improved and simpler operation ... experiments so far have indicated that this means added complications (e.g. two oscillators) and gives a reduced range'.[96] Nevertheless, progress was made, so that by April 1943 the concept was being tested in elementary form. A normal asdic transmitter was used but reception of the echoes was made on two separate asdic receivers. By comparing the amplitude of the echoes heard on each receiver a direct measurement of the bearing of the target was made. This avoided the slow cut-on method of bearing calculation.[97] Not only was this latter method slow, but while the asdic was trained off the target (as each cut-on was located) there were no echoes on the range record. If this record became too sparse, it was more difficult to measure the range rate, and hence to calculate the time to fire which was crucial for the fixed-range ATWs. This problem was being explored at HMA/SEE with an alternative method of using the searchlight asdic to 'step across' the target in the hope of providing a more complete range record, but it seemed that in sea trials the boundaries of the target were more difficult to discern.[98] The split-beam method should overcome this problem and provide a continuous range record, as well as instantaneous bearings for every echo.

Although the priority at HMA/SEE was on modifications to improve existing equipment, they had towards the end of 1945 greatly improved the rudimentary split-beam set of 1943. The research teams working on the direction-finding and depth-determination problems had combined to suggest a single method of solving both problems. The result was a square-faced oscillator that was divided into four independent and identical 5-inch square sub-oscillators, from which it became known as the 'Four Square' (and formally as Type 170) asdic. For echo locations, all four elements transmitted together. For the measurement of azimuth bearing, echo reception from the left and right sub-oscillators was compared on a cathode ray oscillograph (CRO) for phase difference. From this it was possible to determine the training to be applied to the oscillator to align it with the submarine's centre bearing. This could be achieved within a couple of transmissions. Trials show that the horizontal bearing accuracy was $\pm 0.4°$. By simultaneously comparing the upper and lower sub-oscillators, the angular depression could be measured and hence the submarine's depth determined. Range was measured in the normal way. The 'Four Square' set was able to obtain more frequent and more accurate measurements of the range, bearing and depth of a submarine.[99] By the spring of 1946 the set had been tested against a streamlined 'S'-Class at 11 knots by which time HMA/SEE had moved from its wartime location at Fairlie, Scotland, to its former home at Portland and been renamed HM Underwater Detection Establishment (HMUDE).[100] This new asdic, according to Vice-Admiral Hezlet, 'did not do very much more than its predecessors but did it very much better'.[101]

While HMA/SEE and HMUDE were busy with the Type 170 Asdic, HM Countermeasures and Mining Establishment (CMDE) were designing the associated A/S mortar system, and the Torpedo Experimental Establishment (TEE) were continuing development of the 'Bidder' A/S torpedo.[102] The Staff Targets for these weapons were outlined in 1946 by DTASW. The mortar was to be able to fire a projectile to an infinitely variable range between 250 and 2,000 yards, with an accuracy equivalent to that of Squid, and, ideally, with the capability of firing on any relative bearing from the ship. The fire-control solution was to be taken from the underwater detection gear, and the projectile was to have an automatically depth-set fuse capable of operating from 20 feet down to 1,500 feet, and also have a proximity fuse. The total explosive charge was to be adequate to rupture the pressure hull of a submarine capable of diving to 1,500 feet. The lineage of this weapon can be seen in the modifications to the Squid expressed by Captain Prichard in 1945.

It was soon clear that meeting such a requirement within the weight and deck stress constraints of A/S escorts was unlikely and DTASW therefore produced a further requirement for an interim weapon, known as 'Limbo'. This mortar was to fire a pattern of three Squid projectiles to variable ranges between 380 to 1,000 yards, on any bearing from the A/S ships and using information from the asdic.[103] By spring 1949 the design of the weapon was well advanced, after some disappointing results during the previous year (which appear to be related to the fire-control gear).[104] At this point, the individual Limbo and Asdic Type 170 development programmes were combined into a single project at HMUDE, where the largest team of scientists at the Establishment were concentrated on the work.[105] By the middle of the year HMS *Helmsdale* had carried out a brief series of exercises with the 17-knot submarine *Scotsman*, with the aim of proving the contact-holding properties of the experimental Type 170 set with a fast evading submarine under the conditions of a Limbo attack. 'These properties', HMUDE gleefully noted, 'were fully demonstrated and emphasised the advantage of the centre-bearing procedure compared with the step-across procedure.'[106]

Two related projects had been underway for some time which were seen as having a significant effect on the attack of a submarine when high ship speeds were needed. HMUDE (and it predecessors) had, since at least 1944, been investigating means of reducing the interfering HE noise from ship's propellers. The device, known as 'Nightshirt', used a screen of bubbles over the propellers, both as a means of reducing interference to the asdic and vulnerability to submarine-launched homing torpedoes when the A/S ship was at speed. Although initially promising, this system proved ultimately to be disappointing.[107] The second project was the fitting of an asdic dome capable of use at high speed. This 100-inch dome was fitted to HMS *Scorpion* and withstood long periods at speeds over 30 knots and, more significantly, allowed the asdic to be operated during attacks at speeds up to 28 knots, though only in ideal conditions. In a seaway, however, the maximum speed was nearer 20–22 knots.[108] This was an improvement over earlier domes, but hardly adequate against existing submarines capable of 15 knots and with the prospect of future submarines achieving 20 knots or more. The larger high-speed dome would at least allow the fitting of the new asdic without further structural alterations.[109]

1948 saw the fitting of a Type 170 Asdic and Limbo experimental system to *Scorpion* for trials. At the same time the wartime destroyers *Rocket* and *Relentless* were taken in hand for the first conversions to the Type 15 A/S frigate which were also to have this A/S system.[110] *Scorpion*'s trials were planned for 1950 and into early 1951 and reported upon in the autumn of that year.[111] In January and February 1951 *Scorpion*'s Type 170 and Limbo were used in successful tracking and firing trials against *Scotsman* travelling at speed but on a steady course. When these were completed a number of additional runs were made with *Scotsman* making dummy attacks on *Scorpion*, and although no firings were made, these exercises 'gave the basic information necessary to assess the effect on the probabilities of success that evasion by a fast submarine would have'.[112]

The assessment in DTASW was that modern submarines were very likely to have fired their initial torpedo salvo from some distance outside the conventional escort screen of a convoy or battle fleet. At this time it was hoped that a long-range asdic set would be developed, and to make use of detections and to counter these long-range attacks DTASW formulated a Staff Target for a 'target-seeking A/S weapon' in 1946, which was 'To reach the vicinity of a submarine which has been located at a distance by underwater detection gear; the weapon is then to home on to the submarine and destroy it'.[113] The weapon was to complete its homing in three dimensions onto a submarine at any speed between stopped and 25 knots, fitted with the latest propeller-silencing gear and at any depth down to 1,500 feet. Like the mortar it was to have a warhead able to sink a submarine capable of diving to 1,500 feet. It was envisaged that this weapon would be launched singly at an initial range of up to 8,000 yards, or in salvoes against longer-range targets. Considering that the range at which the weapon would be able to home onto a submarine would be limited, it was important to cut down to a minimum the time between the last asdic information and the arrival of the weapon close to the target to begin self-homing.

A number of options were considered to meet this requirement. The weapon could fly to the vicinity of the target, entering the water close enough to allow it to self-home.[114] The alternative was for a weapon that ran out to the target area underwater. This could be made an initial high-speed straight run, before the torpedo slowed down to carry out its homing programme. The possibility of compensating for the long dead-time by providing mid-course guidance was also considered. There was also a brief flirtation with hydrogen peroxide-fuelled torpedoes capable of very high speed, but this type was abandoned after a disastrous explosion in HM Submarine *Sidon* and further technical difficulties in 1959.[115] As far as meeting the requirement for an escort-launched A/S torpedo, the British settled for a passive homing weapon, known as the Bidder (E).[116] Apart from the enormous technical difficulties involved in the development of a effective homing torpedo, the British were somewhat more sceptical than the Americans in this field over the ability of a weapon to home at high speed. At slower speeds, however, a torpedo could have difficulty in intercepting and attacking a high-speed submarine. The British were also concerned that a homing torpedo would not be effective in shallow waters.[117] This illustrates the effect of recent operational experience on the forecast outcome of development programmes. For the British the overwhelming influence was from the last year of the Second World War when they fought an inshore campaign against the U-boat, whereas the Americans had been involved largely in ocean operations.

By 1950 the requirement for Bidder (E) had been refined. Development work had continued at TEE and by 1951 they had successfully run the torpedo during trials. The battery-powered weapon had two speeds, 15 knots for search, and 24 knots for the initial run-out and for attacking. On being fired from the ship, it ran for 500 yards while its electronics were warming up in a 'dead-run', which also avoided the torpedo homing back on the firing ship. It then continued at 24 knots on a 'fore-run' before slowing to 15 knots to begin searching until, in the predicted vicinity of the target, it commenced a circular search pattern. The total endurance of the weapon was sufficient for 6,000 yards at 24 knots or 20,000 yards at 15 knots.[118] TEE saw this weapon as a complement to the Limbo system, 'since a fast moving and therefore noisy target which is difficult to hold by asdics is an easy mark for a well-placed Bidder, whereas the slow moving silent target on which Bidder cannot home is a "sitting bird" for Limbo'.[119] They also saw Bidder (E) as a weapon that could be used to attack contacts gained by the future 'long-range' (really medium-range) asdics now under development.[120] The weapon could therefore be used in two ways: aimed directly at a known target, or as a 'search weapon' in salvoes against a target whose position is not known with precision (such as that gained from HF/DF, enemy torpedo HE, or an aircraft sighting). Bidder (E) was not ready to enter service until 1958.[121] By that time the combination of a medium-range asdic and a weapon-carrying helicopter (the Wasp) seemed to offer better prospects of attacking the more distant targets.

The fitting of Limbo and Type 170 was also planned for the first two Type 15 frigates, HM Ships *Rocket* and *Relentless*, converted from wartime destroyers. Captain Burnett and Commander Ormsby had had great influence on the design of these ships, including – for frigates – the novel idea of an enclosed bridge.[122] These ships were converted fleet destroyers, which if successful were planned to be extended to over thirty other vessels. The original upper works were removed and replaced with a streamlined aluminium superstructure (to save top weight which could then be used for A/S equipment). The Bridge was low down, enclosed and well forward. Immediately aft was a large Operations Room from where the ship was fought. Apart from the Type 170 Asdic and Limbo combination, the ships were equipped with high definition surface search radars for the detection of a submarine periscope or schnorkel mast and for the co-ordination of A/S action. There was also space on the upper deck for the mounting of Bidder A/S torpedoes when they were ready. Improved communications and radio warfare facilities were also provided, with all the sensor information being combined on an A/S plot in the Operations Room, though Captain M. Le Fanu, DSC, RN, a gunnery specialist who now commanded *Rocket*, thought that the detailed co-ordination was too focused on the close-range A/S battle. The captain was therefore provided with up-to-date information from the above and underwater sensors on the progress of the A/S battle, which he could use to manoeuvre his own ship and, if Senior Officer, the movements of the whole group.[123]

Over the summer of 1952, *Rocket* and *Relentless* were operating intermittently from Londonderry in the Third Training Squadron under Le Fanu. Commander R. Hart, DSO, DSC*, RN, commanded *Relentless*. Hart, although not a specialist A/S officer, was one of the more successful Escort Group commanders of the Second World War, with the destruction of seven U-boats to his credit.[124] The normal position for the captain, Le Fanu noted, was in the Operations Room from where he could most effectively conduct the hunt for a submarine. He was, however, unable to quickly appreciate the manoeuvres of the consort ship during a close A/S action, because much of this is derived from recognising the changes in inclination of nearby ships. This could not be done from the radar screen, and although these ships were fitted with a periscope in the Operations Room, it took too long to sweep round nearby ships and assess their movements. With the ships at times steaming at high speed, there was a real risk of collision. For this reason a senior watch-keeping officer (normally the First Lieutenant) was on the bridge during close actions as a safety number and was ready, if necessary, to instantly countermand the captain's helm orders if they put the ship into a dangerous situation.[125]

This had not been a problem during the Second World War when the captain's normal fighting position was on an open bridge, when he could instantly appreciate the changing inclination of a co-operating escort, and could directly sense the impact a change of course would have from the wind and sea conditions. Now, in the 1950s, fighting the Type 15 was a very different matter. The information available to the captain in the Operations Room was entirely adequate for him to fight the ship, but he could only do this effectively once he had acquired absolute confidence in driving the ship from below. The danger was that the captain might fall into a false sense of security, for as Captain Hart noted, 'Ships and waves appear as nice little warm glows on a radar scan.' All this would come with practice, with ensuring the Operations Room teams were well worked up, the bridge watch-keeper was alert and the consort ships was equally efficient. This was not entirely new, for some captains had experimented with controlling the battle from the rudimentary plots fitted in wartime escorts.[126] Now, however, the scale of the use of electronic sensors had dramatically increased and involved a considerable culture change in the way commanding officers approached the A/S battle, a factor easily lost in the fast-moving technical advances.

The great advantage of the Type 15 was that its Limbo system allowed the ship deliberately to 'lie off, hold contact and not wake up the target area'.[127] For urgent attacks, even if the target had been overrun, a Limbo shot could be made 'over the shoulder' on the run out. Contact could be easily held using the Type 170 asdic even when the crossing rates were fairly high. Against a slow submarine, Le Fanu's technique with the Type 15 was 'to spend the maximum time "within the bracket" (i.e. 300–1,000 yds from the submarine) carrying out deliberate attacks [with the Limbo] as often as possible and controlling the consort to guard the other side of the target'.[128] His experience by the autumn of 1952 with fast submarines was extremely limited and he felt able to offer only very tentative opinions as to tactics to be used against them. Le Fanu noted, 'we have had some duels with *Turpin*', a streamlined 'T'-Class, but '*Turpin* won on a technical knockout'.[129] To help guard against these failures, he suggested that at least two Limbo-fitted ships would be needed, possibly with the assistance of a third escort (provided that she also had a turn of speed of at least 20 knots). During the summer of 1952, *Rocket* (under Commander T.F. Halifax) was 'lured over the United States'. There she worked against US Navy Guppy fast submarines, proving the accuracy of the Limbo system by scoring a direct hit with a dummy round on one of the US boats.[130]

These trials nevertheless revealed some limitations to the Type 170 and Limbo system. It had been clear, since the problem of the fast U-boat had first reared its head, that single salvo attacks with a thrown weapon were unlikely to be effective and that any future weapon of this type would have to be in the form of 'an "Asdic-controlled" bombardment'.[131] As the Type 170 and Limbo system was being developed the Admiralty continued to believe that the asdic would have to control such a bombardment.[132] The trials with *Rocket* and *Relentless* had emphasised this too. The tactics that were developed were so that 'salvos continue to be fired at the submarine with reasonable frequency'.[133] These attacks could be placed most accurately if they were fired between the bow and beam of the attacking ship. It was therefore best if the escort approached from the quarter of the submarine and maintained roughly the same base course and speed of the target. The speed of the attacking ship would be dependent on that of the submarine. If this was slow, say below 5 knots, the frigates started to loose steerage way and thus become unmanageable. The ideal was about 5–6 knots, with the firing ship on a steady course (which would allow the fire-control system to settle down). The ship would also be safest operating at this low 'safe' speed which would substantially reduce the homing performance of an anti-escort torpedo.

When the submarine's speed was between about 8 and 11 knots the problem was complicated. On the one hand, this was a good speed for a fast submarine which could maintain this evasion for several hours.[134] However, in this speed range the attacking ship had to exceed low safe speed but was not going fast enough to make her unifoxer effective. To stand less chance of being hit by a homing torpedo she would therefore have to operate at a higher speed and this would take her through the Limbo firing bracket too quickly to maintain a continuous bombardment. If the submarine exceeded 12 knots, it was possible for her HE to swamp the asdic echo (as had been discovered during the trials with *Seraph* and later *Scotsman*).[135] If the engagement had to be conducted at speeds above

15 knots, because of high submarine evasion manoeuvres, the A/S ships' unifoxers would produce a great deal of interference on the asdic which could render it almost impossible to hold contact. The Admiralty's opinion, reflecting wartime practices, was that 'The Senior Officer should then consider ordering unifoxers to be slipped, accepting the risk from homing torpedoes'.[136] Rapid, and hopefully accurate, salvoes would maximise the chance of eventually destroying the submarine and in the meantime provide the best protection against the ever-present threat of a counter-attack by the submarine with an anti-escort homing torpedo by making the submarine concentrate on its own preservation.

A/S ships (including the Type 15) would be at greatest risk if operating alone against a submarine but, if found in this situation, they should make their initial attack without delay, followed by a rapid series of attacks 'to deter the submarine from offensive counter-action'.[137] A hunt with two ships was greatly preferred. The close action area was split into two semi-circles, with the first ship to gain contact becoming the 'Attacking Ship' and claiming one whole semi-circle in which to manoeuvre. The assisting ship was to maintain contact but stand about 1,500 yards clear of the attacking ship and her salvoes. This procedure then combined the best chance of destroying the submarine while providing the highest level of protection to the A/S ships. The Admiralty's sobering assessment in 1953 was that the

> Type 170/Mortar Mark 10 can give a probability of success far above that attained hitherto: even against submarines at speeds up to 18 knots and at depths down to 1,000 feet. Under certain circumstances it can unfortunately give probabilities no better than could be obtained with earlier equipment. The 170/Mortar Mark 10 combination suffers, then, from a marked variability in its probability of success.[138]

Even so Captain Hart, by 1958 commanding his second Type 15, thought that the frigate 'with the Type 170 and Mark 10 Mortar combination, is just about the finest submarine-killing system in the world today and that we are ahead of any other nation in this field'.[139] Speaking at the Fifteenth Torpedo and Anti-Submarine Conference, he cautioned the audience not to be complacent. The 1,000-yard firing range of the Limbo mortar was 'an enormous improvement on depth-charges, the Hedgehog and the Squid firing ranges'. However, realistically, Hart warned his listeners, the submarine, realising she was under threat, would probably have fired her homing torpedoes at the approaching escort at about 3,000 yards. It was, Hart went on, 'this 2,000 yard gap in which the submarine can, at present, if determined enough, have it all her own way before she, herself, is [directly] endangered'. To rub in the point, he added that

> This was the weakness of the modern frigate; it may well be in contact with a submarine, and is fitted with the finest short range A/S weapon there is in the world, but it is liable to be sunk before it can close in sufficiently to bring the latter into action. This is where the importance [lies] of getting, firstly, an effective decoy and, secondly, a longer range weapon into service as quickly as possible.[140]

Recent exercises seemed to confirm that the attrition rate of A/S ships in engagements with submarines would be unacceptably high but, Hart pointed out, not every submarine commander (and especially the Russians) would be that capable and brave in the next war. Aggressive, co-ordinated tactics by the escort groups might just be able to win the day, though the trend by the end of the 1950s by which escort groups rarely exercised together was squandering one of the main lessons of the Second World War. 'History has shown us', Hart said, drawing from his own wartime record,

> that our success against the U-boat was due, in no small measure, to the escort group system; ships worked and fought together months in and months out and developed a mutual confidence and understanding which was of a very high order. I know it is, perhaps, difficult to achieve quite the same results in peace-time but I'm certain that we could do better than we do now.[141]

From Hart's perspective, the battle was not going to be won wholly by technical innovation. He, and others were sure that the human element was equally (some would say, more) important, and that meant that a strong emphasis on realistic training was vital. This, in turn, could illuminate operational deficiencies and hence the need for further innovation.

Conclusions

The Type 170 Asdic and Limbo Mortar illustrate the evolutionary nature of most innovation.[142] This equipment combination grew out of the A/S attack gear whose ancestry stretched back to the First World War, though the key developments occurred during the quest for an effective counter to the slow U-boat throughout the Second World War. The resultant Squid and Asdic Types 144 and 147 came about through incremental developments to improve the asdic's location accuracy and of ahead throwing weapons (themselves not a new idea) – a combination which dramatically improved attack effectiveness against deep-diving U-boats. Meanwhile, the enemy were developing high-speed U-boats to counter British A/S capability. The Admiralty, in conjunction with the operational commands, training and research establishments, rapidly adapted tactics to create an adequate (if temporary) counter, by optimising the use of existing A/S gear. The process also helped to identify shortfalls in attack effectiveness and define future equipment requirements. In the post-war era, the British (and Americans) assumed that the new submarine technology would transfer to the Soviet Navy, though for some time they would be unable to exploit it. This gave the Admiralty a breathing space in which existing A/S gear was retained (with minor modification), while resources were applied to the development of new equipment. Impetus, in a period of financial stringency, was fostered by the creation of a high-level, inter-departmental committee which kept anti-submarine warfare in the forefront of British military priorities. The development of new equipment was a laborious process (even in the heat of war) and many projects proved impracticable. Even successful experimental models required considerable effort to turn them into operational equipment, which could not be considered to be effective until lengthy training programmes were in place. Ironically, just as the Type 170 and Limbo became operational, the nuclear submarine made its debut – so the innovative cycle was set to continue.

Notes

1 The genealogy can, of course, ultimately be traced back to the earliest days of anti-submarine warfare during the First World War. For more detail of the wider developments, see M. Llewellyn-Jones, 'The Royal Navy on the Threshold of Modern Anti-Submarine Warfare, 1944–1949', Ph.D. thesis (King's College, London University, 2004).

2 'The Asdic and its Associated Weapons', W.E. Dawson, ER30, HM Underwater Detection Establishment, Portland, Feb. 1947, Information Centre, DERA Winfrith, Accession No. 15971, p. 2.

3 'Type 144. Trials of Operating Procedure', HMA/SEE, Fairlie, Internal Report No. 159, Dec. 1943, The National Archive (TNA): Public Record Office (PRO), ADM 259/382, p. 7.

4 'Asdic Operating and Control: Supplementary Notes on Procedure and Control', CB4127(4)(45), ASW 304/45, July 1945, Naval Historical Branch, p. 9.

5 'Detection, Attacking, Hunting', CB4097(2)(41), Dec. 1941, Box 468, RG 38, National Archives and Records Administration (NARA), NARA2, para. 77.

6 'The Anti-Submarine Division of the Naval Staff, December 1916–November 1918', Technical History No. 7 (TH 7), CB 1515(7), Technical History Section, Admiralty, July 1919, Admiralty Library, p. 20.

7 Dwight R. Messimer, *Find and Destroy: Antisubmarine Warfare in World War I* (Annapolis, MD: Naval Institute Press, 2001), 59. For another, rather

negative view, see George Franklin, *Britain's Anti-Submarine Capability, 1919–1939* (London: Frank Cass, 2003), 72–3.

8 This idea presumably worked on the same concept as Barnes Wallis's anti-dam 'bouncing' bomb where a relatively small charge placed against a dam would cause more damage than a much larger charge at a distance when the intervening water cushioned the explosive effect. A smaller version of this bomb was intended for use against ships.

9 'Technical History of A/S Weapons', [DUW], R/S.4492A/49, [1949], Naval Historical Branch, p. 86; 'The Asdic and its Associated Weapons', W.E. Dawson, ER30, HM Underwater Detection Establishment, Portland, Feb. 1947, Information Centre, DERA Winfrith, Accession No. 15971, p. 11.

10 Ibid., p. 4.

11 'The Anti-Submarine War, Points which arose at 1st Sea Lord's meeting (27 September 1942 to discuss memorandum by AOC-in-C, Coastal Command', [28 Sept. 1942], ADM 205/21.

12 'Asdic Notebook', Electrical Sub-Lieutenant M. Walford, RNVR; Willem Hackmann, *Seek and Strike: Sonar, Anti-submarine Warfare and the Royal Navy 1914–54* (London: HMSO, 1984), 279.

13 'Creeping Attack', Admiralty Message, DTG 181904A, Aug. 1943, NAA(M): MP1185/8, 1932/3/45.

14 'Creeping Attack', ASCI(2) Amendment Sheet No. 4, [Nov. 1943], NAA(M): MP1049/5, 1866/2/174.

15 Some contemporary documents claim the success rate was as high as 75 per cent, but this may be exaggerated. The overall lethality of the creeping attack seems to have been in the order of 25 per cent. 'The Asdic and its Associated Weapons', W.E. Dawson, ER30, HM Underwater Detection Establishment, Portland, Feb. 1947, Information Centre, DERA Winfrith, Accession No. 15971, p. 6; 'Creeping Attack', Admiralty Message, DTG 101255Z, Feb. 1944, NAA(M): MP1185/8, 1932/3/45.

16 'Direction Finding by High Frequency Beam – Report of Preliminary Experiments', [Feb. 1942], ADM 1/15208. This work may have also contributed to the development of the 'Q' Attachment.

17 'Type 144. Trials of Operating Procedure', HMA/SEE, Fairlie, Internal Report No. 159, Dec. 1943, ADM 259/382; 'Asdic Operating and Control: Echo Operating Procedure', CB 4127(2)(45), A/SW.1031/44, July 1945, Naval Historical Branch, p. 8.

18 'Technical History of A/S Weapons', [DUW], R/S.4492A/49, [1949], Naval Historical Branch, pp. 50–1.

19 Ibid., p. 113.

20 Hackmann, *Seek and Strike*, 283.

21 'The Asdic and its Associated Weapons', W.E. Dawson, ER30, HM Underwater Detection Establishment, Portland, Feb. 1947, Information Centre, DERA Winfrith, Accession No. 15971, p. 11

22 In Britain this fuel was known as 'High Test Peroxide' or HTP.

23 The Type XVII experimental design achieved a submerged speed of 25 knots. Notes taken from 'Walter U-boats – situation at the End of the War' by Foreign Documents Section (FDS 78/55) for Roskill, 12 May 1955, CCAC, ROSK 5/19.

24 'The RAF in Maritime War, Vol. IV: The Atlantic and Home Waters, The Offensive Phase, February 1943–May 1944' (First Draft), n.d., AIR 41/48, pp. 238–40; Karl Doenitz, *Memoirs: Ten Years and Twenty Days*, trans. R.H.

Stevens with introduction by Jürgen Rohwer (London: Greenhill Books, 1990), 265.

25 'Bergen', in 'Report on Interrogation of German Naval Staff Officers of the U-Boat Arm at Flensburg and Bergen', Group Captain Gates, CC/s.17384 A/U Ops., 6 June 1945, National Martime Museum (NMM), NMM(G), Gretton Papers, MSS/93/008.

26 M. Llewellyn-Jones, 'Trials with HM Submarine *Seraph* and British Preparations to Defeat the Type XXI U-Boat, September–October, 1944', *The Mariner's Mirror*, 86(4) (Nov. 2000), 434–51.

27 M. Llewellyn-Jones, 'British Responses to the U-boat, Winter 1943 to Spring 1945', MA dissertation (King's College, London, Dec. 1997), pp. 7–11.

28 Prichard was a specialist A/S officer, who had completed the professional course in 1922. 'The Evolution of the *Osprey*', Lieutenant-Commander F.M. Mason, Summer 1938 (issued 30 Jan. 1942), P.1009, Admiralty Library.

29 'Deep and/or Fast U-boats', DASW, ASW468/44, 24 Mar. 1944, ADM 1/16495; 'Deep and/or Fast U-boats', Captain HMA/SEE, Fairlie to DASW, 10 Apr. 1944, ADM 1/16495.

30 'The Type XXI U-boat – A Provisional Appreciation', in 'Monthly Anti-Submarine Report, August 1944', 15 Sept. 1944, ADM 199/2061, pp. 17–19; 'Type XXI U-boat (A Provisional Appreciation)', E.J. Williams, DOR/44/68, 4 Sept. 1944, ADM 219/150.

31 'Western Approaches Monthly News Bulletin, November 1944', 18 Dec. 1944, Records of the Office of the Chief of Naval Operations: Registered Publications Section, Foreign Navy and Related Foreign Military Publications, 1913–1960, Box 396, RG 38, National Archives and Records Administration 2, College Park, MD; interview, Professor Sir William McCrea, FRS, 17 Apr. 1998; 'Monthly Log of HM Submarine *Seraph*, Month of September 1944', TNA: PRO, ADM 173/18701.

32 Quoted in 'Monthly Anti-Submarine Report, November 1944', 15 Dec. 1944, TNA: PRO, ADM 199/2061, p. 21.

33 'Minutes of the First Meeting of DASW's Sub-Committee of ACNS(UT)'s U-boat Warfare Committee held at the Admiralty on Thursday, 30 Nov. 1944 (Copy)', Folder NSS 1271–22, Vol. 8080, RG 24, NAC.

34 'Notes on A/S Trials with a Fast Submarine', W.H. McCrea, Report No. 72/44, 9 Oct. 1944, ADM 219/154; 'Notes on A/S Trials with a Fast Submarine, "Rockabill", 10–30 Oct. 1944', [W.H. McCrea], Report No. 80/44, 11 Nov. 1944, ADM 219/160; 'Asdic Trials with HM S/M *Seraph* as Target', J.A. Hakes, Research Note No. 53, HMA/SEE Fairlie, Nov. 1944, DERA, AN 28144.

35 H.W. Smith, 'Countering the Fast Conventional Submarine, 1946–1956', in 'Sonar Systems in the RCN, 1945–68', Partial Draft, 15 Jan. 1997, DHH, pp. 5–6.

36 Minute, [Commander] I.M.R. Campbell for Director of Naval Intelligence, 15 Mar. 1945, ADM 116/5202.

37 'Report on Interrogation of Admiral Godt, German Navy, Admiral Commanding BdU Ops. and his Staff Officers, [May 1945], NMM, Gretton Papers, MSS/93/008, National Maritime Museum, Greenwich. In fact, the Germans were not able to complete any Type XXVIs before the war ended. 'Development of the Submarine', Annex A to TASW.021/46, Revised Edition, 4 May 1946, TNA: PRO, ADM 1/20960; 'Submarine Development: Lecture given to Senior Officers' Technical Course on Tuesday 6 May 1947', [A.J. Sims], RNSM A1990/083.

38 'The Use of Squid against the 25 knot U-Boat', Captain N.A. Prichard, DASW, to Captain HMS *Osprey* and Captain HMA/SEE, ASW 945/45, 2 July 1945, TNA: PRO, ADM 1/17591.
39 'The Use of Squid against the 25 knot U-Boat', [Captain N.A. Prichard], DASW, [ASW 945/45], 30 June 1945, TNA: PRO, ADM 1/17591, p. 1.
40 Ibid., p. 2.
41 Ibid.
42 Ibid., p. 3.
43 'Dependence of Submarine Propeller Noise on Depth of Submarine', Director of Scientific Research, SRE/SM/7/0, 19 June 1944, ADM 283/13. See also 'Surface Craft Tactical Countermeasures to Type XXI U-Boats', Research Report No. 93, ASWORG/206 (LO)1380–45, 4 May 1945, TNA: PRO, ADM 1/17588.
44 'The Use of Squid against the 25 knot U-Boat', [Captain N.A. Prichard], DASW, [ASW 945/45], 30 June 1945, TNA: PRO, ADM 1/17591, pp. 4–5.
45 'Deep and/or Fast U-boats', DASW, ASW468/44, 24 Mar. 1944, ADM 1/16495.
46 Minute, G.B.H. Fawkes for Admiral (Submarines), 16 Nov. 1945, TNA: PRO, ADM 116/5500.
47 'Type of German U-boats Required for Post War Experiments and Tests', Admiral (Submarines), Northways, to Secretary of the Admiralty, 15 Oct. 1944, TNA: PRO, ADM 1/16384.
48 'Third Submarine Flotilla Monthly General Letter – July 1945', Captain (S/M), Third Submarine Flotilla, HMS *Forth*, to Admiral (Submarines), No. TSF.1230/3714, 8 Aug. 1945, Royal Navy Submarine Museum (RNSM) A1944/007. The Americans came to the same conclusion.
49 Minute, Director of Operations Division, 2 Nov. 1945, TNA: PRO, ADM 1/18328.
50 Minute, L. Solomon, DNOR, 1 Nov. 1945, TNA: PRO, ADM 1/18328.
51 Minute, Director of Operations Division, 2 Nov. 1945, TNA: PRO, ADM 1/18328.
52 'Submerged Performance Tests on Type XXI U-Boats', Staff Officer (Anti-Submarine) to Director of Torpedo, Anti-Submarine and Mine Warfare, Admiralty, A/S 230–1, 14 Apr. 1947, RNSM A1991/076.
53 'Proposed Evaluation of Present Guppy Submarine Conversion and Equipment', L.R. Daspit, Commander Submarine Squadron Four, to Commander Submarine Force, US Atlantic Fleet, FC5–4/S1, 24 Mar. 1948, Box 98, RG 313, NARA2.
54 'Torpedo, Anti-Submarine and Mine Warfare Division – Institution', H.V. Markham, Office Memorandum No. 394, CE.58514/45, 24 Sept. 1945, TNA: PRO, ADM 1/17743.
55 Minute, DTASW, 10 Nov. 1945, ADM 1/18328; 'Proposal to refit and re-commission *U-2518* on return by the French Navy', Captain Ashbourne, DTASW, TASW 44/47, 7 Feb. 1947, TNA: PRO, ADM 116/5500.
56 The conversion eventually appeared as HMS *Scotsman* in 1948. Minute, E.W. Pratt, for Director of Scientific Research, 18 Dec. 1945, TNA: PRO, ADM 1/18328; Minute, R.C Boyle, for DTM, 4 Jan. 1946, TNA: PRO, ADM 1/18328; Minute, Director of Naval Construction, 15 Nov. 1945, TNA: PRO, ADM 1/18328.
57 Captain G.H. Roberts, RN, Western Approaches Tactical Unit, to C-in-C, WA, 30 May 1945, ADM 1/17561; Letter Report, Captain Gilbert H. Roberts, RN, Western Approaches Tactical Unit, to Commander-in-Chief,

Western Approaches, 30 May 1945, ADM 1/17561; 'Considerations Regarding the Operation of Type XXI, Précis of Text', Grand Admiral Dönitz, [10 July 1944], Section III, 'The Anti-Submarine Report, September, October, November and December 1945', DTASW, CB04050/45(7), 19 Dec. 1945, NHB, pp. 13–19. The full text of the latter document can be found in 'Operation of U-boat Type XXI (Document issued by Admiral Dönitz from Naval Staff Headquarters on 10 July 1944)', Department of Research Programmes and Planning, Admiralty, ACSIL Translation No. 542 (PG.18487), Mar. 1952, FDS, Box 269, NHB.

58 Franklin, *Britain's Anti-Submarine Capability, 1919–1939*, 190.

59 'Operation "Unthinkable", Report by the Joint Planning Staff', G. Grantham, G.S. Thompson, W.L. Dawson, Offices of the War Cabinet, Final, 22 May 1945, TNA: PRO, CAB 120/691.

60 'Russia's Strategic Interests and Intentions', Report by the Joint Intelligence Sub-Committee, JIC(46)1(0) Final (Revise), 1 Mar. 1946, TNA: PRO, CAB 81/132.

61 A.S. Pavlov, *Warships of the USSR and Russia, 1945–1995* (London: Chatham Publishing, 1997), 69, 75.

62 Jürgen Rohwer and Mikhail S. Monakov, *Stalin's Ocean-Going Fleet: Soviet Naval Strategy and Shipbuilding Programmes, 1935–1953* (London: Frank Cass, 2001), 205–6.

63 'Russian Naval Tactics', NID/16, 10 Oct. 1946, TNA: PRO, ADM 1/20030.

64 'Scale and Nature of Attack against Sea Communications', Joint Intelligence Committee, JIC(48)69(0)Final, 11 Aug. 1948, TNA: PRO, CAB 158/4.

65 Minute, Philip Currey, for DTSD, 29 Apr. 1947, TNA: PRO, ADM 1/20030.

66 'Eleventh TAS Liaison Meeting: Minutes', Part 13, 'Paper I – Review of Soviet Naval and Air Forces and their TAS Roles; Paper II – Soviet Underwater Weapons: Discussion', 9–11 Sept. 1952, TNA: PRO, ADM 189/235, pp. 152–7.

67 'Russian Submarines in the Second World War: An Estimate of their Efficiency (Reference: NATO (Secret) ID 0940/1 of 4 January 1955)', Historical Section, Admiralty, Box PT135, NHB.

68 'Soviet Interests, Intentions and Capabilities – General', Report by the Joint Intelligence Sub-Committee, JIC(47)7(Final), 6 Aug. 1947, TNA: PRO, CAB 158/1.

69 'The Overall Strategic Plan, May 1947 (DO(47)44 (Also COS(47)102(0)) (Retained – Cab Off))', Appendix 7, in, J. Lewis, *Changing Direction: British Military Planning for Post-war Strategic Defence, 1942–1947* (London: The Sherwood Press, 1988), 372.

70 'Appreciation of Russian Intentions: Memorandum by the First Sea Lord', Lord Fraser, COS(49)161, 5 May 1949, TNA: PRO, DEFE 5/14.

71 Minute, DNAW, 25 July 1946, TNA: PRO, ADM 1/20045.

72 Minute by D of P, 26 Aug. 1945, TNA: PRO, ADM 1/20045.

73 'Third A/S Tactical Liaison Meeting held in HMS *Vernon* on 1st and 2nd May 1947', A.198/3/47, 17 May 1947, distributed by Op-32-F-45, n.d., Box 102, RG 313, NARA2.

74 'The Development of A/S Warfare', TASW.021/46, Revised Edition, 4 May 1946, TNA: PRO, ADM 1/20960, p. 2.

75 It was assumed that the Russians would capitalise on captured German plans and personnel. 'Russian Naval Tactics', NID/16, 10 Oct. 1946, ADM 1/20030; 'Monthly Intelligence Report, Oct. 1948', NID, 10 Nov. 1948, Directorate of Naval History, Canberra, p. 41.

76 Unmarked Paper of Detailed Comments on Problems at HMA/SEE, [Aug. 1942], 'Papers Re Resignation from HMA/SEE, Fairlie in 1942', KEYN 1, Correspondence: World War II and Radar, Acc. 23/667/669 (Keynes), Box 1, CCAC, KEYN; 'Example C: The Spit Beam Asdic', Draft, n.d., CCAC, GOEV 3/1; 'Half-Yearly Scientific and Technical Progress Report', HM Underwater Detection Establishment, Portland, 1946 (2), TNA: PRO, ADM 213/362.
77 'Progress Report: Shipborne A/S Weapons', TASW.038/46, [5 Sept. 1946], TNA: PRO, ADM 1/20960, pp. 6–9.
78 'Fourth Anti-Submarine Conference', J.D. Price, Vice Chief of Naval Operations, OP 312F/rh A19 Serial 00296P31, 18 Aug. 1949, File 8100.5, Vol. 3734, RG 24, NAC.
79 'Policy Review of Methods of Attacking Submerged Submarines ...', TNA: PRO, ADM 1/20960, p. 3.
80 'Progress in Underwater Warfare, 1947', DTASW, TASW.116/48, CB04050(47), 8 Oct. 1948, TNA: PRO, ADM 239/421, p. 33.
81 'Third A/S Tactical Liaison Meeting held in HMS *Vernon* on 1st and 2nd May 1947'. A.198/3/47, 17 May 1947, distributed by Op-32-F-45, n.d., Box 102, RG 313, NARA2, p. 22.
82 'Progress in Tactics, 1948', ADM 239/144, p. 28; and more particularly, 'Progress in Underwater Warfare, 1947', TNA: PRO, ADM 239/421, p. 33.
83 'Semi-Annual Summary of US Naval Forces Eastern Atlantic and Mediterranean, 1 April 1948–1 September 1948', Commander-in-Chief, US Naval Forces Eastern Atlantic and Mediterranean, to Secretary of the Navy, 14 Oct. 1948, LHCMA, MF 868.
84 Norman Friedman, *US Submarines Since 1945: An Illustrated Design History* (Annapolis: Naval Institute Press, 1994), p. 242.
85 'Exercises with USS *Trumpetfish*', Captain E.A. Gibbs, 11 June 1948, Box 96, RG 313, NARA2, p. 5.
86 Ibid., p. 8.
87 'The First Experience of A/S Actions with Intermediate (B) Submarines', in 'Progress in Underwater Warfare, 1949', CB04050(49), 17 July 1950, TNA: PRO, ADM 239/274, pp. 53, 64.
88 'Progress in Underwater Warfare, 1948', TNA: PRO, ADM 239/422, p. 39.
89 'The First Experience of A/S Actions with Intermediate (B) Submarines', TNA: PRO, ADM 239/274, p. 53.
90 Vice-Admiral Sir Lancelot Bell Davies, KBE, e-mail, 6 January 2001.
91 'Progress in Underwater Warfare, 1948', TNA: PRO, ADM 239/422, p. 41.
92 'The First Experiences of A/S Actions with Intermediate (B) Submarines ...', TNA: PRO, ADM 239/423, p. 2 [emphasis supplied].
93 Leo Marriott, *Royal Navy Destroyers since 1945* (London: Ian Allan, 1989), 87.
94 The author is grateful to Professor Keynes for permission to access his records in CCAC which are normally closed to view.
95 R.D. Keynes, HMA/SEE, Fairlie, to The Director, Scientific Research and Experimental Department, Admiralty, 26 Aug. 1942, 'Papers Re Resignation from HMA/SEE, Fairlie in 1942', KEYN 1, Correspondence: World War II and Radar, Acc. 23/667/669 (Keynes), Box 1, CCAC, KEYN.
96 'The Anti-Submarine War, Points which arose at 1st Sea Lord's meeting (27 September 1942 to discuss memorandum by AOC-in-C, Coastal Command', [28 Sept. 1942], TNA: PRO, ADM 205/21.
97 'Split Beam Direction Finding', R.D. Keynes and R.B. Serle, Internal Report No. 91, HMA/SEE, 16 Apr. 1943, TNA: PRO, ADM 259/359.

98 'Type 144. Trials of Operating Procedure', HMA/SEE, Fairlie, Internal Report No. 159, Dec. 1943, ADM 259/382. It is unclear whether this procedure was adopted, though there are brief references to it in subsequent reports; see 'HMUDE Summary of Progress', 1 Dec. 1949, NAA(M): MP1049/5, 1968/2/800.

99 'The Asdic and its Associated Weapons', W.E. Dawson, ER30, HM Underwater Detection Establishment, Portland, Feb. 1947, Information Centre, DERA Winfrith, Accession No. 15971, p. 16; 'The Experimental Four Square Asdic Set', HMA/SEE, Fairlie, Internal Report No. 230, 9 Nov. 1945, TNA: PRO, ADM 259/429. The latter report was written by Lt-Cdr F. Möller, RNorNVR, T.M. Fry, M.H.J. Hawkins, P.C. Newman, G.A. Smith and Lt O.F. Harbek, RNorNVR (The Split Beam Section (R4) at HMA/SEE).

100 'Half-Yearly Scientific and Technical Progress Report', HM Underwater Detection Establishment, Portland, 1946 (2), TNA: PRO, ADM 213/362.

101 Arthur Hezlet, *The Electron and Sea Power* (London: Peter Davies, 1975), 268. In 1955 Hezlet was Captain (D), 6 Destroyer Squadron, which included the Type 170-fitted HMS Scorpion.

102 The name 'Bidder' was applied to several development weapons at different times. The term is used here for the ship-launched 21-inch torpedo developed after the Second World War. See G.J. Kirby, 'A History of the Torpedo', Part 4, *Journal of the Royal Naval Scientific Service*, 27(2) (1972), 91, 98.

103 'Progress Report: Shipborne A/S Weapons', TASW 038/46, [5 Sept. 1946], ADM 1/20960, pp. 3, 6–8; Norman Friedman, *The Naval Institute Guide to World Naval Weapons Systems, 1991/92* (Annapolis, MD: Naval Institute Press, 1991), 723.

104 'Meetings in UK on Underwater Weapons – Research and Development', DTSR, 28 Apr. 1948, NAA(M): MP1049/5, 1968/2/780.

105 'Underwater Weapons and Equipment – Research Reports – Summary', DTSR, 28 Apr. 1949, NAA(M): MP1049/5, 1968/2/780.

106 'HMUDE Summary of Progress', 1 Dec. 1949, NAA(M): MP1049/5, 1968/2/800.

107 Captain N.A. Prichard, DASW, to First Lord, 24 Nov. 1944, TNA: PRO, ADM 205/36; 'Policy Review of Methods of Attacking Submerged Submarines by Surface Vessels and (Appendix) by Aircraft', Annex B to TASW.021/46, Revised Edition, 4 May 1946, TNA: PRO, ADM 1/20960, p. 3.

108 'Underwater Weapons and Equipment – Research Reports – Summary', DTSR, 28 Apr. 1949, NAA(M): MP1049/5, 1968/2/780; 'Underwater Weapons and Equipment Research Reports', H. Newcomb, DNL, 5 May 1949, NAA(M): MP1049/5, 1968/2/780.

109 'Fitting of High Speed Dome to Destroyers', Ship Design Policy Committee, SDPC(49)14, 25 May 1949, TNA: PRO, ADM 116/5632.

110 'Progress in Underwater Warfare, 1949 Edition', Torpedo, Anti-Submarine and Mine Warfare Division, Admiralty, CB 04050(49), TASW 30/50, 17 July 1950, TNA: PRO, ADM 239/274.

111 'Type 170X Trails Schedule in *Scorpion*', P. Ward, Lieutenant-Commander R. Emden, T.L. Mack, UDE Pamphlet No. 36, May 1950, TNA: PRO, ADM 259/23.

112 'Type 170X-Limbo. Accuracy Determination Trials carried out in *Scorpion*. Part I', T. Mack and D. Addinell, HMUDE, Establishment Report No. 89, 16 Oct. 1951, TNA: PRO, ADM 259/330.

113 'Progress Report: Shipborne A/S Weapons', TASW 038/46, [5 Sept. 1946], TNA: PRO, ADM 1/20960, pp. 9–10.

114 This idea led to the investigation of a number of potential 'Z' weapons. These weapons were not proceeded with. See, for example, ' "Zannet": A Suggested Amphibious Torpedo Carrier to Transport, Aim and Discharge Torpedoes and to carry out A/S Detection and Attack', W.S. Burn, Chief Torpedo Development Engineer, Torpedo Experimental Establishment, Greenock, ACSIL/ADM/47/884, Sept. 1947, TNA: PRO, ADM 290/287. This concept finally resulted in the Ikara system, developed initially by the Royal Australian Navy in the 1960s. Friedman, *The Naval Institute Guide to World Naval Weapons Systems*, 687.

115 The provision of mid-course guidance to a torpedo was via a trailed wire and this system was eventually incorporated into submarine-launched versions of A/S torpedoes. Kirby, 'A History of the Torpedo', Part 4, 100, 102. An outline of the torpedo developments during this period is also to be found in 'Progress in Underwater Warfare, 1951 Edition: Part 3, Torpedo', CB 04050(51), TASW 149/52, 1 Dec. 1952, ADM 239/275.

116 The Bidder (E) was the escort-launched version, while Bidder (S) was the submarine version (which eventually entered service as the Mk 20 Torpedo).

117 'Report of Coordinator of Undersea Warfare and Assistants' Visit to British Naval Activities, Jan. 19–Feb. 12 1947', Forrest Sherman, Deputy Chief of Naval Operations (Operations), Op-31B:ch (SC) A16–3(17) Serial 003P31, 30 Apr. 1947, Records of the Naval Operating Forces: Commander-in-Chief Atlantic (CinCLant) Secret Administrative Files, 1941–1949, Box 90, RG 313, (NARA) p. 2.

118 'Eleventh TAS Liaison Meeting: Minutes', Part 9, 'Paper II – Projects Bidder and Mackle', paper read by Lieutenant-Commander J.P.G. Brooks, RN, Torpedo Experimental Establishment, Greenock, 9–11 Sept. 1952, TNA: PRO, ADM 189/235, pp. 93–4.

119 Ibid., p. 95.

120 'Employment of Long Range Asdic Fitted Ships', Commander T.H.P. Wilson, RN, Undersea Warfare Division, Admiralty, in 'Fifteenth TAS Conference: Minutes', HMS *Vernon*, 6–8 May 1958, TNA: PRO, ADM 189/239, pp. 88–91.

121 'Long Range Submarine and A/S Torpedoes', Captain G.O. Symonds, DSC, RN, Superintendent, Torpedo Experimental and Design, ibid., p. 23.

122 John Mosse, 'Half a Lifetime', Part II, Aug. 1986, Imperial War Museum (IMW) IWM 90/23/1, p. 76.

123 'Eleventh TAS Liaison Meeting: Minutes,' Part 4, 'Evaluation of Fast A/S Frigate Conversions', paper read by Captain M. Le Fanu, DSC, RN, Captain (D), Third Training Squadron, 9–11 Sept. 1952, TNA: PRO, ADM 189/235, p. 37.

124 Axel Niestlé, *German U-boat Losses during World War II: Details of Destruction* (London: Greenhill, 1998), 277, 288.

125 'Eleventh TAS Liaison Meeting: Minutes', Part 4, 'Evaluation of Fast A/S Frigate Conversions', paper read by Captain M. Le Fanu, DSC, RN, Captain (D), Third Training Squadron, 9–11 Sept. 1952, TNA: PRO, ADM 189/235, p. 38.

126 M. Llewellyn-Jones, 'The Pursuit of Realism: British Anti-Submarine Tactics and Training to Counter the Fast Submarine,' in John Reeve and David Stevens (eds), *The Face of Naval Battle: The Human Experience of Modern War at Sea* (Crows Nest, NSW, Australia: Allen & Unwin, 2003), 224.

127 'Eleventh TAS Liaison Meeting: Minutes,' Part 4, 'Evaluation of Fast A/S Frigate Conversions', paper read by Captain M. Le Fanu, DSC, RN, Captain

(D), Third Training Squadron, 9–11 Sept. 1952, TNA: PRO, ADM 189/235, p. 39.
128 Ibid.
129 Ibid., p. 37.
130 'Progress in Tactics, 1953', Tactical and Staff Duties Division, Naval Staff, Admiralty, TSD 71/53, CB 03016(53), 1 May 1953, Records of the Office of the Chief of Naval Operations: Registered Publications Section, Foreign Navy and Related Foreign Military Publications, 1913–1960, Box 444, RG 38, NARA .
131 'Deep and/or Fast U-boats', Captain HMA/SEE, Fairlie to DASW, 10 Apr. 1944, TNA: PRO, ADM 1/16495.
132 Assistant Chief of the Naval Staff to First Sea Lord, ACNS/263, 20 Oct. 1948, TNA: PRO, ADM 205/69, p. 121.
133 'Anti-Submarine', in CB 04050/1953, 'Progress in Underwater Warfare, 1953 Edition', Part 2, TASW 220/53, Torpedo, Anti-Submarine and Mine Warfare Division, Admiralty, 18 June 1954, TNA: PRO, ADM 239/684, p. 37.
134 *Scotsman*, for example, could maintain 12 knots for 4 hours. 'Submarines,' in 'Progress in Underwater Warfare, 1948 Edition,' Chapter 2, Torpedo, Anti-Submarine and Mine Warfare Division, Admiralty, CB 04050(48), TASW 53/49, 10 Sept. 1949, TNA: PRO, ADM 239/422, p. 29.
135 'Notes on A/S Trials with a Fast Submarine,' W.H. McCrea, Report No. 72/44, 9 Oct. 1944, ADM 219/154; 'A/S Practices of HMS *Battleaxe*, HMS *Crossbow* and HMS *Scorpion* with HM Submarine *Scotsman* in the North Channel in November, 1948', in CB 04050(49), 'Progress in Underwater Warfare, 1949 Edition', 17 July 1950, TNA: PRO, ADM 239/274, p. 69; 'Echo and HE Characteristics of the Submarine *Scotsman*', J.W. McCloy, HM Underwater Detection Establishment Report No. 95, Oct. 1951, TNA: PRO, ADM 259/29, p. 7.
136 'Anti-Submarine,' in CB 04050/1953, 'Progress in Underwater Warfare, 1953 Edition', Part 2, TASW 220/53, Torpedo, Anti-Submarine and Mine Warfare Division, Admiralty, 18 June 1954, TNA: PRO, ADM 239/684, p. 37.
137 Ibid.
138 Ibid., p. 38.
139 'Fighting a Modern A/S Frigate,' Captain R. Hart, DSO, DSC, RN, Captain (F), Sixth Frigate Squadron, in, 'Fifteenth TAS Conference: Minutes,' HMS *Vernon*, 6–8 May, 1958, TNA: PRO, ADM 189/239, p. 104.
140 Ibid., p. 105.
141 Ibid., p. 107.
142 This categorisation has been discussed, somewhat theoretically, in Williamson Murray and Allan R. Millett (eds), *Military Innovation in the Interwar Period* (Cambridge: Cambridge University Press, 1996), 308–10.

7

CVA-01

A case study in innovation in Royal Navy aircraft carriers, 1959–1966

Anthony Gorst

A new carrier

In February 1966, as part of the exhaustive defence review undertaken by the Labour Government since its election in 1964, the then Secretary of State for Defence, Denis Healey, announced in Parliament the cancellation of CVA-01,[1] the first of what the Royal Navy had hoped would be a class of three large strike aircraft carriers to replace at two-year intervals Britain's ageing war-built fixed-wing fleet carriers (*Victorious, Ark Royal, Eagle* and *Hermes*) as they successively went out of service in the early 1970s. This decision was taken at the point that shipbuilders were to be invited to tender for the contract, bringing to an abrupt close an exceptionally difficult design and procurement process. Such a momentous decision, dispensing as it did with the capital ship type that had been the centrepiece of the Navy since 1945, was always likely to prove controversial, and so it proved with the resignation of the First Sea Lord and Chief of Naval Staff, Admiral Sir David Luce. This was followed by the resignation of the Minister of Defence (Navy), Christopher Mayhew, over the closely related issue, announced simultaneously, of the end of an independent British intervention capability.

Others, however, felt differently: perhaps surprisingly the project leader of the CVA-01 design team in the Ship Department of the Admiralty from 1962 has been quoted as observing that the 'cancellation [of the project] was the happiest day of my life'.[2] This sense of relief was undoubtedly because CVA-01, at the time probably the single most important, complex and ambitious naval project to be undertaken in Britain since the end of the Second World War, with the exception of the Polaris programme, had been beset with more than its fair share of difficulties since its inception in the late 1950s. Moreover, it has since been argued by one authority that 'it was, perhaps, fortunate that CVA-01 was cancelled before her constraints of size, undue novelty and production problems had led to a costly and unsatisfactory ship'.[3] Others have argued, however, that the design 'had much in it that was good'.[4] Of course, CVA-01 as a case study in innovation poses particular problems precisely because it was never built; the ideas embedded in the first carrier to be built in Britain since the end of the Second World War were thus never put to the acid test to be assessed individually and collectively as either successes or failures. Yet CVA-01 had advanced sufficiently far before its sudden cancellation for an examination of the design and procurement process to shed valuable light on both the driving forces for innovation in ship design and the attitudes of the Naval Staff, responsible for drawing up staff requirements, and the Ship Department, responsible for ship design, to innovation.

This chapter argues that the main driving force behind the novel features contained in CVA-01 was the paramount need, within strict size, volume and weight limits, to design as capable a ship as possible with as many features of the much larger United States Navy strike carriers as possible and able to operate as many fighter and strike aircraft as could be crammed into its hull. It was this delicate balancing act that was to lead to the incorporation of several new ideas – perhaps too many for comfort – into CVA-01, including *inter alia* a new radical design parallel flight deck, new aircraft-handling equipment (including direct-acting arrestor gear) and the use of weight-saving materials that would have posed problems in the production of the ship. Other innovations, such as nuclear power and an all-V/STOL aircraft group, were considered but rapidly dismissed as steps too far, although CVA-01 could have operated a limited number of V/STOL aircraft from four deck spots. Development of these innovations was further hindered by the stop/start nature of the R & D process which merely added to the uncertainties surrounding the programme.

Aircraft carriers have always represented particular challenges to ship designers, as they must balance operating facilities for high-performance aircraft with the sometimes contradictory requirements of a fighting ship. This challenge was particularly demanding in the 1950s and 1960s, a period of rapid change in aircraft design and performance and equally rapid change in ships' weapons systems. The largest Royal Navy carriers, *Eagle* and *Ark Royal*, had been designed from early 1942 to operate aircraft of up to 30,000 lb all-up weight, yet by the time the latter was finally completed in 1955 this already appeared inadequate and they were consequently refitted in the early 1960s to operate Buccaneer and Sea Vixen aircraft at over 40,000 lb all-up weight. Equally, completed with 4.5-inch and 40 mm guns as their defensive armaments, they were subsequently refitted for Seacat surface-to-air missile systems (SAM), although those of *Ark Royal* were never fitted.

Given this rapidly changing environment, in which an aircraft carrier would operate several generations of aircraft over its 25–30-year service life, the design and construction of the first new fleet carrier for the Royal Navy for some twenty years would have posed more than enough difficulties for the Ship Department, overstretched as it was with other projects and deficient as it was in recent experience in carrier design. Yet these undoubted practical difficulties were to be compounded by political problems that no doubt contributed to the weary sense of relief of some at the cancellation of CVA-01 The necessity for a replacement programme of large, complex and inevitably costly strike carriers was by no means accepted by all within the Navy, let alone by a Royal Air Force competing for a similar role and by politicians intent on curtailing the defence budget. There was therefore an inexorable pressure to produce an aircraft carrier that was as small and as cheap as possible in order to avoid the damaging political controversies over size and cost that had stymied the carrier replacement programme in the 1950s.[5] This constraint, together with the natural but conflicting desire to make such a large investment as capable as possible, notably in a departure for the Royal Navy by including area defence anti-aircraft and anti-submarine missile systems, meant inevitable conflicts in the design process that were attempted to be solved by innovations to reduce the size and cost of the ships themselves.

The necessity for a programme of new aircraft carriers arose from the inadequacies, particularly in aircraft complement, of the existing carrier fleet of the Royal Navy in the late 1950s. Although the post-war navy carrier fleet, had served with some distinction through the 1950s, particularly during the Korean War and the Suez crisis, they were fast approaching the limits of their capabilities before necessarily reaching the end of their hull lives. A series of ideas initiated by the Royal Navy, precisely because a combination of small hulls and large aircraft forced the pace of innovation, and perfected in tandem with the United States Navy – the angled deck, mirror landing sight and steam catapult – enabled relatively small carriers to operate aircraft of performance and weights far beyond what had been envisaged when designed; however, such innovations could take intrinsically limited hulls only so far. The basic and inescapable problem was that these ships were far too small to operate modern aircraft without extensive and expensive modernisations; these would still, however, have left them with such small air groups (the modernisation of *Victorious* from 1950–8 meant that she could embark only 36 aircraft while *Hermes* as refitted from 1964–6 could operate but 28) that on any rational cost-benefit analysis, such an exercise for all seven British carriers would have been simply uneconomical. Even the largest of the British carriers, *Eagle* and *Ark Royal*, designed to operate some 80 aircraft, would be able to operate only half that figure by the mid-1960s and probably 36 by the 1970s, should their hulls last that long. What was needed, of course, if the Royal Navy was to retain a fixed-wing operating capability, conferring the ability to operate and intervene beyond land-based air cover, past the early 1970s was a new carrier programme.

By the late 1950s the carrier situation was pressing. As the then Director of Naval Construction (DNC) Sir Victor Shepheard, noted in 1957, the existing carriers

> have been brought to a reasonably satisfactory state for operating the present generation of naval aircraft. We are now in the initial stages of an even greater task in modernising *Eagle*, still further altering *Victorious*, squeezing everything possible into *Hermes*, partially modernising *Centaur* and maybe *Albion* and in doing what we can to *Ark Royal*. By these rather desperate measures, we hope to have reasonable facilities for operating the next generation of naval aircraft ... this programme will take us to the mid-1960s by which time the ships concerned will be becoming of rapidly decreasing value for front-line use. It seems certain that further modification will be uneconomic and aircraft beyond the next generation will probably be ruled out for operation from our present carriers.[6]

Given that a new class of carriers would take some ten years to join the fleet from the point of issuing staff requirements – the theoretical start of the process – time was pressing, not least because *Eagle* and *Ark Royal*, the most capable of Britain's carriers, would reach the end of their lives in the early 1970s, leaving only the much smaller *Hermes* to carry the burden.[7] The features and layout of any new aircraft carrier would inevitably be shaped by the composition of the air group that it was to operate and the characteristics of the aircraft that made up that air group. The air group would be made up of three fundamentally different types of aircraft: a high-performance fighter/strike aircraft comparable in capability with land-based aircraft, a fixed-wing airborne early warning (AEW) aircraft, and helicopters for both 'plane guard' search and rescue duties (SAR) and anti-submarine warfare (ASW). It was the high-performance fighter/strike requirement, the *raison d'être* for the carrier, which would define the ship.

A Fleet Requirements Committee paper of 1958 clearly spelt out that manned fixed-wing aircraft would continue to be required over the operational life of any new carrier for strike reconnaissance and air defence into the 1990s. Future strike aircraft, the largest carrier-borne type, were likely to grow to 60,000 lb all-up weight with a folded length of 65 ft and a folded wingspan of some 30 ft, take-off speed being 150 knots with a landing speed of 120 knots at 30,000 lb; operational research indicated a minimum air group of 12–14 strike aircraft, 18 air defence aircraft and 8 AEW aircraft. These figures were clearly beyond the capacity of even the largest of the existing carriers, and in a prescient note of caution the paper concluded that they might even be difficult to achieve within a new design as: 'A new construction carrier, designed within the limits of strategic and practical considerations, cannot absorb all the equipment and facilities which present-day carriers are attempting to absorb with only limited success.' It was for this reason that initial discussions within the Ship Department considered that 'nothing should be included in a new carrier which does not make an effective contribution towards the operation of heavy fixed-wing aircraft'; thus anti-submarine helicopters, area air defence weapons and possibly fleet command and control facilities might be embarked elsewhere, possibly in an accompanying escort cruiser.[8]

Two potential developments in aircraft technology were of particular relevance for the design of fixed-wing aircraft to be operated at sea which sought to marry maximum performance with the necessity for as low a landing speed as possible: these were Vertical/Short Take Off and Landing (V/STOL) fixed-wing aircraft using vectored thrust and variable-geometry or 'swing-wing' aircraft. There were of course trade-offs: in the case of the former, aircraft performance, particularly reduced range and payload, and in the case of the latter, the likely complexity and cost of the aircraft. With comparatively few aircraft to be deployed, the argument in favour of quality initially carried the day, although the issue of V/STOL continued to raise its head for some years, largely for inter-service political reasons; it was therefore hoped that CVA-01 would be introduced into service simultaneously with a new generation of swing-wing fighter and strike aircraft.

Design commences

Design work on CVA-01 really began with a meeting of the Naval Staff and Ship Department on 10 June 1960; this defined the tasks of the new carrier as being to operate strike and reconnaissance aircraft against land and sea targets and to provide air defence for the fleet and ground forces. Aircraft dimensions overall had grown to 70 ft for both the wingspan and fuselage length with a height of 23 ft, folding to 30 ft, 64 ft and 19 ft 6 in., respectively. A minimum of 42 aircraft (including ancillary aircraft and helicopters) were to be embarked, although the Director of Plans felt strongly that the complement of 32 fighter/strike aircraft was inadequate to meet the defined tasks. It was not, however, merely a question of increasing the aircraft complement by increasing the size of the carrier itself, as extrinsic factors immediately began to constrain the new carrier: anything above 45,000 tons would raise problems with dockyard facilities, particularly those at Portsmouth and Gibraltar, as well as running into political difficulties if the Navy was seen to be asking for replacement carriers significantly larger than HMS *Eagle* and HMS *Ark Royal*. It was agreed that 'the problem was therefore to design a ship as large as possible in order to take the maximum number of aircraft and as small as possible in order to fit into the maximum number of docks'. At the same time financial considerations also came into play, as above 45,000 tons 'all costs concerned with ships rise rapidly'; the Director General (Ships) (DGS), A.J. Sims, was nonetheless instructed to investigate designs below 45,000 tons and up to 55,000 tons. It was also suggested that a maximum speed of 28 knots would suffice as this would allow a three-shaft layout that was likely to be considerably cheaper than the four shafts required to produce the desirable 30 knots fleet speed.[9]

From the beginning of the process, then, constraints of size and cost began to shape the design. Only one month later Sims sounded the first of many notes of caution, pointing out that on a ship of under 45,000 tons 'some of the staff requirements now being discussed cannot be met'; he was understandably anxious to avoid repeating earlier experiences where 'the problem has been to meet, in aircraft carriers of relatively modest size, staff requirements which approach those for the much larger American aircraft carriers'.[10] It was little wonder then that the early design studies conducted in the Ship Department showed an inexorable rise in size and cost as staff requirements were added to meet the desiderata of the various departments of the Naval Staff. By November 1960, it was concluded that the required number of aircraft embarked in an aircraft carrier task group of two ships, to provide air support for land forces and naval forces deployed beyond the limits of land-based air cover, was 64 strike reconnaissance and 32 fighter aircraft, an increase of 50 per cent in the fixed-wing aircraft complement to 48 for each carrier. Moreover it was now thought desirable by the DOR that at least two, and preferably four, surface-to-air guided weapon systems (SAGW), the American Tartar system 'in the absence of any suitable British weapon', should be fitted both for self-defence but also to maximise the number of such systems at sea with the fleet. The DOR also specified a new frequency-scanning three-dimensional air search radar and a comprehensive ASW sensor suite while four anti-submarine hunter-killer single-package helicopters were to be carried.[11]

Design studies conducted thus far in the Ship Department (see Figure 7.1) clearly revealed the wide gap between the desiderata of staff requirements and the realities of dimensional and financial limits that were to continue to plague the design process. None of the studies could meet the ideal complement figure of 48 aircraft and only the largest at 68,000 tons could embark the *minimum* required number of next-generation aircraft together with ASW and AEW aircraft. Only those above 55,000 tons could mount the number of catapults requested by the Director of Air Warfare (DAW), whilst only the 68,000 tons design could incorporate the three lifts, one on the deck edge, specified and accommodate the desired four SAGW systems: the drawback was, of

Design study	*27*	*23D*	*23E*	*29*	*24*	*30*
Flight deck length	770 ft	820 ft	820 ft	860 ft	870 ft	1004 ft
Max. flight deck width	165 ft	165 ft	200 ft	165 ft	200 ft	190 ft
Length waterline	720 ft	764 ft	764 ft	800 ft	810 ft	964 ft
Beam waterline	112 ft	116 ft	116 ft	116 ft	118 ft/120 ft	128 ft
Depth	76 ft 6 in.	83 ft 6 in.	76 ft 6 in.	83 ft 6 in.	83 ft 6 in.	96 ft 4 in.
Displacement (tons)	42,000	48,000	48,000	50,000	55,000	68,000
Draft	31 ft 6 in.	32 ft 7 in.	32 ft 7 in.	32 ft 5 in.	34 ft 6 in.	33 ft 5 in.
Horsepower/shafts	135,000/3	150,000/3	150,000/3	150,000/3	150,000/3	160,000/4
Speed clean/6 months out of dock (knots)	29.8/29.6	30/29	30/29	30/28+	30/28+	30/28
Endurance in miles at 20 knots	6,000	6,000	6,000	6,000	6,000	6,000
'Next generation' aircraft deck park/ hangar/total	8/10/18	8/15/23	13/11/24	8/17/25	14/18/32	13/23/36
Buccaneer aircraft deck park/ hangar/total	13/18/31	15/26/41	23/20/43	15/29/44	23/50/53	22/37/59
Catapults, number/length	2/225 ft	2/225 ft	2/225 ft	2/225 ft	3/225 ft	3/225 ft
Arrester wires/barriers	4/1	4/1	4/1	4/1	4/1	4/1
Lifts	2	2	2	2	2	3
Aviation fuel (gallons)	400,000	550,000	550,000	550,000	750,000	470,000
Armament	4 Seacat	3 Tartar type	3 Tartar type	3 Tartar type	4 Tartar type	4 Tartar type
Radar types	985/978	985/978	985/978	985/978	985\978	985/978
Sonar types	182/185	182/185	182/185	182/185	182/185	182/185
Complement officers/men	210/2,500	260/3,050	260/3,050	260/3,100	290/3,400	290/3,400
Cost of ship in £ millions	43.5	47.5	47.5	48.5	51.0	59.1
Cost of missiles in £ millions	0.55	6.45	6.45	6.45	7.9	7.9
Cost of dock works in £ millions	4.1	4.3	4.6	5.0	5.7	5.7+
Total cost in £ millions	48.15	58.25	58.55	59.95	64.60	72.70+

Figure 7.1 Aircraft carrier design studies, November 1960. (Table derived from NMM, ADM 138/888, FRC(60)7, 'New Aircraft Carrier', 14 November 1960.)

course, that such a design would cost half as much again as the smallest design.[12]

It was clear therefore that the size of the ship in relation to the aircraft complement was to be the contentious issue. On the one hand, as the Chairman of the Fleet Requirements Committee (FRC) noted, 'below a certain minimum the potential of the aircraft that could be embarked would be insufficient to justify the inevitably high cost of constructing the ship'; on the other hand, 'it was idle to assume that three 68,000 ton ships with a full complement of aircraft would be authorised'. Although fresh information on the size of the variable-geometry aircraft led to a welcome increase in the aircraft complement, the issue of a V/STOL air group was placed firmly back on the agenda by the Chairman of the FRC who stressed that future aircraft development for the RAF by the Ministry of Aviation would concentrate on V/STOL aircraft and that the Minister of Defence, Harold Watkinson, was convinced that a common airframe for the Navy and the RAF to reduce development costs was essential. The FRC were less than happy at this reintroduction of a radical concept for overtly political reasons, noting that although V/STOL aircraft might be smaller and would not require arrestor gear, they would still require catapults, would have the same personnel accommodation and maintenance overheads as conventional aircraft, and worse their 'performance would tend to be inferior' in terms of range and payload.[13] Preliminary calculations revealed the scale of the commitment: four 42,000-ton carriers plus their aircraft would cost, including research and development, some £650 million, of which only £180 million was accounted for by the building cost of the carrier, while four 55,000-ton carriers would cost £780 million of which the carriers represented £240 million.[14] The Fleet Requirements Committee (FRC) considered that a design of 48,000 tons, with carrier building costs of around £180 million for four ships, was 'the smallest that made sense'.[15]

In early 1961, the Admiralty Board accepted these broad characteristics but, recognising the likelihood of opposition to expenditure on this scale, spent much time discussing how to seek Government approval. The Vice Chief of the Naval Staff argued that 'the Admiralty should not appear to be pressing for a new generation of carriers but rather as accepting, with some reluctance, the responsibility for providing sea-borne Army support with the concomitant necessity to replace the present carriers'. Moreover it was accepted at least by the Board that

> On grounds of economy, and because Ministers were likely to attach so much importance to it, the aim must be, to achieve common aircraft with the RAF in the next generation of naval aircraft. If necessary some compromise on naval requirements should be accepted for this purpose.

The Controller of the Navy also recommended that an *ad hoc* one-by-one approach to the replacement of the existing carriers should be taken; such an incremental approach would have the advantage of deferring decisions on the later carrier replacements and their aircraft, thus putting off expenditure, allowing them to take full account of new technical developments in VTOL and facilitating agreement with the RAF on a common aircraft.[16]

Sketch staff requirements drawn up over the summer of 1961 envisaged a displacement of around 50,000 tons with an air group built around a new common airframe, with Sea Vixens and Buccaneers being carried in the interim. A fully angled flight deck served by two lifts from a 20 ft high hangar, all stressed to take 60,000 lb loads, was specified together with two 225 ft catapults. Conventional machinery with three shafts was to give 28 knots, 25 knots when catapulting aircraft.[17] A revised draft revealed an alarming tendency by the Staff to add equipment and facilities to what was already clearly a tight design that was expected to cost between £50 million and £60 million at 1961 prices. An extensive sensor suite was envisaged with two 3D surveillance radars now specified. An anti-submarine attack system, based on the Australian Ikara, was now added, albeit at the expense of two of the four CF299 SAGW launchers while the four ASW helicopters were also removed in compensation. Notwithstanding a recognition that these additions would make it difficult to hold to a 50,000-ton limit, the DGS was instructed to examine the possibility of providing three lifts and catapults, reinstating the two CF299 SAGW launchers, and providing increased aircraft stores and fuel for five, rather than three, days of intensive flying operations.[18] A further iteration specified a speed of 30 knots, reintroduced the four ASW helicopters but only *in lieu* of part of the fixed-wing complement, but rejected the call for three lifts and catapults, specifying instead 'at least two' of each.[19] The DGS was clearly anxious about these additions for as he noted, 'we had in mind a ship of *Eagle*'s size into which we are trying to fit many more weapons and equipment than in *Eagle*'. Moreover, a requirement for 30 knots would demand an extra 35,000 horsepower, probably an extra shaft, and would push the carrier over 50,000 tons, calling into question dockyard capacity to support the ship.[20]

Following Defence Committee approval to proceed with design work in January 1962, although explicitly with no commitment to construction,[21] design study A1/1D, the culmination of some forty design studies, was drawn up to meet these exacting staff requirements and emerged as a 50,000-ton design with an 890 ft long angled flight deck with two lifts and two catapults capable of operating 30 of the new common RN/RAF strike/fighter aircraft at up to 60,000 lb all-up weight. However, on these dimensions the new carrier could not be docked at Portsmouth, Devonport or Gibraltar unless a new dock was built at Portsmouth and major works carried out at Devonport and Gibraltar at a cost of £114 million.[22] Presented to the Ship Characteristics Committee (SCC) in early March 1962 by DGS, design A1/1D was greeted with a degree of coolness. In the first place, the sheer cost of the programme was beginning to worry the Naval Staff; the DCNS noted that 'the present naval building programme ... had insecure foundations. The escort cruiser might become vulnerable on this account and it was therefore more than ever necessary to be flexible in regard to the capabilities of the aircraft carrier.'

Consequently the Committee agreed that the new design must accommodate organic ASW helicopters. This therefore reopened the vital question of the number of aircraft carried as 'any reduction in the complement of strike aircraft might in itself call into question the case for the ship'. It was hoped that the common airframe would be kept as small as possible, but 'there seemed little doubt that the aircraft which eventually emerged would be bigger than one, OR346, which would meet the Royal Navy requirements only'.[23] Further discussion, based on new data on the size of the common aircraft, suggested that only 25 of the RAF OR355 version of the common strike/fighter could be carried and that 'if it were to be considered essential that 30 such aircraft were to be carried then the size of the ship would have to be increased' to between 53,000 and 57,000 tons. As the DGS recognised, 'his dilemma was where to draw the limit on displacement' for, as the Deputy-Secretary (G) noted, 'considerable controversy would be excited if the displacement were to exceed about 52,000 tons' not least because of the 'embarrassing' question of the essential dock alterations. Detailed discussion of the extra facilities added in the staff requirements confirmed that the two CR299 SAGW systems (of a different design to the destroyer/frigate version) were necessary, that the second 3D radar was essential and that the Ikara system was desirable. Moreover, the Naval Air Warfare staff were now asking for at least one 250 ft catapult and a third lift. It is no surprise then that the decision of the SCC was to recommend that

> design work should proceed on the basis of a ship of 50,000 tons displacement designed to carry OR346 on the understanding if in the future it became necessary to cater for a bigger aircraft then fewer would be carried: but that a moderate increase in displacement should be accepted.[24]

The Admiralty Board on 2 April 1962 followed the lead of the SCC in registering its concern about the size of the aircraft complement; it was noted that 'a design approaching 60,000 tons would take a disproportionately greater number of aircraft and cost perhaps only £7–£8 millions more than the 50,000 ton design'. This effectively signed the death warrant of the escort carrier as its ASW functions could be transferred to a larger carrier; as the Secretary noted:

> If a case for a carrier bigger than 50,000 tons could be established – and the discussion suggested such a case existed – this could be most effectively linked with the abandonment of Escort Cruisers which might in any case be found ... to be beyond our resources.

The SCC was therefore requested to carry out a quick study of carriers up to 60,000 tons with an evaluation of the number of aircraft that could be embarked.[25]

Over the next two months, therefore, the Ship Department produced a series of design studies of varying displacement (see Figure 7.2).[26] A1/1E was produced to see the effect of embarking the minimum number of OR346 aircraft while A1/5A and A1/6A were produced to evaluate the effect of embarking five ASW helicopters on a cheaper design than 52/A/3. Discussion of these design studies in the SCC ruled out the 52,000-ton design as it 'permitted but little resilience for meeting future needs' while the 58,000-ton design was also discounted as 'its high order of cost compared with other designs made it unattractive'. Discussion therefore centred on the 53,000- and 55,000-ton designs; although 53,000 tons 'was up to the limit for three shafts', this design met the staff requirements, with sufficient stretch to meet future demands while 'there was no positive gains in the 55,000 ton design'.[27] Design 53 was therefore selected to be presented to the Admiralty Board.[28]

Subsequent discussion in the Board foreshadowed future difficulties. The Civil Lord expressed his doubts about the whole carrier programme, chiefly on grounds of escalating costs, which for later units of the new class might reach '£70 or £80 millions'. He argued for 'a design of about 40,000 tons carrying 24 aircraft and costing perhaps £43 millions' with the potential of operating rather more of the space-efficient VTOL aircraft if and when they came into service. Although this was squashed by the rest of the Board, the First Sea Lord arguing against 'a second-rate design' and others pointing out that the Admiralty 'had been criticised in the past for building carriers with an inadequate margin for aircraft development', clear doubts were beginning to emerge, even within the Admiralty, about the escalating size and cost of the new carrier.[29] The presentation of the new carrier to the Minister of Defence on 18 July 1962 therefore focused on the issue of the size and cost:

> So much of the new carrier is taken up by its machinery, workshops, structures, accommodation and fuel that it is not until a displacement of about 35,000 tons has been exceeded that the capacity for carrying aircraft begins to pay a dividend on the

Design study	*A1/1D (50)*	*A1/1E (52)*	*A1/5A (53)*	*A1/6A (55)*	*52/A/3 (58)*
Flight deck length	890 ft	900 ft	920 ft	940 ft	970 ft
Max. flight deck width/angle	177 ft/4.5°	177 ft/6.5°	180 ft/7°	180 ft/7.5°	190 ft/8°
Beam waterline	118 ft	122 ft	122 ft	122 ft	120 ft
Displacement (tons)	50,000	52,000	53,000	55,000	58,000
Draft	32 ft	32 ft	32 ft	32 ft	32 ft 6 in.
Horse power/shafts	135,000/3	135,000/3	135,000/3	160,000/4	180,000/4
Speed 6 months out of dock (knots)	28	28	28	29	29
OR 346 aircraft	30	32	30	30	40
Buccaneer aircraft	36	36	36	36	48
AEW aircraft	4	4	3	3	4
SAR aircraft	2	2	2	2	2
ASW helicopters	0	0	5	5	0
Max. aircraft weight	60,000 lb	70,000 lb	70,000 lb	70,000 lb	70,000 lb
Catapults, number/length	1 × 250/1 × 225	1 × 250/1 × 225	2 × 250	2 × 250	2 × 250
Lifts (ft)	2 × 65 × 30	2 × 70 × 32	2 × 70 × 32	2 × 70 × 32	2 × 70 × 32
Armament	2 × CF299 1 × Ikara	2 × CF299 1 × Ikara	2 × CF299 1 × Ikara	2 × CF299 1 × Ikara	2 × CF299 1 × Ikara
Radar types	2 × 3 D	2 × 3 D	2 × 3 D	2 × 3 D	2 × 3 D
Cost of ship in £ millions	50–60	55–60	55–60	58–63	60–65

Figure 7.2 Aircraft carrier design studies, May 1962. (Table derived from NMM, ADM 138/888, SCC/P(62)28, 'New Aircraft Carrier', 22 May 1962.)

> consequential overheads. As an example of this a 50,000 ton carrier can accommodate almost 100% more aircraft than a carrier of 40,000 tons but it would cost only about 25% more ... the bigger the carrier the better the ratio of military output to overheads, the more safely and efficiently she can operate aircraft and the more stretch for the future can be built into her.... In short as a military concept small carriers are a mistake ... the French Navy recognise that the *Clemenceau*, because she cannot meet the requirements of present aircraft, let alone future ones, is a costly national blunder.[30]

For the moment then, with the approval of the Minister of Defence, the Ship Department proceeded with the development of design 53.

Design under pressure

The first significant change to the design occurred in December 1962 with the adoption of an innovative new flight deck design that aimed to increase the aircraft complement without adding to displacement. Up to this point all the detailed design studies had envisaged conventional angled decks, the landing area of the flight deck being offset at anything up to 8° to port of the centre line of the ship; this innovation, invented by the Royal Navy in the early 1950s and fitted to existing carriers, took the flight path of landing aircraft away from any aircraft parked in the forward deck park. However the new design, produced following a Fleet Work Study, recommended reducing the angle of the flight deck to $2\frac{1}{2}°$ by extending the width of the flight deck aft, thus moving the landing area 50 ft to port and forward. This radical change had the effect of increasing the total flight deck area by 2.8 per cent (some 3,500 square feet) but increased the parking area, clear of landing and launching aircraft, by 32 per cent (10,000 square feet), allowing an extra five aircraft to be parked clear of the landing area, increasing the total complement of OR346 aircraft by two to 32. The new design, by widening the flight deck, also allowed a more flexible movement of aircraft on what was likely to be a crowded flight deck by introducing a two-way traffic stream using an 'Alaskan Highway' outboard of the island and the extra deck space created inboard of the island. Moreover, the new design created space for an engine running-up area, regarded as desirable by the air departments from the beginning, from the hangar deck onto the now open quarterdeck. The cost, however, was the loss of one of the SAGW missile systems, reducing the outfit to one sited on the quarterdeck. Even so this had some advantages, provided two radars could be provided on the island for all-round fire, as the destroyer-type launcher already under development could be adopted saving some £0.75 million in production and development costs for a carrier version.[31] The advantages of this innovative flight deck design were speedily endorsed by the SCC and staff requirements amended accordingly.[32]

The design was finalised in June 1963 and emerged as around 53,000 tons on an 890 ft waterline. The 660 ft × 80 ft hangar, serviced by two lifts of 70 ft × 32 ft, could accommodate two-thirds of the aircraft complement at any one time. Two 230 ft catapults to launch aircraft at 60,000 lb and 150 knots were envisaged while a four-wire direct-acting arrestor gear capable of arresting a 40,000 lb aircraft was specified. The ship was to be powered by a three-shaft layout with three separate and independent units working at 1000 psi and 900°F. Although there were still uncertainties about the radar and communications fit, not least whether all the sets and their associated antennae and aerials could be fitted into the restricted space of the island, it was decided to merge the funnels and masts into 'two combined funnels and structural supports', a so-called mack, to maximise suitable locations. The ship was to be protected against underwater attack by 19 ft of side protection while splinter protection only was to be provided around vital areas including 3 inches over the magazines, $1\frac{1}{2}$ inches around the operations complex and $1\frac{1}{2}$ inches over the hangar. In addition, significant amounts of high-tensile QT35 steel would have to be used in maximum strength areas, notably the flight and hangar decks; as a relatively new development it was noted with some concern that 'this demands from the shipbuilder the use of advanced welding techniques and requires a great deal more Admiralty supervision'.

All in all, although the design was 'considered to meet the staff requirements', it was noted that 'demands for space have made it necessary to ... take up some design margins and a strict control will have to be exercised'.[33] The design was accepted by the SCC, although some concerns were raised at the now £59 million cost of CVA-01.[34] Presented to the Board in mid-July 1963, with a comment by the Controller that 'US Naval authorities had been impressed by many features of the design',[35] CVA-01 was approved for full development, a decision confirmed by the Cabinet and announced in Parliament on 30 July 1963. Even so this good news was accompanied by bad news: *Victorious* was not to be replaced – instead a three-carrier fleet would be maintained with CVA-01 to replace *Ark Royal* in 1972, with, ominously, decisions about the replacements for *Eagle* and *Hermes* to be taken when 'they fall due'.[36]

As the design was firmed up, major problems began to afflict the development of CVA-01; these stemmed not only from the fact that much new and novel equipment, particularly for aircraft handling, had to be specifically developed for CVA-01, but largely from the reluctance of the Treasury to authorise expenditure for research and development and long-lead production of these items, particularly for extra-mural work. An August 1962 memo to the DGS outlined the position: contracts worth some £100,000 needed to be placed by the end of the year with a further £700,000 placed by October 1963 and a further £1.564 million by September 1964, the expenditure itself to be phased over the financial years up to 1966–7. These included contracts for the new direct-acting arrestor gear (from McTaggart Scott), improved steam catapults (from Brown Bros) and new design space-saving 'scissor' aircraft lifts (GEC) as well as design of the main machinery by Y-ARD.[37] This was to be particularly problematic because much of this equipment, such as the direct-acting arrestor gear, was in itself innovative and needed a thorough development and testing process: as Friedman has noted, CVA-01 'incorporated many ... ingenious ideas ... all entailed considerable technical risk ... so that as the design progressed, the design team became more and more nervous'.[38] By December 1962 the DGS was lamenting the reluctance of the Treasury to 'honour any research and development expenditure although this has been placed at an absolute minimum'.[39] The situation did not improve, the First Lord, Lord Carrington, lamenting to the Minister of Defence, Peter Thorneycroft, in March 1963 that consequent delays, particularly on the catapults, were 'crippling the design effort'.[40] A brief for the Admiralty Board spelt out the problem:

> The final design cannot be completed nor can tenders be invited until all contracts ... are completed. These cover the design of the main machinery, electrical generators, catapults, arresting gear, aircraft lifts, etc. and are vital to a balanced ship design. The stage has now been reached where contract work has been virtually halted. To continue with design work ... without this work would become pointless as time goes on with an increasing probability that much of it will prove to be incorrectly based.[41]

Even the support of Thorneycroft, albeit for a reduced sum of approximately £1 million before going to tender, failed to move the Treasury to release funds that the Admiralty argued strenuously had been embedded and authorised in that year's estimates. Indeed the Treasury seized on the decision not to replace *Victorious* to further delay releasing funds, with John Boyd-Carpenter, the Chief Secretary to the Treasury, stating that 'I very much hope that we should not ... think it necessary to bring forward any of the expenditure'. His position was clear: 'We shall be carrying a very heavy burden of defence expenditure in 1964/5 and the following years. We are strenuously looking for economies within the broad framework of present defence policy and any avoidable additions will make our task even harder.'[42]

The continued resistance of the Treasury to release funds was causing real difficulties within the Ship Department. DNC noted in August 1963 that it was vital to design, develop and order long-lead items immediately as 'this ship is a very big technical problem both in design and building. The more thought and work put into the design and specifications the cheaper the job will be.' He also noted, registering concern over the likely delivery date of mid-1972, that 'industry has not been asked to build such a ship for very many years'.[43] This theme was amplified by a member of his Department in a meeting with the Treasury about the release of funds for catapult and arrestor gear development, when he noted that 'this is a very big job indeed for the main contractor and calls for contributions from a wide cross-section of contractors. There will be many technical problems to overcome.'[44] Nor were these difficulties likely to be confined to the shipbuilding industry, as

> There are too few members of the Admiralty, including Ships Department, who can remember just what is involved in developing a design for a large and complicated ship to the building drawing stage. The staffs available in the Design Divisions are by no means over generous and will be progressively stretched as time slips by.[45]

By October 1963 the situation was becoming critical with the DDNC noting that work on the main machinery, catapults, arrestor gear, lifts, generators, transformers and switch gear was 'practically at a standstill' while the stop/start nature of research and development 'is undoubtedly going to have the most unfortunate effects'. As far as the Ship Department was concerned, 'the layout of the ship and the structural design cannot be completed if design work on machinery and important equipment is held up'. For example, Y-ARD had reallocated staff to other projects with the result that there was no information available on the uptakes, machinery and boiler spaces and pie systems.[46]

By December 1963 the DGS was noting that Treasury obstructionism in connection with the extra-mural work 'has retarded the design as a whole and has meant that the Government announcement that the carrier was being designed has never been more than a half truth'. Extra-mural design and development contracts were essential, particularly where 'more novel or more advanced equipment of a certain type is needed for a warship design, firms must be approached and set to work in the design stage if the ship itself is to be effectively designed and described in the building drawings and specifications'. Nor was the picture much happier in relation to work within the Ship Department where much of the work normally being done was not in fact being done. The net result was that, owing to these delays and likely difficulties, an in-service date of mid-1972 was looking increasingly unlikely with early 1973 being the most likely, although at worst this could be 1975.[47] A request for the release of £1.1

million for long-delayed development items, particularly for aircraft-handling gear, main machinery and ship's services, was turned down by the Treasury who offered only half this sum.[48] Alarmingly, the Chief Secretary, noting the conjunction of expenditure on the Polaris and aircraft carrier programmes, cut this to only £238,000, noting that work on aircraft-handling gear could be deferred, leading to reawakened fears for some in the Admiralty that the Treasury, or at least the Chief Secretary, was about to reopen the whole case for the necessity for carriers.[49] Pressure from the Minister of Defence led to a meeting between the First Lord and the Chief Secretary at which it was finally agreed that £600,000 of contracts could be let over the next year provided that they were so placed that the cost of cancellation would not exceed £70,000 before April 1964 and £250,000 by the end of 1964. The major outstanding items included contracts for the production of prototype arresting gear (£117,000), delayed catapult items (£302,000), design of aircraft lifts (£60,000) and main machinery installation design (£70,800).[50] With this agreement secured, DGS was concerned 'to avoid the delays and frustrations to which design work has been subject by the Treasury embargo on extramural work over the last 18 months' by securing authorisation of a further £2.7 million of contracts in 1964 with a further £5.1 million in 1965.[51]

Whilst waiting for a response on these items, the design team turned to the outstanding areas within the design. The aircraft complement had at last been clarified, with the First Lord and the Minister of Defence now thinking of a Rolls-Royce Spey-powered modified American-built Phantom as the fighter aircraft rather than a joint RN/RAF P1154.[52] Discussions between the Minister of Defence and the American Secretary of State for Defence, Robert McNamara, confirmed that this was a feasible development.[53] This, however, called into question flight deck arrangements as a folded Phantom was some 5 ft wider than a P1154, meaning that the outboard Alaska Highway would have to be widened, by moving the island inboard.[54] However, it was already believed that the island needed to be lengthened by at least 20 ft to provide separation between the macks so that radar and communications aerials could be mounted without interference and to provide adequate arcs for the tracker/illuminator radars for the CR299 Sea Dart system, more vital than ever since the dropping of the second 3D radar in early 1963.[55] These two issues also called into question the siting of the Ikara launcher as the proposed site abaft the island would be subject to jet blast from taxiing aircraft while the cramped island would be an unsuitable location for the launcher owing to the complex magazine arrangements this would entail. The only remaining option was to mount Ikara on the quarterdeck, although this would have obvious consequences for the firing arcs of the system, would conflict with the Sea Dart system and would displace the valuable aircraft running-up space.[56] Further consideration revealed a split in the Naval Staff when DGS reported that there was a stark choice between the running-up area and Ikara: those concerned with the anti-submarine defence of the carrier (DUSW) argued for the retention of Ikara, while those concerned with the operation of aircraft from the carrier, notably DNOR and DNTWP, argued for the retention of the aircraft running-up area which was 'an essential requirement for the full exploitation of the ship's potential'. The decision went in favour of the view that 'the operation of aircraft is the primary function of the aircraft carrier' and Ikara was deleted from the Staff requirements in December 1964.[57]

Fittings for the ship were also being firmed up: it was decided in June 1964 that the fitting of fin stabilisers, at a cost of 250 tons in weight and 550 tons of fuel stowage, could not be afforded within the limits of the design.[58] At the same time the fitting of three new-type rudders was also approved in order to save weight.[59] These weight-saving measures were much needed as ballistic protection had been increased in the ship's structure and a total of 1,471 tons had been added for magazine protection which 'cut deeply into our margins' so that 'we cannot be as sure as we would like to be that the 53,000 tons limit will not be exceeded'.[60] A newly established Watch Committee to oversee CVA-01 and the closely associated Type 82 destroyer therefore had the brief of reviewing the rate at which the design was being progressed but also the expected cost and any problem areas that might arise.[61]

The shipbuilders, design issues and cancellation

With the design finally progressing, although still with uncertainties surrounding the aircraft complement,[62] notably the AEW aircraft and ASW helicopters to be embarked, and with an added commando ship role to be worked out,[63] attention turned to the next stage in the process, the contract to be sought with the shipbuilders. As the project leader, Rydill, noted in January 1965, 'the crux of the problem is that for more than a generation neither MOD (N) nor the major warship builders have had the continuity of design for large aircraft carriers, the technical complexity of which has grown enormously'. This difficulty would be compounded by the fact that owing to the delays occasioned by the Treasury embargos, 'the information that will be available for tendering may not be as detailed as such a large project should merit'.[64] All were concerned to run a competitive tendering exercise in order to bring the ship into service on time and on cost.[65] However, from the start of the tender process, there were concerns as to how realistic this would be as few firms were in a position to take on the task of building the ship. The First Sea Lord summarised the position thus: 'there is only one firm, Harland & Wolff, which on its own could build CVA-01'.[66] As the DGS, Sims, summarised the position on 19 March 1965:

> Harland & Wolff are keen to get the carrier and are prepared to tender ... John Brown/Fairfield might tender, although I believe they might find it difficult once the facts are more clearly realised; the Swan Hunter/Vickers consortium are hedging to some extent and, in any case, I doubt whether the Tyne is now capable of building the carrier to the same timescale we have in mind; and Cammell Laird must have a query after their name.

This conclusion was confirmed by an assessment of the shipyard requirements which indicated that none of the firms concerned had the facilities to build and fit out the hull without substantial works being undertaken; again Harland & Wolff were in the best position, not least because they alone possessed the necessary prefabrication shops capable of handling 100-ton sections. Harland & Wolff was probably in the best position in terms of design effort and draughtsmen in its drawing office, although like all firms short of electrical draughtsmen, only 50 compared to the 130 required (although this constituted one-third of those employed by the six major firms).[67] Effectively, then, only one firm was a realistic contender for the contract, something of a drawback for a competitive tendering exercise.

The major production concern, as consideration of the tendering process continued through 1965, was the question of the approximately 8,000–9,000 tons of QT35 steel used in the major strength areas and as splinter protection in CVA-01; although this saved weight, it was both expensive and difficult to weld. In March 1965 it was noted that 'the shipyards concerned are unable to find enough welders of suitable quality' to weld to a high enough standard.[68] As the cost of CVA-01 crept upwards – now reckoned at £66 million in May 1965[69] – and as her weight also increased, likely to be over 53,000 tons, largely owing to an 800-ton increase in the estimated weight of her machinery,[70] attention therefore turned to the question of the amount of QT35 to be used in CVA-01. It was noted in September 1965 that removal of the QT35 used for protection would save £3 million while removal of all QT35 would save £5 million, helping, together with a more austere equipment and electronics fit, to reduce the cost of CVA-01 to somewhere between £51 million and £56 million.[71] Further investigation suggested that retaining 3,000 tons of QT35 steel for protection, 500 tons of which was in the side protection system, the remaining 5,000 tons being replaced by a lower-grade (QT28) steel, would save £2.5 million and make the welding process easier, albeit at a cost of a 7 per cent reduction in ballistic resistance and an increase in weight of 100 tons.[72] This was accepted by DGS in December 1965 as it would 'significantly reduce the welding task and speed up production', an argument of 'overriding importance when industry will be hard put to build this vessel expeditiously'.[73] In January 1966, one month before the cancellation, it was noted that although 'confidence is felt that ... the Navy will have a sound carrier', the estimated displacement had grown to 54,500 tons while concerns were expressed at the ability of the shipbuilders, whoever they were, to bring the ship in on price; therefore a final figure for the first of class, allowing for contingencies, of some £70 million was suggested.[74]

Ultimately, of course, CVA-01 was not cancelled for technical reasons or because it was too innovative; rather it was cancelled because the case for a new large and expensive carrier programme was not made by the Royal Navy in a political environment where the overriding governing constraint was finance and resources. However, the protracted design and procurement process caused by the difficulties surrounding the development of the ship and its equipment no doubt contributed to its demise. The task of designing and building the largest aircraft carrier ever for the Royal Navy, constrained as it was by extrinsic limits that forced the adoption of ever more novel solutions, would have been difficult enough without the constantly changing staff requirements. The innovations within CVA-01 were not adopted for their own sake, they were in a very real sense forced on the designers in an effort to meet the demanding and often contradictory staff requirements while holding down the size and cost of the ship for political reasons. Their work was hampered further by the lack of information on key new equipment occasioned by Treasury reluctance to sanction expenditure on research and development so that the design work after 1963 tended to proceed in a spasmodic and unsatisfactory fashion. This resulted in a less than fully detailed design which, in turn, cast further doubt on the ability – already the subject of reservations in some quarters – of the British shipbuilding industry to produce the ship on time and on cost. Small wonder then that there was a sense of relief at the cancellation of CVA-01; however, this relief must have been occasioned not just by misgivings over the innovations embedded in CVA-01, but also by an undoubted weariness caused by the tortuous and protracted design process.

Notes

1 Although the name HMS *Queen Elizabeth* was earmarked for CVA-01 on the initiative of the Chief of Defence Staff, Earl Mountbatten, with HMS *Duke of Edinburgh* for any follow-on CVA-02, these names were never in fact used. (I am grateful to Eric Grove for this information in The National Archive (TNA): Public Record Office (PRO), ADM 1/29044.) See also D. Hobbs, *Aircraft Carriers of the Royal and Commonwealth Navies* (London: Greenhill Books,

1996), 250. Therefore the well-known acronym CVA-01 will be used to indicate both the class and first of class.

2 Quoted in D.K. Brown, *A Century of British Naval Construction* (London: Conway, 1983), 229–30.

3 Ibid., 229. This observation is given added force, as D.K. Brown was himself a former figure in the Ship Department.

4 Hobbs, *Aircraft Carriers of the Royal and Commonwealth Navies*, 12.

5 See Eric Grove, *Vanguard to Trident* (Annapolis, MD: Naval Institute Press, 1987), chap. 3, and N. Friedman, *British Carrier Aviation* (Annapolis, MD: Naval Institute Press, 1988), chap. 16, for details of the fate of the Royal Navy carrier programmes in the 1950s.

6 National Maritime Museum, Historic Photographs and Ships Plans (hereafter NMM), ADM 138/818, Ships Cover 'Fleet Carriers, New Design 1952', Director of Naval Construction to Controller, 'Aircraft Carrier Policy', Feb. 1957.

7 On the timetabling of the process of design and procurement, see for example NMM, ADM 135/888, 'Ships Cover CVA-01', SCC/P(60)19, 'Timetable for replacement ships and aircraft', 1 June 1960.

8 NMM, ADM 138/888, 'Ships Cover CVA-01', Head of Military Branch I to DDNC, 14 Nov. 1958.

9 NMM, ADM 138/888, 'Minutes of Meeting to discuss the characteristics of New Aircraft Carriers', 10 June 1960.

10 NMM, ADM 138/888, AWD6666/60, DGS to DDNC/S1, 21 July 1960.

11 NMM, ADM 138/888, FRC(60)7, DTWP memorandum 'New Aircraft Carrier', 14 Nov. 1960.

12 Ibid.

13 NMM, ADM 138/888, FRC minutes, 17 Nov. 1960.

14 NMM, ADM 138/888, FRC(60)11(Revised), 'Size of the New Aircraft Carrier', 22 Dec. 1960.

15 NMM, ADM 138/888, Fleet Requirements Committee meeting, 5 Jan. 1961.

16 NMM, ADM 138/888, B1373, Admiralty Board Minutes, 21 Jan. 1961.

17 NMM, ADM 138/888, TWP2025/61, 'New Carrier Sketch Requirements', 5 June 1961.

18 NMM, ADM 138/888, TWP2025/61 Revised, 15 June 1961.

19 NMM, ADM 138/888, TWP2025/61 Revised, 9 Nov. 1961.

20 NMM, ADM 138/888, Minutes of Meeting held in the Admiralty, 9 Nov. 1961.

21 TNO PRO, CAB 131/27, D(62)6, 'Aircraft Carriers', 26 Jan. 1962, approved at D(62) 2nd meeting, 31 Jan. 1962.

22 NMM, ADM 138/888, SCC/P(62)3, DTWP/DGS memorandum 'New Aircraft Carrier Design', 23 Feb. 1962.

23 NMM, ADM 138/888, SCC/M(62)1, 2 Mar. 1962.

24 NMM, ADM 138/888, SCC/M(62)2, 7 Mar. 1962.

25 NMM, ADM 138/888, B5530, Admiralty Board Minutes, 2 Apr. 1962

26 NMM, ADM 138/888A, SCC/P(62)28, 'New Aircraft Carrier: Statement of Design Studies', 22 May 1962.

27 NMM, ADM 138/888A, SCC/M(62)5, 23 May 1962.

28 NMMH, ADM 138/888A, B1421, 'Design of New Aircraft Carrier', 12 June 1962.

29 NMMHPSP, ADM 138/888A, B5535, Admiralty Board Minutes, 20 June 1962.

30 NMMHPSP, ADM 138/888A, DTWP note, 17 July 1962.

31 TNA: PRO, ADM 1/26653, 'Work Study Number 2 – Flight Deck Layout New Aircraft Carrier Design', 1 Oct. 1962.

32 NMM, ADM 138/888A, SCC/P(62)47, 'New Aircraft Carrier Design – Arrangement of Flight Deck', 13 Dec. 1962, approved at SCC/M (62)9, 19 Dec. 1962.
33 NMM, ADM 138/888A, SCC/P(63)21 'New Aircraft Carrier Sketch Design', 5 June 1963.
34 NMM, ADM 138/888A, SCC/M(63)4, 12 June 1963.
35 NMM, ADM 138/888A, B5594, 17 July 1963.
36 *Hansard*, HC Debates 682/158, 30 July 1963.
37 NMM, ADM 138/888A, DGS note '1963/4 expenditure', 23 Aug. 1962.
38 Friedman, *British Carrier Aviation*, 343.
39 NMM, ADM 138/888A, DGS to Controller, 14 Dec. 1962.
40 NMM, ADM 138/888A, First Lord to Minister of Defence, 15 Mar. 1963.
41 NMM, ADM 138/888A, DGS brief for Admiralty Board, 8 July 1963.
42 NMM, ADM 138/888A, Boyd-Carpenter to Macmillan, 4 Oct. 1963.
43 NMM, ADM 138/888A, DNC 'New Carrier date of ordering', 8 Aug. 1963.
44 NMM, ADM 138/888A, Nash to Boyd-Carpenter, 16 Aug. 1963.
45 NMM, ADM 138/888A, ADNC/A 'New Aircraft carrier design', 16 Aug. 1963.
46 NMM, ADM 138/888A, DDNC brief for Controller, 7 Oct. 1963.
47 NMM, ADM 138/888A, DGS to First Sea Lord, 18 Dec. 1963.
48 NMM, ADM 138/888B, Head of Military Branch to Controller, 'Research and Development', 30 Dec. 1963.
49 NMM, ADM 138/888B, Nash note 'Ordering the New Carrier', 3 Jan. 1964.
50 NMM, ADM 138/888A, Mat. Branch 1 4/64, 10 Jan. 1964.
51 NMM, ADM 138/888A, AUS(Mat. N) to Treasury, 8 Apr. 1964.
52 NMM, ADM 138/888B, First Lord minute, 24 Jan. 1964. See Grove, *Vanguard to Trident*, 256–8, for the fate of P1154 in 1963.
53 NMM, ADM 138/888B, Thorneycroft to McNamara, 17 Feb. 1964, and McNamara to Thorneycroft, 22 Feb. 1964.
54 NMM, ADM 138/888B, SCC/M(64)4, 12 May 1964.
55 NMM, ADM 138/888B, SCC/P(64)18, DGS/DGW 'New aircraft carrier design: Island arrangements', 5 May 1964.
56 NMM, ADM 138/888B, SCC/P(64)30, DGS 'Siting of Ikara', 6 Aug. 1964, considered at SCC/M(64)6, 17 Aug. 1964.
57 NMM, ADM 138/888B, SCC/P(64)47, DNTWP 'Revision of Ikara Requirements', 7 Dec. 1964, considered at SCC/M(64)9, 17 Dec. 1964.
58 NMM, ADM 138/888B, ND/E/8/1, 18 June 1964.
59 NMM, ADM 138/888B, ND/Q/3/3, 18 June 1964.
60 NMM, ADM 138/888B, DNC note 'CVA-01 Ballistic protection', 20 Aug. 1964.
61 NMM, ADM 138/888B, OM(N)193/64, 'Establishment of Watch Committee', Oct. 1964.
62 NMM, ADM 138/888B, CWC/M(64)1, 8 Dec. 1964.
63 NMM, ADM 138/888B, SCC/M(64)9, 17 Dec. 1964.
64 NMM, ADM 138/888C, Rydill to DNC, 'Type of Contract', 26 Jan. 1965.
65 NMM, ADM 138/888C, CWC/M(65)1, 23 Feb. 1965.
66 NMM, ADM 138/888C, First Sea Lord to Minister of Defence (Navy), 14 Apr. 1965.
67 NMM, ADM 138/888C, DGS to Controller, 'CVA-01: approaches to possible tenderers', 19 Mar. 1965.
68 Ibid.
69 NMM, ADM 138/888C, DGS to Head of Mat Branch 1 (N), 'CVA-01: Unit Cost', 28 May 1965.

70 NMM, ADM 138/888C, DGS note 'CVA-01: Machinery Weight Estimates', 7 Sept. 1965.
71 NMM, ADM 138/888C, DGS note A1/ND/N/03, 16 Sept. 1965.
72 NMM, ADM 138/888C, A1 note 'CVA-01: Possibility of reducing the amount of QT35 steel', 28 Oct. 1965.
73 NMM, ADM 138/888C, DGS to DNC, 2 Dec. 1965 and 3 Dec. 1965.
74 NMM, ADM 138/888C, AP(66)5 'CVA-01', 21 Jan. 1965.

8

THE ROYAL NAVY AND THE GUIDED MISSILE

Eric Grove

Since the early 1960s guided missiles have played an increasingly dominant part in the capabilities of the Royal Navy. They were first developed in the surface-to-air role to deal with the threat of faster jet aircraft equipped with weapons capable of being fired at long range. Air-to-air and, later, air-to-surface missiles were adopted as the armament of carrier-based fighters while submarine-launched ballistic missiles were deployed for strategic nuclear deterrence. This was followed by the procurement of missiles for the anti-submarine and anti-ship roles. Finally, in the late 1990s, long-range cruise missiles were adopted to allow submarines to carry out precision conventional land attacks.

Seaslug

In the inter-war period the Royal Navy carried out experiments with a radio-controlled pilotless aircraft missile system called 'Larynx', but in the prevailing atmosphere of financial constraint the project proved abortive. The beginnings of development that would lead to deployed systems began in 1943 with a letter from the Admiralty Signals Establishment to the Director of Naval Ordnance. This argued for the virtues of guiding a missile by a continuously tracking radar beam. The idea was transmitted to the Assistant Controller and led to a 'directed projectiles' paper that was 'the first formal staff requirement for guided weapons issued anywhere in the United Kingdom'.[1] This argued that aircraft would soon be flying too fast and too high to be engaged by contemporary gun systems. They would be capable of launching guided weapons while manoeuvring (the Germans already had such weapons operational and had used them with success). Anti-aircraft gun systems would become obsolete.[2] A meeting was held and an inter-departmental 'Guided Anti-Aircraft Projectile' (GAP) Committee held its first meeting on 16 March 1944.[3] A Naval Staff Target was created calling for a system of as small a size as possible, capable of engaging targets at heights up to 50,000 feet and at speeds of up to 700 mph.[4] It was soon named 'Seaslug', a name that stuck despite recommendations at various times to change it (it became 'Triumph' for a period around 1949).

The Air Ministry opposed putting too much effort into systems that would probably not be in service before the war's end and which might delay production of jet aircraft. Development continued slowly, largely under the auspices of the Admiralty and the Ministry of Supply (MoS), with two committees, three technical panels and an executive office. In June 1945 a Director of Guided Projectiles was appointed within the MoS and a Guided Projectiles Establishment founded at Westcott, Bucks. In 1945 Seaslug was given priority over anti-surface weapons and it was hoped a system would be in service within two years. Post-war shortages of staff and materials combined with the dislocation of administrative reorganisation delayed the programme. In 1946 the Guided Projectiles Directorate was subordinated to the Controller of Supplies (Air) and the Royal Aircraft Establishment at Farnborough took over as the main development agency. Westcott became the Rocket Propulsion Department. Two Assistant Directors Guided Weapons were created, one of whom supervised four departments, one concerned with Seaslug.[5]

The new bureaucracy did not work well and the Admiralty chafed at the slow progress being made. In June 1947 it put pressure on the Defence Research Policy Committee chairman Sir Henry Tizard for more 'virile leadership' of the guided weapons programme.[6] The DRPC had just had its first meeting on the direction of guided weapons development. It considered that resources were being spread over too many projects and in July recommended that the MoS report as soon as possible on the efforts needed to solve the design and construction problems of four priority projects to be in service by 1957, the date by which Britain's services were to be ready for war. The four chosen projects were Seaslug, a long-range land-based ground-to-air missile; Red Heathen, a guided bomb; Blue Boar; and an air-to-air missile, Red Hawk.[7] A specification was issued in March 1948.

In July of that year the MoS report was completed. It concluded that there were not enough resources for all four missiles. The Air Ministry, asked for its views on priorities, hardly surprisingly put Seaslug third after Red Heathen and Blue Boar. Its comments on Seaslug were as follows:

> It is doubtful whether the successful development of Seaslug could be classified as an improvement in the top strategic category. Air attacks against shipping in the early stages of a war are not likely to be heavy .... It is perhaps more important to concentrate on anti-submarine warfare, and in any case probably more attractive targets on land in the early stages of war will draw attacks away from shipping.'[8]

Although 'every effort' should be made to develop Seaslug, Red Heathen should receive the majority of research and development effort.

Hardly surprisingly the Admiralty demurred. It 'could not agree with the assumption that guided weapons for the defence of the fleet should not be in the top strategic category'.[9] The Army (in charge of land-based air defence) had suggested that Seaslug be developed as a common medium-range (30,000 yards) sea- and ground-based surface-to-air missile (SAM) with equal priority to Red Heathen, and the Admiralty welcomed this suggestion. The DRPC, worried about the guidance difficulties of the 100,000 yards range Red Heathen, endorsed this view and in September 1948 decided 'as a matter of insurance' to develop Seaslug as a common interim weapon.[10] This achieved top priority in the second 1949 DRPC annual R&D Review accepted by the Defence Committee of the Cabinet in August. The first firings of test vehicles took place that year on the range at Aberporth. Hopes for a relatively small 1,800 lb missile without separate boosters and capable of vertical launch guided by a homing system had to be abandoned in the interests of practicality, given the weapon's high priority. By 1949 Seaslug had become a liquid-fuelled missile with wrap-round solid-fuelled boosters which would be launched from a directable launcher to fly down a radar beam to its target. The system was the joint responsibility of an industrial 'Project 502' group (Armstrong Whitworth, assisted by Sperry for flight controls and GEC for guidance), the MoS and the Admiralty, the last named anxious at the opportunities the organisational complexity still created for delay.[11] In October the Chief Scientist at the MoS warned that 'due to its limited performance and production difficulties' the Armstrong Whitworth missile could not be 'recommended for Army use except in emergency'.[12] Bristol/Ferranti had become involved in Seaslug in 1949 to investigate alternative technical approaches to this priority weapon and its project was continued as Red Duster for land-based use (eventually by the RAF who took over national air defence in 1953). It entered service as Bloodhound in 1958.

In 1950 'guided missiles of all types' were given the highest priority in the Government's Global Strategy Paper.[13] A Chief Executive for guided weapons was appointed but it was clear that Seaslug would not be ready for some time. The Admiralty did consider trying to obtain the more compact American Terrier missile which would be in service more quickly and have less ship impact, but there was uncertainty as to whether the Americans would sell as well as a desire not to be dependent on foreign supplies.[14]

The first firings of Seaslug test vehicles took place at Woomera in 1950 but the next such firings in Australia did not take place until 1953 as the programme suffered from the Conservative Government's slowing down, redirecting and cutting of the Attlee Government's rearmament. The following year Seaslug launchers were built at Woomera and in November the first Research and Development 'motored test vehicle' was fired. This worked well, but the second shot in December 1954 was a 'messy business' and a failure in most respects.[15] The petrol/nitric acid liquid fuel mix proved tricky to handle and guidance and control problems were serious. As money for missile projects was squeezed, cancellation of Seaslug was being considered at the end of the year.[16] The need for a task force air defence weapon in both nuclear and limited war saved it. Public commitment to missile ships would also have made cancellation somewhat embarrassing. In his speeches in 1954 the First Lord, J.P.L Thomas, stressed that development of missile ships would be speeded up and that the three Tiger-class cruisers being completed to modernised designs would probably be the last all-gun major surface warships to be built.[17]

Although American missiles were again being considered if licences could be obtained, Seaslug remained the only realistic and national option. Its technical problems *were* slowly being solved. Solid-fuel sustainers were under development and were available by 1955. They proved their superiority as liquid-fuelled Seaslugs continued to explode both on the launcher and in the air; the solid-fuel Foxhound sustainer motor was officially adopted in 1957. Troubles continued, however, with both guidance and control difficulties and Woomera results remained generally 'dismal', the trials being 'one long struggle'.[18] There was a pause in firings in mid-1957 and better results were finally obtained when they were resumed later in the year. Six missiles flew and two achieved successful beam riding. By the end of 1957 the Seaslug project was being costed at £25–30 million.[19] It was decided by the Cabinet Defence Committee that it should be kept as simple as possible with improvements kept to a minimum to assist its entry into service as early as possible. Improvements would go into a Mark 2 version.

Seaslug was a big weapon, 20 feet long with a wing span of 5 feet. Four boosters were wrapped around the forward part of the rocket with their jet launchers adjacent to the wings. The booster exhausts were angled outwards to avoid the need for wide stabilising fins and to reduce flame envelopment of the ship-borne launcher. It was only suitable for relatively large ships. Installing the system on the battleship *Vanguard* was considered, but by the end of 1950 serious plans were being made for both a slow coastal convoy escort Seaslug ship and a faster fleet vessel. Given the priority for convoy escort the former had priority, and it was hoped that the earmarked Seaslug trials ship, the former maintenance vessel HMS *Girdle Ness*, could double as an operational escort. Difficulties in accommodating a war complement meant, however, that she could only be used for trials. Conversion began in 1953 and she was commissioned three years later with a twin launcher forward.

An early plan for a fleet Seaslug ship was to convert Majestic-class light fleet carrier hulls with a triple launcher at each end, but these were felt to have insufficient speed and the idea was abandoned in 1951.[20] July 1952 saw a decision to develop a new construction ocean-going escort missile ship and, by the following year, designs in the 10,000-ton class were being considered by the Ship Design Policy Committee, which considered them rather large for convoy escort. As strategy began to swing back to fleet work, conversions of cruisers were considered and by 1954 a new build missile cruiser was the preferred option, a high-speed ship of over 10,000 tons of which three were intended in the first instance.

The precise configuration of the new cruiser and its dependence on missiles was a matter of debate. The new Soviet Sverdlov-class cruiser was reasserting the anti-surface role and in 1953 the idea was put forward of a surface-to-surface missile that could outrange the existing 6-inch gun and be usable before carrier air strikes. In the immediate post-war period the Admiralty had proposed for ship-to-ship use both a 50,000-yard low-trajectory missile with underwater impact and a similarly ranged missile for attack at steep angles, together with a 'zonal' ship-launched airborne torpedo weapon.[21] None of these interesting concepts had survived the 1947 prioritisation and now a Blue Slug surface-to-surface variant of Seaslug was proposed. Its hitting power would only be limited and by 1955, therefore, a nuclear warhead was being considered which could also be fitted to Seaslug, the latter for use against formation targets. Nuclear Seaslug could be used in the surface-to-surface role and, with no spare industrial capacity to develop it, the specialised Blue Slug was cancelled in 1956.[22] Nuclear Seaslug was still some years away, so double-ended designs of cruiser were shelved and by 1957 the missile cruiser had become a 687-foot-long, 18,450-ton monster with a Seaslug launcher aft, two twin 6-inch mountings forward and two twin 3-inch guns on each beam. A 984 radar and comprehensive display system analogue computerised action information system was to be fitted.[23] The ship's company was over 1,100.

Time was running out on this ambitious project too, however, and in the context of the Sandys Review in 1957 the ship was cancelled. A more cost-effective platform for Seaslug had been under development since 1955 in the shape of missile-armed fleet escorts built along destroyer lines but increased in size to 6,000 tons, making them, in effect, light cruisers. The ship's companies of these ships would be less than half those proposed for the cruisers. The Admiralty considered that a substantial number of these 'guided missile destroyers' (the first four of which were in the 1955–6 and 1956–7 progammes) together with four aircraft carriers would both be adequate to deal with the air and surface threats and be a programme that could be sold to a defence minister devoted to the rapid development of guided missiles. The cruiser fleet would be run down and eventually disappear.[24]

Aircraft carriers remained the main 'fists of the fleet' and the delayed development of Seaslug meant that the first guided missiles actually to enter service with the Royal Navy were with the Fleet Air Arm in the air-to-air role. The British infra-red homing Firestreak, developed by De Havilland at considerable expense since 1952, entered service for the Sea Vixen all-weather fighter in 1958. The American Sidewinder was, however, adopted for the Scimitar, passing its acceptance trials in 1963; it proved generally superior with greater development potential.

In the immediate post-war period, just as innovative ship-launched weapons were being explored (see above), a number of interesting Naval Staff ideas had also been put forward for guided air-to-surface weapons. One was Nozzle, a 10,000-plus yard range supersonic missile, and another Zoster, a 21,000 yard range flying torpedo.[25] These were casualties of the 1947 setting of priorities. There was also Admiralty interest in the television-guided Blue Boar guided bomb that was eventually cancelled in 1954. An attempt to produce an anti-ship air-to-surface missile with a radar homing head for carrier-based aircraft, codenamed Green Cheese, was cancelled in 1956. The most certain 'Sverdlov' killing device for aircraft reverted to the Red Beard 15 kiloton range nuclear bomb delivered, in the first instance, by Scimitars. Scimitar was also the first platform for the American Bullpup command-guided air-to-surface missile that entered service in 1962.

In 1958 Seaslug seemed at last to be coming good. The First Sea Lord, Lord Louis Mountbatten, reported enthusiastically to flag officers on the success of *Girdle Ness*'s latest firings in the Mediterranean. A new system to gather the missile into the beam had been fitted and subsequently ten missiles had been fired. Two had passed within the lethal radius of the Firefly drone target at 20,000 yards and 15,000 feet, two had been fired at low elevations and short range to achieve a high crossing rate, and two had fired as a salvo. All had successfully ridden the beams and the first of the salvo had hit the Firefly at 21,000 yards and broken it into two parts. The 901 radar had followed the larger piece of wreckage down and the second missile had followed the descending beam until the Seaslug had been signalled to self-destruct. On Sandys' strong recommendation, therefore, the Cabinet's Defence Committee had finally approved Seaslug.[26] Development, however, remained troubled, with half the Seaslugs fired at Woomera in 1959 being failures.[27]

The first of the new guided missile destroyers, HMS *Devonshire* and HMS *Hampshire*, were duly laid down in March 1959. The next two, *London* and *Kent*, followed the next year. They were big ships, 6,800 tons full load, but not big enough to carry the 984 radar and its associated command system. This would have precluded the carrying of guns necessary for peacetime gunboat duties. Two twin 4.5-inch weapons were therefore mounted forward with a twin Seaslug launcher aft fed from a forward magazine through a 'tunnel' in which checks were carried out and the missiles fitted out with wings. Thirty-six missiles were carried with provision for two nuclear-armed weapons to be added in the tunnel, but nuclear warheads were not expected until the Mark 2 missile appeared in the mid-1960s. The destroyers were connected to the command systems of the carriers they were to escort by innovative digital data links. This made up somewhat for the lack of a complete command system in the ships themselves.

Devonshire was launched in June 1960, by which time acceptance trials were in progress at Aberporth and in HMS *Girdle Ness*. Results were better, Aberporth reporting in August that of twenty-one firings against target aircraft, thirteen had been successful. By the time Seaslug Mark 1 development concluded at Woomera in September 1961 the success rate there was 80 per cent.[28] The Seaslug programme had been long and expensive and in July 1960 the Public Accounts Committee had strongly criticised it. Seaslug was now costed at £70 million, more than twice previous estimates that were condemned as unrealistic. The Committee strongly criticised the financial control of the project and stated that the system's delayed entry into service was 'inexcusable'.[29]

Seacat

These new 'Counties' would also carry a second type of guided missile, Seacat, whose development had been neither so protracted nor so expensive. This was a close-range (3,500 yards) anti-aircraft weapon intended for small ships to replace light anti-aircraft guns whose accuracy and hitting power against the latest air threats was becoming suspect. A short-range 'Popsy' missile proposal had been cut in 1947 but development of a similar 'Green Light' began in the mid-1950s, despite attempts to strangle it almost at birth in 1955 (in the same discussions that almost killed Seaslug). Short Brothers and Harland were in charge of the project with an estimated project completion date of 1960–1. Seacat was a relatively simple radio-command subsonic (0.6 Mach) guided weapon. It was carried on a quadruple launcher and operated from a director in which a skilled operator acquired the target visually and then guided the missile by joystick to the target. A tracking radar was later linked to the aimer's binocular sight. Range was 5,000 yards maximum and 1,500 yards minimum, and maximum altitude 3,300 feet.

In 1959, the Daring-class destroyer HMS *Decoy*, one of the four later members of the class fitted with alternating current, began conversion with a Seacat launcher for trials. She went to sea with the new equipment in May 1960 and the system was prepared for entry into service in 1962. It was first fitted in the four Battle-class destroyers converted as radar pickets that were commissioned in the first half of the year. These carried a single quadruple launcher aft. The new County-class destroyers were fitted with two launchers, one on each beam. *Devonshire* commissioned in

November 1962 and the other three the following year. In 1963 it was decided not to fit all four AC Darings with Seacat and the system was removed from *Decoy*.

Seacat remained in short supply. Even the new ships for which it was now primarily reserved suffered delays in fitting. It had been intended to mount it in both classes of new general-purpose frigate, the 'first-rate' Leanders and 'second-rate' Tribals, but only the last of the seven Tribals, *Zulu*, received it on commissioning in April 1964. The first seven Leander-class first-rate frigates that began to be commissioned in 1963 also had to make do with 40 mm guns. HMS *Naiad*, commissioned in March 1965, was the first Leander to carry Seacat. As Seacat became more available in the late 1960s it was retro-fitted to earlier Tribals and Leanders as well as being fitted to older ships, the second batch of Type 12 frigates on their rebuilding to near Leander standard, two of the Type 61 aircraft direction frigates and the last surviving 'C' class destroyers.

Although primarily intended for smaller ships, Seacat was also fitted as close-in defence for larger units. The carrier *Eagle* was fitted with six launchers in her major reconstruction that was completed in 1964 and *Hermes* received two launchers in her 1964–6 long refit. The two assault ships *Fearless* and *Intrepid*, launched in 1963–4, were also fitted with four mountings each around the superstructure and the two helicopter cruiser conversions *Blake* and *Tiger*, commissioned in 1969 and 1972, had two Seacat launchers each, one on each beam.[30]

Two more 'Counties' were laid down in 1962, *Kent* and *Fife*. These were to carry the Mark 2 version of Seaslug. This took shape as a weapon with a performance at least 20 per cent better than its predecessors. It had much greater effectiveness against low-flying aircraft as well as an enhanced range at high altitude of over 20 miles at 65,000 feet. It would also be suitable for anti-surface use at similar ranges. In 1960 it was estimated that 10 per cent of Mark 2s would be fitted with nuclear warheads. These latter plans were finally abandoned in 1962 with doubts over the prospects of warhead release in limited war and the usability of the weapon against many surface targets both afloat and ashore.[31]

The Mark 2 Seaslug was extensively changed. More powerful boosters and sustainers were fitted and different kinds of warhead. The latter could be initiated by proximity (60 metres), by impact or by command. The beam riding guidance was more advanced, being modified to allow missiles to carry out 'up and over' manoeuvres against surface and low-flying air targets as well as engage guided missiles. Development trials of this 'technically ambitious project' took place at Woomera between 1961 and 1964 and despite problems with the new motors were successfully concluded. Acceptance trials were carried out, both at Woomera and Aberporth, in 1965. Of the four firings at Woomera that year, three successfully shot down the targets; the fourth suffered a control system fault.[32] Seaslug Mark 2 entered service with HMS *Fife in* June 1966; *Kent* followed in October. Earlier in the year two sisters had been laid down. They were commissioned as *Norfolk* and *Antrim* in 1970.

Polaris

By this time a much larger missile had entered the naval inventory, Polaris. When first informed of America's Polaris plans the Admiralty had not been too keen on the immediate deployment of a force of strategic nuclear deterrent submarines. The context of the continuing process of defence review advised caution as the RAF could only respond to a naval attack on its V-bombers with a counter-attack on carriers. The arrival of that old enemy of the carrier programme Duncan Sandys as Defence Minister only made the situation potentially more sensitive. When the Board of Admiralty discussed American plans for Polaris in 1957, the First Lord set out the situation with clarity. He argued that the combination of Polaris with the nuclear submarine would be the successor of the strategic bomber and it was only a question of

> when, and not whether, the Admiralty should seek the resources to introduce the combination into the Royal Navy. Nevertheless he felt that the present time was not the moment at which to raise the subject in discussions of defence policy. Such a move made at an early stage might present the Minister of Defence with an opportunity of setting one service against another, perhaps to the detriment of the Navy's position, in the forthcoming deliberations of the defence committee. The Board agreed that it would be inexpedient for the present to urge any claim to equip Royal Naval submarines with ballistic missiles, though there would be advantage in drawing attention discreetly to such publicity as might be given in the USA to the progress of the Polaris missile.[33]

Mountbatten was a strong supporter of Polaris in principle but, as he told the flag officers in 1958, 'we have made no bid for Polaris because we cannot afford this weapon out of navy votes. If opinion swings towards putting the deterrent to sea, we want the money for Polaris to be found from the overall defence vote.'[34] The situation was made more difficult still by the Admiralty's views on the whole question of the nuclear deterrent. In its opinion, 'from a strictly military point of view we do not believe the requirement for an independent nuclear deterrent to exist'. There was, however, from the 'political' point of view the need to make 'some contribution to the Western deterrent as a whole', about commensurate with the existing V-force, but 'not with the enormous missile programme designed to overlap and eventually replace it' (i.e. the land-based Blue Streak).[35] A relatively small Polaris force could be such a deterrent, but the first priority was 'first rate equipment' for conventional forces.

In 1959 the Admiralty carried out a study that vindicated Polaris as a practical and invulnerable nuclear deterrent system, but inter-service politics advised going along with the decision to obtain Skybolt air-launched ballistic missiles as the interim replacement for Blue Streak. Polaris might have to wait until the 1970s but, in mid-1960, the Director General Weapons, Rear-Admiral Michael Le Fanu, wrote contingency plan for Polaris procurement that argued the case for an executive organisation that would cut across functional responsibilities.[36] As Skybolt began to look doubtful later in the year, Mountbatten, now Chief of Defence Staff, pushed the Polaris case with Defence Minister Harold Watkinson who agreed that if Skybolt was cancelled Polaris would be procured.

These circumstances came to pass in late 1962 and as a result of the Kennedy–Macmillan summit agreement at Nassau it was agreed that the United States would supply Polaris missiles to Britain. The Board of Admiralty agreed to put into effect the basic architecture worked out by Le Fanu (now Third Sea Lord) two and a half years before. A Polaris Executive was set up under a distinguished submariner, Rear-Admiral H.S Mackenzie. A sales agreement was signed in Washington in April 1963 that was on very favourable terms for the British: retail cost plus 5 per cent as a contribution to development. The missiles would be the latest Polaris A3s. Using modern management techniques the Polaris executive ran a model programme both on time and at £350 million within 5 per cent of estimated cost. HMS *Resolution*, the first British ballistic missile-firing nuclear-powered submarine (SSBN), fired the first UK Polaris on 15 February 1968. She carried out her first deterrent patrol in June. A year later, with two more SSBNs in commission, the Royal Navy officially took over the strategic deterrent role from the RAF.

There was a cost to this success, however. The RAF had indeed felt forced to attack the naval programme to carve out a role for themselves in limited war 'East of Suez'. The carrier programme was cancelled and in 1966 significantly, in a frosty meeting with the Admiralty Board after this had been decided but not yet announced, Secretary of State for Defence Denis Healey had specifically mentioned the Navy's responsibility for the strategic deterrent as a basis for a 'firm and assured' naval future.[37] Mountbatten's hopes were borne out in extra resources for Polaris coming from the defence programme as a whole, but the opportunity costs for the rest of the Navy were not negligible. In 1971, with an upgrade programme beginning (see below), the Admiralty Board set out the situation with alarming clarity. The Polaris programme, they said, 'showed considerable increases which could not be cut without prejudicing the maintenance by the Navy of the British nuclear deterrent. The high priority rightly accorded to this part of the Naval programme inevitably reflected adversely on the remainder.'[38]

Ikara

Development of three key new tactical missiles for 'the remainder' of the naval programme had begun in the 1960s. The first, chronologically, was the anti-submarine missile Ikara designed for the rapid delivery of a lightweight homing torpedo over a submarine detected at 20 kilometres or more by long-range sonar. This had originated in 1959 in Australia as Blue Duck and a basic design was drawn up by 1960. It was powered by a solid-fuel booster/sustainer and was computer guided by a two-way command link from the firing ship. The missile was first launched at Woomera in 1963 and the Royal Australian Navy began sea trials. The Royal Navy was enthusiastic and in March 1965 a formal agreement on Ikara's development for RN service was signed.[39] Its first platform was to be the new 'small escort', the Type 82 'frigate' (later 'destroyer'), of which eight were planned with initial entry into service in 1970–1. The new ship was a high priority in order to get Ikara and the new Sea Dart surface-to-air-missile to sea as soon as possible.[40]

The end of the carrier saw the Type 82 programme reduced to one ship, HMS *Bristol*, whose survival had much to do with her new weapons systems. The month she was laid down, November 1967, the Admiralty Board still wanted to get as many Ikara launchers to sea as quickly as possible and decided that the five Leanders should be converted to carry the system with the missiles mounted forward instead of the guns.[41] This programme was later increased by three hulls to eight ships in all. The opportunity was taken to mount a much heavier Seacat armament with three launchers in place of one. Beginning with *Leander* herself, the conversions were completed between 1972 and 1978. The Ikara Leanders were advanced ships with data links to integrate their weapons with task forces, but they turned out to be over-specialised and not very suitable for general service on their own. None was sent to the Falklands. Although the missile was a technical success, the Royal Navy preferred a more versatile helicopter as a means of ASW torpedo delivery and the system was not maintained beyond the end of the Cold War.

Sea Dart

The other system intended for the Type 82 was Sea Dart, development of which was begun as CF299 in 1963. Designed to be both more compact and longer ranged than Seaslug (over 40 miles), and a replacement for both it and Seacat in ships that carried it, Sea Dart was developed as a two-stage missile with a solid-fuel booster and a ramjet sustainer.[42] The guidance is semi-active with two 909 radars being carried to illuminate the target, the missile homing on the reflections. Development trials at Woomera were carefully planned and began in 1965, but many technical problems were faced and overcome before they were completed at the end of 1968. Acceptance trials were also delayed by problems, one being a serious fire in HMS *Bristol* shortly after commissioning in 1973. By March 1974 the system was in service, but trials at Woomera in 1975–6 continued to improve reliability and performance against low-altitude targets. A new generation of smaller 4,000-ton Type 42 'destroyers' was being built for the system and the first, HMS *Sheffield*, was commissioned in 1975. Sea Dart complement was only 22 missiles compared to 40 in *Bristol*. Sea Dart was also intended for the new large cruiser, with a forward mounting. The decision to convert these ships into 'proto carriers' with 'through decks' did not see the end of Sea Dart and all three 'Invincibles' were completed with the system on the starboard bow.

Sea Wolf

The advent in the 1960s of an increasingly formidable array of anti-ship missiles in the hands of Cold War enemies stimulated both the development of chaff rockets as countermeasures for 'soft kill' and the development of an improved short-range missile for 'hard kill' of incoming hostile missiles. Work on the latter had begun in 1963 with the British Aircraft Corporation's Confessor programme. More detailed design work was carried out in 1966 and in 1968 a development contract was placed with a consortium of BAC, Vickers, Ferranti and EMI. Sea Wolf, as it became, is an unpowered dart rapidly boosted to supersonic speed by a solid-fuelled booster. The missile is automatically guided by radio command to the target by the guidance radar tracking both target and missile; back-up TV guidance is also fitted. Technical and programming difficulties had delayed Sea Wolf by a year by 1970 but trials began at Aberporth that year.[43] The radar continued to give trouble and not until 1973 were successful firings being carried out with consistency. The programme moved from development to evaluation in 1974 and this was completed at Woomera in 1975. The disarmed Leander-class frigate HMS *Penelope* was then used as trials ship and the system was ready for service in 1979.[44] Sea Wolf, once developed, demonstrated impressive capabilities, including an ability to engage shells in flight.

A new Type 22 frigate had been designed around a double-ended Sea Wolf installation with a sextuple launcher fore and aft, but the delays to the system by 1970 caused the Admiralty Board to add two more ships to the Type 21 programme of frigates to be launched in the early 1970s to replace older 'second-rate' ships. These eight vessels carried the latest

GWS24 version of Seacat on a single quadruple launcher aft. The missiles could be fired from the ship's operations room using both television and the ship's radar. The first Type 22, HMS *Broadsword*, was laid down in 1976 and one a year followed for the rest of the decade.

Exocet

Both these types of frigate carried the French-made Exocet surface-to-surface missile. The forthcoming demise of carrier strike aircraft had led the Royal Navy to put some emphasis on the development of specialised anti-ship missiles for surface and submarine launch. Admiralty Board minutes of 1970–2 show great enthusiasm for them.[45] The missile chosen for surface launch was the MM38 Exocet sea-skimming radar homer being developed by Aérospatiale in France. Its early trials were observed with close interest at Board level and joint evaluation with the French and West Germans began in 1973. Some modifications were necessary, but in 1974 the thirty rounds fired scored 91 per cent hits.

In 1972 the County-class missile destroyer HMS *Norfolk* had been taken in hand for conversion to carry four Exocets in place of the 'B' 4.5-inch forward gun mounting. In 1974 she took part in the trials on the French range, becoming the first RN surface ship ever to fire a surface-to-surface missile. Her three Seaslug Mark 2 sisters, *Antrim, Glamorgan* and *Fife*, were also soon converted to Exocet, the Mark 1 ships not being considered suitable investments because of the obsolescence of their main armament. Exocet was added to new Type 21s from the third unit HMS *Active*, commissioned in 1973, and a second batch of Leanders was converted to carry four missiles instead of the forward 4.5-inch gun mounting from 1975; like the Ikara ships these also had three Seacat launchers, one forward and two aft. Also like the Ikara Leanders they had no guns bigger than 40 mm and were effectively all-missile ships, a pattern followed by the Type 22s and the last batch of broad-beam Leanders that began conversion in 1977. The latter had four Exocets and a single Sea Wolf installation, both forward. Plans to fit Exocet to the new cruisers were abandoned as their Sea Harriers were more potent strike systems. The effective surface-to-surface capability of Sea Dart also meant that Exocet was not necessary in the Type 42s.

Sub-Harpoon

Providing an undersea guided weapon (USGW) took longer than procurement of the ship-launched missile, although the need to supplement Britain's disappointingly limited torpedo capability was so urgent that nuclear-tipped torpedoes were even being considered. A version of the Anglo-French Martel air-launched missile, intended for the Royal Navy's

Buccaneers and Sea Harriers, had been under consideration at the end of the 1960s. A project definition study was approved by the Admiralty Board in 1972. The submarine-launched version of the long-range American Harpoon missile was eventually chosen, but this took time and it was only in 1980 that HMS *Churchill* carried out trials. Sub-Harpoon finally entered service in 1982 in HMS *Courageous*.

Operations: Falklands to the Gulf 1991

The Royal Navy's first missile war took place in 1982 around the Falkland Islands. No British Exocets were fired and the missile, largely air launched, got a spurious reputation for lethality. It was easily decoyed away by chaff and only hit ships that either took no countermeasures (HMS *Sheffield*) or that could not take such measures (*Atlantic Conveyor*). The two available Sea Wolf ships, *Broadsword* and *Brilliant*, spent much time acting as 'goalkeeper' anti-Exocet protection for carriers, but the software problems of the missiles acting outside their designed performance envelope (the missiles had been designed for directly closing, not crossing, targets) prevented them acting as successfully as hoped with Type 42 destroyers in electronically linked 'combo' tactics. The Type 42s being given close-range protection were damaged (HMS *Glasgow*) or sunk (HMS *Coventry*). Sea Dart acting at the proper range did, however, shoot down six Argentine aircraft (and, accidentally, one British helicopter). Sea Wolf missiles accounted for four with a contribution to a fifth. Seacat shot down at least one aircraft and contributed to other kills, but its malfunctioning contributed to the loss of Type 21 frigate *Ardent*. No Seaslugs were fired in the anti-air role but HMS *Glamorgan* did fire some against the shore. The ships' missile defences played a key role in victory. They kept the Argentine aircraft at very low altitude, thus preventing most of their bombs from exploding. Missiles, however, had their limitations and light guns had played an important role. It was also found that medium calibre artillery was still a necessity for shore bombardment. The design of the last batch of Type 22s was altered to include a 4.5-inch gun and the new Type 23 frigate was also to be fitted with a similar weapon.

The main individual key to victory had, however, been the Fleet Air Arm's air-to-air missiles. Firestreak had been succeded by the improved Red Top in the Sea Vixen Mark 2 in the carriers of the 1960s, and the arrival of the Phantom in *Ark Royal* the following decade saw the entry into RN service of the radar-guided long-range American Sparrow missile as a complement to Sidewinder.[46] The Naval armaments facility at Beith became the single point reception facility for both Sparrow and Sidewinder, doing work for the RAF as well as the Fleet Air Arm. Sidewinder was the chosen air-to-air weapon of the Sea Harrier; the latest AIM-9L more than proved itself in the Falklands. Provided in large quantities by the Americans, its ability to be fired at all angles demoralised the enemy from the start. Eighteen aircraft were shot down by it against only three with cannon fire and a transport aircraft with both.[47]

Another system that had its combat début in the Falklands was the helicopter-borne air-to-surface missile. Following the sinking of the Israeli destroyer *Eilath* by missile-armed fast attack craft in 1967, the Wasp helicopters of RN frigates were equipped with French-made wire-guided AS-12 missiles for use against these threats. The missiles were used by Wasp helicopters from the ice patrol ship HMS *Endurance* to help disable the Argentine submarine *Santa Fé*. The advent of the more advanced Lynx with its surveillance radar increased the anti-small surface vessel role of ships' helicopters and a new 15 km range semi-active radar-guided missile, Sea Skua, was developed. Project definition began in 1972 and the first airborne firing of a guided round was in 1979.[48] The weapon was used to damage Argentine patrol vessels in the Falklands and came into its own in the Gulf War of 1991 when it sank four Iraqi boats and damaged another twelve.[49] Although the lethality of the warhead is limited, the advent of Sea Skua greatly increased the operational potential of the small-ship helicopter.

Chevaline and Trident

By the time of the Falklands War the defence debate was being dominated by the future of the British nuclear deterrent. The 1970s had seen considerable expenditure on this core capability. The need to modernise had been considered as early as 1967 but the obvious next step, the Poseidon missile with its multiple independently targeted re-entry vehicles (MIRVs), was turned down for political and financial reasons. Poseidon was offered again in 1970 but again a decision was delayed and by 1972 Prime Minister Heath was told that arms control considerations made it undesirable for Britain to ask for the missile. A project definition study was therefore carried out on a Polaris improvement programme that it was estimated would take five years and cost £175 million. The requirement was to penetrate the anti-ballistic missile defences around Moscow. At the beginning of 1974 it was decided to proceed and the decision was reaffirmed by the new Wilson government. Final approval for the programme was given in September 1975.[50]

Thus was born Chevaline, which replaced the warhead triplet of the earlier A3 with two hardened warheads, one of which was carried on a manoeuvring space vehicle. A large number of decoys made the interception task impossible, especially if many missiles were fired at the same target area. The Navy had its doubts about Chevaline; it would have preferred Poseidon, which it felt its connections with the US Navy would allow it to receive. Relations with the Atomic Weapons Research

Establishment at Aldermaston that was put in charge of the project were not good.[51] The Chevaline project was a technical success. The quality of its technological innovation led to the United States, which gave some access to its own thinking on 'Antelope' modifications to Polaris, requesting its exact details remain classified lest they be copied to defeat its projected ballistic missile defence system. Chevaline, however, did not come cheaply. When it was officially announced in 1980 the cost was over £530 million at 1974 prices or over a billion 1980 pounds. The first Polaris A-3TK missiles with 'Improved Front Ends' went to sea in the summer of 1982.[52]

By then the decision had been taken on a fully fledged new successor system. Working parties convened in 1978 which recommended retention of the nuclear force and set out technical options. Submarine-launched missiles remained the best option and although there was some support for cruise missiles, a MIRVed ballistic missile was the strongest contender. In 1980 it was decided to procure the Trident C-4 system in a new generation of SSBNs. The Navy had mixed feelings about this as it soon became clear that the Naval budget would bear even more of the cost than it had previously. The First Sea Lord referred to the programme as 'the cuckoo in the nest'. The Trident piority made it even more difficult to fit the Navy's long-term costings into expected defence provision. The budget was already under strain. Impressive new Type 43 destroyers had been designed to combine improved Sea Dart (with four 909 channels of fire) with Sea Wolf in ships comparable in capability to the 'Aegis' ships being built for the US Navy. These were abandoned around 1980 and the Navy fared badly in the following year's defence review. Exocet and Seawolf upgrades of Leanders were curtailed. Full modernisation of the Sea Dart system to increase its range and the number of targets the Type 42s could engage (along the lines of the 'New Threat Upgrade' modernisation of older missiles taking place in the United States) was cancelled.

When it became clear that the Americans were going to go for the D-5 version of Trident, the overriding need to prevent a future national Chevaline-type upgrade for C-5 forced Britain to follow suit. The short-term funding implications were, however, positive as the revisions to the programme and the decision to use American storage facilities allowed the retention of the two assault ships, even before the Falklands War had reasserted their utility. The Trident programme came to fruition in 1995 when the first of the four 16,000-ton SSBNs, HMS *Vanguard*, launched in 1986 went on her first operational patrol. The Cold War, for which the system had been designed, was over and the multiple warhead capability designed to penetrate further improved Moscow defences was unnecessary. The flexibility and accuracy of the system, however, allowed the Trident fleet to take over all Britain's nuclear delivery needs, both 'strategic and 'sub-strategic', and in 1995 it was announced that Trident would replace the

RAF's free-fall bomb capability. A low-yield option was added to its warhead.[53]

The end of the Cold War, modernization and Tomahawk

The shortcomings of Exocet were reflected in its replacement in new construction in the late 1980s by a longer-ranged weapon. The 60-mile range Sea Eagle, a British development of the Martel air-launched missile, was considered, but the already operational American Harpoon with a proven range capability of more than 70 miles was chosen in 1984. Exocet finally disappeared from service at the turn of the century. 1990 also saw the introduction of the vertically launched Sea Wolf, which solved the problem of having to reload the sextuple launchers by hand. Range was also slightly increased from 2.7 to 3.3 nautical miles. The new system was carried in the Type 23 frigates, sixteen of which were commissioned into the twenty-first century. The end of the Cold War, however, saw the demise in 1991 of a plan to develop a lightweight Sea Wolf system to give enhanced point defence capacity to the later Type 42s and the carriers (former 'cruisers'). The diminishing air threat also saw the latter eventually lose their residual Sea Dart launchers, so enhancing aircraft-carrying potential for power projection.

After the Falklands, Sea Dart received a series of incremental improvements, to guidance, motors, warhead and fusing, but it remained essentially limited to a 42-mile range and in the numbers of targets the ship could engage. This was due respectively to battery capacity and the need for the missiles rapidly to pick up the received energy of the two 909 radars. The continued utility of Sea Dart was, however, shown in the successful engagement of a Chinese-made coastal defence missile by HMS *Gloucester* while defending the American battleship *Wisconsin* in the 1991 Gulf War.[54] By the 1980s, however, it was already becoming obsolescent given the capacity of the American Aegis system to track and engage large numbers of targets. Aegis was offered to the British as part of US Secretary of the Navy John Lehman's 'Naval Defence Initiative' but was turned down because of an unwillingness to become totally committed industrially to the United States. A European approach was preferred with the development of the Principal Anti-Air warfare Missile System (PAAMS) developed by France, Britain and Italy. Using French Aster command-guided and active homing missiles of two sizes and ranges, this system was originally intended for the 'Project Horizon' ships to be built by the whole consortium. Britain eventually pulled out of the troubled combined project to build a PAAMS-equipped Type 45, the first of which is due in 2007. About nine ships of this class are likely; their individual engagement capacity will be many times an equivalent number of Type 42s.

In the 1980s Sea Eagle, rejected as a ship-launched weapon, was added to the carrier-based anti-shipping strike inventory for the RN's Sea Harriers. The following decade the combination of AMRAAM (Advanced Medium Range Air-to-Air Missile) with the Blue Vixen radar in the Sea Harrier FA-2 gave the Royal Navy probably the finest fighter capability in Europe with the possibility of beyond visual range (BVR) multiple engagements. The changed strategic environment and the disappearance of the main Soviet land-based air threat meant that this capability was doomed to a relatively short life. The FA-2 had a relatively disappointing land attack capability.

Power projection against the shore became ever more important to naval capability in the post-Cold War world. In the early 1990s, ideas of 'conventional deterrence' that had previously been unwelcome in the higher echelons of the Royal Navy were revised. A paper was written on the utility of precision conventional attack for coercion. The result was the announcement as a 'sweetener' to the Defence Costs Study of 1994 of the procurement of Tomahawk long-range land attack cruise missiles for the Royal Navy's submarine force. The Strategic Defence Review of 1997 announced that all ten of Britain's SSNs would be fitted for Tomahawk. In 1998 HMS *Splendid* became the first British submarine to fire Tomahawk and she was the first to receive a full war load. She went into action the following year in the air campaign against Serbia. Tomahawk was also fired by British submarines against Afghanistan in 2001 and Iraq in 2003. *Splendid* built up something of a record as having fired the largest number of Tomahawks of any submarine in the world. She contributed to the total of 24 Tomahawks fired in the attack on Iraq in 2003 before being decommissioned. The need for greater weapons capacity in cruise missile-firing submarines was reflected in the design of the new Astute class ordered in 1997, 38 as opposed to 25 in 'S' and 'T' class boats. As an interim measure Sub-Harpoon was taken out of service to make space for more Tomahawks. Modern torpedoes are at last sufficient to cope with the limited surface ship threat.

The twenty-first-century Royal Navy had become wholly or partly dependent on guided missiles for almost all its major roles, strategic and sub-strategic nuclear strike, long-range conventional land attack, air defence both long and short range, and (together with submarine-launched torpedoes) anti-surface ship warfare. Ikara had been something of a false start for anti-submarine warfare, although guided torpedoes launched in other ways remained the key to this capability. The gun still dominated short-range land attack, although the missile and the rocket-assisted guided shell promised much in this area also. The emphasis in the near term would be on providing surface warships with enhanced land attack capabilities, including more flexible land attack missiles on more platforms. Missiles would also remain at the heart of medium and close-in air defence. Although the procurement of missiles had sometimes been limited by technical and industrial infrastructure and by the resources that could be made available, the record in providing innovative capabilities stood comparison with other navies. The Royal Navy had – within overall national resources and capabilities – maintained its record for being at the forefront of technological innovation.

Notes

1 S.R. Twigge, *The Early Development of Guided Weapons in the United Kingdom* (Chur, Switzerland: Harwood, 1993), 95.
2 Ibid.
3 Ibid., 96.
4 E.J. Grove, *Vanguard to Trident* (Annapolis, MD: Naval Institute Press, 1987), 119. For sources on Seaslug development see The National Archive (TNA): Public Record Office (PRO), DO(49) 62 in CAB 131/7, DO(50) 96 in CAB 131/9, ADM 205/69, and Ships Cover 789, 'Guided Weapon Ship'.
5 Grove, *Vanguard to Trident*, 107–17.
6 Ibid., 117.
7 Ibid., 140.
8 Quoted ibid., 141.
9 Ibid., 142.
10 Quoted ibid., 146.
11 Ibid., 28–9.
12 Quoted in Twigge, *The Early Development of Guided Weapons in the United Kingdom*, 29.
13 TNA: PRO, DO(50) CAB 131/9.
14 Grove, *Vanguard to Trident*, 121, 343.
15 P. Morton, *Fire Across the Desert: Woomera and the Anglo-Australian Joint Project 1946–1980* (Canberra: Australian Government Publishing Service, 1989).
16 See Twigge, *The Early Development of Guided Weapons in the United Kingdom*, 177–81.
17 D. Wettern, *The Decline of British Sea Power* (London: Jane's, 1982), 99–100.
18 Morton, *Fire Across the Desert*.
19 Table from TNA: PRO, DEFE 7/266, in Twigge, *The Early Development of Guided Weapons*, 183.
20 See illustration on p. 123 of Grove, *Vanguard to Trident*.
21 See table of 10 June 1947 in DEFE9/9, quoted in Twigge, op. cit., 136–7.
22 For Blue Slug and nuclear Seaslug, see R. Moore, *The Royal Navy and Nuclear Weapons* (London: Frank Cass, 2001), 110–12.
23 See p. 205 of Grove, *Vanguard to Trident*, for a drawing.
24 TNA: PRO, ADM 167/150.
25 See note 21.
26 TNA: PRO, ADM 205/172.
27 Morton, *Fire Across the Desert*, 344.
28 Ibid.
29 Wettern, *The Decline of British Sea Power*, 180.
30 For fittings and dates see contemporary *Jane's Fighting Ships*.
31 Moore, *The Royal Navy and Nuclear Weapons*.
32 Morton, *Fire Across the Desert*, 344–5.

33 TNA: PRO, ADM 167/149.
34 TNA: PRO, ADM 205/172.
35 Ibid.
36 See Grove, *Vanguard to Trident*, for a more detailed account; this was based in large part on the then unpublished insider's account by P. Nailor. This has since been published as *The Nassau Connection* (London: HMSO, 1988).
37 TNA: PRO, ADM 167/166.
38 TNA: PRO, ADM 167/171.
39 Morton, *Fire Across the Desert*, 350–2, gives a good description of Ikara.
40 TNA: PRO, ADM 167/164.
41 TNA: PRO, ADM 167.
42 Morton, *Fire Across the Desert*, 353–4.
43 Ibid. and TNA: PRO, ADM 167/170.
44 Ibid., 354–5.
45 TNA: PRO, ADM 167/170–2.
46 A History of the Department of the Chief Inspector of Naval Ordnance (prepared by the University of Hull for MoD, 2003), 107.
47 Grove, *Vanguard to Trident*, 381.
48 N. Friedman, *The Naval Institute Guide to World Naval Weapons Systems* (Annapolis, MD: Naval Institute Press, 1997), 249.
49 Ibid.
50 Grove, *Vanguard to Trident*.
51 Conversations and witness seminars with participants.
52 Grove, *Vanguard to Trident*, 348.
53 D.J. Hawkings, *Keeping the Peace: The Aldermaston Story* (London: Leo Cooper, 2000), 61.
54 Friedman, *The Naval Institute Guide to World Naval Weapons Systems*, 410.

9

AMPHIBIOUS OPERATIONS, 1945–1998

Ian Speller

Prior to 1945 Britain had not maintained a significant specialist amphibious capability in peacetime. No such capability existed before 1914 and none was retained after the conclusion of the First World War. In the inter-war period the British adopted a policy of developing prototype equipment and a basic doctrine for amphibious operations without maintaining any forces specifically devoted to this mode of warfare. As such, they could avoid the cost of maintaining a standing force for what was seen as a low priority while retaining the ability to generate amphibious forces in future should the need arise.[1] Prior to the fall of Norway and France in 1940 the British did not anticipate conducting major landings in a future war against Germany or Japan and in this sense the policy was logical. The German victories in 1940 overturned the existing strategic reality and it became apparent that if Allied troops were to return to mainland Europe, some form of amphibious operation would be required. As a result, amphibious capabilities were expanded until by 1944 the Allies possessed a range and scale of forces that was unprecedented in the history of warfare. This, associated with a new proficiency in this field gained through training, experimentation and hard-won experience, provided the Allies with a war-winning instrument that was wielded with decisive effect in both the European and Pacific theatres of operation. By the end of the war the British possessed an understanding of amphibious operations rivalled only by the United States and had an amphibious fleet that included over 5,000 ships, craft and landing barges and over 100 amphibious vehicles.[2]

Despite this success, the British displayed a remarkable inconsistency in their approach towards amphibious operations in the years after 1945. In the late 1940s and early 1950s amphibious operations were generally accorded a very low priority, and amphibious capabilities suffered accordingly. From the late 1950s amphibious capabilities underwent something of a renaissance and during the 1960s amphibious operations once again became a high-priority activity for the armed forces. However, by 1975 this situation had been reversed, amphibious capabilities were cut back and it appeared possible that Britain might relinquish entirely its ability to conduct specialist amphibious operations. Although this situation did not in fact arise, amphibious operations continued to receive a relatively low priority throughout the 1980s. In yet another major change amphibious capabilities gained a new priority in the 1990s and this led to a second 'renaissance' akin to that which had occurred in the 1960s. The commissioning in 1998 of a new amphibious helicopter carrier (LPH), HMS *Ocean*, provided firm evidence of this change.

In the introduction to this book, Richard Harding defined innovation as a process that takes an idea or invention and converts it into a new product, structure or operational activity. Using this definition, the period 1945–98 was characterised by a considerable degree of innovation in British approaches to amphibious operations. This mode of warfare changed from being viewed as an inter-service responsibility relevant to major war operations to an essentially single-service responsibility linked to limited war contingencies. In the process the type of amphibious capability that was required changed, the institutional structure was altered and the style of operational activity envisaged was revised fundamentally. This chapter will examine this process in an attempt to show the reasons for and the impact of these changes. The process of innovation was the result of a variety of complex interacting factors that can be categorised broadly as strategic, technological, and institutional. Using these categories this chapter will examine the evolution of British policy towards amphibious operations in the period 1945–98 and will assess the impact of these factors on the process of change and innovation.

Strategy

Victory in the Second World War did not solve all of Britain's security problems. As early as 1944 the Chiefs of Staff had identified the Soviet Union as a potential future enemy and events after the war only served to reinforce this impression.[3] Given the numerical superiority of the Soviet army to the British and US occupation forces in Germany, and the weakened condition of the countries of Western Europe, British decision-makers were pessimistic about the possibility of stemming any Soviet offensive. In these circumstances, in the late 1940s Britain adopted a maritime/air strategy based upon defending the UK and vital overseas territories and waging a major strategic air offensive. Prior to the formation of the North Atlantic Treaty Organisation (NATO) in 1949, British and US forces planned to retreat in the face of overwhelming odds and withdraw from mainland Europe to either the UK or the Mediterranean. Eventually, once allied resources had been mobilised and the Soviets were sufficiently weakened, it would be possible to return to liberate the continent of Europe in a similar fashion to 1943–5. In such circumstances amphibious operations would have an important role to play. Amphibious raiding might be required in the rear and flank of the advancing enemy and in order to harass and tie down troops along the occupied coastline of Europe. Amphibious forces would play an important part in the evacuation of allied forces from the mainland, although, surprisingly, this role did not figure prominently in British assessments of their likely uses. Most notably, amphibious operations would be required to return the allied armies to Europe in a re-run of the Anglo-American landings of 1943–4.[4]

British thinking about post-war strategy was influenced profoundly by the experience of war and this was particularly true in the field of amphibious operations. In 1944 a joint committee on Inter-Service Responsibility for Amphibious Warfare had been established under the chairmanship of Air Marshal Sir Norman Bottomley to examine the requirements for post-war amphibious capabilities. The committee's conclusions, contained in a report that was submitted to the Chiefs of Staff on 29 June 1944, established the basic principles that would dominate British thinking about amphibious operations for the next ten years. The committee prepared and submitted their report at the same time that the Normandy landings of 6 June 1944 were being planned and executed. Perhaps inevitably, they used the model provided by recent Anglo-American operations in Europe as the basis for future planning. They sought to ensure that Britain's peacetime armed forces would remain ready to conduct similar operations in the future. Post-war economies pared down the ambitious organisation that they recommended; however, the basic strategic priorities that they established remained unchanged for a decade.[5]

The recommendations of the Bottomley Committee were centred on the belief that operations on a similar scale to the Normandy landings might be necessary in future. The scale and range of forces required for such operations were beyond the reach of any specialist amphibious force that Britain could afford to maintain and so it was accepted that the armed forces as a whole would have to become proficient in this mode of warfare. Thus, amphibious operations would be but one of the many different skills that all soldiers would learn. It would not be an activity confined to specialists. In order to achieve this, new training and educational establishments would need to be set up in addition to a large amphibious training fleet capable of embarking an entire division during a summer training period. The committee explicitly ruled out maintaining amphibious forces for circumstances short of major war. They believed that there would be little need for amphibious operations in such circumstances and any that should arise could be met by local army units utilising such craft as were available.

Unfortunately the committee's ambitious plans proved far beyond British resources in the 1940s. Plans for a Naval Assault Force capable of lifting a division were scaled down in 1947 to an 'Assault Training Force' able to embark a brigade group.[6] Even this reduced requirement remained unfulfilled and no standing amphibious force existed until 1951 when an Amphibious Warfare (AW) Squadron capable of embarking a battalion group was established, based at Malta in the Mediterranean.[7] The world-wide training organisation was never set up. A Combined Operations (later Amphibious Warfare[8]) Centre was created at Fremington in North Devon, consisting of a School, a Signals School and an Experimental Establishment. This centre, in conjunction with the Headquarters in London, attempted to maintain and develop British expertise in the field of amphibious warfare and provided instruction to officers from the UK and overseas. They also maintained a valuable liaison with their equivalents in the United States.[9] However, the policy of keeping the armed forces, as a whole, proficient in amphibious operations remained unfulfilled and there were few opportunities for unit-level training.

A key problem was that, although amphibious operations were expected to play an important part in a future war, major operations would not be required until the later stages of any conflict. Large-scale production of ships and craft could therefore be delayed until after mobilisation.[10] As such it was inevitable that amphibious capabilities would receive a lower priority than forces required during peacetime and in the early stages of war. This situation was exacerbated in the early 1950s when Soviet possession of a growing stockpile of atomic weapons posed an obvious threat to traditional-style amphibious operations. In these circumstances the requirement to conduct major landing operations was given even less priority. More emphasis was placed on the use of amphibious forces for the administrative discharge of cargo into the UK or troops into Europe after conventional port facilities had been devastated by atomic attack.[11]

Soviet possession of atomic weapons did little to affect the utility of amphibious raiding and a Royal Marine commando unit was raised specifically to conduct raiding operations during the Korean War.[12] However, even in this respect the lack of priority showed. The marines in Korea were equipped by the Americans and landed from American ships, craft and submarines. In the UK it was accepted that raiding operations in the first months of any war would be circumscribed by the failure to stockpile equipment needed for the rapid conversion of merchant ships into Landing Ships, Infantry.[13] The parlous condition of the amphibious fleet was demonstrated during the Abadan crisis in 1951 and again during the Suez crisis in 1956.[14] Britain still possessed a large number of ships and craft built towards the end of the war, but most were kept in low-priority reserve and could not be made available for operations at short notice and, increasingly, problems were experienced in the carriage of new heavier and bulkier army equipment.[15] The Amphibious Warfare Centre also suffered, being subjected to a series of reviews that resulted in cuts to manpower and funding.[16]

By the mid-1950s the extent to which nuclear weapons had changed the strategic environment was becoming more apparent. Military and civilian decision-makers were beginning to appreciate that a nuclear stalemate made major war in Europe less likely. At the same time there was a growing danger of instability in the rest of the world, not least due to the potentially destabilising effect of decolonisation in Africa and Asia. In these circumstances British defence priorities began to change. Avoiding 'global war' remained the highest priority, although this was increasingly viewed as a matter of nuclear deterrence. Beyond this, the ability to protect British interests overseas and to win any limited war should it break out was given a higher priority than the ability to wage global war should it actually occur. This shift in priority was apparent even before the Suez crisis demonstrated the danger of relying almost exclusively on forces designed mainly for major war and ill-suited to the requirement for rapid and effective intervention overseas.[17] The changing emphasis became more apparent after Britain's humiliation in Egypt and lay at the heart of Macmillan's defence policy.[18]

Inevitably these changes had an impact on attitudes towards amphibious operations. In June 1954 the Chiefs of Staff established an inter-service working party under the chair of the Vice-Chief of the Naval Staff, Vice-Admiral W.W. Davis, to review the future role of amphibious warfare.[19] The Davis Working Party built upon a position established by a Joint Planning Staff study in March.[20] They believed that the advent of the hydrogen bomb meant that in major war the requirement for amphibious operations was limited to raiding. As such, training in peacetime could be limited to the study of the staff work and techniques required for a brigade group assault, with exercises up to the strength of a reinforced battalion. There was no longer any requirement for the army as a whole to be trained in amphibious operations and they recommended that the Royal Marines, as amphibious specialists, should become the parent arm for such operations. The report was endorsed by the Chiefs of Staff and became the basis for future policy.[21]

The existence of growing numbers of atomic and hydrogen bombs in Soviet arsenals had made Normandy-style landings obsolete. The US Marine Corps had already reached a similar conclusion with respect to traditional-style assaults against a nuclear-armed opponent. With no obvious requirement to conduct major landings against an enemy during peacetime, it was inevitable that the conclusions of the Bottomley Committee would be overturned. The strategic environment had changed. As a result of this change amphibious operations became the primary concern of a small specialist corps and attempts to keep the armed forces as a whole conversant in this form of warfare were abandoned. This was a major change in policy, although in reality very few army units had been able to conduct serious amphibious training. As recommended, the inter-service Amphibious Warfare Centre at Fremington closed on 1 October 1956. It was replaced by a Joint Services Amphibious Warfare Centre at the Royal Marines establishment at Poole.[22] This centre remained under the overall control of the Chief of Amphibious Warfare until that post was abolished, along with Amphibious Warfare Headquarters, in 1962.

The immediate impact of the new strategic circumstances was thus to reduce the apparent utility of amphibious operations in major war. However, almost simultaneously there was a growing appreciation that amphibious forces could have utility in situations short of major war. Amphibious forces began to be viewed as a key means of exerting British influence overseas. They could provide a mobile and flexible intervention capability able to counterbalance the inevitable reduction in fixed land bases upon which the British presence in Africa and Asia had previously been founded. The Royal Navy's response to the changing strategic environment was encapsulated in a document entitled 'The Future Role of the Navy', submitted to the Chiefs of Staff Committee for consideration in July 1956, immediately prior to the Suez Crisis.[23] The paper articulated a shift in priority away from forces devoted to fighting a global war against the Soviet Union, with a new emphasis placed upon Cold War and limited war tasks. At the heart of the concept was to be the creation of a task group based at Singapore and centred on an aircraft carrier and a helicopter-equipped commando carrier. The utility of amphibious forces as a means of protecting British interests and projecting British power without undue reliance on overseas bases was to form a major part of British defence policy for the area east of Suez.

This change in emphasis was reflected in the 1957 Defence White Paper which stated that the role of the navy in major war was now 'somewhat uncertain' but that the navy and the Royal Marines provided a means of 'bringing power rapidly to bear in peacetime emergencies or limited hostilities'.[24] It was also reflected in the so-called 'Autumn Naval Rethink' of 1957.[25] By 1961 Admiralty[26] plans were based upon deploying four aircraft carriers,[27] two commando carriers and two assault ships east of Suez. This was based on the premise that Britain would retain all of its current bases. If this were not the case and no bases were available east of Suez except in Australia, they advocated what was called the 'double stance'. This provided for the permanent availability of an amphibious task force able to land and support a balanced brigade group, backed up by carrier-borne aircraft and the associated warships and supply ships. For rotational purposes and in order to guarantee the permanent availability of the force, a total of four commando carriers, four assault ships and six large aircraft carriers[28] would be required. The First Sea Lord, Admiral

Caspar John, sought to establish the inter-service credentials of the force, calling it the Joint Services Seaborne Force. It was clear that the 'double stance' would require a significant increase in resources for the navy, and although the Chiefs of Staff recognised that it was a desirable strategy given the uncertain tenure of Britain's overseas bases, it was ruled out on the grounds of cost.[29]

Despite this, the 1962 Defence White Paper announced that a fully effective joint services amphibious force would be maintained east of Suez.[30] The Admiralty planned to form an Amphibious Group consisting of three major vessels permanently in theatre, based at Singapore.[31] The 1962 Navy Estimates demonstrated the extent to which priorities had changed. Amphibious warfare was identified as the key role. All other activities were discussed in relation to their support for this mode of warfare.[32] Policy was supported by action. In 1959 the aircraft carrier HMS *Bulwark* underwent conversion into a helicopter-equipped 'commando carrier' capable of embarking and supporting in action a battalion-sized commando unit. In 1962 *Bulwark's* sister ship, HMS *Albion*, underwent a similar conversion. The obsolescent ships of the AW Squadron were replaced by two new assault ships (LPDs), HMS *Fearless* and *Intrepid*, commissioned in 1965 and 1967 respectively. Follow-on and logistic support was provided by the construction of six new Landing Ships Logistic (LSLs), launched between 1963 and 1967. In addition to this the number of Royal Marine commando units expanded from three in 1956 to five by 1961 and the Commando Brigade was enhanced by the inclusion of organic artillery and logistic units provided by the army.[33]

Unfortunately, by the time that all of this new equipment had entered service, the role for which they had been built had begun to change. Under pressure of economy the Labour Government elected to office in 1964 was forced to curtail defence expenditure. The immediate result was a cap on defence spending that resulted in an effective cut of £400 million on Conservative long-term spending plans. The inevitable result was a defence review conducted by the new Secretary of State for Defence, Denis Healey. From a naval perspective the most high-profile result of this review was the announcement in 1966 of the cancellation of plans to build a new large aircraft carrier, codenamed CVA-01.[34] From a broader perspective what was more significant was the rationale behind this decision. Although it was intended that Britain should maintain a 'major military capability' for operations outside Europe, three key constraints would apply: Britain would not undertake military operations without the aid of allies; it would not accept defence obligations to another country unless that country provided the facilities necessary to make such assistance effective; and there would be no attempt to maintain defence facilities in an independent country against its wishes. Significantly, the report also announced that:

> Only one type of operation exists for which carriers and carrier-borne aircraft would be indispensable: that is the landing or withdrawal of troops against sophisticated opposition beyond the range of land-based air cover. It is only realistic that we, unaided by our allies, could not expect to undertake operations of this character in the 1970s.

The cancellation of CVA-01 and the associated decision to phase out fixed-wing aircraft carriers in the 1970s had a major impact on naval policy, only partially offset by the eventual emergence in the 1980s of the small *Invincible*-class support carriers.[35] In the short term, however, the decisions of the defence review reinforced the need for amphibious capabilities. Reliance on a declining number of bases raised the value of mobile and flexible intervention forces. In 1967 a major study into future operations was conducted by the Intervention and Amphibious Capability Working Party at the request of Healey. The study concluded that air transport provided the quickest method of intervention where entry points were secure and where only a small, light force was required. However, it accepted that for larger operations where forces of brigade strength were needed or where entry points were not secure, a combination of amphibious and air transport was preferable.[36] As such, amphibious forces remained an important part of the special 'military capability' announced in July 1967 and designed to offset further cuts in the permanent British military presence east of Suez.[37]

By the late 1960s Britain's entire role east of Suez was beginning to be questioned.[38] In the aftermath of the November 1967 devaluation of sterling the government was forced to accept a further reduction of commitments with the announcement in February 1968 that all British forces would withdraw from the Middle East and Asia by 1971. In addition no special military capability for intervention was to be maintained, only a 'general capability' based on forces devoted to NATO would be retained.[39] This new approach survived the change in government in 1970 relatively unscathed. The 1975 Mason defence review carried its logic further, withdrawing almost all of the few forces that remained east of Suez and concentrating British assets in Central and Northern Europe.[40] John Nott's 1981 defence review forcefully reaffirmed these priorities and emphasised that the navy's primary area of interest was the Eastern Atlantic and the North Sea.[41]

This had major implications for amphibious policy. Up to this time it had been accepted that there was no requirement for an amphibious capability west of Suez.[42] Fortunately the new NATO concept of flexible response had begun to place a renewed emphasis on conventional forces in Europe and Britain's amphibious forces were to find a new role in this strategy. A Supplementary Statement on Defence in July 1968 announced a new role for the marines and amphibious ships in support of NATO's northern and southern flanks.[43] The role on the southern flank was abandoned in the 1970s but Britain maintained a commitment to the defence of Norway and it was this role that formed the primary justification for the retention of amphibious forces until the end of the Cold War.

A renewed emphasis on European contingencies led to a reduction in priority on amphibious forces. Capabilities were cut back. Both HMS *Albion* and *Bulwark* were decommissioned in the 1970s without a dedicated replacement.[44] The Commando Brigade contracted from five to three commando units by 1982. Both new LPDs remained in service with one ship operational, although replacement vessels were removed from the Long Term Costings in 1975.[45] The Conservative Secretary of State for Defence, John Nott, initiated his 1981 defence review with a very sceptical attitude towards amphibious operations. He contemplated abolishing the Royal Marines, but eventually settled for scrapping the specialist ships, the LPDs. In the event this decision was reversed prior to the Falklands conflict, partially in response to international pressure.[46] That conflict demonstrated the utility of amphibious operations and the value of amphibious forces. It did not lead to a change in strategic policy. Europe remained the primary focus for British defence policy and, despite occasional studies into the issue, there was no new construction of amphibious shipping in the 1980s except for a replacement for the LSL *Sir Galahad* destroyed in the Falklands. Amphibious operations were accorded a low priority.

This situation did not change until the end of the Cold War brought yet another shift in strategic priorities. With a major war in Europe now perceived as very unlikely, there was more opportunity to devote resources to contingencies on the periphery of Europe and beyond. This, coupled with a desire for Britain to retain a security role in the wider world, led to increased emphasis being placed on expeditionary capabilities, including amphibious forces. This process was initiated by the Conservative Government of John Major and was reinforced and reconfirmed by the new Labour Government in their 1998 Strategic Defence Review. The Secretary of State for Defence, George Robertson, neatly summed up future requirements by stating that 'In the post Cold War World, we must be prepared to go to the crisis rather than have the crisis come to us.'[47] The review codified existing developments, articulated an emphasis on joint operations and expeditionary warfare and placed a premium on rapid reaction capabilities. In the aftermath of this the armed forces adopted the concept of Joint Rapid Reaction Forces based upon a flexible pool of powerful and adaptable units from all three services that could be put together to meet the challenges posed by individual circumstances.[48] At the end of the twentieth century the British armed forces placed a new emphasis on mobile, flexible and deployable forces. This was reflected in both doctrine and procurement.[49]

Amphibious operations were accorded an important role in this new strategic approach. In the 1990s the Royal Navy began to list amphibious forces as one of its three core capabilities, alongside nuclear submarines and the *Invincible*-class aircraft carriers. As early as 1986 the government announced plans to procure two new Aviation Support Ships, similar to the commando carriers decommissioned in the 1970s. However, lack of priority meant that no progress was made until 1992 when the project was revised and invitations to tender for the contract were issued. Budgetary restraint saw the order reduced to one such vessel. In May 1993 VSEL received the contract to build this ship, now classified as an LPH. The resulting vessel, HMS *Ocean*, was commissioned in 1998.[50] By this time the old LPDs HMS *Fearless* and *Intrepid* were fast approaching the end of their useful lives. In 1992 a project definition study was undertaken for the replacement of these ships and in July 1996 a contract was placed with VSEL for the construction of two new and improved vessels, to be named HMS *Albion* and *Bulwark*.[51] HMS *Albion* entered service, after some delay, in June 2003. *Bulwark* is scheduled to follow suit in August 2004.[52] The third element of the amphibious fleet, the LSLs, are also to be replaced, in this case by a smaller number of larger and significantly more capable vessels.[53]

A study of this period illustrates the important role that strategy has played in the British approach towards amphibious operations. Broadly speaking, when defence policy concentrated on European contingencies and placed little emphasis on the need to project military power overseas, amphibious operations received little priority. Over time this had a deleterious effect on amphibious capabilities. Conversely, when British defence policy was focused on the projection of power overseas, with less emphasis placed on the defence of mainland Europe, amphibious operations were recognised as a useful tool of national policy and received funding commensurate with this. During such periods amphibious forces were employed to good effect, for example at Kuwait in 1961, East Africa in 1964, during the withdrawal from Aden in 1967 and at Sierra Leone in 2000. However, it is notable that the two occasions since 1945 when the British conducted brigade-scale amphibious operations against an active and hostile opponent, 1956 and 1982, both occurred at a time when defence policy was explicitly Euro-centric in focus.[54] Amphibious forces had received little priority prior to both conflicts and in each case success was dependent on equipment and techniques that had only recently been largely discounted.

Technology

The current state of technology in any given field has an important impact on overall policy. It establishes what is and is not possible within a given budget. Policy towards amphibious operations was formed within the boundaries set by existing technology, but the nature of that technology was never the most important determining factor. Indeed, technology, in the form of ships, craft and specialist equipment, was developed in response to changing policy and not vice versa. However, the manner in which the navy sought to use amphibious forces to support government policy did reflect the changing nature of technology within the field. In addition, by affecting the cost of maintaining a capability, the nature of existing and emerging technology could act as both an enabler and a constraint on the development of policy and thus the relationship between the two was never entirely one-way.

The boundaries set by technological limitations in the field of amphibious operations underwent two major changes in the twentieth century.[55] First, during the Second World War, the British and Americans developed a new range of equipment to enable them to land large, modern, balanced forces on an enemy-occupied coast in the face of determined and sophisticated opposition. This represented a quantum leap in capability and enabled successful operations such as those conducted at Normandy, Iwo Jima and Okinawa. The second major change occurred after the war and received its operational début at Port Said in 1956. This was the employment of helicopters in amphibious operations or, more specifically, the co-ordinated employment of large numbers of helicopters operating from aircraft carriers or similar vessels. This, in addition to incremental advances in the speed, sea-keeping, endurance, payload and habitability of conventional amphibious ships, greatly enhanced the ability of amphibious forces to meet the changing requirements of government policy during times of 'armed peace'.

By the end of the Second World War a series of successful operations had shown that well-balanced amphibious forces could secure a beach even against the most determined opposition. Unfortunately, this required a large number of specialist ships and craft. The post-war Naval Assault Force recommended by the Bottomley Committee in 1944, designed to land a single army division, included 64 ships, 135 major landing craft and 256 minor landing craft. The personnel requirement for the force was for 16,250 men.[56] This was to prove completely beyond British resources after 1945. The AW Squadron, formed in 1951, actually consisted of only three ships and four major landing craft.[57] The problem was not one of overall availability. By the late 1940s most of the huge wartime amphibious fleet had been returned to the United States under the provisions of the Lend-Lease agreement, reconverted back to civilian use, or scrapped due to a combination of age, obsolescence and general wear and tear. However, the Royal Navy still possessed a large number of British-built Landing Ship Tank Mk3s, Landing Craft Tank Mk8s and minor craft, and these sufficed for most peacetime requirements. Unfortunately, the majority of these vessels were held in reserve status, where rust slowly combined with age to undermine capability. The critical problem was that it was simply impossible to maintain, in commission or high-priority reserve, the number and range of landing craft required to conduct Normandy-size operations. Even the US Navy had difficulties in this respect and this was illustrated by their need to requisition Japanese-operated landing ships to support the landing at Inchon in 1950.[58]

Given British defence priorities, this was not seen as a serious problem. Large-scale amphibious operations would not occur until the latter stages of any major war and thus, providing a nucleus capability existed and key skills were maintained, the full range of specialist shipping and equipment could be built after mobilisation. Unfortunately, this meant that the amphibious fleet available for operations in peacetime would lack many of the ships and craft that had proved useful during the Second World War. Furthermore, the decision to maintain an AW Squadron capable of embarking only a battalion group, expanding to a brigade group at 30 days' notice, meant that there would be a considerable delay before shipping sufficient to embark and land a larger force could be made available. This was to have a serious impact on potential military action during the 1951 Abadan crisis and again during the Suez crisis in 1956. An additional problem was that the old ships and craft were slow and had rather poor living conditions. It took the old vessels of the AW Squadron six days to sail from Malta to Port Said in November 1956.[59] This had an impact on the timing of the seaborne landing, which had to wait the arrival of these ships despite the growing political pressure to complete military operations quickly. The ships could only afford to sail for seven or eight days before putting into harbour to re-provision and re-fuel.[60] They thus lacked the ability to poise offshore for any length of time before landing their embarked force. The remnants of Britain's Second World War amphibious fleet did not offer a fast, responsive and flexible intervention capability able to meet unforeseen contingencies in situations short of major war.

The new generation of amphibious ships built in Britain during the 1960s remedied this situation. The decision to maintain four major amphibious ships, plus the decision to build six new LSLs, meant that Britain would have available at short notice sufficient specialist shipping to land and support in combat a brigade-sized force. This capability was provided by four Royal Navy ships and six Royal Fleet Auxiliaries. In 1951 it had been estimated that 22 ships and 24 major landing craft would be required to land a brigade.[61] To some extent this reduction represented the reduced requirement. In the 1960s there was no longer any expectation that troops would be landed on a strongly defended beach and thus, for example, the requirement for specialist rocket-firing support ships could be dropped. In addition, the assault ships HMS *Fearless* and *Intrepid* had command and control facilities designed for a brigade-scale operation, removing the need for separate headquarters vessels, and the landing craft carried in their docks removed the need to deploy Landing Craft Tanks. It also reflected the fact that the more modern amphibious ships were larger, faster and more versatile than their predecessors. By relying on fewer but more capable vessels the Royal Navy was able to maintain a high degree of capability and readiness without denuding the rest of the fleet of manpower and resources. There was one drawback in that one ship, no matter how capable, could only be in one place at a time. On numerous occasions during the 1960s the navy was to find that their specialist ships were at the wrong end of the Indian Ocean when trouble broke out.[62]

The increased speed, endurance, payload and habitability of the new generation of amphibious ships made them far more suitable for peacetime service than their war-built predecessors. In technological terms they represented an incremental improvement of existing capabilities. The LPDs and LSLs built by the British were, in essence, simply updated versions of the wartime Landing Ship Dock and Landing Ship Tank. In contrast, the employment of helicopters in amphibious operations provided an important new capability. The US Marine Corps had pioneered the use of helicopters in this role. In response to the apparent threat to traditional, concentrated amphibious operations posed by atomic weapons, the US Marines sought new ways to add speed, flexibility and dispersal to amphibious warfare. After some initial investigations into the use of seaplanes they eventually harnessed the potential of helicopters and in doing so contributed to the second major technological change relating to amphibious operations.[63] Although initially intended for use in major operations against first-rate opposition, the helicopter later proved to be ideally suited to support the kind of low-intensity operations that were central to British requirements in the 1960s. They offered the ability to land a light military force quickly without reliance on landing craft and regardless of beach conditions or coastal terrain. Utilising the concept of 'vertical envelopment', enemy strongpoints on the beach could be avoided or outflanked and key installations inland could be seized in the initial assault. Unlike traditional airborne troops, helicopter-landed infantry could also be re-embarked at short notice should the need arise.

The best platform to support helicopter operations proved to be a vessel with a large flight deck able to launch numerous aircraft simultaneously, an aircraft hangar to store and maintain the helicopters, and sufficient room to comfortably accommodate the embarked military force. Redundant aircraft carriers proved well suited to this role and the United States began conversion of the first helicopter assault ship (LPH), the former escort carrier USS *Thetis Bay*, in 1955. An additional advantage of this type of ship was that without any of the structural compromises associated with traditional amphibious vessels they could maintain high speeds unusual for amphibious ships.[64] In 1959 the US

Navy began work on a new, purpose-built class of LPHs. Displacing 18,000 tons, these *Iwo Jima*-class ships could embark 2,000 marines and around 30 medium-lift helicopters.[65] The LPH, and subsequent developments of this concept,[66] have remained central to US amphibious capabilities while the vertical assault capability offered by helicopters, and potentially by new tilt-rotor aircraft, is vital to contemporary concepts of sea-basing and ship-to-objective manoeuvre.[67]

The British were slow to appreciate the value of the helicopter. In 1948, one year after the US Marines had formed their first helicopter squadron, Combined Operations HQ (COHQ) reported that the unloading of stores by helicopters in an assault 'could not be regarded as a feasible proposition within the foreseeable future'.[68] Both COHQ and the Admiralty displayed a cautious attitude towards this emerging technology.[69] The performance of helicopters at this time did not inspire confidence and neither organisation could spare major resources for experimentation in this field. During the 1950s the increased performance of these aircraft and their employment on counter-insurgency operations in Malaya illustrated their potential. Unfortunately, despite numerous requests from both Amphibious Warfare HQ (AWHQ) and No. 3 Commando Brigade, no helicopters were made available for amphibious training. Their employment in Malaya reduced availability and the Admiralty was reluctant to divert any of their limited stocks of these aircraft away from anti-submarine and air–sea rescue work. An additional need to preserve scarce engines and limitations on their use, imposed as part of US sale agreements, further reduced availability.[70]

The British were aware of US developments in this field through the close liaison that still existed with the US Marines. Indeed, even before the Suez crisis the Admiralty were planning to convert an old aircraft carrier into an LPH. This decision was boosted by events during that crisis. At Port Said on 6 November 1956 the Royal Marines of No. 45 Commando conducted the first ever helicopter landing during an amphibious operation. The troops that landed received limited training immediately prior to the operation and were landed in 22 rather inadequate Whirlwind and Sycamore helicopters from the aircraft carriers HMS *Ocean* and *Theseus*. The original plan had been to land them in the rear of the town to seize two vital bridges. This was cancelled due to a fear about the vulnerability of troops and aircraft operating in this novel way and landing in a defended area. Instead, the marines were landed on the beach in the same place that conventional landing craft would have put them. The bridges were secured by a low-level French parachute drop.[71]

The utility of helicopters in an amphibious role was demonstrated on a number of occasions. The tactical reach and flexibility of the helicopter, allied to the speed, endurance and support capabilities of the LPH, made a potent combination, particularly when devoted to limited war contingencies. The commando carrier HMS *Bulwark* made a vital contribution to the success of Operation 'Vantage' in 1961 when No. 42 Commando, landed by helicopter on 1 July, was the only complete unit in Kuwait during the critical first day of the operation.[72] Similarly, the operation to disarm mutinous Tanganyikan troops in January 1964 was founded on the ability of sea-based helicopters to land marines quickly and effectively directly at the main rebel barracks. In this case the assault force was made up of an improvised combination of RAF and Royal Navy aircraft embarked on the conventional aircraft carrier, HMS *Centaur*. *Centaur* was used in lieu of the commando carrier HMS *Albion* which, rather inconveniently, was at the wrong side of the Indian Ocean when the crisis broke out. The operation was successful despite the cramped conditions endured by the marines on the voyage from Aden to Dar-es-Salaam. Once the marines were disembarked and the flight deck was clear, HMS *Centaur* was even able to provide air cover with its complement of *Sea Vixen* fighter/ground attack aircraft.[73]

The fact that the commando carrier concept had proven to be a useful tool in limited war scenarios did not guarantee its relevance to British defence needs. In July 1974 HMS *Hermes*, recently converted to replace the commando carrier HMS *Albion*, used its helicopters to land No. 41 Commando in Cyprus in order to safeguard the security of the British sovereign base areas following the Turkish invasion of that island.[74] However, the decision to abandon the military presence east of Suez undermined the case for retaining this capability. By 1984 the helicopter assault capability had been lost. HMS *Albion* was decommissioned in 1973 and *Bulwark* relinquished the commando carrier role in 1976 and was decommissioned in 1981 after a brief period operating as an anti-submarine warfare (ASW) carrier. In 1977 *Hermes* was re-designated as an ASW carrier and underwent conversion to enable it to operate Sea Harrier fixed-wing aircraft.[75] The ship retained a secondary role as a commando carrier, although it was employed in its new primary role during the 1982 Falklands conflict, and therefore no commando carrier was available for operations in the South Atlantic. This had an impact on the planning and conduct of the amphibious landing by No. 3 Commando Brigade and significantly reduced the tactical mobility and flexibility of the force once ashore.[76]

HMS *Hermes* was reduced to a training ship in April 1984 and then sold to India in 1986. To alleviate this loss of capability, the new *Invincible*-class aircraft carriers were given a secondary role as LPHs in the 'fast dash' role and HMS *Invincible* exercised this role in 1984.[77] Use of carriers in this role provided some capacity for vertical envelopment, although their limitations soon became apparent. Experience in exercises demonstrated that the lack of a dedicated LPH represented a serious gap in capability. An additional problem was that as the Royal Navy had only three *Invincible*-class ships, it was questionable whether any of these scarce and high-value assets would be spared from their primary role in war.[78]

The helicopter requirement identified by the navy and marines was for a two-company-group lift capability. This implied one, or preferably two, vessels capable of operating twelve medium-lift helicopters. In 1986 the Ministry of Defence approved the allocation of £200 million for the construction of two new helicopter-capable ships, dubbed Aviation Support Ships, or £160 million for the conversion of two ships to this role. There was considerable speculation that conversion rather than new construction might be the favoured option. In the absence of a spare aircraft carrier hull, one possibility was conversion of the container ship *Contender Argent,* sister ship to the *Contender Bezant* which had been given a flight deck and converted into the Air Training Ship RFA *Argus*. There was even some idea that in order to reduce costs the ships might be manned by civilian crews. In October 1988 tenders were invited for the construction of two ships and bids were received from three consortia. Lack of priority meant that the project was shelved and then reduced to just one vessel, now being described by the more conventional title of LPH. The end of the Cold War saw the project revived. In May 1993 VSEL was awarded a contract to build one new LPH at a cost of £143.9 million. The ship, christened HMS *Ocean*, was commissioned in September 1998.[79]

HMS *Ocean* was the Royal Navy's first purpose-built LPH. Able to embark and operate a support squadron of twelve medium-lift helicopters and six attack helicopters, it was designed to embark a full Royal Marine commando unit with an overload capacity for 303 additional personnel. It has proven to be an extremely valuable and versatile amphibious vessel. In many ways the ship represents a compromise between cost and capability. Although a new Royal Navy ship rather than a cheaper civilian conversion, construction costs were kept to a minimum. The hull was based upon the existing *Invincible*-class design and costs were further reduced by accepting Merchant Navy as opposed to more stringent military build requirements where appropriate. In order to reduce manpower costs the ship was designed to be 'lean manned', with a complement of only 254 personnel. In addition, the ship was not fitted with a comprehensive command and control suite and is thus not suitable for use as a headquarters in any large-scale operations. Space was provided for such facilities to be fitted at a latter date should funding become available. The result was an innovative compromise that reflected a flexible approach to attain capability at an acceptable cost.

The changing nature of technology had an impact on British policy. During the late 1940s the difficulty of maintaining, in commission, the full range of ships and craft required to embark a division or even a brigade group provided an additional reason to accept the policy whereby such capabilities were not required during peacetime. The new amphibious capability built during the 1960s provided a new flexible and affordable means of projecting power without undue reliance on static garrisons. In the short period between the 1966 defence review and the decision taken in 1968 to abandon the east of Suez role, amphibious forces, together with long-range land-based aircraft, appeared to offer the government a means of maintaining a credible intervention capability at an acceptable cost. In a similar fashion, in the 1990s the British government rediscovered the utility of amphibious forces as useful means of projecting limited power overseas. In all of these cases the state of existing technology provided or constrained options. It influenced the way in which policy was implemented. In no case did it determine the general direction of policy. The fact that the commando carrier, in conjunction with its air group and an embarked commando unit, provided a valuable and flexible means of exerting limited military force overseas did not guarantee that British policy would follow in any particular direction. It may have made it easier to adopt that policy within a given budget and it may have influenced the decision to allocate maritime resources to certain contingencies rather than land or air assets. However, once defence policy changed, the commando carrier role was dropped and was not reinvigorated until defence policy once again changed to re-emphasise power projection beyond Europe. Strategic priorities were far more important than any technological development in the evolution of policy towards amphibious operations.

Institutional

The link between strategy and defence priorities is a necessary one. It is difficult to see how any policy could be logical without it. However, the process by which alternative choices are identified can sometimes be less than entirely objective. A study of British attitudes towards amphibious operations during this period illustrates that strategic considerations were often influenced by other factors. Indeed, the way in which strategic priorities were identified and the degree to which different issues were resourced appears to have had as much to do with bureaucratic politics and institutional priorities as it did with a dispassionate study of national requirements. Thus, the idea of change and innovation in the field of amphibious operations being driven exclusively by strategic priorities is, in reality, misleading.

The conclusions of the Bottomley Committee in 1944 were based upon the principle that amphibious operations would remain an inter-service activity. No one service would have primary responsibility. In line with these recommendations COHQ was retained as an independent, inter-service headquarters based in London with overall responsibility for amphibious advice, training and development. At the head of this organisation was the Chief of Combined Operations,[80] who had the right to sit as a member of the Chiefs of Staff Committee when relevant issues were discussed. This post originated with Admiral of the Fleet Sir Roger Keyes, who had been appointed as Director of Combined Operations in 1940, and it had gained prominence under his successor, Lord Louis Mountbatten. Mountbatten had originally been appointed as Adviser on Combined Operations under the general direction of the Chiefs of Staff with the rank of Commodore. It was a reflection of the importance of amphibious operations to Britain's war effort that by March 1942 he had been advanced to the acting rank of Vice-Admiral with the new title of Chief of Combined Operations.[81]

In 1943 Mountbatten left COHQ to become Supreme Allied Commander South-east Asia and was replaced by Major-General Robert Laycock, an Army officer with extensive experience of commando operations. Laycock remained in the post until 1947 when he was replaced by Major-General Wildman-Lushington, a Royal Marine. There were four more Chiefs of Combined Operations/Amphibious Warfare before the post was abolished in 1962. All of these were Royal Marines.[82] Despite the theoretically inter-service nature of amphibious operations, Laycock was the only Chief from outside the naval service.

The inter-service nature of the organisation was reflected in the staff of COHQ and the Combined Operations/Amphibious Warfare Centre at Fremington. It was also reflected in the students attending courses at the Centre. The Centre maintained an important liaison with allied countries and provided amphibious training to NATO and Commonwealth personnel. The most important relationship was that with the armed forces of the United States and particularly with the US Marine Corps. The United States was the only other nation with comparable experience in amphibious operations and a close relationship was fostered by the maintenance of exchange officers at the Amphibious Warfare Centre and the Marine Corps Schools at Quantico. A system of annual visits between these centres was established and appears to have been highly valued by all participants. The British were careful to ensure that co-operation with other allies was never so complete that it might preclude the closest relationship with the United States.[83]

COHQ's institutional position was not strong. As an independent organisation within the newly created Ministry of Defence it faced a number of challenges. Prior to the reforms of the 1960s, the Ministry of Defence had a relatively weak central organisation and the three individual services retained much authority. COHQ and its attendant organisation was funded out of central funds, but the amount of resources that could be devoted to this field was under constant scrutiny. For anything beyond the daily upkeep of the organisation as a whole, such as large-scale exercises or the provision of new equipment, manpower and funding was required from the three services. The problem that the Chief of Combined

Operations faced was that although he was represented on the Chiefs of Staff Committee, he could not force the other Chiefs to devote resources to amphibious priorities. He could make recommendations and bring pressure to bear, but success depended on getting at least one other Chief to support his case. Inevitably support from the Chiefs tended to depend upon their perceptions of their own service's self-interest.

In the immediate post-war years the army remained very interested in this mode of warfare. The Chief of the Imperial General Staff, Field-Marshal Montgomery, had commanded 21st Army Group during the Normandy landings on 6 June 1944 and retained an active interest in amphibious operations. In 1947 he issued a 'Blue Book' outlining his views on amphibious operations, stating that 'Training in Combined Operations must form a normal part of the peacetime instruction of the Army.'[84] Army interest in amphibious operations was demonstrated by Exercise Spearhead conducted at Camberley in May 1947. Spearhead was only the second major post-war exercise conducted by the War Office and was attended by all the general officers of the army. In his final address to the exercise group Montgomery reaffirmed the army's interest in amphibious operations, declaring that 'The Army considers that the torch of Combined Operations must be kept alight.'[85] The army frequently defended the Combined Operations organisation in the Chiefs of Staff Committee, countering an Admiralty suggestion that the navy should assume responsibility for amphibious operations by stating that if any one service should assume primary responsibility, it should be the army.

The Admiralty's attitude to amphibious operations was less enthusiastic. The navy had gained extensive experience of amphibious operations in Europe during the war. However, although vital for victory, such operations were never really accepted as the navy's core business which remained focused on the battle for sea control. In many ways amphibious operations conflicted with this primary role, requiring manpower and assets that could be employed elsewhere. Unlike in the Pacific where amphibious operations made a direct and vital contribution to the war at sea, in Europe major operations were conducted in order to return the army to Europe so that it could conduct a conventional land campaign. These operations could only have an indirect benefit for the war at sea. As such, amphibious operations tended to be viewed as an onerous duty rather than an exciting opportunity. They were something that was done by the navy on behalf of the army. The Admiralty attitude was summed up perfectly by their response to a suggestion by Laycock that, in order to provide new amphibious shipping, some reduction in the ability to retain control of the sea might be accepted.[86] At a time when Soviet maritime capabilities could at best be described as primitive, the Admiralty rejected this proposal as 'basically unsound and utterly inadmissible'. Laycock was provided with a brief lesson in maritime strategy:

> Nothing could be more unsound than to risk our ability to gain and maintain control of the sea communications, by which alone can the movement of our fighting forces to the points where they can be most effectively used be ensured, in order to provide the actual means, i.e. the ships and craft, of carrying out these movements.[87]

The Admiralty's attitude was exacerbated by the difficult relationship that it had with COHQ. Problems had occurred in this relationship ever since Keyes had moved his staff out of the main Admiralty building in 1940 in order to set up a separate headquarters. Keyes' approach alienated the Chiefs of Staff in general and the First Sea Lord in particular.[88] Similarly, Keyes' successor, Mountbatten, encountered a degree of hostility due to his personal style and his rapid advancement at the behest of Churchill.[89] However, in reality the problems that existed in the relationship with the Admiralty went beyond that of personalities. The tension that existed in the relationship between the two organisations persisted after the war despite numerous changes in their leadership. The main problem was that COHQ trespassed into an area that the Admiralty believed to be its own. It made constant demands for naval manpower and resources, demands that the Admiralty could not control and were generally reluctant to meet. In an attempt to reverse this situation the Admiralty made numerous attempts to abolish COHQ, replace it with an inter-service committee under the control of the Chiefs of Staff, or have it absorbed within the organisation of the Royal Marines.[90] The prevailing view of amphibious operations as an inter-service activity undermined such attempts and ensured that the Admiralty did not have a firm institutional stake in the maintenance of amphibious capabilities. The opposite was the case. Manpower and resources devoted to amphibious operations could only be provided at the expense of traditional naval tasks. The key problem at this time was that although COHQ had an interest in maintaining amphibious capabilities and expertise, it had a very limited ability to act on this interest. The Admiralty had the latter but not the former.

The situation that existed in the United States at this time was very different. The US Marine Corps had had primary responsibility for amphibious warfare since the 1930s.[91] Unlike the Royal Marines, who were an integral part of the Royal Navy and subject to the rulings of the Board of Admiralty, the US Marines were a fourth service and its Commandant held equal rank to the Chief of Naval Operations. The Corps represented a powerful organisation with an institutional imperative to promote amphibious capabilities. US observers were unimpressed by the inter-service structure adopted by the British. In 1948 one commentator, a serving US Marine Corps officer who had worked with the British at Fremington, articulated the view that 'since amphibious operations are not squarely the responsibility of one service, the subject tends to take on the aspects of an orphan child dependent on the indulgence and the generosity of the older members of the family'. He was rather unflattering about the existing organisation, calling it 'neither fish nor fowl nor yet good red herring'.[92]

AWHQ retained overall responsibility for amphibious policy and advice until it, and the post of Chief of Amphibious Warfare, were disbanded in 1962. Amphibious operations had achieved a new importance, but they were now one of a number of different types of operations that required close inter-service co-operation. In 1961 the Joint Planning Staff completed a report calling for a joint authority responsible for promulgating and directing new policy on joint (i.e. inter-service) operations.[93] In order to better co-ordinate inter-service activity, both AWHQ and the existing Land/Air Warfare Committee were disbanded and replaced by a Joint Warfare Committee responsible to the Chiefs of Staff and made up of senior representatives from the three services and the Ministry of Defence. The Committee, which met for the first time on 17 January 1962, was supported by a small Joint Warfare Staff which acted as a secretariat and submitted an annual report, and a Joint Warfare Establishment was set up by combining the Amphibious Warfare School at Poole with the School of Land/Air Warfare at Old Sarum. An Amphibious Warfare Sub-Committee of the Joint Warfare Committee was responsible for advice and recommendations on policy, techniques, tactical developments and joint-service training in this mode of warfare.[94]

As an inter-service committee responsible to the Chiefs of Staff, the Joint Warfare Committee was clearly subordinate to the services in a way that AWHQ had not been. The last Chief of Amphibious Warfare, Major-General R.D. Houghton, became the first Director of the Joint Warfare Staff, a position that lacked the direct access to the Chiefs of Staff Committee that had previously been available. Nevertheless, amphibious capabilities prospered. Of rather more import than the institutional structure was the fact that the Admiralty was now keen to exploit the amphibious role. Unlike COHQ/AWHQ, they also had the means to act on this interest.

By the mid-1950s the growing belief that major war in Europe was unlikely, but that if it occurred it would be characterised by a nuclear exchange, undermined the rationale for a fleet designed primarily to win the battle for sea control against Soviet air and maritime assets. In such circumstances the Admiralty was forced to find a new role in order to justify their share of the defence budget. The Board of Admiralty discussed the implications of this in June 1956. Some members of the Board expressed concern at the reduction in emphasis on traditional sea control, and the Board was only willing to countenance a reduction in anti-submarine and minesweeping efforts on the assumption that 'very heavy' defence cuts in these areas were inevitable. The shift in emphasis away from sea control and towards power projection was adopted as the 'least damaging to naval interests of all the possible modifications of policy'.[95] It was seen as a means of limiting damage to the shape and size of the fleet.

Despite this rather begrudging attitude, the new approach did prove useful to the navy. It provided them with a means of justifying a large, balanced fleet. The range of assets that could be supported with reference to amphibious operations is illustrated by the following extract from the 1962 Navy Estimates:

> The commando ships and the assault ships put ashore the spearhead of the land forces with their guns, tanks and vehicles. The aircraft carriers provide reconnaissance and tactical strike ahead of the landing; air defence for the seaborne force; and close support for the troops ashore – especially when this cannot be done, either adequately or at all, by land-based aircraft. Cruisers and escorts reinforce the air and anti-submarine cover, direct our aircraft and give warning of the enemy's and use their guns for bombardment if required. Submarines provide additional protection against hostile submarines and carry out reconnaissance and minelaying. The minesweepers clear a way to the land. The Royal Fleet Auxiliary tankers and store ships keep the whole seaborne force supplied.[96]

The navy's case in support of CVA-01 was built upon this vessel's role in support of the expeditionary strategy east of Suez and particularly its utility in support of amphibious operations.[97] It is hardly surprising that the Admiralty supported amphibious capabilities enthusiastically while opposing Royal Air Force schemes to rely primarily on air transport.

The Royal Marines had an important role to play within this strategy, providing the specialist amphibious infantry. In 1944 the Bottomley Committee had rejected the idea of creating a small, specialist amphibious corps similar to the US Marine Corps.[98] After 1945 the Royal Marines had retained a Commando Brigade consisting of three commando units. The army disbanded all of the commando units that it had raised during the war and thus the marines did provide a distinct capability, although the army could reasonably point out that their own units had performed at least as well as their marine counterparts during the war. The position of the marines remained somewhat precarious. The 1948 Harwood Report had recommended that as a cost-cutting measure the commando units should be abolished and that the marines could either be disbanded or transferred as a regiment into the army.[99] The Admiralty refused to consider either proposal.[100] Nevertheless, their own support for the commando idea could be equivocal. Major-General Moulton, both a former commanding officer of No. 3 Commando Brigade and a Chief of Amphibious Warfare, was of the opinion that 'if the board had the choice between a new ship and a Commando, they would go for the ship every time'.[101]

This approach did not change in the 1960s. The mobility of the commando and amphibious ship combination provided politicians with a versatile military tool that could be employed without the need to negotiate local basing agreements or overflight rights. Buoyant recruitment at a time when the army faced manpower difficulties made the marines doubly attractive and saw the number of active commando units rise from three to five by 1961.[102] In that year the Chiefs of Staff approved Admiralty proposals to increase the size of the marines by 500 men in order to provide air control teams and a naval gunfire support section to each commando unit and to create two Administrative Group Elements. Both measures were designed to allow the commandos to fulfil their new expeditionary role more effectively. Capabilities were further enhanced by the allocation of 105 mm pack howitzers of 29 and 95 Commando Light Regiments, Royal Artillery, to the commando carriers HMS *Bulwark* and *Albion*.[103]

The Royal Marines were an integral part of the Royal Navy and the Commandant General was subordinate to the First Sea Lord and the Board of Admiralty. The weakness of this position was illustrated in 1962. The Secretary of State for Defence, Harold Watkinson, was eager to exploit the strengths of the Royal Marine commandos and advocated raising a sixth commando unit.[104] Surprisingly the Admiralty were not enthusiastic. At this time they were seeking to gain approval for the construction of a new aircraft carrier. In order to succeed they required the support, or at least the acquiescence, of the army in order to overcome opposition from the RAF. The War Office had viewed the increase to five commando units with some alarm, seeing it as an uncalled-for expansion at a time when the army faced cuts. As a result, the Admiralty concluded an agreement with the War Office not to form a sixth commando unit and to disband the fifth. The opposition of the Commandant General was ignored.[105] The agreement was contrary to the views of the Secretary of State and against the logic of contemporary defence policy, and it was soon revised. In 1964 a new deal was agreed. The marines would retain five active commando units and in return the Admiralty accepted that these were specialist amphibious troops. Both parties accepted that it would be wrong to make army infantry battalions redundant by using commandos in a purely land role or to make marines redundant by the excessive employment of army units at sea.[106]

This agreement did not bring an end to the issue. When the defence reviews of the late 1960s threatened cutbacks in military expenditure, the army once again discovered an interest in amphibious operations. In the aftermath of the 1966 defence review the army suggested that they should provide one of the two battalions now required for the amphibious force to be maintained east of Suez. They also suggested that command of the Commando Brigade should rotate between the army and the Royal Marines. Army commitment to the cause of amphibious operations could perhaps be gauged by their suggestion that the helicopters assigned to the commando carriers could be assigned primarily for counter-insurgency operations ashore, with amphibious operations as only a secondary role. The First Sea Lord opposed these proposals, citing the marines' expertise and experience in amphibious operations and contrasting this with the army's obvious inexperience.[107]

The army case was based on a desire to protect themselves from defence cuts. Unlike the Royal Marine policy of trickle drafting between UK and overseas units, the army approach to overseas drafting was to rotate one overseas battalion with three other units. Thus, by replacing one Royal Marine commando unit allocated to amphibious operations, a role could be found for three or four army battalions. Regardless of the disparity in experience and specialist amphibious expertise, this approach would clearly have been wasteful in terms of the overall defence budget. In September 1966 the Chief of the General Staff accepted that the two infantry units allocated to the Amphibious Group should be provided by the Royal Marines. Despite this, the army resurrected the issue the following year when further defence cuts were proposed.[108] It is difficult to regard this as anything other than a cynical attempt to maintain army battalions at the expense of the marines, despite any impact that this might have on operational efficiency.

There was an appreciation within the Admiralty that allowing greater army participation in the amphibious role might prove dangerous to the marines as it could reduce the requirement for commando units and possibly even lead to army claims that the Royal Marines could be entirely replaced by army infantry battalions.[109] This was counterbalanced by a realisation that greater army involvement in this role might help to cement their support for the navy's overall maritime strategy east of Suez and limit their support for the RAF's alternative based on air transport. In such circumstances some form of compromise may have been advantageous. In May 1967 the Commander-in-Chief, Plymouth, Vice-Admiral Sir Fitzroy Talbot, expressed this view in a letter to the Vice Chief of the Naval Staff, writing: 'I must admit that, while I fully appreciate the reasons for our party line, I do have some doubts whether it is 100% in the best interests *of the ships* as well as the Royals [i.e. Royal Marines].'[110] In the real world of inter-service politics, defence policy could be influenced by the need to secure the support of another service. Compromise was sometimes necessary. In this case the dispute was resolved by changing policy as the role that was being fought over was abandoned with the withdrawal from east of Suez.

During the 1970s and 1980s yet another change in defence priorities brought a renewed emphasis on sea control operations in major war. The main role of the navy was the provision of ASW support for SACLANT.[111] The pared-down amphibious force retained a limited role in support of the Northern Flank. They could support maritime operations by occupying ports and airfields that might otherwise be seized by Soviet forces, but amphibious operations were no longer at the heart of naval strategy. In the circumstances, amphibious capabilities were reduced and there was increasing concern within the Royal Marines that their colleagues in the navy had turned their back on amphibious operations.[112] By the late 1970s responsibility for amphibious operations was vested in the Flag Officer 3rd Flotilla.[113] Under this officer a Commodore Amphibious Warfare commanded the UK/Netherlands Amphibious Group[114] and provided advice as Chief of Staff (Amphibious Warfare) in support of the admiral's role as Fleet Amphibious Warfare Authority. It may be indicative of naval attitudes to amphibious warfare that the position of Commodore Amphibious Warfare was abolished in the late 1970s, before a decision was taken to re-establish it with a smaller staff.[115]

Despite the experience of the Falklands conflict in 1982, amphibious operations retained their Cinderella status within the navy until the next change in strategic priorities in the 1990s. Once again the Admiralty embraced the amphibious role as part of a general expeditionary strategy.[116] Once again it has proven to be a useful way of protecting the navy's share of the defence budget and ensuring the maintenance of a relatively large, balanced fleet. Amphibious operations moved from being a rather peripheral activity to being central to the business of the Royal Navy. This approach has undoubtedly been driven by the change in strategic requirements. The navy could claim, with some justification, that their advocacy of the new maritime expeditionary role was simply a rational response to the new strategic priorities. Recent history suggests, however, that the navy's response was also influenced by a shrewd appreciation of the best way to protect the enduring interests of the navy as well as to meet the needs of government policy.

Conclusion

If innovation is defined as a process that takes an idea or invention and converts it into a new product, structure or operational activity, then British approaches to amphibious operations in the period 1945–98 can be described as innovative. The development of amphibious capabilities that had occurred during the Second World War, and their employment in large-scale opposed landings, represented a major innovation in both method and technology. This process had been supported in the UK by the establishment of a new institutional structure, encompassing the Chief of Combined Operations, COHQ and the wider Combined Operations organisation. In the immediate post-war years the British sought to retain an element of this capability and laid plans for an ambitious peacetime amphibious fleet and a world-wide training organisation. The maintenance of amphibious capabilities on this scale in peacetime would have been a new development in British practice, although in reality a combination of factors meant that the plans would be largely unfulfilled. In retrospect, British approaches in the late 1940s appear rather backward-looking as elements of the armed forces sought to maintain the ability to conduct Second World War-type operations in Second World War-type scenarios using Second World War-type equipment. This is a little unfair. In reality, British planners sought to harness the potential of what was still a relatively new capability and apply it to what were then considered to be the most likely wartime contingencies.

By the 1950s the growing availability of atomic weapons raised serious questions about the tactical vulnerability of large-scale opposed landings. It also contributed to a major strategic reappraisal as to the likelihood of a conventional war in Europe. In the new strategic environment, where war in Europe appeared unlikely but there was an enhanced possibility of limited conflict overseas, amphibious forces had a new relevance. The realisation that Normandy-style operations were unlikely to be either possible or necessary led the British to fundamentally change their approach to amphibious operations. The attempt to prepare the armed forces as a whole for Second World War-type operations was abandoned and responsibility for this mode of warfare was vested in one service, the Royal Navy.[117] Institutional structures and responsibilities adapted to meet changing requirements. The navy developed a new concept for the employment of amphibious forces as part of a wider maritime expeditionary capability designed to support government policy overseas. The re-concentration on major war contingencies in Europe in the 1970s and 1980s threatened the role and utility of British amphibious forces despite their employment on NATO's Northern Flank. However, the new role adopted in the late 1950s and 1960s proved equally well suited to meet changing needs after the end of the Cold War, and both the navy and the government recognised the value of amphibious operations as part of a wider expeditionary strategy.

The varying degrees of priority accorded to amphibious operations closely reflected broader assumptions about the strategic environment. At times when defence policy focused on major war in Europe, amphibious forces were seen as peripheral to immediate defence requirements and were accorded a low priority. At other times, when more emphasis was placed on the projection of power and influence overseas, amphibious operations played an important part in mainstream defence policy and amphibious capabilities received increased interest and funding. In this sense, changing policy towards amphibious operations reflected changes in overall defence policy. These adjustments in policy were driven by a variety of strategic factors largely unconnected with the utility of amphibious operations or the capabilities of amphibious forces. Critical among these factors were the perceived likelihood of future war in Europe, changing assessments of Britain's role in the world, and the inevitable pressure of economy.

Innovation does not occur in a vacuum. The fact that a change in approach can occur does not mean that it will, particularly if that change has an impact on entrenched interests. In the 1950s the Board of Admiralty's acceptance of the new expeditionary role was somewhat reluctant. The change in emphasis was accepted on the basis that it was the 'least damaging' of all possible courses of action. The new approach was thus designed to support British interests given the new strategic priorities, but the interpretation of what those interests were was interwoven with an appreciation of the naval requirement to develop a strategy that would facilitate the protection of the naval share of the defence budget. Throughout the late 1940s and early 1950s the Admiralty had opposed the ambitious plans of COHQ/AWHQ in order to devote the maximum resources to the conventional sea control navy. In the 1960s the amphibious role was adopted, at least in part, as a key means of justifying the maintenance of a balanced range of sea control assets. A similar pattern of behaviour appears to have emerged in the 1990s. With the old role of anti-submarine operations against Soviet forces now redundant, the new expeditionary approach offered a means of both supporting government policy and protecting naval interests. A definitive account of naval and defence policy in the 1990s must await the opening of the relevant records. However, it would be naïve to assume that the navy was not once again influenced by self-interest in its rediscovery of the utility of amphibious operations.

Innovation in the use of technology has always played an important part in maritime warfare. Britain had been at the forefront of technological developments in amphibious operations during the Second World War and these enabled the successful operations of 1943–5. After 1945, with limited priority and limited funding, the British were unable to match progress achieved in the United States. Innovation was reflected in the requirement to adapt existing vessels to fulfil new roles in the absence of more suitable ships, or in the need to incorporate merchant ship design standards in HMS *Ocean* in order to keep costs down to an acceptable level. New developments such as the employment of helicopters in amphibious operations, conversion of aircraft carriers into LPHs or, more recently, radical new concepts such as Operational Manoeuvre from the Sea, originated in the US rather than the UK. Nevertheless, the adoption of new techniques and new equipment in the 1960s was central to the navy's ability to offer a realistic intervention capability at an acceptable cost. This would have been difficult to achieve with a 1940s-style amphibious fleet. More fundamentally, although changing technology acted as both a constraint and an enabler on both tactics and strategy, it was never the key determinant in British attitudes towards amphibious operations. Technology was harnessed to support policy. The reverse was not the case.

One intriguing aspect of British policy during this period is the way in which major military operations did not provide an impetus for change after 1945. The large Royal Navy commitment to United Nations operations during the Korean War did not have a significant impact on Admiralty policy in the early 1950s.[118] Furthermore, the employment of a Royal Marine commando unit in raiding operations did not have an immediate impact on the prevailing view that there was little requirement to prepare for amphibious operations in situations short of major war. Similarly, the inability of the British armed forces to mount an effective military response in the first months of the 1951 Abadan crisis did not lead to a change in policy. All of the difficulties that the British experienced in providing amphibious ships and craft during the Suez crisis in 1956 had been previewed in Abadan five years earlier. Even the Suez crisis itself did not lead to the change in policy towards a more expeditionary focus, rather it reinforced and accelerated a process that was already underway. Most obviously, the 1982 Falklands conflict did not change the overall direction of British defence policy and did not bring a renewed emphasis on amphibious capabilities. It was to take another ten years, and the end of the Cold War, for the first stirring of the new amphibious renaissance to become apparent.

Notes

1 See D. R. Massam, 'British Maritime Strategy and Amphibious Capability, 1900–1940' (Ph.D. dissertation, Oxford University, 1995).

2 UK Public Records Office, Kew [henceforth PRO]: ADM 210/17, Admiralty Green List, 3 Sept. 1945.

3 P. Cornish, *British Military Planning for the Defence of Germany, 1945–1950* (London: Macmillan, 1996).

4 These issues are examined in detail in Ian Speller, *The Role of Amphibious Warfare in British Defence Policy, 1945–1956* (Basingstoke: Palgrave, 2001).

5 The National Archive (TNA): Public Record Office (PRO), CAB 80/44, COS (44) 166, 'Report by Committee on Inter-Service Responsibility for Amphibious Warfare', 29 June 1944.

6 Ibid.; TNA: PRO, CAB 84/75, JP (45) 259, 'Post War Naval Assault Forces', 26 Jan. 1946; TNA: PRO, CAB 79/44, COS (46) 18 mtg, 1 Feb. 1946.

7 TNA: PRO, DEFE 6/20, JP (52) 1, report by the Joint Planning Staff, 14 Mar. 1952; TNA: PRO, DEFE 4/53, COS (52) 45 mtg, 31 Mar. 1952.

8 The British armed forces did not officially adopt the term 'amphibious warfare' until 1951. Prior to this the official term for this mode of warfare had

been 'combined operations'. In this chapter I shall use the term 'amphibious warfare/operations' throughout except when referring to a specific post or organisation prior to 1951.

9 TNA: PRO, DEFE 2/1452; DEFE 2/1561; DEFE 2/1673; DEFE 2/1654; DEFE 2/1655; DEFE 2/1739; DEFE 2/1579.

10 For an example of this approach, see TNA: PRO, DEFE 2/1903, folio 4, docket AW 558/56.

11 See TNA: PRO, DEFE 5/42, COS (52) 391, memorandum by the Chief of Amphibious Warfare, 30 Apr. 1952; PRO, DEFE 5/42, COS (52) 645, note by the War Office, 25 Nov. 1952; PRO, DEFE 2/1900, 'A Short Review of the History and Development of British Amphibious Warfare', 23 Aug. 1954.

12 No. 41 (Independent) Commando Royal Marines. The existing Commando Brigade, No. 3 Commando Brigade, Royal Marines, was fully employed ashore in Malaya. For further details see D. B. Drysdale, '41 Commando', *Marine Corps Gazette*, Aug. 1952, 28–32; TNA: PRO, ADM 202/459, 41 Independent Commando, RM. – War Diary; PRO, ADM 1/21882, Royal Marine Commando Operations in Korea.

13 TNA: PRO, DEFE 5/43, COS (53) 649, report by the Chief of Amphibious Warfare, 29 Nov. 1952.

14 Ian Speller, 'A Splutter of Musketry? The British Military Response to the Anglo-Iranian Oil Dispute 1951', *Contemporary Military History*, 17(1) (Spring 2003); TNA: PRO, ADM 116/6209, Naval Report on Operation Musketeer; K. Kyle, *Suez* (London: Weidenfeld & Nicolson, 1992).

15 TNA: PRO, DEFE 2/1477, folio 6(a), docket 725/47, 'Implications of the rising dimensional limits of War Office heavy equipment'; PRO, DEFE 2/1866, folio 10 docket co. 1887/50.

16 TNA: PRO, DEFE 5/17, COS (49) 336, 11 Oct. 1949; PRO, DEFE 2/1845; PRO, DEFE 5/49, COS (53) 527, report by working party, 29 Oct. 1953; PRO, DEFE 5/53, COS (54) 228, report by working party, 9 July 1954.

17 For example, see TNA: PRO, DEFE 5/59, COS (55) 176, 25 July 1955.

18 TNA: PRO, CAB 131/18, D (57) 6 mtg, 31 July 1957.

19 TNA: PRO, COS (54) 228.

20 TNA: PRO, DEFE 5/51, COS (54) 79, report by the Joint Planning Staff, 12 Mar. 1954.

21 TNA: PRO, DEFE 4/71, COS (54) 82 mtg, 14 July 1954.

22 TNA: PRO, DEFE 7/1455.

23 TNA: PRO, DEFE 5/70, COS (56) 280, 'The Future Role of the Navy', 20 July 1956.

24 Cmnd 124, *Defence: Outline of Future Policy*, (London: The Stationery Office, 1957).

25 See TNA: PRO, ADM 167/150, B.1163, 'The Role of the Navy', Memorandum for the Board, 30 Aug. 1957.

26 During the 1964 reorganisation of the Ministry of Defence, the Board of Admiralty was replaced by a renamed Admiralty Board of the Defence Council. For ease of reference the term 'Admiralty' will continue to be used throughout this chapter.

27 But only three air groups, guaranteeing that a maximum of three aircraft carriers could be available for operations at any one time.

28 With four air groups.

29 TNA: PRO, ADM 205/192, 'Presentation of Alternative Long Term Naval Programme', 17 May 1961; PRO, DEFE 7/2235, D (61) 1 mtg, 12 Jan. 1961; PRO, CAB 131/27.

30 Cmnd 1639, *Statement on Defence 1962: The Next Five Years* (London: The Stationery Office, 1962).
31 TNA: PRO, DEFE 5/150, COS 109/64, 2 Apr. 1964; PRO, DEFE 4/167, COS 26 mtg/64, 2 Apr. 1964.
32 Cmnd 1629, *Explanatory Statement on the Navy Estimates 1962–1963* (London: The Stationery Office, 1962).
33 For further details see Ian Speller, 'The Royal Navy, Expeditionary Operations and the End of Empire, 1956–1975', in Greg Kennedy (ed.), *Britain's Maritime Strategy East of Suez, 1900–2000: Influences and Actions* (London: Frank Cass, 2003).
34 Cmnd 2901, *Statement on the Defence Estimates 1966. Part 1. The Defence Review* (London: The Stationery Office, 1966).
35 HMS *Invincible*, the first of three such ships, was commissioned in 1980.
36 TNA: PRO, DEFE 13/479, Report of the Working Party on Intervention Operations and Amphibious Capability, 1967.
37 Cmnd 3357, *Supplementary Statement on Defence Policy 1967* (London: The Stationery Office, 1967).
38 S. Dockerill, *Britain's Retreat from East of Suez: The Choice Between Europe and the World?* (Basingstoke: Palgrave Macmillan, 2002).
39 Cmnd 3540, *Statement on the Defence Estimates 1968* (London: The Stationery Office, 1968).
40 Cmnd 5976, *Statement on the Defence Estimates 1975* (London: The Stationery Office, 1975).
41 Cmnd 8288, *The United Kingdom Defence Programme: The Way Forward* (London: The Stationery Office, 1981).
42 TNA: PRO, DEFE 7/2235, COS (61) 488, 20 Dec. 1961; PRO, CAB 131/27, D (61) 1 mtg, 12 Jan. 1962.
43 Cmnd 3701, *Supplementary Statement on Defence Policy 1968* (London: The Stationery Office, 1968).
44 The aircraft carrier HMS *Hermes* operated as a commando carrier between 1974 and 1977 and retained this as a secondary role until it was sold to India in 1986.
45 Cmnd 5976, *Statement on the Defence Estimates 1975*.
46 E. Grove, *Vanguard to Trident: British Naval Policy Since World War Two* (London: Bodley Head, 1987), p. 355.
47 Cmnd 3999, *The Strategic Defence Review* (London: The Stationery Office, 1998).
48 'Joint Rapid Reaction Forces – Special Report', *Defence Review*, Winter 1998, 38–48.
49 For example, see *BR1806. British Maritime Doctrine*, 2nd ed. (London: The Stationery Office, 1999).
50 *Warship World*, 3(2) (Spring 1992), 8; R. Scott, 'Ocean's Wave is Set to Roll', *Jane's Navy International*, 104(7) (Sept. 1999), 26–35.
51 *Jane's Navy International*, 101(7) (Sept. 1996), 6.
52 Information taken from the official Royal Navy website, www.royal-navy.mod.uk. Downloaded on 6 Dec. 2003.
53 'RFA Crucial in Expeditionary Warfare', *Jane's Navy International*, 106(1) (Jan.–Feb. 2001), 19–23.
54 Defence policy had begun to change and to place increasing emphasis on 'limited war' operations immediately prior to the Suez crisis, but this had not had an impact on operational capabilities.

55 One might also suggest that there has been a third such development, namely the introduction at the end of the century of the concept of Operational Manoeuvre From the Sea and supporting concepts such as Sea Based Logistics and Ship to Objective Manoeuvre. However, it remains to be seen to what extent these approaches will truly alter the employment and utility of amphibious forces. Detailed examination of these concepts is beyond the scope of this study.
56 TNA: PRO, COS (44) 166.
57 TNA: PRO, DEFE 4/53, COS (52) 45 mtg, 31 Mar. 1952.
58 M.W. Cagle and F.A. Manson, *The Sea War in Korea* (Annapolis, MD: Naval Institute Press, 1957), 95–6.
59 TNA: PRO, ADM 116/6209.
60 Kyle, *Suez*, 240.
61 TNA: PRO, DEFE 5/29, COS (51) 146, memorandum by the Chief of Amphibious Warfare, 19 Mar. 1951
62 For example, in December 1962 when the Brunei revolt broke out, HMS *Albion* was off the coast of Kenya. It took six days for this ship to sail to Brunei.
63 A.R. Millett, *Semper Fidelis: The History of the United States Marine Corps* (New York: The Free Press, 1991), chap. 15; R.B. Asprey, 'The Fleet Marine Force in the early 1950s', in M.L. Bartlett (ed.), *Assault from the Sea: Essays on the History of Amphibious Warfare* (Annapolis, MD: Naval Institute Press, 1983) 354–9.
64 For example, the commando carrier/LPH HMS *Bulwark* had a top speed of 28 knots compared to a (rarely achieved) design speed of up to 13 knots for the Landing Ship Tank Mk3, 17 knots for the new LSLs, or 21 knots for the LPD HMS *Fearless*.
65 D. Steigman, 'Amphibious Forces', in R. Gardiner (ed.), *Navies in the Nuclear Age: Warships since 1945* (London: Conway Maritime Press, 1993), 110–20.
66 For example, the US-built LHD and LHA which are also equipped with a protected dock for landing craft and air cushion vehicles.
67 'Operational Maneuver From the Sea', *United States Naval Institute Proceedings*, Jan. 1994; 'A Concept for Ship to Objective Maneuver', *United States Marine Corps Gazette*, Nov. 1997.
68 TNA: PRO, DEFE 2/1697.
69 Ibid.
70 TNA: PRO, DEFE 4/74, COS (54) 132 mtg, 15 Dec. 1954; PRO, DEFE 2/1890; PRO, DEFE 2/1891; PRO, DEFE 5/55, COS (54) 372, report by the Chief of Amphibious Warfare, 2 Dec. 1954.
71 TNA: PRO, ADM 116/6209; PRO, ADM 202/455, Operation Musketeer – 45 Commando, Unit Report.
72 TNA: PRO, DEFE 5/118, COS (61) 378, Report by the Commander in Chief Middle East on Operations in Support of the State of Kuwait in July 1961, 18 Oct. 1961.
73 TNA: PRO, ADM 1/29063, Operations in East Africa; Lt-Col. T. Stephens, 'A Joint Operation in Tanganyika', *Journal of the Royal United Services Institute*, CX (637) (Feb. 1965), 48–55.
74 Grove, *Vanguard to Trident*, 337–8.
75 Ibid., 311, 323.
76 For further details see J. Thompson, *No Picnic: 3 Commando Brigade in the South Atlantic, 1982* (London: Leo Cooper, 1992); and M. Clapp and E.

Southby-Tailyour, *Amphibious Assault Falklands: The Battle of San Carlos Water* (London: Leo Cooper, 1996).

77 The role was described as 'fast dash' because the ships had insufficient space to comfortably accommodate large numbers of troops and their equipment for anything but a short voyage.

78 M. Wells, 'Purple Warrior: Most Ambitious Joint Exercise since 1945', *Navy International*, Feb. 1988, 77–81.

79 J.J. Lok and R. Scott, 'Shipshapes for Amphibious Age: The Worldwide Renaissance of the Multirole Amphibious Ship', *Jane's International Defense Review*, No. 5 (1999), 41–7; Scott, 'Ocean's Wave is Set to Roll'.

80 Also known as the Chief of Combined Operations Staff (COCOS) for a period before adopting the title of Chief of Amphibious Warfare in 1951

81 Phillip Ziegler, *Mountbatten: The Official Biography* (London: Collins, 1985), chaps. 11–16.

82 Major-General V.D. Thomas (1950–4), Major General C.F. Phillips (1954–7), Major-General J.L. Moulton (1957–61) and Major-General R.D. Houghton (1961–2).

83 TNA: PRO, ADM 1/21178.

84 *War Office Exercise Spearhead. Annexure to Report (Blue Book)*; copy accessed in the library at the UK Joint Services Command and Staff College at Bracknell in 1999.

85 TNA: PRO, WO 216/202, War Office Exercise Spearhead.

86 TNA: PRO, DEFE 5/4, COS (47) 129(o), 'An Appreciation of our Capabilities and a Review of our Requirements in Combined Operations', 14 June 1947.

87 TNA: PRO, DEFE 5/5, COS (47) 157(o), memorandum by the Admiralty, 6 Aug. 1947.

88 C. Aspinall-Oglander, *Roger Keyes: The Biography of the Admiral of the Fleet Lord Keyes of Zeebrugge and Dover* (London: Hogarth Press, 1951), 400; Ziegler, *Mountbatten*, 154–5; Bernard Fergusson, *Watery Maze: The Story of Combined Operations* (London: Collins, 1961), 74–5.

89 Ziegler, *Mountbatten*, chaps 11 and 12.

90 TNA: PRO, DEFE 2/1178, COS (44) 414(o), 11 May 1944; PRO, CAB 79/54, COS (46) 190 mtg, 31 Dec. 1946; PRO, DEFE 5/3, COS (47) 55(o), 14 Mar. 1947; PRO, DEFE 5/25, COS (49) 236, 15 July 1949; PRO, DEFE 4/27, COS (49) 182 mtg, 8 Dec. 1949; PRO, DEFE 11/277, COS (50) 87, 9 Mar. 1950; PRO, DEFE 4/60, COS (53) 21 mtg, 10 Feb. 1953; PRO, DEFE 5/47, COS (53) 357, 22 July 1953.

91 Millett, *Semper Fidelis*, 328–30.

92 Lt-Col. R. Tomkins, USMC, 'British Combined Operations', *Marine Corps Gazette*, Dec. 1948.

93 TNA: PRO, DEFE 5/123, COS (62) 12, report by the Joint Planning Staff, 4 Jan. 1962.

94 TNA: PRO, DEFE 5/124, COS (62) 84, 28 Feb. 1962; PRO, DEFE 5/144, COS 365/63, 8 Nov. 1963; PRO, DEFE 4/148, COS (62) 68 mtg, 30 Oct. 1962.

95 TNA: PRO, ADM 167/146, Board of Admiralty Meeting, 7 June 1956.

96 Cmnd 1629, *Explanatory Statement on the Navy Estimates 1962–1963*.

97 TNA: PRO, ADM 205/192; E. Grove, 'Partnership Spurned: the Royal Navy's Search for a Joint Maritime-Air Strategy East of Suez, 1961–63', in N.A.M. Rodger (ed.), *Naval Power in the Twentieth Century* (London: Macmillan, 1996), 227–41.

98 TNA: PRO, COS (44) 166.

99 TNA: PRO, DEFE 2/1440, folio 1, docket CO(o) 7/49 (special folder), 'Report of Inter-Service Working Party on Shape and Size of the Armed Forces', 28 Feb. 1949.
100 TNA: PRO, DEFE 5/4, COS (49) 143, 23 Apr. 1949.
101 J.L. Moulton, *The Royal Marines* (Eastney: Royal Marines Museum, 1981), 111.
102 Ibid., 121 In 1960 No. 41 Commando and in 1961 No. 43 Commando were formed.
103 TNA: PRO, DEFE 7/1681.
104 Ibid.
105 TNA: PRO, ADM 205/185; PRO, ADM 205/191.
106 TNA: PRO, DEFE 5/150, COS 133/64, 15 Apr. 1964.
107 TNA: PRO, ADM 201/135.
108 Ibid.
109 Ibid.
110 Ibid. Letter from Vice-Admiral Sir Fitzroy Talbot to the Vice-Chief of the Naval Staff, 10 May 1967.
111 Grove, *Vanguard to Trident*, chap. 9.
112 I am indebted to Major-General Julian Thompson, RM, Major-General Andrew Whitehead, RM, and Commodore Mike Clapp for their advice on this matter.
113 Flag Officer 3rd Flotilla had previously been known as Flag Officer Carriers and Amphibious Ships.
114 The UK/Netherlands Amphibious Force was created in 1973. Under this arrangement a Royal Netherlands Marine Corps battalion operates as an integral element of No. 3 Commando Brigade for NATO contingencies.
115 The post was re-established 'about two years' before the Falklands conflict in 1982 when Rear-Admiral Derek Reffell was Flag Officer 3rd Flotilla. Clapp and Southby-Tailyour, *Amphibious Assault Falklands*, 1–9.
116 *Navy Strategic Plan 2000–2015*, www.royal-navy.mod.uk. Downloaded 14 Jan. 2002.
117 Including the Royal Marines.
118 Grove, *Vanguard to Trident*, 150.

10

ELECTRONICS AND THE ROYAL NAVY

1945 and after

Norman Friedman

Postwar modernization of the Royal Navy

Beginning in World War II, electronic systems came to dominate naval warfare. Thus the story of post-1945 British naval electronics is, to a considerable extent, the story of the technological development of the postwar Royal Navy. Britain ended World War II with some of the most sophisticated military electronic technology in the world, but with only a limited production base. With the country impoverished by the war and without a foreign market for advanced consumer technology (such as television), there was no mass market to feed a postwar electronic industry. Nor does there seem to have been an understanding, on the part of the British Government, of just how important such devices as electronic computers were likely to become. That was not a unique situation, but the scarcity of research money in post-1945 Britain (compared, say, to in the United States, meant that projects that, in the United States, would have received some money got none in Britain.[1] What money there was for civilian firms had to be allocated to specific systems, such as radars or sonars, rather than to broader industrial research. New naval concepts seem to have come virtually entirely from the array of Admiralty Laboratories.[2] By way of contrast, the U.S. approach seems to have been to combine internal research (which was considerable) with contracts to major companies. Until about 1949 it could be argued that the British approach was far superior, because companies were unlikely to risk their resources for small returns in a starving defense sector. Once it was generally understood that the Cold War had begun, however, companies in the United States realized that defense could be a major source of income, and their internal laboratories suddenly became an important defense resource.

As electronic systems developed, the character of warship design changed dramatically. Past warships had been "weight-critical," their internal components taking up relatively little volume. Very crudely, a ship's hull was generally the smallest that would support the weights of her main components (aircraft carriers were the main exception, because they were largely designed around the considerable volumes represented by hangars). Modern warships are generally "volume-critical": their components are not very heavy, but they take up considerable volume. That is why so many modern warships look so boxy. For the Royal Navy, this shift had unfortunate consequences. In 1945 the Royal Navy faced poverty, but it had enjoyed a considerable wartime windfall in the shape of numerous new warships, particularly carriers, cruisers, destroyers, and frigates. Its misfortune was that these ships had been designed very tightly in a weight-critical world. Moreover, their designs reflected missions and technology, particularly electronic, that was rapidly becoming obsolete. They lacked the volume for the new technology, and the Royal Navy lacked the funds for development of new systems. Considerable efforts were made to adapt war-built destroyers to some (albeit not all) new postwar roles, but attempts to adapt cruisers generally failed.[3] A lack of volume (and electric generating capacity) also probably limited the extent to which the Royal Navy could exploit technology and systems offered by the U.S. Navy. The need to build an entirely new fleet could not be met, given limited money, with very visible consequences from the late 1950s on. Carriers were successfully adapted, and that put off the decision to build new carriers until the 1960s – when they proved unaffordable.

In 1949 First Sea Lord Admiral Sir Bruce Fraser laid out what he considered the three main issues that postwar Western navies had to solve:

- countering fast aircraft and missiles;
- countering fast submarines and their long-range (including homing) torpedoes;
- countering pressure mines.

An additional issue, which Fraser presumably assumed was being solved, was how to overcome the modern defenses that enemy fleets could be expected to erect. In effect, Fraser was arguing that existing forces were no longer sufficient, and that new development was urgent.[4]

Admiral Fraser's threats were much like those the contemporary U.S. Navy faced, with one interesting exception. The Royal Navy had been forced into an implicit agreement with the Royal Air Force not to contemplate direct attacks from the sea against land targets, or at least against inshore land targets. On its part the Royal Air Force seems to have made no parallel agreement not to seek capabilities offshore, and indeed Coastal Command existed for exactly that purpose. This asymmetry would shape much of the British inter-service rivalry of the postwar period.

It might seem odd that as late as 1949 Admiral Fraser seemed to be speaking abstractly. By that time the future, or at least near-term, adversary was clearly the Soviet Union. The Soviets had known capabilities – but their future capabilities were essentially unknown. World War II had introduced several radical technologies, the best known being radar, jet aircraft, guided missiles, and nuclear weapons. To this list navies would add fast submarines, homing and pattern-running torpedoes, and pressure mines. Except for the atomic bomb, all had been developed in Germany, and thus examples of the new technology had all been seized by the advancing Red Army at the end of the war in Europe. Fraser's assumption, which proved accurate, was that the Soviets would exploit the new technology. However, technology was changing so fast that whatever was known of the enemy in 1949 would not be relevant by, say, 1959. Yet whatever countermeasures the Royal Navy could hope to deploy by 1959 had to be well in train a decade earlier. These problems applied equally to the other Western navies.

These issues in effect shaped modern Western naval systems. In each area the Royal Navy made vital contributions, many of them in the area of command and control. As in the invention of the turbojet, it can be argued that the British contributions were overtaken by others, particularly by the United States, because the British internal market was small and because it proved difficult to gain market by export. This situation can be contrasted with that before 1914, when the British internal naval market was the largest in the world, and when most navies trying to import technology bought British.

In 1949 the Royal Navy was in the early years of what was envisaged as a modernization program to be completed in 1957. The latter year was predicated on a Joint Intelligence Committee estimate, made about 1948, that the Soviets would not be in any position to fight a major war before 1957, which was denoted the "year of maximum danger." The concept of such a deadline for modernization was not actually new. In 1934, in view of the growing strength and bellicosity of Nazi Germany, the year 1939 had been chosen as the target date for defense modernization, the "year of maximum danger" (probably on the basis that the previous ten-year guarantee of no war should be replaced by a five-year danger horizon). This time the choice of 1957 was based on several factors, one being the expectation that Soviet recovery from the devastation of World War II would take about a decade. Another was that Stalin would not have an atomic bomb until 1952, and that it would then take the Soviets about five years to build up a sufficient stockpile to devastate the United States, and thus either to destroy it or at least to keep it out of a European war.[5]

The 1957 modernization schedule had important implications for British defense policy. Postwar Britain did not have the resources to develop new technology while mass-producing the latest existing equipment. For at least the first five years of the planning period, say 1948–53, the emphasis would be on new development, at the cost of operational effectiveness. Interim equipment, such as first- and second-generation jet fighters, just would not be bought, so that development of the later ("ultimate") systems could be pursued. Of course, planning concepts often prove inaccurate. When the Soviet-backed North Koreans invaded South Korea in June 1950, it seemed to many that the "year of maximum danger" had just been moved up seven years. The British tried to mobilize. Nothing had changed the calculus of resources and costs, and full mobilization proved impossible. What did happen was that investment in many of the 1957 systems was badly slowed. One visible symptom was that aircraft that should have been available in quantity in 1957 had still to fly in prototype form at that time.

The failure of mobilization triggered a major rethink of overall British strategy. It coincided roughly with the advent of the hydrogen (fusion) bomb. Where in 1948 it seemed likely that a future war might proceed for some time after fission bombs had severely damaged both sides, now it seemed far less likely that such a war could proceed at all. If H-bombs were used, both sides would effectively cease to exist. It followed that general war might not be possible at all, that it would be closed off by deterrence. In that case future warfare would probably be much more limited. The scope of the 1952 review was limited. For example, reserves maintained to fight the post-nuclear phase of the war were maintained, at considerable cost. The underlying assumption, that a future war would be a repeat version of World War II using newer weapons, was not really overthrown.

The entire 1948–57 program had been a response to what would now be called a revolution in military affairs heralded by wartime weapon developments, including the fission bomb. Under the pressure of the Cold War, by 1957 further revolutionary weapons were at hand, most notably the hydrogen bomb, the ballistic missile, and the nuclear submarine. Weapons that might have seemed adequate for the future when they were projected about 1949 now seemed obsolete. British policy had to be recast. The review was triggered by the failure at Suez in 1956: British forces had succeeded, but not quickly enough to avoid being pushed out of Egypt when the United States intervened. The mechanism by which the United States intervened was a threat to sterling. It might be argued that Britain was vulnerable because of the imbalance in her economy due to the cost of maintaining large standing forces – which had proven insufficient at Suez. In any case, the review that followed rejected expensive standing forces and changed the basis for British defense calculations. Now the assumption was that, for the moment, deterrence foreclosed the possibility of central war. It did not end the East–West hostility, but warfare would probably shift towards the Third World, including much of the Commonwealth. The central role of the Royal Navy would be to project force into the Third World, quite possibly in the face of modern Soviet-supplied weapons. The great example of just such a conflict was the confrontation with Indonesia. The new concept of defense ultimately justified a shift in defense spending towards mobile, particularly naval, forces, such as those that were to be built around a new generation of aircraft carriers.

The other side of the equation was that deterrence had to be maintained in Europe. That meant the connections with the United States and with overall NATO strategy. In the 1960s the U.S. view changed. Pure deterrence might fail. NATO had to be able to fight a lower-level war in Europe. To the extent that such a view was accepted, it meant that the earlier theme of a large-scale fight for sea control in the Atlantic was, if anything, more important. Thus, by the mid-1960s, the Royal Navy had two vital roles. One was sea control in the context of a major war short of central nuclear exchange. The other was power projection in the Third World, which generally meant "East of Suez."

In 1962 a third central role was added. The U.S. Government had agreed to supply Britain with a stand-off ballistic missile, Skybolt, which would have maintained the viability of the British strategic bomber force for at least another decade. Then Skybolt was cancelled. Given the rising capability of Soviet air defense missiles, it seemed that the British bombers were no longer likely to reach their assigned targets. The British choice was to shift the burden of deterrence to the Royal Navy, in the form of ballistic missile submarines. Unfortunately this new program coincided with the planned new-carrier program. The combination was deemed unaffordable. In 1965–6 the British Government decided first to abandon carriers in favor of long-range bombers (which were soon abandoned in their turn) and then to abandon the East of Suez policy, which was no longer viable. That left the Royal Navy with the Atlantic support role, which survived to the end of the Cold War. This role in turn shaped British naval investment in the 1970s and beyond.

Atlantic support had several aspects. The most publicized was anti-submarine warfare, particularly in the Greenland–Iceland–United Kingdom Gap which led from Soviet Arctic bases to the North Atlantic. A related role was amphibious support, to help keep the Soviets from seizing the Norwegian coast – which would have made NATO blockage of the Gap difficult or impossible. That justified continued operation of British amphibious forces, but it also required some degree of fire support. Ultimately that role was filled by Sea Harriers, which were fitted to deliver nuclear weapons. It was also necessary to protect British and other NATO surface units blocking the Gap, not only from Soviet submarines but also from surface and air forces. The latter role could have justified retention of large carriers, but at a governmental level it was accepted that land-based RAF interceptors would suffice. The anti-surface role caused the Royal Navy to adopt an anti-ship missile, Exocet, in 1974, and presumably explained efforts, using electronic surveillance methods (ESM), to detect Soviet surface ships beyond the horizon.

Successive British Governments had to balance various kinds of military power. In 1945 it was generally accepted that the United Kingdom was a great power, but what did that mean? If it meant the existence of a worldwide Empire and Commonwealth, then effort had to be expended to defend that entity against enemies both internal and external. To the extent that a world Communist movement, directed from Moscow, was fomenting the internal problems, the two were nearly identical. In either case, imperial security required substantial numbers of troops, which were expensive not only in direct terms but also in their opportunity cost to the British economy. There was also the direct threat to Britain. In the years immediately after 1945 the wartime experience of missile bombardment loomed large. It seemed that one countermeasure against future Soviet missile bombardment would be to keep the Soviet army out of missile range – which in turn meant maintaining a substantial modern army in Germany. The cost of modern mechanized forces was quite high. Finally, given the existence of nuclear weapons, it seemed that to remain a great power, Britain must possess them. The cost of developing a British bomb and British means of delivering it must have accounted for a large fraction of overall British defense spending in the immediate postwar period. Once the Soviets had their own bomb, in 1949, air defense became a more urgent issue, and it was also quite expensive. All of these factors limited resources available to the Royal Navy, and that limitation in turn pushed the Royal Navy towards missions that the other services could not perform, mainly anti-submarine warfare and mine countermeasures.

To some extent, the United States helped. Very close U.S. naval relations with the Royal Navy survived the end of World War II, and some of the new equipment being developed by the U.S. Navy was passed to the Royal Navy for tests. With the formation of NATO, the United States Government wanted to rebuild the European defense establishments so as to help the Europeans resist Soviet pressure. One mechanism was MDAP, the Mutual Defense Assistance Program, under which U.S. equipment was transferred directly. Another was a program of Offshore Purchases (OSP), under which the United States underwrote the production of foreign arms, and thus helped the various European (including British) arms industries revive. OSP included buying British equipment for other countries. After MDAP and OSP lapsed in the 1950s, the United States had bilateral agreements with the Royal Navy for development projects of mutual interest, such as certain sonars, and there were also special agreements to provide particular weapons.

At least through the mid-1960s, moreover, the British view was that weapon systems had to be compatible with U.S. equivalents so that, in wartime, as in World War II, the Royal Navy could exploit the much larger U.S. productive resources. The most obvious example was the decision to pursue a common caliber, 3in/70, for the initial postwar anti-aircraft weapon. Thus the Royal Navy could, in wartime, obtain both ammunition and replacement barrels. However, commonality did not mean adopting the U.S. gun mounting, or relying on U.S. ammunition in peacetime. In the case of torpedoes, it was necessary that British submarine fire controls be able to control both U.S. and British weapons. In the analog era, that entailed considerable complication. The British solution was to embrace more flexible digital technology, probably earlier than in the United States. One particular advantage, in the early 1960s, was that in wartime British submarines could be furnished with the futuristic Subroc anti-submarine missile – a weapon not adopted in peacetime.[6]

By the early 1960s there was apparently a feeling within the British Government that the United Kingdom could no longer develop major new military systems on an independent basis; the home market was too small to support escalating costs. Aggressive attempts were therefore made to find industrial partners, and the Government was apparently often willing to make sacrifices in order to gain customers for British products. For example, in the early 1960s the Royal Navy planned to buy a Dutch three-dimensional radar (Broomstick) for the new carrier and her accompanying destroyers in return for Dutch purchase of the new British Sea Dart missile. The Dutch rejected Sea Dart. Although surviving papers show no *quid pro quo*, the British did abandon Broomstick. Later, the Royal Navy adopted a version of the Dutch LW-08 radar (in preference to a British [Marconi] set) and the Dutch bought British Olympus gas turbines for their new-generation frigates. Such attempts did not approach the French policy of developing equipment specifically to attract export sales, then adopting the same equipment for their own forces.

The emergence of numerous small navies after 1945 offered a real possibility that exports of versions of key systems could make up at least in part for the shrinkage of the British home market. The prestige of British naval construction did survive World War II, and many navies retained strong ties with the Royal Navy. Quite possibly, however, much of the new technology, particularly in the electronic area, did not seem nearly as vital to potential export buyers as it did to the major navies who developed it (and some key systems were probably deemed unexportable for security reasons). This question is of more than academic interest.

There is a new interest in networked forms of warfare (Network-Centric Warfare in the United States, Network-Enabled Capability in the United Kingdom). Naval command and control, particularly as it developed after World War II, seems to be a small-scale model of the application of such ideas to more complex kinds of warfare ashore. The great question is whether armies and air forces adopt the new kind of warfare, which often seems counter-intuitive. Several major Western navies, particularly those of the United States, the United Kingdom, and the Netherlands, showed early appreciation of what was needed. The export market seems to have been far less responsive. Is that an unhappy indication of what will happen as the same ideas are offered outside the naval sphere?

Fleet air defense

In 1945 the existing naval air defense system was barely adequate to handle mass attacks such as those mounted by the Japanese Kamikazes. The system consisted of sensors, mainly (but not only) radars, feeding Action Information Organizations which maintained a tactical picture. Using various forms of that picture, incoming attackers were assigned to guns or to intercepting fighters (either deck-launched or on Combat Air Patrol). The Kamikazes stressed the system for several reasons.

First, unlike conventional attackers, they were not deterred by gunfire. A conventional attacker, no matter how brave, would be shaken by the sheer volume of fire. That would reduce his accuracy, so that more attackers had to concentrate to obtain a given number of hits. Concentration in turn reduced the number of separate raids the fleet had to handle. Conversely, if the attackers were not deterred, they had to be destroyed in order to protect the fleet. Anti-aircraft gunfire typically destroyed only a small fraction of the incoming attackers.

Second, because they did not have to concentrate to achieve hits, Kamikazes could split up, arriving from many directions. It was well known that a split attack was more effective against terminal defenses, but normally it had to be carefully coordinated. Coordination would both protect the attackers and insure hits. Kamikazes generally were not well enough trained to achieve much coordination, but then again they also did not have to concern themselves with survival. The net effect was to overwhelm the defensive system.

Third, the Kamikazes tended to approach at low altitude, which minimized warning time for the fleet. Just as fleet radars would not detect the attackers until quite late, the attackers had to be cued into position. That was difficult in the open sea. It was far easier when the fleet was tied to a specific objective, as at Okinawa. It could be assumed, then, that future low-level attackers would rely on cueing by "snoopers" equipped with long-range radar. Much would therefore depend on whether the fleet could either detect and destroy such aircraft at sufficient range, or at least could frustrate their own observation by jamming and decoying.

The Kamikazes seemed to be a glimpse of the future. From 1943 on, the Germans employed anti-ship guided missiles. Like Kamikazes, but unlike conventional attack aircraft, they could not be deterred by gunfire. The only direct defense was to neutralize them, either by directly destroying them or by somehow negating their guidance systems. An indirect defense would be to destroy the bombers launching such weapons, but that would have to be done at a considerable distance. Moreover, the threat offered by nuclear weapons was, in a way, analogous to that offered by guided missiles, in that the attacker would likely toss the bomb at the fleet from a considerable distance, perhaps ten miles or more. The weapon would not need guidance, because it would have an area effect.

One obvious countermeasure was to extend fleet anti-aircraft range. In 1944 the Royal Navy began work on its first anti-aircraft missile, LOP-GAP, which evolved into the postwar Seaslug. At least in theory, such weapons could be directed by extended versions of gunfire control radars. Indeed, the Type 901 control radar for Seaslug seems to have evolved out of the postwar long-range gunfire control system, the abortive LRS 1. The Seaslug effort itself suffered badly from the exodus of technicians and engineers at the end of World War II. As in the United States, there seems to have been little or no attempt to coordinate it with ongoing land-based air defense missile programs, despite the limited number of engineers who had to be spread over both broadly similar efforts.

As during World War II, the Royal Navy hoped that coordination with the parallel U.S. effort would help. By about 1954 it was clear that Seaslug would be a massive system; indeed, attempts to fit it into existing cruisers had been abandoned. Moreover, the missile's beam-riding guidance technique precluded effective low-altitude performance. The British claim that they convinced the U.S. Navy to take on the problem of producing a small-ship (destroyer) missile suited to low-altitude operation.[7] At this time the U.S. naval missiles (Terrier and Talos) both used beam-riding guidance, hence were expected to suffer from the same basic limitations as Seaslug (none of these missiles had yet entered service). The U.S. response was to develop a smaller semi-actively guided missile, Tartar. Presumably the Royal Navy planned to adopt Tartar, but that never happened.[8] The cost proved unacceptable. The British second-generation missile, Sea Dart, might be seen as an Anglicized Tartar, albeit with a very different airframe and engine.[9]

In the late 1970s the Royal Navy planned a Sea Dart improvement program which would have been broadly equivalent to the contemporary U.S. New Threat Upgrade, the missile being fitted with a commandable autopilot. Given this feature, a ship with a limited number of fire control channels could have commanded multiple missiles, to defeat saturation raids. In the event, this Sea Dart Mk 2 program was cancelled in 1981 in the aftermath of a defence review. Although many of the review's recommendations were reversed following the Falklands War, Sea Dart was never upgraded as planned. The Royal Navy will not get an anti-saturation weapon until the Type 45 destroyers, armed with the Aster missile, enter service.

In effect Seaslug and Sea Dart replaced long-range anti-aircraft guns. Initially it seemed that the Royal Navy would continue to buy short-range automatic weapons, and the standard weapon of the 1950s was to have been the new 70-caliber version of the 40 mm Bofors gun. However, a missile alternative appeared: Seacat, derived from a command-guided anti-tank missile. This type of guidance made it possible to adapt existing gunfire control systems to control Seacat. Seacat was adopted because it represented a technology at the beginning of its development, whereas the 40 mm/70 was seen as the last gasp of gun technology. Seacat was considered effective against subsonic targets, thanks in part to its continuous-rod warhead. In particular, it was likely to be able to shoot down the first-generation Soviet air-launched anti-ship missile, Komet (NATO AS-1), which by 1957 figured prominently in threat assessments. The Royal Navy never did buy the new Bofors. As an effective alternative to a small anti-aircraft gun, Seacat was very widely exported; for many navies it provided an entrée into the missile age.

Seacat was unlikely to be able to counter anti-ship missiles. As the Soviets continued to proliferate such weapons, a new small-ship defensive missile was needed. It entered service as Sea Wolf, a short-range supersonic command-guided weapon that is still in service.

A second effort was to improve sensor performance. By the end of World War II the Royal Navy had a combination of very broad-beam search radars, such as the Type 281 and Type 291 air warning sets, and much shorter-range microwave sets, such as Type 277 (which could function as a height-finder) and Type 293 (the "cheese"). Typical practice was to use the broad-beam sets for initial warning, passing targets to short-range Target Indication sets (293), which then passed them on to fire control sets. This technique contrasted with that used by the US Navy, whose narrower-beam search sets could pass targets directly to fire control. In 1945 the Royal Navy was developing a new generation of radars, comprising a new wide-beam set (Type 960), a new target indication set (Type 992), and a pair of shorter-range microwave sets for fighter control (Types 980 and 981, which later gave way to 982 and 983).[10] Of the latter pair, one would locate a target in range and bearing, the other measuring that target's height. The tacit assumption was that targets would be presented in relatively slow succession, so that height could be measured on one before the height-finder had to switch to another. Unfortunately, as the Kamikazes showed, targets might present themselves in all directions in very quick succession. The Admiralty Signals Research Establishment (ASRE) devised an alternative, which was designated Type 984. It was a true three-dimensional radar, in that it measured target altitude while it scanned for new targets. To do this Type 984 created a stack of vertically scanning beams produced in a single nacelle which rotated. The nacelle was mechanically stabilized against ship motion. It was the most sophisticated air-search radar of its time.[11]

Progress beyond Type 984 was far less satisfactory. By 1957 ASRE was working on an electrically scanned radar, Type 985, but that was abandoned in favor of a Dutch set, Broomstick (Type 988) – which would have equipped the abortive aircraft carrier of the 1960s, CVA-01. It would also have equipped the corresponding Type 82 escort. In the event, both the carrier and 988 were abandoned. Unfortunately, so was any effort to provide fleet escorts with modern three-dimensional radars. Several candidate replacement radars were evaluated, but none was chosen, presumably because the requirement was not considered urgent. The lack of such sets may have been considered acceptable given the improved performance of the Sea Dart missile, the missile's fire control set scanning in the vertical to lock onto a target indicated by a two-dimensional radar.

Escort radar was a vexed issue. In the early postwar period a distinction was drawn between anti-submarine escorts (Types 12 and 14), which needed only surface-search sets and short-range air defense sets; air defense frigates (Type 41), which needed similar gun air defense sets; and air direction frigates (Type 61), which needed much better air-search sets so that they could direct fighters. To the extent that any of these ships was fitted with a long-range air-search set, it was Type 960, a direct descendant of the wartime broad-beam sets. Type 61 had the new pair of fighter control radars (982/983). About 1954, however, the idea arose of a general-purpose frigate that would have some air control capacity, but would not be equipped with the full fighter control system. Such a ship would need a two-dimensional radar with much better beam definition than the wartime sets. There was initial interest in obtaining the contemporary U.S. destroyer radar, SPS-6C, under MDAP, but by this time the MDAP program was running down. Ultimately, a Marconi radar conceived for land-based air defense, which was designated Type 965, was chosen, and for years many British warships showed its distinctive "bedstead" antenna.

Type 965 had the important virtue of long range, thanks to its use of longer (metric) wavelengths. However, it had some important drawbacks. Its beam was still fairly broad. It also lacked any provision for moving target indication (MTI). MTI was relatively unimportant in the open ocean, but during the Falklands War the absence of such capability made it impossible for ships to detect Argentine aircraft flying over land before emerging over Falkland Sound to deliver their attacks. Type 965 was ultimately abandoned not because of its inherent limitations but because, with the development of television, it could no longer be used near land because its emissions interfered with those of television stations. The replacement, Type 1022, combined the electronics of the Dutch LW-08 air-search set with a new Marconi antenna planned for a more advanced (but abortive) radar.

This was hardly the end of efforts to develop a new advanced British air-search radar. The key question seems to have been whether to invest in a radar embodying contemporary technology or to try to jump to the next kind of radar technology. The choice seems to have fallen on the latter, which was active-array technology. Existing radars used a single transmitting tube which fed an antenna. In the late 1970s the most advanced antennas, like that of the U.S. SPY-1 of the Aegis system, used phase-shifters to move their beams electronically. Such beams could move extremely rapidly, but the radars could create only one beam at a time. Beam shaping was also somewhat limited by the technique used to form the beam. Thus the beam could not, for example, "null out" a jammer in order to negate its effects. The alternative was to form the antenna itself out of small radars. Coordinating the outputs of the elementary radars in the antenna would create one or more beams. This active array (active because its elements separately produced emissions) could also null out jammers.

The Admiralty Research Establishment (ARE) and Plessey began development of a single-face active-array radar, MESAR (Multifunction Electronically Scanned Adaptive Radar), in 1982, trials beginning in 1989. MESAR in turn developed into the Sampson radar which is to equip the new Type 45 destroyer. Like Type 984, it will probably be among the most advanced radars in the world when it emerges.[12] However, it is also noteworthy that until it appears, the Royal Navy will have had to make do with rather ancient radar technology.

The Admiralty was not the only radar developer in Britain. The combination of entirely commercial and official naval radar developers may have been unique to Britain.[13] From the mid-1950s on, both Marconi and Plessey marketed their own lines of commercial naval radars with some considerable success. Decca produced a line of commercial surface-search radars that for a time dominated the world market. These efforts supported British warship exports; in some cases British commercial radars equipped existing warships or ships built abroad.

By the mid-1950s ASRE was also developing another type of air defense sensor, a passive radar detector. Such devices had seen wartime service, but the postwar ones seem to have been new developments rather than derivatives of existing types. Radar detectors offered two complementary capabilities. One was to detect the sea-search or targeting radars of approaching bombers. Another was to detect surface radars, such as those submarines might use before firing torpedoes. The two roles entailed different emphases. For bomber detection, it was most important to achieve the earliest possible detection. Since the bomber would begin radiating at a considerable distance, and would keep doing so continuously, what mattered was sensitivity. That in turn required a narrow scanning beam. The beam might well miss many pulses, but if there were enough, it would pick up its target. The same was true of electronic sensitivity. A very sensitive receiver scanned a narrow frequency window over a wide range. Again, it would miss many pulses, but given enough pulses it would pick some up at long range. Surface radars were a different proposition. Submariners, for example, learned to turn their radars on only very briefly, sometimes sending out only a single pulse. To catch that elusive signal the receiver had to be available at all times: wide-open in both bearing and frequency, albeit at a considerable cost in maximum range. The British choice was the latter; the U.S. Navy chose the longer-range option.[14] ASRE produced a series of different sets, working over different frequency ranges, and by the early 1960s British surface warships were typically fitted with this equipment.[15]

The corresponding electronic weapon was the jammer, which was developed in two complementary ways. One was intended for the escort role. In the late 1950s and the early 1960s the main Soviet missile threat to ships came from bombers carrying stand-off missiles. The missile was typically locked onto its target before launch. The bomber therefore had to be able to distinguish the high-value target before firing. The escort (screening) jammer was intended to make this impossible, by producing an electronic target far larger than that of the ship being escorted.[16] The bomber could distinguish real targets only by approaching relatively closely, giving the fleet a far better chance of defending itself. Eventually ships were fitted with chaff projectors, to produce decoy targets. Later yet, there was a self-defense jammer intended to divert an incoming missile into a chaff cloud.[17]

All of these weapons could be classed as tactical. The Soviets used a variety of reconnaissance measures to coach missile-carrying bombers, ships, and submarines onto their targets. For example, ships and submarines firing some types of anti-ship missiles relied on special radar-equipped aircraft (Bear D, Tu-95Ts) to provide them with over-the-horizon data. These aircraft would operate outside the fleet's anti-aircraft missile range, but they could be attacked by sea-based fighters.[18] The existence of the Bear D helps explain the retention of fleet fighters in the form of the Sea Harrier. Presumably a Bear D would be located and tracked using passive electronic detectors. Later the Soviets tried to replace the Bear D with a satellite (they used both passive and active radars for this purpose). During the 1980s the Royal Navy fielded a new jammer,

Type 675 (Millpost), which was apparently intended to generate false targets so as to confuse either a Bear D or a satellite. It is not yet clear to what extent efforts were made to frustrate passive Soviet ship-detection satellites.[19]

A subtler counter was to automate the fleet control system built around the Action Information Organization created during World War II. By 1947 a team at ASRE, led by Professor Ralph Benjamin, CB, was developing the Comprehensive Display System (CDS), an analog combat direction system.[20] CDS seems to have been the first of its kind in any fleet. It envisaged automatically entering radar or other data into a central series of memories, the contents of which could be displayed to the many users of such data, including fighter controllers. The two central advances that made CDS possible were a technique for storing information in a bank of capacitors, and a means of transmitting information written on a display by one operator to others in the system. The CDS project included a data link between CDS ships, or between CDS and non-CDS ships. Although clearly system capacity was limited by the analog memory mechanism (one set of elements per track: the operational version could handle only 48 target tracks, and even the largest version envisaged was limited to 96), CDS enormously outperformed its manual predecessors. It became operational in HMS *Victorious* in 1958, and it also figured prominently in the British land air defense system. An improved version was very nearly adopted by the U.S. Air Force in 1952–3 (the digital alternative, SAGE, was bought instead). CDS demonstrated its capability spectacularly when *Victorious* exercised against U.S. aircraft on a 1958 visit to the United States.

CDS was associated with a three-dimensional radar, Type 984, which was developed in parallel with it. This radar in turn inspired what would now be called a network-centric approach to fleet air defense. It was soon clear that the Seaslug missile needed three-dimensional (height as well as range and bearing) information. By 1955 plans called for two distinct types of Seaslug ships, a very large cruiser and a missile destroyer. The cruiser could easily accommodate Type 984. However, the destroyer could accommodate the radar only at the cost of her 4.5-inch guns. Given the strategic situation – that the Royal Navy would often be used to put down minor Third World wars – the guns would often be at least as important as the missiles. How could the lack of three-dimensional radar coverage be made up?

The solution was to think of the destroyers working with the Type 984 ship as extensions of her surveillance system. If the destroyers were netted with the larger ship, they could share her three-dimensional radar picture. The first group of Seaslug destroyers had a less capable form of CDS fed by a CDS link receiver, DPT (digital picture transmission, sometimes rendered digital picture translation). This netting became, if anything, more important when the Seaslug cruiser was cancelled in 1957.[21]

CDS and 984 established a concept of operations. About 1957 ASRE began work on the successor radar, tentatively designated Type 985, which would have substituted electronic scanning for the mechanical scanning of 984.[22] At about the same time it also began work on a CDS successor in which a digital computer would replace the parallel analog memories of CDS. The new system was called Action Data Automation (ADA). In the event, Type 985 never materialized. However, by 1959 ADA was mature enough for installation on board the carrier HMS *Eagle*, working with her new Type 984 radar. By this time a second series of Seaslug destroyers was in prospect. Again, to be effective they had to be tied to a 984 ship. Digitization made the system much more compact than CDS, to the point where it could clearly fit on board a large destroyer. There was not, however, space or weight to accommodate both the new system and the usual fire control systems. The combat system computer, therefore, was programmed to control the ship's weapons. The combination system was called ADAWS (Action Data Automation Weapons System).

As in other systems of this type, much depended on the characteristics of the central computer. Ferranti developed the combat system computer, but the Admiralty served as system integrator, at least until the last few versions. A 24-bit configuration was chosen (at about the same time the U.S. Navy chose 30-bit computers).[23] As in other computer applications, overall size shrank dramatically and performance improved. The original British computer was Poseidon, and it was succeeded by an FM1600 series and then by F2420. The latter was credited with six times the processing power of its predecessors.[24]

ADA and ADAWS were developed at about the same time the U.S. Navy introduced its own digital combat direction system, NTDS (Naval Tactical Data System). It is clear that the two navies had close contact, but it is not at all clear that the developers of the two systems had much interaction. Indeed, basic operating concepts were different. NTDS was conceived as the core of a federated system, using existing fire control systems. Detection, moreover, would be manual, operators inserting data on targets they saw. That was much the way CDS had operated. For ADAWS the Royal Navy was considerably more ambitious. It wanted automatic target detection by the ship's radars, and it wanted integration between the new system and the ship's fire controls.[25] It turned out that automatic radar detection (plot extraction) was quite difficult; it was quite some years before it could be implemented. Integrated fire control was a simpler proposition, and indeed one the U.S. Navy adopted in the 1960s (apparently without reference to British practice).

Both navies expected to continue to operate in close conjunction. Both therefore wanted to be able to exchange tactical data. In the past, that had meant sharing common codes and common radio frequencies. Now it also meant sharing data links. Discussions of data links (which included the

Canadians as well) began in 1954. By 1958 they were being formalized by a TIDE (Tactical Information Data Exchange) committee, which ultimately adopted the current NATO-wide Link 11.[26]

About 1960 the Dutch began developing a new three-dimensional radar using a combination of electronic and mechanical scanning. The Royal Navy agreed to joint development, the British version being designated Type 988 (Broomstick). The new radar was conceived from the first as suited to destroyers, and that may be why the Royal Navy abandoned 985 in its favor. Also, by 1960 the Royal Navy was developing the Seaslug successor which later materialized as Sea Dart. There was hope that the Dutch would share development costs, both navies adopting a common 988–Sea Dart weapon system. With the new radar and the new weapon went a new version of ADAWS. It was to be produced in both a missile destroyer and a carrier version (ADAWS 2 and ADAWS 3).

Both the carrier and the destroyer also had a long-range ASW weapon, the Australian-developed Ikara. It was essential because the carrier battle group would be spread out over far too wide an area for existing weapons to cover. Although the group would employ ASW helicopters, they could not react instantly to a submarine approaching the group, which might be armed with anti-ship missiles. Like Sea Dart, Ikara was to be controlled by ADAWS.

In the event, the agreement over 988 broke down; only the Dutch ever adopted it, as SPS-01 for their *Heemskerck* class. Nor, to British disappointment, did the Dutch adopt Sea Dart; they preferred the U.S.-supplied Tartar. For their part, the British did not proceed with the new carrier, and they built only one of the envisaged carrier escorts, HMS *Bristol*.

However, the post-carrier Royal Navy still had to deal with enemy air attacks, and it still had to conduct anti-submarine warfare. By 1966, when the carrier force was cancelled, carrier-based helicopters with dipping sonars were a major factor in the latter. The Royal Navy was planning to move the helicopters off its carriers in order to free their decks for fighters and strike aircraft. It called its projected helicopter ships escort cruisers. In the aftermath of the carrier decision, the escort cruiser survived because it supported a vital fleet mission. The fleet air defense mission would be taken over largely by shipboard missiles, so the post-carrier fleet needed missile destroyers. Because Sea Dart did not require a three-dimensional radar, these ships, unlike the Seaslug destroyers, could operate effectively without relying on a carrier with a special radar. Moreover, they could function without the expensive 988. Thus a new small destroyer, Type 42, was developed, armed with Sea Dart.

In order to keep the destroyer small, its armament had to be limited quite drastically. Thus it could not carry Ikara. Plans for the post-carrier Royal Navy initially envisaged a common hull which could be built in either Sea Dart or Ikara versions. In the end it was simpler to rebuild existing *Leander* class frigates to carry Ikara.

Meanwhile the VSTOL Harrier, which could operate from the escort cruiser, became viable as a tactical aircraft. By about 1975, then, the Royal Navy could once more contemplate operating sea-based fixed-wing aircraft, and the escort cruiser was seen as a small aircraft carrier, albeit with much more limited capabilities than the earlier carriers. Unlike the carriers, it was armed with a long-range air defense missile, Sea Dart.

All three new warship classes were equipped with computer command systems in the ADAWS series: ADAWS 4 for the Type 42 destroyer, ADAWS 5 for the Ikara *Leander*, ADAWS 6 for the *Illustrious* class carrier.[27] These versions had a new feature, an austere data link (Link X, later called NATO Link 10), which was less demanding than the earlier Link 11. Operating with other NATO forces, particularly the U.S. Navy, required a gateway between the two links, which would have been provided by the carriers and by HMS *Bristol*. As built or as converted, Type 42 and the Ikara *Leander* were limited to Link X.

Later versions of ADAWS were upgrades. Thus ADAWS 7 was an upgrade of Mk 4 which added a data link processor (full Link 4 and Link 11 capacity) and a captain's console offering a summary view of the tactical situation. ADAWS 8 was for the final Batch 3 series of Type 42 destroyers, which had a digital sonar (Type 2016). ADAWS 10 was a carrier upgrade version, and ADAWS 12 was a further destroyer upgrade (ADIMP, the ADAWS Improvement Programmme).[28]

By the late 1960s it was clear that automated command systems were vital not only for fleet air defense or for area ASW defense, but also for other kinds of warfare. The Royal Navy therefore invested in a more austere system, CAAIS (Computer-Aided Action Information System), initially for frigates. It will be described below, under the heading of anti-submarine warfare. CAAIS used the same computer as ADAWS but had much more limited capability. By the 1970s ASW was as complex as anti-air warfare had been, and a new generation of systems was being developed to replace CAAIS in new frigates and in destroyers: CACS (Computer Aided Command System). That CACS was in effect an ADAWS replacement is shown by the fact that one of its versions was intended to replace ADAWS in Type 42 destroyers; another was destined for an abortive new missile destroyer, Type 43.

As might have been imagined, a combination of destroyers and small VSTOL carriers was not equivalent to the larger carriers that were discarded. In particular, the conventional carriers supported not only higher-performance interceptors, but also airborne early warning aircraft. These aircraft were important both for fleet air defense (they could detect targets beyond the fleet's horizon) and to support anti-ship strikes. As long as the Royal Navy was limited to operations in the North Atlantic and in the Norwegian Sea, it could be argued that land-based radar aircraft could replace the carrier-based ones. As it turned out, however, even after the abandonment of the "East of Suez" role the Royal Navy still had to operate on a global basis. The first post-carrier experience of this type was the war in the Falklands. As in the Soviet-strike scenario, the first stage in attacking the fleet was the appearance of a snooper operating beyond easy engagement range: in one case, an Argentine Boeing 707 airliner, in a second, a Neptune. In the first case the Argentine Air Force attacked the fleet, but without much success. In the second, the Neptune cued an Argentine Etendard fighter-bomber which hit HMS *Sheffield* with two Exocets, fatally damaging her. This and other experience in the Falklands convinced the Royal Navy that the VSTOL carriers needed some form of airborne early warning. As it happened, there had already been a proposal to place a Searchwater radar (derived from that on board the land-based Nimrod maritime patrol aircraft) on board the existing Sea King helicopter. It was quickly implemented under the pressure of war.

The war also demonstrated that the Sea Harrier was an effective fleet air defense aircraft. Prior to the war, it had been accepted as a strike asset, but apparently there had been skepticism as to its value, given its relatively low maximum speed. War experience thus ultimately led to a program to upgrade the Sea Harrier with a much more effective air-to-air radar and with the AMRAAM radar-guided missile. Thus equipped, Sea Harrier FA.2 was the most sophisticated air-to-air aircraft in Europe, albeit by no means the fastest. On the other hand, its upgrade was limited to electronic improvements, and it was not re-engined, so its payload suffered badly. To maintain their striking capability, the carriers had to take on board RAF Harriers suited only to ground attack. This practice had two consequences. One was a decision to amalgamate the RAF and Royal Navy Harrier forces, on the theory that they would have to operate together much of the time in any case. A second was to retire the Sea Harrier prematurely, on the theory that in a post-Cold War world the air threat to the fleet seemed to be waning. It would thus be a reasonable calculated risk to put off restoring Royal Navy air-to-air capability until the advent of the new Joint Strike Fighter, at least five years after the retirement of the Sea Harrier.

The question of strike warfare without carrier radar aircraft will be taken up below.

Anti-submarine warfare

As in air defense, the response to the increasing submarine threat came on several different levels. One was strategic. The main British World War II response to the U-boat threat was convoying, and the great problem at the end of the war was that existing escorts could not be expected to counter the new fast U-boats, let alone the even faster HTP type then in prospect. Their sensors and their weapons lacked sufficient range, and, at least as importantly, they were slower than the new U-boats. That is, submerged, the new U-boats could outrun them, precluding the sort of sustained hunting that had doomed earlier U-boats attacking convoys. Unfortunately faster escorts equipped with new weapons and sensors would necessarily be far more expensive than their World War II predecessors. Convoy was a strategy of numbers, because there had to be a fixed number of escorts for each group of ships to be protected. To some extent the problem could be solved, on a temporary basis, by converting wartime destroyers into escorts, but even then the numbers available would be limited at best.

The alternative was to try to pare down the threat closer to its source. Both the Royal Navy and the U.S. Navy became interested in using their submarines, the only platforms they had that could operate in waters nominally controlled by the Soviets, to attack Soviet submarines transiting to their operational areas. This new mission placed great stress on long-range detection and on the use of homing torpedoes, and both navies developed new sonars and weapons for this purpose.

As in fleet air defense, efforts can be divided into three categories: sensors (in this case, mainly sonars), weapons, and coordinating command/control systems.

British sonar development in the early postwar years was predicated on three considerations. One was that existing searchlight sonars were unlikely to be able to track fast submarines, which would flash into and out of their single beams. A second consideration was that passive operation would probably become increasingly important, the perception being that the new fast submarines would necessarily be quite loud.[29] This turned out to be false, but it shaped the new generation of British sonars. Moreover, the British considered listening vital as a means of torpedo detection and warning. Considerable early postwar effort went into developing hard-kill torpedo countermeasures.[30] A third was that range had to be increased, which meant that frequencies had to be reduced substantially. The first and third, but crucially not the second, considerations were shared by the U.S. Navy.

Work began in 1945 on a generation of sonars, to be ready over the next five years, to deal with the Type XXI and similar submarines (15 knots submerged, diving depth 1,000 ft).[31] The British view was that these were intermediate submarines; within a few years much faster submarines powered by closed-cycle engines would be in service.[32] In 1950 a new Staff Target was set: 25 knots submerged, 1,500 ft diving depth. Although the new closed-cycle submarines which would have reached such figures did not materialize, by the late 1950s nuclear submarines with just such characteristics were entering service.

Wartime sonars were searchlights. They projected a single beam. Normal practice was to send out a ping and to wait for its return before pointing the sonar in another direction. In 1945 a typical frigate had a pair of searchlight sonars, one for search and the other tiltable, to find the depth of a target. Given three-dimensional information, the ship could fire an ahead-thrown weapon such as Squid to burst near the submarine. The first postwar sets were extrapolations of this practice, with somewhat longer range to suit them to the new generation of underwater weapons. Thus the tiltable set became a target tracker (Type 170), with four elements. Comparison of returns in the different elements made it possible to keep the transducer pointed at a target submarine, both horizontally and vertically. Type 170 was associated with the successor to Squid, the longer-ranged Limbo (Mortar D). Associated with Type 170 was a new search sonar, Type 174.[33]

Searchlight operation greatly limited a sonar's ability to search for a submarine, particularly a fast one. Such sonars were most effective as means of maintaining contact with a submarine once she had been located, e.g., once she had revealed herself by firing a torpedo. The faster the submarine, as noted above, the less likely it was that a succession of pings in different directions would necessarily either locate her or maintain contact with her.

The solution was somehow to project multiple beams more or less simultaneously. The beam associated with an array of several transducers could be made to point in any desired direction by adjusting delays (phases) between its elements. That had long been known. As early as World War I both the Germans and the Americans had arrays of low-frequency transducers whose effective direction was set by adjusting delays (the Germans called the approach "electric water," because the delay lines were equivalent to moving the elements around in the water). The concept seems not to have been applied to sonars because there was little perceived need for anything much more complex than a rotatable searchlight. By late in World War II that was no longer the case.

The British approach was to wire multiple sonar transducers together to form several receiving beams working continuously.[34] A broad-beam ping could be sent out. In effect it would cover a broad range of bearings. The submarine's bearing would be indicated by which beam received the echo. This approach would later be called preformed beams. Its great advantage was that such a sonar could also listen in many directions effectively simultaneously, and thus was likely to pick up and to track a noise source, such as a loud submarine or an approaching torpedo. When implemented in analog form, the preformed-beam approach was clearly quite complex, and the number of beams it could support was quite limited. The sonar could not handle more than one target per beam. However, a single target caught in a beam could be located within the beam by phase comparison among the transducer elements. This rather complex technology seems to have been justified by the interest in passive operation (detection of what was then called "hydrophone effect"). In effect a preformed-beam sonar was always listening; it stared at the underwater environment rather than scanning through it.

That this was a distinctive approach is demonstrated by the fact that the U.S. Navy adopted a very different one, scanning sonar, in which a spinning commutator formed one narrow beam at a time in very rapid succession. Scanning was much easier to implement, but it was unlikely to detect transient sounds. It was adapted mainly to active operation.[35]

The first operational British preformed-beam sonar, Type 177, was conceived about 1949 and entered service in the 1970s. It could detect targets at a range of about 10,000 yds, but it was a planar rather than a cylindrical array. It was therefore limited to only a 40-degree sector.[36] That seemed adequate against the sort of fast submarines the Germans had introduced in 1945, but not the much faster craft that seemed likely to appear postwar. That is, a very fast submarine might well spend too little time in even a 40-degree sector to be tracked and attacked. The next step, then, was to substitute a cylindrical transducer capable of detecting submarines over something close to a 360-degree sector (it would still be limited by the ship's own noise, in a narrow sector pointing aft). This sonar, Type 184, began as a large-ship self-defense set, but was soon transformed into a standard surface ship set. It was specifically associated with automated data handling (ADAWS).

Type 177 equipped the first new-construction postwar escorts, such as Type 12 and Type 14 frigates and "County" class missile destroyers. Later units of these types, such as the *Leander* class frigates, had Type 184 instead.[37]

The initial postwar generation of British submarine sonars was Types 186 and 187. Type 187 was a bow-mounted attack (active) set operating at low and medium frequencies (2.5 and 10 kHz). Type 186 was a fixed passive sonar mounted in the submarine's ballast tanks. In effect it was a mobile equivalent of the contemporary British fixed underwater system, Corsair (see below).[38] Thus it had a narrow listening beam, so the submarine had to maneuver to listen in different directions. A digital multi-beam version with the same transducers was Type 2007.

The submarine sonar corresponding to the preformed-beam surface sets was Type 2001. It was developed specifically for the new nuclear submarines. Operating at a lower frequency than the surface sonars, it employed a massive fixed array of flat staves on the outside of the hull. Like the surface ship sets, it was wired to form a number of beams covering the space around it. Type 2001 produced a flood of data, far beyond what had previously been available. This flood in turn was expected to overwhelm manual plotting techniques, so in an important sense Type 2001 inspired the British project to develop submarine action data automation systems.[39]

The step beyond the analog preformed-beam sets was digital technology. A lower-frequency transducer using the new technology became Type 2016 (the ultimate development of this technology was Type 2050). Digital technology made it possible to combine the virtues of both multi-beam techniques. Beams were formed not by wired networks but rather by a computer incorporating the appropriate phase relationships. The computer was powerful enough to form many more beams (typically as many as there were staves or even transducer elements), so that the sonar could handle many more targets. On the other hand, each element was always open, so that the system could operate passively.

Surface ship hull sonars were limited in that they could not effectively search below the surface layer, which was typically about 300 ft deep in the winter North Atlantic. The Royal Navy adopted a Royal Canadian Navy variable-depth sonar (VDS), which it called Type 199 (using a Type 170 transducer); this set could be towed below the surface layer.[40] A more extreme version of the same concept was to use a nuclear submarine as, in effect, a self-powered VDS. This concept in turn required the submarine both to transmit sonar data to the surface force it supported and to keep track of the movements of that force (surface ships as well as submarines would register in its sonar picture). This latter concept was similar to, but seems to have considerably preceded, the U.S. practice of direct support of surface forces by submarines.[41]

These were all sonars fitted to individual ships. The British also developed sonobuoys for aircraft and fixed sonars for broad-area coverage. Aircraft sonobuoys, passive and active, were broadly comparable to those developed in the United States, and employed similar technologies. For example, the two countries shared the central postwar passive sonar invention, LOFAR – narrow-band low-frequency analysis – which for many years was not shared with other NATO countries.[42]

The British fixed-sonar project was Corsair. It was generally described as less sophisticated than the contemporary U.S. SOSUS system, with a shorter maximum range.[43] The political significance of Corsair was that, if it were successful, it could be used to cue RAF land-based maritime patrol aircraft to attack submarines within sonar range of the British Isles. These aircraft could, in effect, replace British naval forces. Corsair was not particularly successful. However, in the early 1970s the U.S. SOSUS system was extended to the Eastern Atlantic. The main barrier to that effort had been the problem of canceling out the strong shipping noise in the area.

A third application of passive sonar technology emerged: towed arrays. It appears that the towed array concept originated with the U.S. Navy, but that the Royal Navy applied it very differently. The basic concept was that a line array of hydrophones was towed well abaft a ship, so far abaft as to be isolated from much of the ship's own noise. The U.S. Navy distinguished between relatively short tactical arrays with limited range and much longer surveillance arrays intended to substitute for SOSUS arrays on the sea floor. The Royal Navy placed tactical arrays on board some submarines, but it was reluctant to buy both tactical and surveillance arrays for surface ships. Instead, it bought long arrays for frigates assigned to surveillance duty in the Greenland–Iceland–UK Gap.[44] The frigates would detect submarines at considerable ranges, and they would cue other forces – largely maritime patrol aircraft – to intercept them. An important British electronic contribution was a new processing architecture (the Curtis architecture), which apparently made shipboard handling of data from long arrays practicable.

The combination of Eastern Atlantic SOSUS and the towed arrays in the Gap made land-based patrol aircraft, at least in theory, far more effective. This possibility was an important factor in the 1981 defence review, which entailed a drastic reduction in British naval forces (and was itself partly reversed due to the outcome of the Falklands War).

Ultimately, sensors are valuable only insofar as they support weapons. In 1945 the two principal ASW weapons were depth charges and ahead-thrown weapons (Hedgehogs and Squids). ASW homing torpedoes had been used, but only in limited numbers. Depth charges were unlikely to be effective against future fast submarines, so attention focused on ahead-thrown weapons, Squid and a new Limbo. Their bombs were time-fused to explode at a set depth, so fire control required a sonar that could tilt to measure that parameter (and, incidentally, to maintain contact with the target as the attacking ship approached).[45]

Limbo represented the effective limit of an unguided ship-fired weapon. By about 1949 it seemed that the future lay with homing torpedoes, which it was hoped would be available by about 1957. In fact development was quite protracted, and although many escorts of the 1950s and 1960s were to have had torpedo tubes, in fact few did.[46] British full-size homing torpedoes were carried only by submarines. Surface ships eventually received U.S.-supplied lightweight torpedoes, which could also be delivered by helicopter and by a command-guided missile, the Australian-developed Ikara.[47] As an alternative to air-delivered lightweight torpedoes, the Royal Navy had nuclear depth bombs. The chief argument in their favor was electronic. As the Soviets introduced increasingly faster submarines, it was by no means clear that homing torpedoes running fast enough to catch them could use their sonar seekers. Torpedo designers generally seek a 50 percent speed margin over their targets. That is why the 30-knot Mk 44 air-launched torpedo was considered adequate against diesel submarines, which probably would not exceed 20 knots submerged, but grossly inadequate against nuclear submarines, whose nominal speed was 30 knots. The Mk 46 torpedo (45 knots) could, at least in theory, deal with most nuclear submarines. However, when the Soviets introduced much faster types, such as the "Alfa" (40-plus knots), even Mk 46 was inadequate, and it could be argued that the limit achievable with a small-diameter sonar had been reached. Hence the interest in nuclear depth bombs.

Helicopter and Ikara delivery offered surface ships an ASW weapon whose range matched that of the new lower-frequency sonars. Two quite different kinds of helicopter delivery were developed. The first involved a relatively large helicopter (Wessex) with its own dipping sonar, hence capable of independent search. The Royal Navy experimented with a U.S.-supplied dipper, AQS-4, but then developed its own Type 195, which in design was a higher-frequency equivalent to the contemporary Type 177.[48] Wessexes and their Sea King successors were generally operated from carriers, but Wessexes also operated from 'County' class missile destroyers. They were considered too massive for frigates.

The frigate solution was a lightweight helicopter that the frigate combat system could command into place to drop a homing torpedo. The helicopter could also deliver a small anti-ship missile, and thus could provide the ship with limited over-the-horizon capability. This Match system differed considerably from its U.S. counterparts. It was, in effect, a smaller-ship alternative to Ikara.[49]

Ultimately sensors drive weapons through a combat direction system. By 1948 the Royal Navy was well aware that success against fast submarines would require cooperation among several platforms, probably including aircraft. A broad requirement was stated for a system that would display the positions and sonar data of several platforms simultaneously. Those developing CDS at ASRE realized that this was the air defense problem, but on a smaller and slower scale. In 1951 ASRE proposed that the new CDS technology be applied to the ASW problem. Project Cambria was initiated, and a prototype of the new Automatic Surface Plot (ASP) went to sea for tests in 1953. It appears not to have been adopted in any quantity, probably because the data storage element would have been fairly massive.[50] Instead British escorts were fitted with an enhanced version of the existing plotting table, JYA. However, Cambria demonstrated that the technology developed for fleet air defense could be applied to multi-platform ASW.

By the late 1960s, digital technology was mature enough and inexpensive enough to be installed in frigates. In effect Cambria was now affordable, and digital computers offered far greater capacity than what had been envisaged in 1953. The Royal Navy bought a single-computer system, CAAIS (Computer Aided Action Information System), for its frigates. Unlike ADAWS, CAAIS was a track-keeper and target designator separate from any fire control system. In existing ships, it could be connected to existing analog fire controls. In new ships, it could feed into a separate digital fire control system.[51] Like ADAWS, CAAIS envisaged a data link, in this case the simplified Link X. The initial Operational Requirement, for the system to be installed on board the new Type 21 frigate, was issued in 1966. It limited unit cost to £100,000. The first version actually produced was for the Argentine carrier *25 de Mayo* (1968), so that the ship could work with the new Type 42 destroyers, with their ADAWS and Link Y (export version of Link X) that the Argentines were buying. CAAIS entered British service in 1974, on board frigates. The system enjoyed considerable export success.[52]

ASW also prompted the Royal Navy to automate submarine tactical data handling, probably well before the U.S. Navy took that step. It is not clear to what extent such automation was seen as necessary for a submarine operating in direct support of surface units.[53]

Mine countermeasures

The Royal Navy was well aware of the potential of mine warfare. In 1945 much of the internal traffic supporting Britain was carried by coastal shipping. Shutting down the Port of London, for example, might well starve the capital. War experience showed that vast numbers of sweepers were needed to keep channels clear. One major problem was that the cleared channel had to be marked. An enemy could then see what had been cleared, and could concentrate on mining just that channel. It seemed, moreover, that the chief mine threat would be enemy aircraft. Electronics offered some solutions. The Royal Navy developed what it called leader cable, which could be laid on the seabed to indicate a clear channel, without making that indication visible to an enemy bent on re-mining. A simple indicator on board a merchant ship would allow it to follow the cable. Another electronic measure was shore radar specially adapted to mine-watching, i.e., to detecting where mines had been laid.

Unfortunately the new mines, particularly pressure mines, presented much greater problems. The initial approach, begun during World War II, was to seek some means of detonating pressure mines by imitating the pressure signature of a passing ship. Efforts included building large but nearly unsinkable objects, running groups of barges, and also using explosives to project a pressure pulse over the mine. None was particularly successful. Ultimately, both the Royal Navy and the U.S. Navy came to the same conclusion, that pressure mines had to be detected and neutralized one by one. This was mine-hunting, and it required an electronic solution in the form of a precision sonar that could distinguish a mine from other objects on the sea bottom, particularly after the mine had been covered by marine growth. It is not clear which navy first developed such a sonar, but the Royal Navy was certainly a leading developer with its Type 193.[54]

Surface warfare

Through the post-World War II period, the Royal Navy continued to maintain a strong interest in surface warfare. That might seem odd, given that before 1939 all navies agreed that their primary wartime role would be to sink each other's ships. However, in 1945 it seemed that the Western navies had gained sea control. At least to Americans, it seemed that the future primary naval roles would be to strike shore targets and to neutralize the enemy's sea denial forces, his submarines and his naval bombers. The Royal Navy seems to have maintained a much more respectful position with regard to Soviet naval surface forces. Presumably that was partly due to its own experience of Arctic operations during World War II, when weather limited the extent to which aircraft could counter surface ships. Also, the postwar Royal Navy had very limited numbers of carriers and carrier-based aircraft. It did lay down an operational requirement for an air-launched anti-ship missile, but that project was not pursued very far. The project to arm British Scimitar fighters with nuclear weapons was justified on anti-ship grounds.

The central question was probably to what extent potential convoy escorts could be provided with effective anti-ship weapons. That was key because it seemed unlikely that the Royal Navy could maintain sufficient numbers of larger ships to deal with potential surface raiders. In the past, it had been assumed that the torpedoes on board destroyers would suffice. However, successful surface torpedo attacks were quite rare during World War II, and it seemed likely that, with the advent of surface search radar, few if any destroyers would be able to penetrate to within torpedo range. There were really three possibilities. One was superior gunfire control, which might make it possible for a smaller ship to defeat a larger, albeit lightly armed one, using weapons with high rates of fire. A second was to develop anti-ship homing torpedoes, which could be effective at far longer ranges. A third was missiles, which initially seemed to mean anti-ship capability in missiles designed primarily to defeat aircraft. All three were pursued, with varying degrees of success.

In effect, gunfire control was a predigital electronic solution. By 1945 the Royal Navy considered its surface fire control systems far advanced. By 1948 the Royal Navy was working on a rapid-fire 5in/70 gun, roughly in parallel with a U.S. project (which latter, however, was not pursued).[55] By that time the Admiralty was beginning to consider what ships it wanted to have by the end of the modernization period, 1957. Initial studies showed that both destroyers and cruisers incorporating modern weapons and sensors would be prohibitively expensive. The Controller, Admiral Edwards, proposed an alternative: a cruiser-destroyer intermediate between the two categories, practicable if it was armed with the new gun controlled by the new systems. This concept was pursued for the next six years. It died for several reasons, among them the collapse of the 5in/70 project and the discovery that a hull of the desired small size could not accommodate sufficiently powerful machinery. In a programmatic sense the successor was the 'County' class missile destroyer – whose Seaslug missile, at least in its Mk 2 version, did have a significant anti-ship capability.

In the early 1960s a new surface threat appeared in the form of torpedo and missile boats that the Soviets exported widely throughout the Third World. Given the range of their weapons, such craft had to be dealt with at considerable range. By this time the Royal Navy was planning to equip frigates with small helicopters, primarily to deliver lightweight torpedoes against submarines (Match). It was relatively simple to provide the same helicopters with a lightweight anti-ship missile, initially the French-supplied wire-guided AS 12, later the British-developed Sea Skua. Presumably the frigate was expected to detect the missile boat using ESM. Note that it took a manned helicopter to deliver an anti-ship missile, since judgment was involved. Thus it was fortunate for the Royal Navy that it had not adopted a drone like the U.S. Navy's Dash for remote torpedo delivery. The attack boat threat would have been emphasized by the events of the confrontation with Indonesia, but the decision to arm the helicopters with anti-boat missiles seems to have predated that crisis.

By the late 1960s Western companies were developing their own anti-ship missiles, examples being the French Exocet and the Swedish Rb08. The Royal Navy decided to adopt such a weapon, choosing the French Exocet over a British project on the basis that Exocet would be available sooner at much the same price. Because these weapons had limited ranges, they did not need a new ship detector; the ship's usual ESM systems would suffice.

For longer ranges the Royal Navy depended on carrier-based Buccaneer aircraft, which could use their onboard ESM sets to locate their targets. Initial location would be either by carrier-based radar aircraft (otherwise used for early warning of enemy attack) or by offboard sensors, presumably the British shore-based HF direction-finder net.[56] Neither system was likely to be effective in the event the Royal Navy could no longer operate carriers. Thus a Royal Navy position paper on a carrier-less fleet, prepared when the construction of new carriers was questioned, argued that surface-launched anti-ship missiles of sufficient range could certainly be built, but that the most expensive element of the system employing them would be the means of localizing enemy warships sufficiently well.

Although the Royal Navy lost its large-deck carriers, it did obtain smaller ones capable of operating VSTOL Sea Harriers. The new ships could not, at least at first, support radar aircraft, but the Sea Harriers could accommodate radars and ESM receivers broadly comparable to those that had equipped the Buccaneers. They could, moreover, deliver new Sea Eagle stand-off missiles using those sensors. The advent of the small carriers and of the Sea Harriers coincided roughly with the advent of computerized ship tracking, by means of which data from existing sensors could be collated centrally. Satellites could provide a reliable channel between the collation center (FOCSLE, the command center at Northwood) to the deployed carriers. As it happened, the Royal Navy was the first to deploy naval satellite communication systems. It is not clear to what extent the decision to deploy such systems was connected with the creation of a computerized command center ashore. However, the Royal Navy did have a long history of such operations. It had long seen the shore center as an operational headquarters, collecting intelligence that would be used to create an operational picture, on the basis of which operational orders could be given.[57] The particular form taken, and the use of satellites, may be traceable to a U.S. initiative of the mid-1970s, the creation of ashore Fleet Command Centers (FCCs) communicating with comparable afloat centers (Tactical Flag Command Centers, or TFCCs). A central role of the FCC was to create a usable picture of world shipping movements on the basis of intelligence sources such as shore HF direction-finders.

Notes

All papers are from The National Archives: Public Record Office (TNA: PRO) unless otherwise identified.

1 Accounts of efforts by Ferranti Bros. to attract government funding suggest this; note also that the Ferranti computer contribution to DATAR, the Canadian digital combat direction system (the first of its kind in the world), seems to have been very much at the behest of Ferranti rather than at that of the Canadian Government. There seems not to have been any British equivalent of the U.S. Navy-financed Whirlwind real-time computer, which proved pivotal in the development of North American air defense (SAGE, the Semi-Automatic Ground Environment). Early British digital computers seem to have been developed within universities, as scientific tools rather than for the British military. SAGE in turn was in effect the proof-of-concept for the later U.S. NTDS (Naval Tactical Data System). DATAR was key because its existence led a 1954–5 U.S. working group on extending SAGE to call for the U.S. Navy to adopt it. Instead the Navy developed the far more powerful NTDS. For the working group papers, at the Lamplight conference (which British representatives attended), see DEFE 7/2084. Ferranti in turn played a key role in naval combat system development, ultimately becoming the principal developer of combat direction systems, until the collapse of the CACS system for the Type 23 frigate in the 1980s.

2 Like the U.S. Navy, in 1945 the Royal Navy relied mainly on its internal resources for research. Thus its warships were designed, in their early stages, almost exclusively by the Royal Corps of Naval Constructors under the Director of Naval Construction, which was backed by the Admiralty

Experimental Works (AEW); AEW in turn operated the large model tank at Haslar. The parallel Director of Naval Engineering (machinery) department had its own experimental laboratory, although apparently on a considerably smaller scale (British naval machinery was developed largely by civilian industry). It is not clear to what extent the Director of Naval Ordnance had his own research arm, at least before World War II. Most guns and mounts were privately developed, although torpedoes were an Admiralty responsibility, and there was a Royal Navy Torpedo Factory. During World War I an Admiralty Research Department was formed, apparently largely to deal with the new problems of radio and of underwater sound. It created the Admiralty Research Laboratory (ARL). During World War II a variety of specialized laboratories were created. They included the Admiralty Signal Establishment (ASE, 1941), which became the Admiralty Signal and Radar Establishment (ASRE) in 1948. ASRE was responsible for postwar combat direction system development. An Admiralty Anti-Submarine Experimental Establishment was created in 1940; it became the Admiralty Underwater Detection Establishment (AUDE) in 1947. A separate Admiralty Mining Establishment was created in 1946. An Admiralty Gunnery Establishment (AGE) was created in 1943, to develop both new weapons and new fire control systems. An Admiralty Underwater Weapons Launching Establishment was created in 1947. There were also new establishments for hull and machinery research, such as the Admiralty Underwater Explosion Research (UNDEX) establishment, for full-scale ship tests (mainly against underwater weapons), set up in 1943; the Admiralty Naval Construction Research Establishment (1946–78); and a unique Admiralty–private company combination, the Yarrow Admiralty Research Department, set up in 1946 to develop new warship machinery.

Many of these organizations were heirs to particular wartime establishments, and postwar there was considerable pressure for consolidation. Thus an Admiralty Underwater Countermeasures and Weapons Establishment (AUCWE, 1951) incorporated, for example, the Admiralty Mining Establishment. In the wake of a major review of naval shore establishments in 1957 (the 'Way Ahead' review) there were further consolidations. AGE and ASRE merged into a new Admiralty Surface Weapons Establishment (ASWE) in 1959. AUDE, AUCWE, and the Admiralty Torpedo Experimental Establishment (set up, 1943) merged into a new Admiralty Underwater Weapons Establishment in 1959–60. From about 1977 on, the purely naval laboratories merged into a single Defence research organization, DERA. There was also increasing emphasis on leaving development to industry. Past practice had been to develop at least brassboard models of new electronic equipment in Admiralty (or, later, Defence) establishments, usually leaving detailed development to industry. That gave way to setting Cardinal Points specifications, leaving the entire technical development to industrial competition – supported by basic research at DERA (and by companies' own research). This evolution is basically similar to what has happened in the United States; it is not clear which country led in reducing the role of internal government laboratories. In the case of torpedoes, as in the United States, a major developmental disaster (in this case, Tigerfish/Mk 24) led to the demise of in-house development. For the decision to amalgamate laboratories into underwater and above-water groups, see the 1957 Admiralty Board papers, ADM 167/150, memorandum B.1147.

3 In particular, cruisers could not be adapted to carry the new British anti-aircraft missile, Seaslug, so a new generation of very large destroyers

("County" class) had to be built. By way of contrast, the US Navy deployed its first-generation anti-aircraft missiles, Terrier and Talos, aboard eleven existing cruisers (it also built numerous new Terrier ships). Such deployment brought the missiles into service earlier than would otherwise have been the case, and in greater numbers. In the British case, the inability to modernize cruisers, beyond limited improvements in anti-aircraft fire control and armament, led to early disposal of ships completed in 1945. A second case in point is the unhappy state of British anti-aircraft fire control systems at the end of World War II. The only satisfactory system was the new Mk 6/Flyplane, which was fitted in new "Battle" and later destroyers. Only ships refitted with it, such as the "C" class (as modernized), could be considered capable of standing off even propeller-driven aircraft. The gap in fire control limited the value of the very large fleet of war-built destroyers.

4 Possibly Admiral Fraser's earliest statement of these priorities was a 14 October 1948 memo he sent the Controller, laying out his three research priorities: (a) pressure mine countermeasures; (b) guided missiles; (c) torpedo countermeasures (on the assumption that the new submarines would often be able to fire unimpeded). ADM 205/69.

5 The U.S. Government seems to have adopted the British concept. The dependence on the date of the Soviet nuclear bomb shows in the U.S. shift to 1954 as the "year of maximum danger" after the Soviets tested their bomb in 1949. It appears that the British Government did not adopt this new calculation. See ADM 116/5966.

6 See, e.g., ADM1/27977, a 1961 paper on the armament of future British submarines, including Subroc.

7 See ADM 220/737, "Report on the Low-Altitude Target Symposium and Other Discussions in the United States," January 1953 (report dated 22 May 1953). The U.S. Navy had recently issued a Staff Requirement for a new small-ship missile, suited to a destroyer, to achieve a maximum range of 15,000 yds. It would use a Raytheon CW Doppler homer, presumably the semi-active system ultimately adopted for Tartar. According to the British report, the initial BuOrd study "was initiated largely as a result of British encouragement, and the specification employed owed much to BJSM [British Joint Services Mission to Washington]."

8 No documents bearing on this decision have been found. The U.S. Navy did provide Tartar to several allies: the Italians, the French, the Dutch, the Japanese, and the Spanish, in roughly that order. It is possible that the British decision to adopt several U.S. ASW weapons, including the Mk 44 torpedo, consumed the dollars that might otherwise have been spent on Tartar. There also may have been a conscious decision that it was vital to preserve the British missile industry. The French made just such a decision when they rejected a U.S. offer of Terrier in favor of completing development of their own Masurca (which, in its final version, was virtually an enlarged version of Terrier). They then accepted Tartar in order to gain access to its new semi-active guidance technique, which they applied back to an improved version of Masurca. Other recipients of Tartar had no surface-to-air missile programs of their own, hence did not face the issue the British and the French faced.

9 By this time the requirement that British weapon systems be able to use U.S. ammunition had clearly been abandoned. The 1960 deliberations on what would become Sea Dart (CF 299), recounted in ADM 1/27647, indicate that Tartar was considered too massive and too expensive; the British wanted a system that could replace a frigate gunnery system (gun mount and director)

in a 3,000-ton warship. Tartar was described as being at the end of its development lifetime, a judgment that would presumably surprise those currently using versions of the U.S. Standard Missile descended from Tartar. Nowhere in the 1960 British document does the issue of ammunition commonality arise, presumably because by then the notion of protracted large-scale war had gone.

10 Types 980 and 981 in turn superseded two late-war projects, Types 294 and 295.

11 In effect, then, Type 984 was a combination of several radars, each scanning simultaneously in the vertical. Of more or less contemporary long-range 3-D radars, the U.S. SPS-2 and the French DRBI-23 also used stacked beams, but neither scanned the stacked beams vertically. Almost all 3-D radars (such as the British Type 983 or the U.S. SPS-8 or -30 or -39) scanned a single beam vertically as they rotated. That limited their effective range, because the beam spent very little of its time staring in any one direction. The U.S. Navy eventually solved the problem by stacking multiple scanning beams in its SPS-48.

12 The Germans and the Dutch have already fielded an active-array shipboard radar, APAR, on board their missile frigates. However, it operates at X-band and hence lacks the range of the S-band Sampson. The U.S. Navy is developing an active-array successor to the SPY-1 of the Aegis system, but it will probably go to sea sometime after Sampson.

13 In most countries a single entity created the country's naval radars and exported versions of them. That certainly applied to France (Thomson-CSF), to Italy (Selenia), and to the Netherlands (Signaal). In the United States, different companies were credited with various radars, but basic radar research was all done by the Navy, and there were no commercial radars produced only for export.

14 See Admiral of the Fleet Sir Edward Ashmore in the Foreword to D.G. Kiely, *Naval Electronic Warfare* (London: Brassey's, 1988). This distinction lasted into the late 1960s, the standard U.S. set being the scanning (in both direction and frequency) WLR-1. Only with the current SLQ-32 did the U.S. Navy adopt a wide-open system (it already had some wide-open threat warners).

15 The British systems were designated in a UA series, different units operating with varying degrees of sophistication in signal processing. The simplest, UA-1 through -4, converted the pulse rate of the detected radar into an audio signal, which the operator heard through earphones or through a loudspeaker. With earphones he could measure the pulse rate by varying the sound in one ear for comparison with the radar signal coming in through the other. The use of such devices explains why some Soviet radars received NATO code-names like Owl Screech. The first of the series, UA-1 was tested in 1953 (see ADM 220/1209). The last, the submarine UA-4 (Naive), was tested in 1960 (see ADM 220/1251). The loudspeaker technique became useless as the number of radars that might be detected simultaneously in a given frequency band rose dramatically. It then became necessary for the receiving system to sort out the trains of pulses it received. The next step was to replace the wideband crystal-video receivers of the UA-1 through -4 series with broadband superheterodyne receivers that could measure signal frequency within a band. Signals could then be sorted by frequency into trains of pulses, the system measuring the pulse rate electronically. Ultimately the received signal could be compared with those in a library. This series (Porker) was UA-8 through -10 for, respectively, S-, C-, and X-bands. The first in the series, UA-9, ran sea trials in 1960 (see ADM 220/1252). The series also included intelligence-gathering sets. In 1952 there

was an urgent need for a portable battery-operated video detector, for use at sea, presumably on board ships that might not be recognized as intelligence-gatherers. Battery operation proved impossible, but the required set, which was produced by ASRE in ten days, could be powered by a ship's electrical system. These systems became UA-6 for S-band and UA-7 for X-band. See ADM 220/1224 and 1225. The UA-10 series was later extended in frequency down to UHF (UA-13) and up to J-band (UA-15); UA-11 and -12 were submarine sets. The next step was a single integrated system, Abbey Hill (UAA-1), covering the full radar band up to J-band. It was introduced in the 1970s for Type 42 destroyers and Type 21 frigates. It incorporated instantaneous frequency measurement (IFM). The next major advance was UAF, for the 'Duke' class (Type 23) in the 1980s; it introduced a color display.

16 The British systems were Types 667 and 668, both code-named Cooky. Both were spot noise jammers producing 30-degree beams. Type 667 could jam both S- and X-band; 668 was limited to X-band to save internal space. Cooky could make it impossible for the standard S-band air-to-surface radar, APS-20, to detect a carrier beyond 25–35 nm, and it could screen an aircraft carrier against X-band radar to 10 nm. It could screen a destroyer to 5 nm in S-band, and completely in X-band. The idea was to force an enemy to within range of fleet air defense missiles by screening to within that range. Thus Cooky became an integral part of the British fleet air defense system. The U.S. Navy used an equivalent 'blip enhancer' described as making all the ships in a group seem to be carriers. Lore had it that too many crewmen knew too much about its function, and therefore that it proved quite unreliable in practice. The successor broadband jammer was Type 670 (Heather).

17 Soviet anti-ship missiles, at least early ones such as Styx (SS-N-2), sought the centroid of the radar target. The British developed a radar repeater that bounced its signal off the sea near the ship (its antenna resembled a searchlight at the top of the ship's mast). At least in theory, the missile would choose the centroid, which would lie somewhere between the ship and the bounced reflection. More sophisticated jammers exploited the fact that the missile set a range gate around the target and ignored signals from outside. It was possible, at least in theory, to capture the range gate and to send spurious signals that would cause the missile to "walk" the gate away from the target. If such range-gate stealing worked, the missile could be diverted into a chaff cloud or other decoy (in the 1980s the Royal Navy and then the U.S. Navy began to use floating decoy made of corner reflectors).

18 During the Falklands War the Argentines used a Neptune patrol bomber in much the same way, to coach an Exocet-firing Super Etendard into place to attack HMS *Sheffield*. The Super Etendard, though possibly not the Neptune, was detected passively. The advantage of passive detection was that the fleet could limit its radar emissions so as not to allow the enemy platform to detect it at long range. It is not clear whether any specific British ESM device was associated with the Bear D threat, since new systems were associated with advances in ESM technology.

19 The contemporary U.S. Navy standardized on one air-search radar, SPS-49, specifically to prevent the Soviets from distinguishing frigates from aircraft carriers. Standardization entailed reversing a frequency-diversity policy under which the U.S. Navy had deliberately used several different types of radars (to keep one kind of jammer from overcoming all of them). The Royal Navy also standardized at this time, but it is not clear to what extent the passive threat was involved.

20 For the ASRE proposal, see ADM 1/20401. See also its inventor's autobiography: Prof. Ralph Benjamin, *Five Lives in One: An Insider's View of the Defence and Intelligence World* (Tunbridge Wells: Parapress, 1996). See also Eric Grove, "Naval Command and Control Equipment: The Birth of the Late Twentieth Century 'Revolution in Military Affairs,'" in Robert Bud and Philip Gummett (eds), *Cold War, Hot Science: Applied Resarch in Britain's Defence Laboratories 1945–1990* (Amsterdam: Harwood Academic Publishers, 1999).

21 See ADM1/26038, a 1955 paper. At this time, plans called for DPT in all new British warships of frigate size or above, but that did not happen.

22 ASRE published details of an electronically scanned (frequency-scanned) radar in 1957; see ADM 220/1009.

23 The Dutch also chose 24 bits when they developed their SEWACO systems. It is not clear to what extent the choices were coordinated. The word size seems to have determined the optimum word size in data links, which is why the Anglo-Dutch Link X/Link 10 uses 24-bit words, whereas the U.S.-developed Link 11 uses 30-bit words.

24 Ferranti entered the computer business in collaboration with the University of Manchester; in 1951 the firm delivered the world's first commercial computer to the university. In 1950–59 it accounted for 26.4 percent of the British computer market, but that understates its share of the more sophisticated end of the market. Ferranti Canada produced the digital computer of the first digital combat direction system, the Canadian DATAR, which was tested in 1953. FM1600 was an integrated-circuit version of the F1600 used in early British naval systems. FM 1600B was used in CAAIS systems and in submarine tactical systems. Memory was 4 kwords, expandable to 64 kwords, and memory cycle time (a measure of speed) was originally 1 microsec (reduced to 0.6 microsec in 1969). FM1600D was a less expensive equivalent introduced in 1972. FM1600E was a larger version (32 to 256 kwords, 0.75 microsec memory time) using the same medium-scale integration technology (1977). F2420, originally FM1600E, had four times the computing speed and 1 Mword of memory. It superseded the FM1600 series in the CACS and ADIMP combat direction systems. These computers were supplemented by smaller-scale (16 bit) Argus-series minicomputers.

25 This distinction is made clear in papers written for the First Sea Lord, Admiral of the Fleet Lord Louis Mountbatten, in 1958 in connection with TIDE; see ADM 205/178. Understanding on both sides was apparently limited. A May 1958 letter from Mountbatten to CNO Admiral Arleigh Burke suggests that the British thought that NTDS was a version of their CDS; the British considered that both were limited because they were semi-automatic. Burke answered that NTDS might currently be semi-automatic, but that it would ultimately be an automatic system, and that it differed from CDS because it was built around a programmable digital computer. This and other letters in the file suggest that the TIDE links had not yet been defined, and some of the British internal memoranda in the file indicate a fear that NTDS would be incompatible with CDS because it operated so differently, with separate ships contributing their plots to the picture that would be broadcast jointly.

26 The name TIDE was contributed by a British participant, who consciously adopted the name of a popular US detergent, the idea being that sharing the link would clean up the tactical picture. It seems to follow that the British adopted Link X as an affordable alternative to what they considered the overly expensive Link 11, in analogy to detergent commercials, in which the less

expensive Brand X is compared with the preferred alternative, such as Tide. For the origins of the term TIDE, see Capt. (N) D.N. Macgillivray and Lt (N) G. Switzer, "Canadian Naval Contribution to Tactical Data Systems and Data Link Development," in the Commemorative Edition (1985) of (Canadian) *Maritime Warfare Bulletin*. Link X development was more protracted. A November 1962 British report on data links, ADM 220/1312, describes Link 11 and also indicates a hope (not realized) that NATO navies would agree on a more austere alternative. Link X seems to have been an Anglo-Dutch development of a link initially designated Link 13.

27 Initially, about 1961, there was a proposal to equip all *Leanders* with ADAWS. It was adjudged too expensive; it was also pointed out that to date there had been no experience of using ADA or ADAWS to maintain a surface or subsurface plot. The new short-range missile then in prospect (Confessor, which became Sea Wolf) would probably need some sort of automatic plotting system, but not necessarily the one suited to typical *Leander* duties. The ASW issue was resolved only with the advent of CAAIS some years later. See ADM1/28514, a proposed Staff Requirement for a *Leander* class version of ADA.

28 The identities of ADAWS 9 and 11 are unknown. It is possible that they were re-designated CACS, as various versions of CACS would have equipped upgraded Type 42 Batch 1 and 2 destroyers and also the abortive Type 43. In that case ADAWS 9 was probably the version for the Type 42 upgrade, and ADAWS 11 was probably intended for Type 43.

29 The assumption that fast submarines would inevitably be noisy appears in late-war documents describing tactical counters to the new submarines. The Allies became aware of their character through intelligence, probably primarily through intercepted signals. To develop the necessary tactics, the Royal Navy rebuilt the small S-class submarine *Scotsman*, drastically streamlining her and installing far more powerful motors. The resulting underwater target could indeed make the necessary speed, but her small-diameter high-speed propellers were quite noisy. It was not appreciated until after the war, when real Type XXI submarines fell into Allied hands, that the Germans had managed to achieve both high speed *and* a reasonable degree of silencing.

30 The two systems under development by 1950, which were incorporated in postwar warship designs, were Ruler and Camrose. Ruler was a rocket projector intended to place proximity-fused weapons near an oncoming torpedo. Camrose was a mini-torpedo, which would be fired in salvo. The projects were abandoned in 1954 when analysis showed that, owing to the high probability of false alarms, an escort crossing the Atlantic would generally carry more anti-torpedo ordnance than anti-submarine ordnance. Moreover, at least in theory, by that time sonar ranges had so increased that there was a very reasonable chance of killing a submarine before she had a chance to fire her weapons. The hard-kill concept returns periodically, usually with the caveat that it is difficult to avoid false alarms.

31 Willem Hackmann, *Seek and Strike: Sonar, Anti-submarine Warfare and the Royal Navy 1914–54* (London: HMSO, 1984), 333.

32 This view is reflected in the Ships' Covers for submarines preserved in the Brass Foundry branch of the National Maritime Museum. Because the development of such craft was considered so imminent, the Royal Navy did not operate the Type XXI submarines it had been assigned at the end of World War II, and did not begin work on upgrading its existing battery-powered submarines until 1948. It turned out that the German closed-cycle (Walter) power plant on

which such expectations had been built had been far less mature than imagined, and such submarines never entered service in any navy. The Soviets did have a small closed-cycle submarine (Project A615, the 'Quebec' class), but it was neither particularly successful nor did it enjoy particularly impressive performance. For the 1950 target, see Hackmann, *Seek and Strike*, 329.

33 At the end of World War II the Royal Navy had two primary surface ship sonars, Types 144 and 147; 147 was a tilting sonar to maintain close contact, and 144 was a conventional searchlight. Probably because it was assumed that the new submarines would be quite noisy, Type 160 was developed, consisting of a Type 144 for listening only and a second set, with deep (Q) attachment, for attack. The listening sonar could rotate rapidly to give all-round coverage. The two hydrophones were housed in a single 100-inch dome, occupying separate shafts. Type 144 was updated to become Type 164, which entered service in 1950. Range scales were 3000 yds for search and 1500 yds for attack. Type 174 was an upgraded passive sonar used with 164; for example, Daring class destroyers had Type 166, consisting of Type 164B plus Type 174. The successor set, used with Type 177, was Type 176, a dual-frequency (12–15 and 39 kHz) listening set. Both beams (8 deg wide at 39 kHz, 35 deg for 12–15 kHz) rotated continuously. Type 176 was designed to give at least twice the range of Type 174.

34 The British scanning-sonar prototype, which would have been Type 172 had it been produced, sampled its 72 stave transducers at a rate of 1 kHz, and fed the sampled data into a fixed set of preformed beams. Hackmann, *Seek and Strike*, 345.

35 A scanning sonar sent out a long pulse and, in effect, sampled what might be picked up in each direction. Much of the received signal was necessarily lost, as the scanning head spent only a small fraction of its time forming a beam in any one direction. The corresponding loss had to be factored into any calculation of how well the sonar worked (it was called scanning loss). However, because the system was quite simple, it was quickly implemented. By 1945 the U.S. Navy had a scanning alternative, QHB, to its standard destroyer hull sonar. This set was widely installed postwar. The Royal Navy tested it postwar on board the trawler *Icewhale*. The Royal Navy never deployed a preformed-beam set as a direct alternative to its wartime searchlights, although it did build the prototype mentioned above. Both navies pursued lower-frequency operation in roughly parallel steps. Thus the British Types 177 and 184 correspond (in frequency) to the U.S. SQS-4 series of the 1950s, but with more complex waveforms. They entered service slightly later. Type 2016 corresponded to the U.S. SQS-23 in frequency, but it was a much later set, in design more like the U.S. SQS-26 (but operating at a considerably higher frequency). The Royal Navy never had an active low-frequency surface ship set comparable to SQS-26, although the Type 2001 submarine sonar would have filled that niche (and it was tested on board surface ships).

36 Type 177 searched simultaneously in four 10-degree-wide beams. The group of beams could be trained to cover 160 degrees in 40-degree steps. The array was 4 ft wide and 3.5 ft deep. The staring concept made it possible to use complex waveforms, since the beam would be looking in the same direction throughout transmission and reception. That would not have been possible with a US-style scanning set.

37 Type 184 was initially expected to replace Type 177 altogether by 1966. Its main stated advantage was that it fed directly into ADA or ADAWS. Thus it was installed for tests on board the ADA carrier *Eagle*, as well as the CDS

carrier *Hermes* and the frigate *Penelope*. Initial tests were apparently disappointing, so by 1964 it was scheduled only for three carriers (presumably *Ark Royal* in addition to the first two), the four missile destroyers with ADAWS (second series of the "County" class), and four frigates. Later it became the standard British surface ship sonar.

38 Knout was first tried aboard HMS *Thule* in 1954. According to Hackmann, the Royal Navy tried but rejected the ex-German array sonar (GHG, which became the postwar BQR-2 and -4) which the US Navy adopted; it also rejected the U.S. rotating line hydrophone (JP, which was modified into the postwar BQR-3). Instead it planned a three-step submarine program. The first phase used only wartime sets: an improved version of the wartime searchlight sonars (Type 129 active, Type 138 passive: Types 169 and 168) plus a submarine version of Type 170 (Type 171) for mine detection and a US-supplied underwater telephone (Type 173). The intermediate submarine fit would be Type 171 plus two new passive sets, Types 718 and 719. Of these, Type 718 was a passive scanner, operating at low frequency at low speed and at higher frequency at higher (noiser) speed. Type 719 was a torpedo detector, a keel-mounted set consisting of a parabolic reflector with a microphone at its focus. The set actually adopted was Type 187, which was Type 718 plus a low-power active mine detector. Its 5 ft flat transducer was rotated mechanically. Type 171 was cancelled, according to Hackmann, because it had no unique value. The third stage was presumably Type 2001, work on which began in 1957.

39 See, for example, ADM 302/348 and 349, which give specifications for the projected automated tactical data-handling systems for the improved *Valiant* class (1967). Other Admiralty papers make it clear that some such automation was being considered as early as 1962; probably work was delayed because of the advent of the strategic submarine program, which delayed work on nuclear attack submarines.

40 Type 199 was the Canadian SQS-504 using a Royal Navy rig. The first was received in May 1962 for tests on board the 'Captain' class frigate *Collingwood*, the first operational one being fitted to HMS *Leander*. As of 1964 it was scheduled for six more *Leanders*: *Dido*, *Aurora*, *Arethusa*, *Naiad*, *Phoebe*, and *Cleopatra*.

41 Both navies certainly toyed with surface–submarine cooperation during the 1950s. The fire control systems on board U.S. and British second-generation nuclear submarines included provision for a surface consort. However, by the mid-1960s the U.S. Navy seems to have regarded direct support as an exotic concept, whereas it was well entrenched in the Royal Navy.

42 ADM 1/26861 is a 1951 report on standardization of U.S. and British sonobuoys. Slightly later French archival records (Service Historique de la Marine, series of Conseil Supérieure de la Marine papers) show how furious the French were to be excluded from Anglo-American ASW cooperation. They also show that the French were fobbed off: they were told that LOFAR was low-frequency active sonar, as in the U.S. SQS-23 of the late 1950s. LOFAR apparently did not become generally available within NATO until the 1970s. Early British sonobuoys were certainly distinctive; it is not clear to what extent those of the 1960s and later were independent designs. By the 1960s there were formal agreements on standardization, which applied to sonobuoy size and to output format. British active sonobuoys, in the CAMBS (Command Active Multibeam Sonobuoy) series, are certainly different from their U.S. DICASS (Directional Command Activated Sonobuoy System) counterparts.

43 Corsair relied on broadband correlation between pairs of hydrophones, whereas SOSUS relied on narrowband analysis of received signals. When it became clear that Corsair was not living up to expectations, British efforts turned towards active sonars. For the history of Corsair, see ADM 204/2547, ARL/R43/L, E.J. Risness, "Some Thoughts on the Recent History, Present Status, and Future Prospects of Passive Acoustic Submarine Detection," May 1961. Risness argued that the passive situation was hopeless. Not only were existing systems ineffective, but the Royal Navy had just demonstrated, in the new *Porpoise* class, that it could silence diesel submarines very effectively. Surely the Soviets would follow suit within a few years. Risness argued, moreover, that SOSUS only seemed successful because it was used to detect U.S. "Guppies" which had unusually well-suited acoustic signatures; European submarines (including Soviet ones) with direct-drive diesels were likely to be far less detectable.

44 This duty imposed considerable stresses on the frigates' hulls, and wore out many of the *Leanders* prematurely. The early history of the Type 23 frigate is in effect an illustration of the surveillance array concept. Type 23 was conceived as the least expensive possible towed array platform, to cost about two-thirds as much as a Type 22 general-purpose frigate in 1981 terms, with a much smaller complement (150 vice 250). The array would detect submarines at a considerable distance, and they would be prosecuted mainly by Nimrod maritime patrol aircraft; a group of Type 23 frigates would be, in effect, a mobile SOSUS field. The surveillance role explains why so much attention was given to silencing the ship at low speeds (up to about 12 knots) – which would not have been the speeds used in, say, screening a carrier or a convoy (this limitation could be finessed: in group operations the ship would dash ahead of the force, then listen at low speed). After the Falklands War, Type 23 was considerably upgraded towards general-purpose capability with, among other things, a 4.5-inch gun that had not previously been envisaged.

45 A fixed sonar projected a beam at a fixed depression angle. As the attacker approached, at some range (depending on target depth, the deeper the greater) contact was necessarily lost. The wartime solution was the "creeping" attack, in which one ship maintained contact and coached the other into attacking position. A single-ship attacker had to accelerate once contact was lost, in hopes of dropping weapons before the submarine got away. Acceleration in turn alerted the submarine to begin evasion.

46 In 1947 the Royal Navy was funding a variety of exotic weapons in a Z-series: Zeta (air-launched 30-inch diameter anti-submarine torpedo, 5,000 yds at 58 knots); Zombi (submarine-launched 30-inch diameter anti-ship homing torpedo, 10,000 yds at 60 knots or 20,000 yds at 35 knots, homing at 30–40 knots, using an oxygen/alcohol/seawater cycle); Zonal (30-inch diameter ship-launched anti-ship torpedo flying through the air at 500 knots [50,000 yds], then re-entering to run at 55 knots for 5,000 yds); and Zoster (30-inch air-launched anti-ship torpedo flying through the air at 500 knots as in Zonal [range 21,000 yds], then running through the water for 5,000 yds at 55 knots, as in Zonal; compared to the others in the series, it had a smaller warhead [520 vs. 800 lb]). These late-war projects did not last much beyond 1947 (the Royal Navy never had 30-inch tubes), but they give some indication of what the Royal Navy thought the new technology could offer. In 1947 the two primary torpedoes were the 21-inch Mk 8** launched by submarines and Mk 9** launched by surface ships; both were straight-runners. Airborne torpedoes (18-inch diameter), which were also carried by torpedo boats, were designated in a

separate series, the main late wartime type being Mk 15. The Germans had introduced hydrogen peroxide (HTP) propulsion, and both they and the U.S. Navy had developed a variety of homing weapons. Thus the Royal Navy sought interim replacements for the two existing torpedoes with much higher performance (10,000 yds at 50 knots) using HTP, and it actually adopted the HTP-powered Mk 12 (Fancy). This weapon was abandoned after one exploded, sinking the submarine *Sidon* in 1955. Mk 11 was an adaptation of the wartime German electric torpedo, also for submarines.

The two main projects for homing weapons were Bidder (ship or submarine vs. submarine, 18-inch diameter, 8,000 yds at 20–25 knots) and Dealer (aircraft vs. submarine, 18-inch diameter, 5,000–6,000 yds at 12–15 knots). Others, which were soon abandoned, were Bootleg (20-inch diameter, air vs. ship, no homing, at 70 knots), Dewlap (30-inch diameter, for torpedo boats, presumably descended from a Z-weapon, running 10,000 yds at 40 knots to home on a surface ship), and Barmaid (21-inch diameter, ship vs. ship, 25,000–40,000 yds at 40–50 knots). Data are from a report of a visit to the UK, 19 January to 12 February 1947, by Capt. Stryker, USN, in the post-1 January 1946 Command File of the U.S. Navy Operational Archives. Of the two main weapons, Bidder became the Mk 20 homing torpedo, which was made in both submarine and escort versions, as Mk 20(S) and Mk 20(E). Mk 20(E) was less than successful, and its protracted failure explains why plans to put torpedo tubes on board most British postwar frigates were abandoned. Reported range was 12,000 yds at 20 knots. Mk 21 was an abortive companion anti-ship torpedo for submarines (Pentane, 12,000 yds at 30 knots). Mk 22 was an abortive wire-guided version of Mk 20(S). The wire-guided Mk 23 did enter service, replacing Mk 20(S). It in turn was superseded by Tigerfish (Mk 24), a faster wire-guided torpedo initially produced only in anti-submarine form (submarines carried the unguided Mk 8** to fire at surface ships) but ultimately capable of attacking surface targets. Mk 24 can be considered broadly equivalent to later versions of the U.S. Mk 37. In the 1960s the Royal Navy began work on a much faster internal-combustion torpedo, Spearfish, which was adopted during the 1990s. It is generally described as broadly equivalent to the U.S. Mk 48 ADCAP.

47 The main British lightweight homing torpedo project was Mk 30 (Dealer B); it could run 2,500 yds at 19 knots. Work was abandoned in 1955 when it was decided to replace Gannet ASW aircraft with helicopters, which could not have delivered it. The Royal Navy bought lightweight U.S. Mk 43s as replacements. Mk 31 was an abortive small-diameter ASW torpedo. The Royal Navy bought the U.S. Mk 44 as an interim weapon, and Mk 31 was finally cancelled in 1971. Not long afterwards work began on a further British lightweight ASW torpedo, which was adopted about 1980 as Stingray. It is generally described as somewhat superior to the U.S. Mk 46 which the Royal Navy bought as an interim weapon.

48 The British version of the U.S. AQS-4 was designated Type 194. It was replaced in 1965–6 by the British Type 195. Type 194 was a searchlight sonar with a 21-degree-wide beam; Type 195 scanned over a 90-degree-wide sector. Maximum transducer depth was 250 vs. 50 ft for the earlier set. Effective range was 8,000 vs. 3,000 yds.

49 In the late 1950s the US Navy developed a drone helicopter, Dash, as a similar torpedo-delivery device. Like Match, Dash allowed a ship that could not accommodate a missile (in the U.S. case, ASROC) to deliver a torpedo at maximum sonar range. Dash ultimately failed because it had no feedback circuit; it was an early and failed UCAV. Match succeeded because the

onboard crew solved that problem. Neither had any way of re-acquiring a submarine target. Thus Match could not prosecute the more ambiguous (and more distant) contacts obtained by towed array ships. The Royal Navy did not, for example, develop a version of its second-generation Match helicopter (Lynx) with sonobuoys or with a dipping sonar, as the French Navy did with the same helicopter.

50 Successive editions of the annual official Confidential list of British warship characteristics, CB 1815, carried mention of UCSF Mk 1 Mod 2, "which may include Project Cambria." Ships so equipped were the frigates *Brighton*, *Falmouth*, and *Lowestoft*. Note also that the 1965 AIO handbook (ADM 239/688) associates the JYA and JYB tables with Automatic Surface Plot, which was another name for Cambria.

51 CAAIS was thus comparable in concept to the earlier U.S. NTDS (which also did not include fire control functions), except that it had a smaller track capacity and it handled a much simpler data link.

52 All Royal Navy versions were designated in a DBA series. DBA(1) was for *Leander* Batch 1 frigates (32k FM1600B computer). DBA(2) was for Type 21 frigates (which had a WSA 4 digital fire control system associated with it, built around a second FM1600B computer). These versions used six displays. DBA(3) was for the carrier *Hermes* as modernized (CDS and Type 984 radar having been removed). This was probably the version in the Argentine carrier *25 de Mayo*, which was the first export sale and also the first installation. DBA(4) was for "Hunt" class minehunters, and was probably the first approach to automatic ship control in a mine countermeasures ship. The setting of the ship's autopilot could be changed via CAAIS. DBA(5) equipped Type 22 Batch 1 frigates, using an FM1600E computer (128 kwords of memory). System capacity is 60 tracks. CAAIS 400 is the export version for Brazilian *Niteroi* class frigates, which are similar in weapon system terms to the British Type 21. CAAIS 450 was an upgraded export version capable of handling 120 tracks (using an FM1600E computer). It was installed in the Brazilian *Inhauma* class, in the Egyptian *Ramadan* class, in the Kenyan *Nyayo* class, and in Korean frigates (fourth and later *Ulsans*, and in the later KCX class). This version is also probably on board the Omani *Al Sharquiyah*. CAAIS (version uncertain) was installed on board the Chilean *Almirante Williams* class destroyers during modernization and it was probably installed on board the *Leander* class frigates built for Chile while they were under construction.

53 The U.S. Navy introduced a digital computer into the *Thresher* class, the first of which was completed in 1961, but it was used to refine a fire control solution on a single target rather than to maintain situational awareness. The Royal Navy sought from the first to devise a situational awareness system. The U.S. Navy moved in that direction from about 1967 on, but it is not at all clear why. The close relationship between the two navies may have been the cause of the U.S. shift, which was quite dramatic.

54 This sonar was tested in 1957; see ADM 259/156.

55 ADM 1/25240, "5in MCDP – Design, Development, and Manufacturing of Prototype," gives a history of the project. It began with a British 1943 project for a new 5.25-inch dual-purpose mount, considered the largest practical weapon with such performance. Wartime progress was minimal, with only 10 percent of the initial budget spent by June 1945. By 1947 a new dual-purpose gun was wanted to rearm some existing cruisers ("Town" and "County" classes), for missile ships, for a new cruiser, and for a new fleet destroyer. The

5.25-inch weapon seemed to be the best choice. However, by June 1948 the Royal Navy was insistent that gun and ammunition be standardized with the U.S. Navy, to insure wartime supplies. The closest U.S. project was the new 5in/54, and at the Fourth U.S./UK Gun Standardization Conference (February 1949) the two navies had fixed the caliber of the new gun at 5 inches. British work would be directed towards a single mount suited to a British 2,500-ton destroyer, but there would also be a twin cruiser version. The 5.25-inch gun was abandoned, but design work on its mounting would contribute to a British 5-inch project. The US gun was being tested by August 1950. In November 1951 the British selected a 5in/62 as the best medium-caliber dual-purpose gun, rejecting the 5in/54 for its low muzzle velocity and low rate of fire, hence its poor anti-aircraft performance. At this stage the 5-inch gun was rated superior to the 6-inch gun planned for the *Tiger* class cruisers. However, the British 5-inch project was tied directly to the cruiser-destroyer project. According to a note in the file cited, the Treasury was reluctant to spend limited funds on R&D, given the need for production (due to the Korean War mobilization). Ministry of Supply orders for the 5-inch prototype were therefore formally closed in September 1952, and the contract was terminated in May 1953. The project was formally cancelled in September 1953 "consequent on decisions recently taken on future new construction," i.e., the decision not to proceed with the cruiser-destroyer. Other files show that the cruiser-destroyer died because it had become too expensive. Instead, an attempt was made to upgrade the *Daring* design to modern standards. In 1955 this "Super *Daring*" became the basis for the "County" class missile destroyer.

56 Buccaneer tactics are described in the 1969 edition of the *Fighting Instructions*, superseding the 1961 edition (ADM 239/785, PRO). This account makes the role of the external HF/DF net explicit.

57 See the author's forthcoming account of naval command and control as a model of network-centric warfare. OPCON was in effect an automated messaging center with only a very limited ability to send data. The later FOCSLE is designed to transmit an automated picture of ship movements, providing a commander at sea with what amounts to over-the-horizon vision. Presumably the difference is that ships now have powerful enough computers on board.

SELECT BIBLIOGRAPHY

Anon., *The Origins and Development of Operational Research in the Royal Air Force* (London: HMSO, 1963).

Aspinall-Oglander, C., *Roger Keyes: The Biography of Admiral of the Fleet Lord Keyes of Zeebrugge and Dover* (London: Hogarth Press, 1951).

Baker, R., *The Terror of Tobermory: Vice-Admiral Sir Gilbert Stephenson, KBE, CBE, CMG* (London: W.H. Allen, 1972).

Bartlett, M.L. (ed.), *Assault from the Sea: Essays on the History of Amphibious Warfare* (Annapolis, MD: Naval Institute Press, 1983).

Beeler, J., *Birth of the Battleship: British Capital Ship Design, 1870–1881* (London: Chatham Publishing, 2001).

Benjamin, R., *Five Lives in One: An Insider's View of the Defence and Intelligence World* (Tunbridge Wells: Parapress, 1996).

Behrens, C.B.A., Merchant Shipping and the Demands of War (London: HMSO, 1955).

Bialer, U., *The Shadow of the Bomber: The Fear of Air Attack and British Politics, 1932–1939* (London: Royal Historical Society, 1980).

Bidwell, S. and Graham, D., *Fire Power: British Military Weapons and Theories of War, 1904–1945* (London: Allen & Unwin, 1982).

Blake, G., *Lloyd's Register of Shipping 1760–1960* (London: Lloyd's, 1960).

Bond, B., *Liddell Hart: A Study in Military Thought* (London: Cassell, 1977).

——, *British Military Policy Between the Two World Wars* (Oxford: Clarendon Press, 1980).

Brewer, J., *The Sinews of Power* (London: Unwin, 1989).

Brown, D.K., *Conway's All the World's Fighting Ships 1922–1946* (London: Conway, 1980).

——, *Nelson to Vanguard: Warship Design and Development 1923–1945* (London: Chatham Publishing, 2000).

——, *Aircraft Carriers* (London: Macdonald & Jane's, 1977).

——, *Carrier Air Groups: HMS Eagle* (Windsor: Hylton Lacy, 1972).

——, *Carrier Operations in World War 2*. Vol. 1: *The Royal Navy* (Shepperton: Ian Allen, 1974).

——, *The Genesis of Naval Aviation: Les marines de guerre du Dreadnought au nucléaire* (Paris: Service Historique de la Marine, 1988).

Bud, R. and Gummett, P. (eds), *Cold War, Hot Science: Applied Resarch in Britain's Defence Laboratories 1945–1990* (Amsterdam: Harwood Academic Publishers, 1999).

Burns, T. and Stalker, G.M., *The Management of Innovation* (Oxford: Oxford University Press, 1962).

Buxton, I.K., *Warship Building and Repair During the Second World War* (Glasgow: University of Glasgow Business History Unit, 1977).

Cagle, M.W. and Manson, F.A., *The Sea War in Korea* (Annapolis, MD: Naval Institute Press, 1957).

Campbell, J., *Naval Weapons of World War Two* (London: Conway Maritime Press, 1985).

Clapp, M. and Southby-Tailyour, E., *Amphibious Assault Falklands: The Battle of San Carlos Water* (London: Leo Cooper, 1996).

Clark, R., *The Rise of the Boffins* (London: Phoenix House, 1962).

Clifford, K.J., *Progress and Purpose: A Developmental History of the United States Marine Corps, 1900–1970* (Washington, DC: USMC, 1973).

——, *Amphibious Warfare Development in Britain and America from 1920 to 1940* (New York: Edgewood, 1983).

Columb, P., *Naval Warfare: Its Ruling Principles and Practice Historically Treated* (Annapolis, MD: Naval Institute Press, 1990).

Cooling, B.F. (ed.), *Case Studies in the Development of Close Air Support* (Washington, DC: Office of Air Force History, 1990).

Corbett, J.S., *Some Principles of Maritime Strategy* (London: Longman, 1911).

Coutau-Bégarie, H. (ed.), *L'Evolution de la Pensée Navale* (Paris: Commission Française d Histoire Maritime, 1990).

Cowman, I., *Dominion or Decline: Anglo-American Naval Relations in the Pacific, 1937–1941* (Oxford: Berg, 1996).

Croizat, V.J., *Across the Reef: The Amphibious Tracked Vehicle at War* (London: Arms and Armour Press, 1989).

Dockerill, S., *Britain's Retreat from East of Suez: The Choice Between Europe and the World?* (Basingstoke: Palgrave Macmillan, 2002).

Edgerton, D., *Science, Technology and British Industrial Decline, 1870–1970* (Cambridge: Cambridge University Press, 1996).

Elster, J., *Explaining Technical Change: A Case Study in the Philosophy of Science* (Cambridge: Cambridge University Press, 1983).

Fergusson, B., *The Watery Maze: The Story of Combined Operations* (London: Collins, 1961).

Fletcher, D., *Mechanized Force: British Tanks Between the Wars* (London: HMSO, 1991).

Franklin, G., *Britain's Anti-Submarine Capability, 1919–1939* (London: Frank Cass, 2003).

French, W. L. and Bell, C.H., *Organization Development: Behavioural Science Interventions for Organization Improvement* (New York: Prentice-Hall, 1995).

Friedman, N., *British Carrier Aviation* (London: Conway Maritime Press, 1988).

——, *Carrier Air Power* (London: Conway Maritime Press, 1981).

——, *The Post War Naval Revolution* (London: Conway Maritime Press, 1986).

——, *The Naval Institute Guide to World Naval Weapons Systems, 1991/92* (Annapolis, MD: Naval Institute Press, 1991).

——, with Hone, T.C. and Mandeles, M.D., *American and British Aircraft Carrier Development 1919–1941* (Annapolis, MD: Naval Institute Press, 1999).

——, with Honnor, A.F. and Andrews, D.J., *HMS Invincible: The First of a New Genus of Aircraft Carrying Ships* (London: Royal Institution of Naval Architects, 1981).

Gardiner, R. (ed.), *Navies in the Nuclear Age: Warships since 1945* (London: Conway Maritime Press, 1993).

Gardner, W.J.R., *Anti-Submarine Warfare* (London: Brassey's, 1996).

——, *Decoding History: The Battle of the Atlantic and Ultra* (Basingstoke: Macmillan, 1999).

Gordon, A., *The Rules of the Game: Jutland and British Naval Command* (London: Murray, 1996).

Gordon, G.A.H., *British Seapower and Procurement Between the Wars: A Reappraisal of Rearmament* (London: Macmillan, 1988).

Green, E. and Moss, M., *A Business of National Importance: The Royal Mail Shipping Group 1902–1937* (London: Methuen, 1982).

Grove, E., *Vanguard to Trident: British Naval Policy Since World War Two* (London: Bodley Head, 1987).

Hackmann, H., *Seek and Strike: Sonar, Anti-Submarine Warfare and the Royal Navy 1914–54* (London: HMSO, 1984).

Hague, A., *The Allied Convoy System; Its Organization, Defence and Operation* (London: Chatham Publishing, 2000).

Hamel, G., *Leading the Revolution* (Cambridge, MA: Harvard Business School Press, 2000).

——, and Prahalad, C.K., *Competing for the Future: Breakthrough Strategies for Seizing Control of Your Industry and Creating the Markets of Tomorrow* (Cambridge, MA: Harvard Business School Press, 1994).

Hannah, L., *The Rise of the Corporate Economy* (Baltimore, MD: Johns Hopkins University Press, 1983).

Harris, J.P., *Men, Ideas and Tanks: British Military Thought and Armoured Warfare, 1903–1939* (Manchester: Manchester University Press, 1995).

Hattendorf, J.B. (ed.), *Ubi Sumus: The State of Naval and Maritime History* (Newport, RI: Naval War College Press, 1994).

——, *Mahan is Not Enough: Proceedings of a Conference on the Works of Sir Julian Corbett and Admiral Sir Herbert Richmond* (Newport, RI: Naval War College Press, 1993).

——, *Doing Naval History: Essays Towards Improvement* (Newport, RI: Naval War College Press, 1995).

Hawkings, D.J., *Keeping the Peace: The Aldermaston Story* (London: Leo Cooper, 2000).

Headrick, D.R., *The Invisible Weapon: Telecommunications and International Politics, 1851–1945* (Oxford: Oxford University Press, 1991).

Hezlet, A., *The Electron and Sea Power* (London: Peter Davies, 1975).

Hobbs, D. A., *Aircraft Carriers of the Royal and Commonwealth Navies* (London: Greenhill Books, 1996).

——, *Royal Navy Escort Carriers* (Liskeard: Maritime Books, 2003).

——, *Aircraft of the Royal Navy since 1945* (Liskeard: Maritime Books, 1982).

——, *Ark Royal – The Name Lives On* (Liskeard: Maritime Books, 1985).

Howard Bailey, C., *The Royal Naval Museum Book of the Battle of the Atlantic: The Corvettes and their Crews: An Oral History* (Stroud: Alan Sutton Publishing, 1994).

Howse, D., *Radar at Sea: The Royal Navy in World War Two* (Basingstoke: Macmillan, 1993).

Hume, J.R. and Moss, M.S., *Beardmore: The History of a Scottish Industrial Giant* (London: Hutchinson, 1979).

Isely, J.A and Crowl, P.A., *The US Marines and Amphibious Warfare: Its Theory and Practice in the Pacific* (Princeton: Princeton University Press, 1951).

Johnman, L. and Murphy, H., *British Shipbuilding and the State since 1918: A Political Economy of Decline* (Exeter: Exeter University Press, 2002).

Johnston, I., *Beardmore Built* (Clydebank: Clydebank District Libraries, 1993).

Jones, L., *Shipbuilding in Britain; Mainly Between the Two World Wars* (Cardiff: University of Wales Press, 1957).

Jones, R.V., *Most Secret War: British Scientific Intelligence, 1939–1945* (London: Hamish Hamilton, 1978).

Kaplan, F., *The Wizards of Armageddon* (New York: Simon & Schuster, 1983).

Kiely, D.G., *Naval Electronic Warfare* (London: Brassey's, 1988).

Kingsley, F.A., *The Development of Radar Equipments for the Royal Navy, 1935–1945* (London: Macmillan, 1995).

—— (ed.), *The Application of Radar and Other Electronic Systems in the Royal Navy in World War 2* (London: Macmillan, 1995).

Kransdorf, A., *Corporate Amnesia: Keeping Know-How in the Company* (Oxford: Butterworth, 1998).

Kuhn, T.S., *The Structure of Scientific Revolutions* (Chicago: University of Chicago Press, 1962).

Ladd, J.D., *By Sea By Land: The Authorised History of the Royal Marine Commandos* (London: HarperCollins, 1998).

Lambert, A., *The Foundations of Naval History: John Knox Laughton, the Royal Navy and the Historical Profession* (London: Chatham Publishing, 1998).

Landa, M. de, *War in the Age of Intelligent Machines* (New York: Zone, 1991).

Lansdown, J.R.P., *With the Carriers in Korea 1950–53* (Worcester: Square One Publications, 1992).

Layman, R.D., *Before the Aircraft Carrier* (London: Conway Maritime Press, 1989).

Lewin, R., *Complexity: Life at the Edge of Chaos* (New York: Macmillan, 1992).

Lewis, J., *Changing Direction: British Military Planning for Post-war Strategic Defence, 1942–1947* (London: The Sherwood Press, 1988).

Liddell Hart, B., *The British Way in Warfare* (London: Faber, 1932).

MacIntyre, D., *Aircraft Carriers: The Majestic Weapon* (London: Macdonald, 1968).

Marder, A.J., *The Anatomy of Power: A History of British Naval Policy in the Pre-Dreadnought Era, 1880–1905* (London: Frank Cass, 1964).

Marriott, L., *Royal Navy Aircraft Carriers 1945–1990* (Shepperton: Ian Allen, 1985).

Marwick, A., *The Deluge: British Society and the First World War* (London: Bodley Head, 1965).

Maund, L.E.H., *Assault from the Sea* (London: Methuen, 1949).

McLachlan, D., *Room 39: Naval Intelligence in Action 1939–1945* (London: Weidenfeld & Nicolson, 1968).

Millett, A.R., *Semper Fidelis: The History of the United States Marine Corps* (New York: The Free Press, 1991).

Morison, E.E., *Men, Machines and Modern Times* (Cambridge, MA: MIT Press, 1966).

Mortimer, J.E., *History of the Boilermakers Society*, 3 vols (London: Verso, 1973, 1981, 1994).

Morton, P., *Fire Across the Desert: Woomera and the Anglo-Australian Joint Project 1946–1980* (Canberra: Australian Government Publishing Service, 1989).

Moskin, J.R., *The Story of the US Marine Corps* (London: Paddington Press, 1979).

Moulton, J.L., *The Royal Marines* (Eastney: Royal Marines Museum, 1981).

Murray, W. and Millett, A.R., *Military Innovation in the Interwar Period* (Cambridge: Cambridge University Press, 1996).

—— and ——, (eds), *Calculation: Net Assessment and the Coming of World War II* (New York: Free Press, 1992).

Niestlé, A., *German U-Boat Losses during World War II: Details of Destruction* (London: Greenhill, 1998).

O'Brien, P.P. (ed.), *Technology and Naval Combat in the Twentieth Century and Beyond* (London: Frank Cass, 2002).

Overy, R., *Why the Allies Won* (London: Cape, 1995).

Palmer, S. and Williams, G., *Charted and Uncharted Waters: Proceedings of a Conference on British Maritime History* (London: National Maritime Museum, 1981).

Pavlov, A.S., *Warships of the USSR and Russia, 1945–1995* (London: Chatham Publishing, 1997).

Polmar, N., *Aircraft Carriers* (London: Macdonald, 1969).

Poolman, K., *The Winning Edge: Naval Technology in Action, 1939–1945* (London: Sutton, 1977).

——, *Allied Escort Carriers of World War Two in Action* (London: Blandford Press, 1988).

Pratt, L.R., *East of Malta, West of Suez: Britain's Mediterranean Crisis, 1936–1939* (Cambridge: Cambridge University Press, 1975).

Price, A., *Aircraft versus Submarine: The Evolution of the Anti-Submarine Aircraft, 1912 to 1980* (London: Jane's Publishing, 1980).

Pugh, P., *The Cost of Seapower: The Influence of Money on Naval Affairs from 1815 to the Present Day* (London: Conway, 1986).

Ranft, B. (ed.), *Technical Change and British Naval Policy 1860–1939* (London: Frank Cass, 1977).

Reid, J.M., *James Lithgow, Master of Work* (London: Hutchinson, 1964).

Reeve, J. and Stevens. D. (eds), *The Face of Naval Battle: The Human Experience of Modern War at Sea* (Crows Nest, NSW, Australia: Allen & Unwin, 2003).

Reynolds, C.G., *The Fast Carriers* (Annapolis, MD: Naval Institute Press, 1992).

Rodger, N.A.M. (ed.), *Naval Power in the Twentieth Century* (London: Macmillan, 1996).

Rogers, E., *Diffusion of Innovations* (New York: Free Press, 1983, 3rd ed.).

Rohwer, J. and Monakov, M.S., *Stalin's Ocean-Going Fleet: Soviet Naval Strategy and Shipbuilding Programmes, 1935–1953* (London: Frank Cass, 2001).

Rosen, S.P., *Winning the Next War: Innovation and the Modern Military* (Ithaca, NY: Cornell University Press, 1991).

Rosenburg, N., *Inside the Black Box: Technology and Economics* (Cambridge: Cambridge University Press, 1992).

Roskill, S., *Naval Policy Between the Wars*, 2 vols (London: Collins, 1968, 1976).

Rössler, E., *The U-Boat: The Evolution and Technical History of German Submarines* (London: Arms and Armour Press, 1981).

Royen, P.C. van, Fischer, L.R. and Williams, D.M. (eds), *Frutta di Mare: Evolution and Revolution in the Maritime World in the 19th and 20th Centuries* (Amsterdam: Batavian Lion International, 1998).

Schofield, B., *The Attack on Taranto* (Shepperton: Ian Allen, 1973).

Schumpeter, J., *Capitalism, Socialism and Democracy* (London: Allen & Unwin, 1976).

Schurman, D.C., *Julian S. Corbett, 1854–1922: Historian of British Maritime Policy from Drake to Jellicoe* (Woodbridge: Royal Historical Society, 1981).

Searle, G., *The Quest for National Efficiency: A Study of British Politics and Political Thought 1899–1914* (Oxford: Blackwell, 1971).

Smith, K., *Conflict over Convoys: Anglo-American Logistics Diplomacy in the Second World War* (Cambridge: Cambridge University Press, 1996).

Smith, M., *British Air Strategy Between the Wars* (Oxford: Oxford University Press, 1984).

Speller, I., *The Role of Amphibious Warfare in British Defence Policy, 1945–1956* (Basingstoke: Palgrave, 2001).

Stern, R.C., *Type VII U-Boats* (London: Arms and Armour Press, 1991).

Sturtivant, R., *Fleet Air Arm 1929–1939* (London: Arms and Armour Press, 1990).

Sumida, J.T., *Inventing Grand Strategy and Teaching Command: The Classic Works of Alfred Thayer Mahan Reconsidered* (Baltimore, MD: Johns Hopkins University Press, 1997).

Thompson, J., *No Picnic: 3 Commando Brigade in the South Atlantic, 1982* (London: Leo Cooper, 1992).

——, *The Royal Marines: From Sea Soldiers to a Special Force* (London: Pan, 2001).

Tidd, J., Bessant, J. and Pavitt, K., *Managing Innovation: Integrating Technological, Market and Organisational Change* (London: Wiley, 2001).

Till, G., *Air Power in the Royal Navy 1914–1945* (London, Jane's Publishing, 1979).

——, *The Future of British Sea Power* (Annapolis, MD: Naval Institute Press, 1984).

Twigge, S.R., *The Early Development of Guided Weapons in the United Kingdom* (Chur, Switzerland: Harwood, 1993).

Urick, R.J., *Principles of Underwater Sound* (New York: McGraw-Hill, 1983).

Waddington, C.H., *OR in World War 2: Operational Research against the U-Boat* (London: Paul Elek Scientific Books).

West, M.A. and Farr, J.L. (eds), *Innovation and Creativity at Work: Psychological and Organisational Strategies* (London: Wiley, 1990).

Wettern, D., *The Decline of British Sea Power* (London: Jane's, 1982).

Williams, K.B., *Secret Weapon: US High-Frequency Direction Finding in the Battle of the Atlantic* (Annapolis, MD: Naval Institute Press, 1996).

Williams, M., *Captain Gilbert Roberts R.N and the Anti-U-Boat School* (London: Cassell, 1979).

Wilson, J.F., *British Business History, 1720–1994* (Manchester: Manchester University Press, 1995).

Winton, H.R. and Mets, D.R. (eds), *The Challenge of Change: Military Institutions and New Realities, 1918–1941* (Lincoln: University of Nebraska Press, 2000).

Ziegler, P., *Mountbatten: The Official Biography* (London: Collins, 1985).

INDEX

Page numbers in italics, e.g. *35*, indicate figures or tables.

An environmentally friendly book printed and bound in England by www.printondemand-worldwide.com

This book is made entirely of sustainable materials; FSC paper for the cover and PEFC paper for the text pages.

#0422 - 280813 - C0 - 234/156/17 - PB